The Status of Legal Ethics

WARSAW STUDIES IN PHILOSOPHY
AND SOCIAL SCIENCES

Edited by
Tadeusz Szawiel and Jakub Kloc-Konkołowicz

VOLUME 1

*Notes on the quality assurance
and peer review of this publication*

Prior to publication,
the quality of the work
published in this series is reviewed
by one of the editors of the series.

Paweł Skuczyński

The Status of Legal Ethics

Translated by Katarzyna Popowicz

PETER LANG
EDITION

Bibliographic Information published by the Deutsche Nationalbibliothek
The Deutsche Nationalbibliothek lists this publication in the Deutsche Nationalbibliografie; detailed bibliographic data is available in the internet at http://dnb.d-nb.de.

The publication was financially supported by the Ministry of Science and Higher Education - National Programme for the Development of Humanities.

NARODOWY PROGRAM ROZWOJU HUMANISTYKI

Library of Congress Cataloging-in-Publication Data

Skuczynski, Pawel, author.
[Status etyki prawniczej. English]
The status of legal ethics / Pawel Skuczynski ; translated by Katarzyna Popowicz.
pages cm. — (Warsaw studies in philosophy and social sciences ; v. 1)
"The present work has been completed on the basis of my doctoral thesis, only editorially changed, entitled "Philosophical and Methodological Status of Legal Ethics", prepared and defended at the Faculty of Law and Administration of Warsaw University" — Introduction.
ISBN 978-3-631-64133-0
1. Legal ethics—Philosophy. I. Popowicz, Katarzyna, translator. II. Title.
K123.S5813 2013
174'.3—dc23

2013026121

ISSN 2196-0143
ISBN 978-3-631-64133-0 (Print)
E-ISBN 978-3-653-03089-1 (E-Book)
DOI 10.3726/978-3-653-03089-1

Peter Lang – Frankfurt am Main · Bern · Bruxelles · New York · Oxford · Warszawa · Wien

www.peterlang.de

Table of contents

Introduction

The increasing interest which has been observed in recent years in legal ethics[*] is often a starting point for modern reflection on this subject. This attitude seems fully justified for at least two reasons. First of all, research directions, especially in practical sciences, to a significant extent are, and should be, determined by the needs of practice. Secondly, practice continually provides data which may form arguments for or against a specific thesis, conception or scientific theory. For the theory presented in the following work and the applied methodology it primarily means increased sensitivity to the needs of practice. Simultaneously, an assumption is being made that, in the case of practical philosophy, practice that should be taken into account covers not only the way in which people act, but also whether and how they justify their actions. In the most developed branches of practical philosophy, singular justifications as well as whole sets of them may be found in ideologies and doctrines and they also should become subjected to explanation and criticism.

As far as legal ethics is concerned, even superficial knowledge of literature allows us to draw the conclusion that a basic problem of practice, in its broad sense, is the conceptual confusion, manifesting itself not only in ambiguity of terms – which seems unavoidable in a branch on the border of law and morality – but primarily in ignoring the fact of this ambiguity. This ambiguity is also disregarded in theoretical considerations, which leads to the situation where scientific theses and concepts are not different views of the same subject, but rather they are studies on completely different subjects[1]. The basic aim of this study is to describe this ambiguity in such a way that it may be next used as a starting point for further research. Therefore, the study is not limited to the analysis of concepts but undertakes the attempt of creating such a theory of legal ethics that would not only accept the ambiguity, but also employ it to explain the

* In the present work, the term "lawyer" essentially refers to a broad variety of law-trained persons, and not only to defence lawyers or attorneys as it is in the American context. Accordingly, the term "legal ethics" refers to professional ethics of lawyers in this broad sense.

1 See P. Skuczyński, "Wieloznaczność w teorii etyki prawniczej", ["Ambiguity in Legal Ethics' Theory"], in: *Etyka prawnicza. Stanowiska i perspektywy*, ed. H. Izdebski, P. Skuczyński, Warsaw 2008, p. 103.

phenomenon of legal ethics and to formulate research program for more specific problems.

Attaining this goal will be possible through explaining the status of legal ethics on the basis of two principles expressing the adopted methodology. The first principle may be characterised by the requirements of adequacy, which marks the division of the work on the analytical-empirical part and the part on moral philosophy and philosophy of law. This results from the fact that the fundamental, though not sole, ambiguity in legal ethics is a consequence of the ambiguity of the term "ethics" itself. Basic classification of its meanings relies first of all on distinguishing descriptive ethics, whose subject is values and duties regarded as moral, but also on the issue whether they are justified, and if so, how. Descriptive ethics does not concern the entirety of moral practice, which is conduct and its possible justification, but only those justifications of the conduct that refer to values and moral duties. Secondly, normative ethics is distinguished with its subject being values and duties of moral nature – from the perspective of rationality understood one way or another – and their justification. Finally, critical ethics (meta-ethics) is singled out. Its subject is language and justifications which are used and should be used in descriptive and normative ethics. Thus, critical ethics does not directly concern specific values and moral duties, but provides methods and criteria to discern what is value and moral duty and what is not on the grounds of morality theories formulated within its framework[2].

Legal ethics shares with ethics as such this fundamental ambiguity, and therefore its tasks are of descriptive and normative as well as critical character. While the thesis that legal ethics may be practised in the two indicated ways is relatively uncontroversial – but still, it requires justification – the place of legal ethics within meta-ethics proves significantly more complicated. On one hand, it has to be determined to what extent legal ethics has its own language and methodology – in other words, what is its status – whereas such problems are usually being solved on the grounds of specific morality theories. On the other hand, reduction of conceptual confusion related to legal ethics may be attained only with a comprehensive theory of legal ethics which will be autonomic in relation to specific morality theories.

The problem thus concerns relations between a general ethical theory and a theory of legal ethics. However, it would be an oversimplification to accept that

2 A. Kojder, "Etyka – przedmiot i stanowiska", ["Ethics – Subject and Views"], in: *Etyka zawodów prawniczych. Etyka prawnicza*, ed. H. Izdebski, P. Skuczyński, Warsaw 2006, pp. 16-18. Cf. R.B. Brandt, *Etyka. Zagadnienia etyki normatywnej i metaetyki*, [*Ethics. The Issues of Normative Ethics and Meta-Ethics*], Warsaw 1996, pp. 15-24.

this is only a problem of a relation between moral philosophy and philosophy of law since both premises and conclusions of arguments with which one may solve the problem of necessity have a wider scope. This is related exactly to the criteria of adequacy, which means in this case carrying out reflections so that their scope agrees with the scope of a problem with the same subject and methodology, and so if the problem concerns all professional ethics, then it should be approached as such. For this reason, the argument will fundamentally be developed from the perspective of moral philosophy and not philosophy of law, though the latter is necessary to understand what legal ethics is.

The second principle on which the study is based may be called the principle of historicality. Founded on the adequacy claim, the search for a model relation between a general ethical theory and a theory of legal ethics sets the perspective for the principal goal of this paper. The analysis would not be complete if it was not supplemented with some general assumption on the rationale of all ethical theories that I accept. The assumption, which I believe should be made *explicite*, is the proposition that all knowledge is historical in character — of course, it does not mean that necessarily historically conditioned — and therefore such terms as "tradition", "paradigm" or "research program" may be used in our reflection.

It is worth remarking that the view saying a paradigm is a basic structure of scientific thought comes from Thomas S. Kuhn, who maintained that this term must, "suggest that some accepted examples of actual scientific practice — examples which include law, theory, application, and instrumentation together — provide models from which spring particular coherent traditions of scientific research."[3] It may thus be said that a paradigm encompasses everything that in a certain society and certain time makes scientific thought, and that helps solve specific research problems, which Kuhn calls "puzzle-solving." When a certain paradigm becomes ineffective, it undergoes a crisis, which may lead to a scientific revolution and establishing a new paradigm[4].

In moral philosophy, the ideas of Alasdair MacIntyre, which may be seen as equivalent to Kuhn's standpoint, make "the beginning of some peculiar 'Copernican Revolution' in meta-ethics."[5] Ethical theories, like scientific

---

3 T.S. Kuhn, *The Structure of Scientific Revolutions*, in: *International Encyclopedia of Unified Science*, vol. II, no. 2, London 1970, p. 10.

4 P. Skuczyński, "Czy sprawiedliwość jest cnotą prawników?", ["Is Justice a Virtue of Lawyers?"], in: B. Wojciechowski, M.J. Golecki, *Rozdroża sprawiedliwości we współczesnej myśli filozoficznoprawnej*, Toruń 2008, p. 292.

5 A. Chmielewski, "Filozofia moralności Alasdaira MacIntyre'a", ["The Philosophy of Morality of Alasdair MacIntyre"], in: A. MacIntyre, *Dziedzictwo cnoty. Studium z teorii moralności*, Warsaw 1996, p. XXV.

paradigms, should help solve ordinary and daily – though, of course, often very complicated – problems of normative ethics. If they fail in this task, it may bring on a calamity more dangerous than a crisis – according to Kuhn's terminology – of normal science operating within the framework of a certain paradigm because a different type of relations occurs between moral philosophy and morality than between philosophy of science and science.

The idea of moral tradition – a key term of this view – is based on the assumption that history of moral philosophy and history of morality are disciplines that are very strongly interconnected[6]. This, naturally, results in many problems arising from the relation of tradition and modernity and its related concept of practical rationality. The problems will have to be solved and, eventually, will lead to a perspective that overcomes some limitations which stem from solely adopting the point of view of particular traditions. This will be made possible as legal ethics becomes a part of an extensive modernising project – as it was understood by some great thinkers of the Frankfurt School.

In the first part of my presentation I begin with the analysis of the state of legal ethics, which includes elements of lawyers' conduct and its justifications (moral practice) – especially justifications referring to what in a given age and society is regarded as values and moral duties of lawyers. It has to be emphasised that a longstanding tradition connected with the domination of the category of virtue in moral thought on one side, and on the other, of ideas and principles of Roman law in legal thought, requires a separate discussion of the legal ethics beginnings. Subsequently, three most important traditions of legal ethics will be presented: the French, basing on the categories of virtue and independence, the American, related to the ideas of loyalty and professional duties, and the German, referring to professional roles and obedience. Equal treatment of all three, and only these three traditions, is justified by their fundamental meaning not only for the discussion in legal ethics, but also by the fact that all of them are objects of the globalisation, professionalisation and juridisation processes, which occur nowadays in legal ethics. These traditions are also present, relatively equally, in modern Poland.

The aim of this presentation will be to study whether and to what ideas there has been an *explicite* or *implicite* reference made in practice, and also what is the nature of the ambiguity present in legal ethics – namely, the ambiguity related to the term "legal ethics" itself. I will make an attempt to show that traditions of legal ethics and their modern transformations allow us to distinguish three basic meanings in which the term "legal ethics" is used. Then, this will serve as a foundation to build a theory of legal ethics that would not only take this

---

6 P. Skuczyński, "Czy sprawiedliwość…", p. 290.

ambiguity into consideration, but also make use of it. It appears appropriate to assume that in the case of ideas so complicated one should avoid reduction, which would limit or obscure the analysed subject, and thus lead to consequences opposite to scientific explanation. With the whole attachment to the value of simplicity in scientific theories, a more appropriate direction is to undertake the effort to find relations between particular meanings of the analysed idea and to make them a basis for subsequently formulated theories. In other words, the idea is to achieve a transition from an ambiguous term to a multidimensional theory, which will order this ambiguity[7].

In the second part, various concepts of legal ethics present in theoretical literature will be critically discussed. The conceptions will be arranged by the two criteria, namely cognitive value and practical value which legal ethics possesses on the ground of these views. However, the adopted criteria do not allow a logical division but only a typology organising conceptions so that any new perspective is a theoretical reaction to deficiencies in the preceding one. Within the framework of empirical and analytical conceptions, these are conceptions of legal ethics as the lawyer's ethos, as myth, as ideology and as professional deontology. Whereas normative and critical perspectives include legal ethics as applied ethics, the lawyer's situational ethics and critical professional ethics, the latter being further developed in the present study.

In part three, carrying out my reflections on the grounds of moral philosophy I will try to construct a multidimensional theory of legal ethics. The starting point will be a discussion of issues of validation crisis in ethics and the relation between moral traditions and practical rationality. The essential problem in ethics relating to particular groups or practices is the status of broadly understood standards or moral obligations formulated by this ethics, which status is characterised by constant lack of sufficient validation. If such ethics, on one hand, repeals some obligations of general ethics in relation to certain groups or practices, and, on the other, establishes some special obligations going even further, then it may be said that it modifies general ethics[8]. The acceptable scope and profundity of these modifications require validation. The thesis whose truth I will try to defend is the following: three fundamental meanings of "legal ethics" correspond with three planes of its theory in which every successive plane contains premises for decisions taken on the lower plane, thus providing for its validation. Accepting the point that a theory of legal ethics should have

7 P. Skuczyński, "Wieloznaczność...", p. 104.

8 M. Michalik, "Społeczne przesłanki, swoistość i funkcje etyki zawodowej", ["Social Premises, Specificity and Functions of Professional Ethics"], in: *Etyka Zawodowa*, ed. A. Sarapata, Warsaw 1971, pp. 17-23.

critical and reflective character will lead to assuming the perspective going beyond traditions of legal ethics and to determining planes of a theory of legal ethics not only on the basis of elementary, traditional meanings of this idea, but also of ones relating to – connected with the Frankfurt School – modern views on Kantian categories i.e. pragmaticality, ethicality and morality. From this perspective the subject of legal ethics consists of three planes – deontological, social and a moral one. Guided by the requirements of the critical theory, the multidimensional theory of legal ethics describes relations between its planes as reflective validation and critical limitation. On the highest plane the theory is validated by reference to reflection as a procedure included in transcendental pragmatics for validation of all normative ethics. For this reason, on the moral plane of legal ethics, the principle of lawyers' responsibility for the law as social practice has been formed.

Part four examines, on the philosophy of law grounds, whether chosen legal-philosophical conceptions – selected on the basis of practical importance – contain, *explicite* or *implicite*, any legal ethics conceptions, and what is their relation to the multidimensional theory of legal ethics. In relation to this, basing on each of the analysed views, conclusions on the content of the lawyers' responsibility for the law principle – meaning that lawyers should maintain and develop law – have been drawn. Among the discussed conceptions there are some in whose case one may speak of corresponding law paradigms, and therefore they may be treated as theoretical models closely related to legal practice. From these models the following will be analysed: the positivist model in its classical but also modern version, characterised by the social thesis and the separation thesis, the juriscentric model[9], related to interpretivism and for this reason including integral theory of law as well as the institutional view, and, lastly, the discursive model, containing topical-rhetorical approach, in which legal discourse is treated as an exemplary one, and procedural approach, in which it is assumed that legal discourse is a special case of general practical discourse.

Finally, the fifth part analyses the status of legal ethics as a scientific discipline which not only has its theory, but also can be practised systematically. For it is not evident and one can imagine a situation in which moral practice and a theory of legal ethics exhaust the forms in which legal ethics is represented. I will also discuss the relations of legal ethics to other legal sciences – dogmatic and general ones – and to what extent its original research program permits its

---

9 This term was introduced by A. Kozak, see: *idem*, *Granice prawniczej władzy dyskrecjonalnej*, [*The Limits of Discretionary Legal Power*], Wrocław 2002, p. 156 ff., and chapter 4.4.2 of the present work.

distinction as a separate discipline. An attempt will be made to answer the question to what extent legal ethics is interdisciplinary.

Both the adopted methodology and the structure of the study require making an important terminological remark at the outset. On one hand, if the starting point of the present study is the legal ethics concept's ambiguity, which will be used to construct a theory in this scope, then it seems very difficult to accept one meaning of the term only for the use of the argument. However, on the other hand, the term must necessarily be used as a fundamental category referring to the subject of the study. Therefore, it will be used in different meanings depending on the context, whereby some additional qualifications like "traditions of legal ethics", "legal ethics conceptions" or "multidimensional theory of legal ethics" will serve as guidelines.

The present work has been completed on the basis of my doctoral thesis, only editorially changed, entitled "Philosophical and Methodological Status of Legal Ethics", prepared and defended at the Faculty of Law and Administration of Warsaw University. To the thesis supervisor, professor Tomasz Stawecki, to the thesis advisers – professor Hubert Izdebski and professor Marek Zirk-Sadowski I owe a deep and sincere debt of gratitude for their invaluable support and always a factual critique. I also want to thank my parents especially for the faith in successful accomplishment of my research and for creating the ideal conditions for it.

*

It has been several years since the creation of this book in the original, Polish version. During this time, some drawbacks of the text have been discovered. They concern both its content – the theses presented and the argumentation, which, from a time perspective, seem to me insufficient, and the form – the way of presenting the theses is often too complicated and requires too much effort from a reader. Also the cited literature should be updated since every year there are new positions being published. Despite all this, I have decided to publish the book in English in an unchanged version. I have assumed that if I tried to eliminate the flaws by changing the text, this would only complicate it and make it completely unreadable. I hope that, in spite of this, the publication in English will make the book a noteworthy position for all those interested in legal ethics and professional ethics in general. At the same time, I want to thank Katarzyna Popowicz for her patience and the effort she has put into translating the book as well as the Polish Ministry of Science and Higher Education for financial support.

Chapter 1
Traditions and transformations of legal ethics

1.1. Preliminary remarks

A discussion of the legal ethics situation includes first of all elements of lawyers' conduct and its justifications referring to what in a given period and a given society is considered as values and moral duties. By this one does not mean studying whether lawyers of a certain age acted morally or not, though this would perhaps solve the problem of the 'moral crisis of legal professions', which is the focus of attention of some part of the discussion on legal ethics[1]. This solution could consist of showing that, historically, lawyers acted more or less morally than today and so one could speak of worsening or improving of their moral condition. However, there is no sort of research tools to attain this objective, and therefore just posing the problem should be regarded as faulty and solution-finding efforts as pointless. Here, it is more about indicating what lawyers' conduct was considered reprehensible or desired, what criteria were used in this regard and what justifications were offered. Naturally, from the fact that some types of lawyers' behaviours were either continually subjected to regulations, condemned in moral philosophy works or just were a subject of constant complaint, one may presume that such types of behaviour were very common despite efforts to fight them. Nevertheless, these will always be only presumptions and not fully justified conclusions.

Traditions and transformations of legal ethics are categories with which one can organise and briefly present the richness of moral thought on lawyers' conduct in many countries over the centuries. Up to a certain historical moment one may speak of only certain elements of such thought, which includes, on the one hand, forms of determining correct conduct of lawyers, and on the other, substantial content of these elements. They may be seen as a kind of a beginning of legal ethics and discussing them will help indicate those elements from which traditions of legal ethics have further developed as stable and coherent linking

---

1 R. Sarkowicz, "O tzw. moralnym kryzysie profesji prawniczej", ["On the so-called Moral Crisis of Legal Profession"], in: *Studia z filozofii prawa 2*, ed. J.Stelmach, Kraków 2003, pp. 159-164.

structures created out of these elements. Both structures that are formal in character and those determining legal ethics content as well.

One may point to three traditions of legal ethics established in the recent couple of centuries that even today in many countries influence the identity and understanding of the legal profession. This is first of all, based on virtue and independence, ethics of the French bar. Secondly, American lawyers' ethics, which refers to obligation and loyalty. Thirdly, German lawyers' ethics, founded on obedience and fulfilment of social roles. Of course, this assignment of particular ethic traditions to specific countries is fully conventional and refers only to the traditions' origins and by no means suggests that their scope was limited to these countries and professions. As it has already been mentioned, even today these traditions impact on how one thinks of legal professions, the best example of this influence being Poland, where combined and mixed elements belonging to each of the mentioned traditions are found.

Contemporary transformations of legal ethics, occurring in each of its traditions, are juridisation, professionalisation and globalisation. These transformations may be viewed in many ways and a commonly discussed perspective in this matter is the view that the effect of changes will be the domination of one of the traditions of legal ethics, which will either absorb or marginalise the others. American legal ethics is indicated as the one with greatest chances for this, and contemporary transformations of legal ethics are referred to collectively as "Americanisation"[2]. Another possibility is to accept that one deals not with the absorption and marginalisation of one tradition by another but with a specific blending of all traditions into one, relatively homogeneous, normative and theoretical structure, in which particular traditions will completely lose their identity.

Irrespective of how it is in reality, attention should be paid to the following circumstances that will help better understand these transformations. Firstly, juridisation, professionalisation and globalisation of legal ethics should be considered as only aspects of some broader social processes, which go far beyond the issue of lawyers' moral conduct. Additionally, they are not independent but interrelated processes that express some deeper aspirations of lawyers and of societies of which they are a part – processes often having a very clear political character. Secondly, it has to be remembered that all traditions of legal ethics have common roots in the processes of Western legal culture

2 T. Stawecki, "Od perfekcjonizmu moralnego do ścisłych reguł odpowiedzialności zawodowej: droga ku globalnej etyce prawniczej?", ["From Moral Perfectionism to Precise Rules of Professional Responsibility: The Way to Global Legal Ethics?"], in: *Etyka prawnicza. Stanowiska i perspektywy*, ed. H. Izdebski, P. Skuczyński, Warsaw 2008, pp. 131-157.

formation, and that they are in fact only different views on the same problems arising from the tension between moral thought and legal thought. Strong development of national elements in this culture over last centuries cannot reverse what is common in it and what, probably because of present transformations in legal ethics, regains its former significance.

1.2. The beginnings of legal ethics

The history of legal ethics is closely connected with the history of: legal professions, the system of justice and law itself. Therefore, the origins of legal ethics may be searched in the origins of social groups that deal with the law, and hence these groups should be, at least roughly, discussed. Of fundamental significance in this matter is the appearance of people to whom law is the main occupation, and also the internal diversity of this group depending on the nature of their work. In other words, the focus is on the development of the legal community together with its professional structure with a reservation that, here, both aspects "community" and "professional" should be interpreted broadly. This reservation is necessary since the present concept of "profession" does not seem appropriate in relation to ancient or medieval lawyers.

These processes have begun as far back as Antiquity, primarily accompanying the development of Roman law. Other legal systems have never developed enough to reach the level enabling clear isolation of legal occupations. The reason for that was the blending of the law as normative order with custom and politics and, consequently, its complete lack of autonomy together with related lack of legal thought or legal methods as such. The appearance of law in a legal sense in Roman times lead to a more precise and clear differentiation of lawyers' groups[3]. Great importance must be ascribed here to the organisation and civil trial rules, which enabled the formation of representation. It is unclear whether representatives made some stable group since a party could assign this role to virtually anyone[4]. Also in criminal trials there has been a great progress made which enabled legal community development often described as "the birth of the lawyers' profession"[5]. This group is important because it gave rise to many rules that exist until today such

3 R. Pound, *The Lawyer from Antiquity to Modern Times*, Minnesota 1953, p. 35.

4 G. Holly, *Geschichte der Ehrengerichtsbarkeit der deutschen Rechtsanwälte*, Frankfurt am Main-Bern-New York-Paris 1989, pp. 11-12, R. Pound, *The Lawyer...*, pp. 37-41.

5 F. Payen, *O powołaniu adwokatury i sztuce obrończej*, [*On the Bar's Vocation and the Art of Defence*], Warsaw 1938, p. 37.

as the privilege of wearing a toga[6] and many regulations being the subject of present legal ethics. One should also mention notaries, who became a very dynamically developing group mainly because of the Hellenistic influence. They were a considerably varied community but what they had in common was the fact that they prepared documents of special status, which, in time, became public documents, and the notaries themselves started to be regarded as practising a profession of public trust[7].

However, the most significant group were jurisconsults, about whom Harold J. Berman writes that among Roman lawyers, "[...] these were the only professionals. It was their chief task to give legal advice to praetors, judges, to advocates, to litigants, to clients wishing to engage in legal transactions."[8] What was characteristic of their professionalism was that in the opinions they voiced "no elaborately reasoned justification was needed, for to persons outside the elite group the jurist's own authority was enough and those inside would understand the reasons well enough"[9]. This dualism in the lawyers-society relations in time will become something common and spreading throughout all groups of lawyers. In the case of jurisconsults it is also significant that they did not engage in legal proceedings but consultancy only, which is why schools of law and professional literature could be created.

The professional structure of legal community that originated in Antiquity has survived until today because of the reception – with more or less modifications – of Roman law. Still, the Middle Ages and the early modern era have brought two major changes, namely the beginning of legal education of academic type and the inclusion of judicial state into the legal community. The creation of a law school in Bologna in the end of the 11th century and the adoption of its curriculum by other universities in the following centuries is significant not only because, "trained in the new legal science, successive generations of university graduates went into the chanceries and other offices of the emerging ecclesiastical and secular states o serve as counselors, judges, advocates, administrators, legislative draftsmen,"[10] and that it, "[…] brought together legal scholars teachers and students from all over Europe, brought them

6 This is why they were also called *togati*, G. Holly, *Geschichte der Ehrengerichtsbarkeit...*, p. 8.

7 A. Oleszko, *Ustrój polskiego notariatu*, [*The Structure of the Polish Notary*], Kraków 1999, pp. 22, 24-25.

8 H.J. Berman, *Law and Revolution: the Formation of the Western Legal Tradition*, Cambridge Massachusetts-London 1983, p. 135.

9 J.P. Dawson, *The Oracles of the Law*, Ann Arbor 1968, pp. 116-117, after: H.J. Berman, *Law and Revolution…*, p. 129.

10 H.J. Berman, *Law and Revolution…*, p. 120.

into contact not only with one another but also [...] made them a calling or, in today's terminology, a profession," but also because law itself, "was no longer, as it had been before the rise of the universities, a branch of rhetoric, on the one hand, and of ethics and politics, on the other. While in the Roman Empire the autonomy of legal thought had been maintained by practitioners, especially praetors and professional legal advisers, in Western Europe that autonomy was maintained by the universities." The universities could fulfil the task as long as they simultaneously met conditions of social and axiological nature according to which the community of scholars was a privileged group that enjoyed much freedom and was guided by a "scientific code of values" such as integrity, objectivity, impartiality and adopting a position of doubt or organised scepticism[11]. The relationship between rationality and autonomy of law and between meeting certain ethical conditions by those who practised law is present in legal ethics even nowadays.

University education of lawyers allows us to speak of them as professionals in a broad sense of this term. However, it does not mean that typical legal occupations have been practised uniquely by them from the beginning. Especially – so characteristic of lawyers – the judge's role became a legal profession relatively late since, due to its political significance, justice administration was directly in the hands of monarchs and, in time, it was committed to the representatives of higher social classes appointed by monarchs to judicial posts. A turning point in this matter – at least in Continental Europe – was the founding of the Imperial Chamber Court (*Reichskammergericht*) in 1495, whose composition in large proportion involved people with legal education[12]. Since that moment in a growing number of courts it was required for judges to have an appropriate education, so that after some time the judge's profession started to be referred to as a legal profession. It is worth mentioning that since the beginning of the 20th century the increasing interest in judicial ethics is observed, which fact may signify a shift of focus in legal ethics from lawyers' ethics – in a broad sense – to a judicial one.

From the beginning, practising main legal occupations was subject to regulation and control, at whose bases lay quite precisely determined standards and more general ethical ideals. One may indicate several sources in which these two categories were formulated. First, there were regulations by courts, being the result of the wide-ranging subordination of lawyers acting before them to the

---

11 *Ibidem*, pp.122,161-162, 155, resp.

12 H. Conrad, *Deutsche Rechtsgeschichte, Band II, Neuzeit bis 1806,* Karlsruhe 1966, pp. 163-165.

authority of judges in proceedings[13]. This form of regulation is present nowadays in countries in which relationships between judges and lawyers remain strong; that is the situation in the United States, where one may speak of good relations between the bar and the bench[14], and in Germany, where not long time ago lawyers were assigned to particular courts. In both cases, characteristic high level of legal professions integration manifests itself in daily cooperation in courts, but also in common standards of education and recruitment.

Secondly, lawyers came under a number of statutes starting with those regulating whole branches of substantive and procedural law, especially starting with the Corpus Iuris Civilis and the laws connected with political structure or proceedings in specific courts to those that regulated only issues belonging to lawyers' conduct[15].

Thirdly, together with the beginnings of professional organisations, with which lawyers associated more or less voluntarily, and which often had rights to recruit for a given profession as well as exercised disciplinary powers over those who already practised the profession, legal acts issued by their organs appeared[16]. In this case, it is difficult to speak of codes of professional ethics in the present sense of this word, but certainly one may discern here self-regulation, which is one of the conditions of professional ethics codification.

Fourthly, a great importance should be ascribed to all kinds of professional oaths: those taken as a pledge at the admittance to a particular profession and those taken periodically, for instance yearly, before a court or a professional organisation that exercised power over a particular lawyer[17]. Even today oaths are an important source of legal ethics, though not so much of its standards – those are usually included in regulations made by courts, the legislator or professional organisations – as of its ethical ideals.

Fifthly, this normative structure composed of many elements of different types was completed with sentences from normative ethics. Their special status stemmed from a typical to scholasticism tendency to ascribe to them a status of authoritative sources of knowledge. As an example one may point to the reflections on lawyers by Cicero and Thomas Aquinas. The former, in his work *On the Laws*, raises important issues of combining legal practice and legal science suggesting that what is necessary for satisfying needs of ordinary people

13 R. Pound, *The Lawyer…*, pp. 26, 50, G. Holly, *Geschichte der Ehrengerichtsbarkeit...*, pp. 19-20.

14 J. Leubsdorf, *Man in His Original Dignity. Legal Ethics in France*, Aldershot-Burlington USA-Singapore-Sydney 2001, pp. 6-7.

15 G. Holly, *Geschichte der Ehrengerichtsbarkeit...*,pp. 17, 28, 37.

16 *Ibidem*, p. 39.

17 *Ibidem*, pp. 10, 25, 26, 35, 37.

in scientific approach gives little effect[18], and he signalises problems connected with the monopoly of clerks of the court on authenticating legal acts and with private motives in playing prosecutor's function. He acknowledges that being driven by such motives makes one expect real severity from indictment[19].

Reflections of Aquinas on legal ethics are contained in one volume of *Summa Theologica* devoted to the issue of justice. The reflections include three points, the first of which concerns judicial ethics, the second prosecutors' ethics, and the third lawyers' ethics[20]. Particular subjects are divided into more specific questions as, for example, "whether a judge may pronounce a sentence on the basis of presented evidence in spite of the truth known to him?", which question raises the issue of judges' impartiality. Similarly, questions like, "can accusation be a duty?", "does accusation become unjust due to libel, embezzlement or accusation withdrawal?", or, "does a prosecutor accusing unjustly deserve to be punished with revenge?", concern prosecutors' impartiality problem. Yet, the most inspiring even today may be questions related to the defenders' work such as, "whether a lawyer is obliged to defend the poor?", "is it just that the law forbids some people to play the role of defenders?", "is a lawyer sinning by defending an unjust case?", "can a lawyer take remuneration for defence?"[21]

Posing these theoretical questions as well as the content of regulations on lawyers make it possible to identify several issues that have been virtually always present in this regard. From the earliest times lawyers' loyalty was under consideration – loyalty, both to courts, clients and colleagues – as well as the possibility of non-disclosing evidence known to the defence – which is the issue of confidentiality – the admissibility of accepting fees and charges for providing legal aid, including the question of reasonable fees for the services. Lawyers were expected to have impeccable characters[22] and necessary competence, to show honesty and litigation fairness. They were also bound to provide legal advice for the poor[23]. Different standards, which in history have been set for

---

18 Cicero, *O prawach*, [*On Laws*] I, 14, Kęty 1999.

19 *Ibidem*, III, 47-48.

20 St. Thomas Aquinas, *Suma teologiczna*, [*Summa Theologica*], vol. 18, *Justice*, questions 67, 68 and 71.

21 Cf. T. Stawecki, "Etyka prawnicza a filozofia prawa", ["Legal Ethics and Philosophy of Law"], in: *Etyka zawodów prawniczych. Etyka prawnicza,* ed. H. Izdebski, P. Skuczyński, Warsaw 2006, pp. 138-142.

22 For modern interpretations of this requirement see M. Laskowski, "Ustawowe pojęcie 'nieskazitelność charakteru'", ["Statutory Term 'Character Impeccability'"], in: *Prokuratura i Prawo* 2008, no. 6, pp. 50-65.

23 C.R. Andrews, "Standards of Conduct for Lawyers: An 800-Year Evolution", *Southern Methodist University Law Review* 57, Fall 2004, pp. 1385-1458. Cf. also R. Pound, *The*

lawyers in relation to particular issues together with the way of justifying these standards and also specific relations in which various forms of standards regulation – all these in time have contributed to the establishment of traditions of legal ethics[24].

1.3. Traditions of legal ethics

1.3.1. The French tradition

The central element of the French tradition of legal ethics are behaviour standards of one profession, namely of lawyers (*avocats*). Naturally, this does not mean that in France there is only one legal profession or that other groups of lawyers do not encounter any moral problems in their practice, to which they answer with their own standards of professional behaviour. On the contrary, each of the professions may be characterised by its own list of duties and virtues, history rooted in Roman times and by socially important roles ascribed to these professions[25]. Nevertheless, they have always stayed on the sidelines and under the influence of lawyers' ethics, though often in opposition to it, and in the recent decades they are being gradually and systematically absorbed by the bar. The influence of French lawyers' ethics has never been limited to their homeland but has spread far beyond its borders. However, it was always accompanied with the saying that, "this estate is far more esteemed in France than in other countries."[26]

The factors considerably determining the French tradition of legal ethics are the system of justice organisation and the form of judicial proceedings in France. Many times in history, the great influence of political powers on judges and prosecutors as well as the principle of inquisition have imposed on lawyers the role of uncomfortable opposition taking it as a point of honour to defend due rights of the clients. The first standards of lawyers' conduct were instituted with a royal order from 1274, which commanded them to accept only just cases,

---

Lawyer..., pp. 43, 52-53, and G. Holly, *Geschichte der Ehrengerichtsbarkeit*..., pp. 6, 9-10, 17, 21-22, 25, 27, 29, 35, 40 and 74.

24 Further reflections on traditions of legal ethics were published as P. Skuczyński, "Tradycje etyki prawniczej a nowoczesne zawody prawnicze", ["Traditions of Legal Ethics and Modern Legal Professions"], in: *Etyka-deontologia-prawo,* ed. P. Steczkowski, Rzeszów 2008, pp. 355-369.

25 J. Leubsdorf, *Man in His*..., , p. 93.

26 D. Torosiewicz, *Myśli o powołaniu obrońców sądowych*, [*Reflections on the Court Advocates' Vocation*], Warsaw 1822, reprint 1917, pp. 13-14, updated spelling.

defend them carefully and loyally and not to charge clients excessively[27]. In time, greater significance in relation to the control of lawyers' actions was given to their associations, which over time transformed into a self-governing professional organisation with the right of controlling admission and discipline. It served internal functions by taking care of an appropriate ethical level of its members as well as external ones by defending a political or even constitutional role of a buffer between the state and citizens. It may be said that French lawyers by the 16th century have formed their ethos, if not professional ethics, which over next centuries was developed and consolidated, with a golden age in the 18th and the 19th centuries[28].

French lawyers have claimed – and to a great extent they claim it even today – that correct fulfilment of their role is possible only after meeting specific conditions. The most important of them is full independence in practising their profession. As a general standard, it is taken very broadly and is a source of many more specific norms. Firstly, it is primarily independence from the state, with limitations or simply a ban on holding state positions while practising in the profession, but also clear separation of lawyers from other legal professions, judges and prosecutors especially, who are considered government functionaries. In addition, regulation and control of legal practice essentially by a professional self-governing organisation is justified by the independence principle as a need of removing all political powers' influence on lawyers[29].

Secondly, lawyers should be independent from their clients. Among other things, it means that lawyers have complete freedom of choice of their clients, and only they decide whether to plead a particular case. It is perfectly acceptable and normal that lawyers in this respect will consider moral assessment of the case and of the client. In this sense lawyers are their clients' first judges[30]. With the above conditions met, the act of accepting a case means, on one hand, that it will be run with more dedication than a case which a lawyer would accept in spite of himself, and on the other, that in the eyes of the public opinion and the court the case itself gains support of an authority.

Furthermore, while conducting the case lawyers should retain their independence from the client since their task is not to, "expose before the judge all of the client's claims whatever they might be. Instead, lawyers' task is first of all to separate the wheat from the chaff," and to, "present the outcome of their

27 J. Leubsdorf, *Man in His...*, p. 61.

28 *Ibidem*, p. 62; G. Holly, *Geschichte der Ehrengerichtsbarkeit...*, pp. 31-41. Cf. also J. Leubsdorf, "On the History of the French Legal Ethics", *University of Chicago Law School Roundtable* 2001, no. 8, pp. 341-352.

29 J. Leubsdorf, *Man in His...*, pp. 4-11.

30 *Ibidem*, p.15.

inquiry and inspection as the expression of his own thoughts." Therefore, lawyers are not bound by any guidelines or commands from the client, but also none of their declarations is binding to the client but they are formulated only on the lawyer's own behalf. Great significance is ascribed to the rejection of representation as a relation between the lawyer and the client. It is claimed that by "separating the assistance principle and the mandate principle the French bar was constituted and it reached positions that cannot be compared to anything."[31]

The independence from the client principle manifests itself also in the standards related to the confidentiality and financial relations. The former is so expanded that, on one hand, it is also directed 'against the client' and covers information which the lawyer received from the opposite party's lawyer, and, on the other, even the client's consent does not dismiss the lawyer from the obligation to keep the secret. In financial matters lawyers should never let themselves become dependent on the client; for example, it is unacceptable to take any deposits. It is forbidden to settle the amount of remuneration depending on the case verdict, which is traditionally called *pactum de quota litis* (contingent fee, success fee), or pursue debts from the client in court. This is why, with reference to ancient terminology, one rather speaks of remuneration than amount due[32].

Thirdly, lawyers should remain independent from other lawyers. This would also entail the command to provide services in the form of individual practice and a ban on going into partnerships, establishing joint law firms or employing one lawyer by another. The relation between lawyers should be based on equality, so that the independence of each one of them strengthens the independence of the bar as a whole, and on companionship together with goodwill of almost familial character[33].

The other side of French lawyers' absolute independence was to demand from them very high ethical requirements. They should act not only independently and according to defined standards, but they should also be equipped in a whole array of virtues enabling them to take right decisions and discern just conduct. The most important virtues were: dignity, conscientiousness, honesty, honour, loyalty, delicacy, self-restraint, kindness, impartiality and tact[34]. Thus, virtues were equally certain qualities of every lawyer, which their individual moral conduct should consist of, and certain behaviour standards flouting of which would make lawyers responsible

---

31 F. Payen, *O powołaniu…*, p. 50.

32 G. Holly, *Geschichte der Ehrengerichtsbarkeit...*, p. 40. More on independence from clients see J. Leubsdorf, *Man in His...*, pp. 13-28.

33 J. Leubsdorf, *Man in His...*, pp. 29-38.

34 *Ibidem*, p. 39.

disciplinarily. Virtues did not have to be precisely defined and to a significant extent they lasted unwritten since the bar constituted a kind of moral community, in which individual and social aspects of morality were in an inseparable relation. On one hand, the fact that particular lawyers possessed these virtues and were guided by them was the reason why the entire bar enjoyed trust and great esteem. However, on the other hand, possession of these virtues was possible only within the framework of an independent community of all lawyers. It should be specially emphasised that the bar thus understood was to forever remain an exclusive occupation and the lawyers themselves were to function as the elite of the elite. As far as independence is concerned, "it was considered a point of honour for them to remain not merely independent, but the most independent of all people," while in relation to virtues, "impeccable honesty was probably even more expected from them than skill."[35]

1.3.2. The American tradition

Another great modern tradition of legal ethics is related to American lawyers. However, it must be noted that it has undergone significant evolution and today it remains one of the most influential on a global scale. Contrary to the European continent, the number of legal professions in American tradition is limited. The basic dividing line is marked by separating the bar and the bench, which means the lawyers are on one side and the judges on the other[36]. This line also divides legal ethics and judicial ethics. Nevertheless, it is noteworthy that the relations between these two professional groups and their standards of conduct are much closer than, for instance, in the French tradition. Both the significant level of legal community integration and its considerable openness make the American lawyers the most numerous legal profession in the world.

Specificity of American legal ethics in great part results from the character of legal procedures, which, on one hand, require from lawyers much more activity in the adversary trial system, and, on the other, create the need for precise delimitation of acceptable and forbidden conduct, which is due to the significant role of the court in control over lawyers' action in the proceedings. The beginnings of American legal ethics may be traced to the first half of the 19th century, and more exactly, in 1836 and 1854 in the works by David

35 F. Payen, *O powołaniu adwokatury...*, pp. 15-16.

36 Cf. R. Tokarczyk, "Charakterystyka ogólna amerykańskich profesji prawniczych", ["General Characterisation of American Legal Professions"], *Palestra* 1995, no. 5-6, pp. 128-143.

Hoffman – who is considered a pioneer in the field of legal ethics[37] – and by Georg Sharswood, respectively. To this day, both of them are cited in the introduction to *Model Rules of Professional Conduct*, even though modern standards, like their justifications, diverge much from these authors' views. Despite some differences between the two, legal ethics was in both cases, as a rule, based on an array of Republican virtues, of which self-restraint was the most important. Being guided by these virtues was to lead to the attainment of the ideal of a good life[38]. Moralism of this perspective was evident since the boundaries of acceptable action for the client were set by moral standards, and thus accepting unjust cases by lawyers or using immoral methods, even if they seemed legal, was excluded. Only rejection of concepts based on close relationship between law and morality – concepts in which law served as a tool for forming good and virtuous citizens – and their replacement with a more formalistic approach has resulted in the reinterpretation of the problem of the limitations of American lawyers' acceptable activity for their clients.

Already for G. Sharswood – though his view relies on the justice-centred legal practice model – of great importance was the problem of distinguishing legal and moral limits on lawyers' acceptable conduct and each citizen's rights to have his case examined uniquely on the basis of the currently binding law[39]. However, only after the American Civil War and under the influence of industrialisation and urbanisation processes a turnabout towards the client-centred model took place, namely loyalty to the client was chosen as the fundamental principle of the American legal ethics. Theoretical and regulatory efforts were directed to define clear, and as far as possible procedural, rules determining limits of this loyalty. Though American lawyers are familiar with lawyer-client relations models that are based on a kind of legal paternalism, the dominating model seems to be the one in which a lawyer is considered to be a hired gun – a lackey that loyally carries out all client's orders not undertaking their assessment[40]. Thus conceived loyalty is not only acceptable, but is also a

---

37 R.L. Rotunda, M.I. Krauss, *Legal Ethics in a Nutshell*, St. Paul 2003, p. 1.

38 Cf. N.W. Spaudling, "The Myth of Civic Republicanism: Interrogating the Ideology of Antebellum Legal Ethics", *Fordham Law Review* 2003, no. 71, pp. 1410-1419.

39 M.H. Hoeflich, "Legal Ethics in the Nineteenth Century: the 'Other Tradition'", *University of Kansas Law Review, Special Issue on Professional Responsibility* 1999, no. 47, pp. 803-806; N.W. Spaudling, *The Myth of Civic Republicanism...*, pp. 1419-1423.

40 For further discussion of lawyer-client relation models see T.L. Shaffer, R.F. Cocharn, Jr., *Lawyers, Clients and Moral Responsibility,* St. Paul 1994, pp. 5-56. In Polish literature see R. Sarkowicz, *Amerykańska etyka prawnicza,* [*American Legal Ethics*], Kraków 2004, pp. 57-71.

lawyer's duty, and so, with the origin of this model, the problem of zeal or overzealous representation – in criminal cases called "zeal advocacy" – arises. Because of it, the loyalty to the client principle is often employed to justify exceptionally fierce rhetoric used by American lawyers, which is a source of their constant criticism by public opinion.

The aforementioned efforts to settle limits of the loyalty principle have found their most characteristic expression in ethical codification, which started with the enactment of the *Code of Ethics* by the lawyers of Alabama in 1887. The very place of the code origin indicated this event's ambiguity. The ambiguity is expressed in the multitude of goals which the authors of the code wanted to attain. It was not solely about curbing some excesses caused by lawyers' overzealousness, but also about something just the opposite, namely protecting the clients from incidents of disloyalty or inappropriate practice of the profession. Here, an important role is ascribed to the social context of the southern states, including Alabama, having lost the war and a newly arisen necessity to open the legal profession to the masses of those to whom the admission to the profession was previously barred. Since then radical demographic changes among lawyers have been present in American ethical codes, which are criticised for their conservative, if not exclusive, character[41].

Codes of ethics have soon spread over the whole territory of the United States appearing in particular states as well as on the federal level. As early as in 1908, the *American Bar Association* adopted *Canons of Professional Ethics*, which in 1969 was replaced with *Model Code of Professional Responsibility*, which in turn was replaced in 1983 with *Model Rules of Professional Conduct.* In the codes' titles as well as in their content there may be observed a gradual withdrawal from ethical terminology and opting for technical and procedural terms instead. This process is related to the change in the status of norms that are included in the codes – norms that evolved from sanction-free standards towards "black letter rules" backed by institutions of disciplinary responsibility[42]. Recently, within the framework of *Ethics 2000* program – expressing the need for further improvement and more precision in American lawyers' rules of conduct – a broad revision of norms contained in the code of 1983 was carried out. It has to be stressed that a major part of the theoretical discussion and legal

41 Cf. A. Marston, "Guiding the Profession: the 1887 Code of Ethics of the Alabama State Bar Association", *Alabama Law Review* 1998, no. 49.

42 See P. Skuczyński, "Metoda i przedmiot etyki prawniczej", ["Legal Ethics Method and Subject"], in: *Etyka zawodów prawniczych. Etyka prawnicza*, ed. H. Izdebski, P. Skuczyński, Warsaw 2006, pp. 59-61; T. Stawecki, *Od perfekcjonizmu...*, pp. 133-139. More also in the chapter on legal ethics juridisation.

education in the field of legal ethics focuses on these rules and responsibilities derived from them[43].

The aforementioned precision together with technical and procedural character of American legal ethics rules may be judged by the codes' volume. Especially from the European perspective, it is striking that so much place is given to the confidentiality problem or the conflict of interests[44]. Characteristic is the regulation of these and other issues that takes into account that lawyers' practice in law firms, where they face quantitatively and qualitatively different moral problems than in the case of working in the form of individual practice. To a large extent legal practice is treated as a business-like activity as evidenced – *inter alia* – by the following: allowing legal service advertising and other commercial forms of attracting clients, the possibility of flexible charging for lawyers' services depending on the lawsuit being successful or not, which is known as the "contingent fee", providing regulation on selling a law firm and the subordination of one lawyer to another. Lawsuits involving lawyers and their former clients concerning due payment or the inappropriate quality of legal services are possible and they actually often take place.

Finally, the democratic character of American legal corporation and the close relationship of American lawyers with the economic life in their country have to be emphasised. Even though lawyers are often criticised for, "commercial attitude towards their profession, unjustifiably high prices, instrumental treatment of clients, continual attempts to shirk any external control and responsibility in regard to quality, reliability and competence of their services,"[45] it is absolutely justified to say that – because of continuous debate on practice rules and constant reforms and revisions of professional duties – the American tradition of legal ethics is vital and thriving even nowadays.

1.3.3. The German tradition

The German tradition of legal ethics, in comparison to the other ones discussed in the present study, seems to have the shortest but simultaneously the most stormy and dramatic history. In the scope of the professional structure and task

---

43 Critically on this phenomenon B.H. Barton, "The ABA, the Rules, and Professionalism: the Mechanics of Self-Defeat and a Call for a Return to the Ethical, Moral, and Practical Approach of the Canons", *North Carolina Law Review* 2005, no. 83.

44 See M. Jurzyk, "Wybrane zagadnienia kolizji interesów w amerykańskiej praktyce prawniczej", ["Selected Issues on Conflict of Interests in the American Legal Practice"], *Radca Prawny* 2002, no. 3, pp. 58-73.

45 R. Sarkowicz, *Amerykańska...*, p. 12.

division between particular professions it does not differ from the solutions found in other European countries. Thus, one may distinguish professions within public service, namely judges and prosecutors, and professions, such as lawyers, practised on a similar to freelance professional basis. As far as notaries are concerned, the situation is more complex because this profession may be practised while remaining in public service, separately or combined with a lawyer's practice. What is significant is that the system of German lawyers' education is under total control of the state and that the requirements before candidates for a legal profession – within the framework of two state examinations – are the same for candidates for each of the professions.

In spite of the similarity of the structure and task division to those in other countries, the very understanding of these tasks as well as the lawyers' position in relation to the state and society are specific of German legal professionals. Historically, this understanding was influenced by two factors. The first one rested on the rivalry between the forming German bureaucracy and the system of justice: rivalry occurring on various levels, ranging from the material and social status of the officials and legal professionals to the issues of their independence from the monarchy. Despite partial successes, the justice system usually lost in this rivalry, which resulted in its being regarded as occupying a place aside the mainstream of legal life, and therefore, as unattractive[46].

Another factor influencing the development of the German tradition of legal ethics was the constantly changing political situation, which simultaneously meant radical re-evaluations of the legal system. Starting with the Wilhelmian epoch, through the Weimar Republic and the Nazi totalitarianism, the liberation system of the Federal Republic and the communist totalitarianism – German lawyers used to find themselves in a completely new, totally different political situation every ten or fifteen years or every couple of decades. Every system change meant not only a crisis of law (*Rechtskrise*) but also a crisis of lawyers (*Juristenkrise*)[47] by making them face some exceptional dilemmas. Attitudes in response to these dilemmas were varied and, on one hand, included active involvement in the re-building of a new political and systemic reality, but, on the other, manifested in a withdrawal from professional life or in heroical adherence to the values they believed in. However, it is noticeable that the latter

46 K. Scheider, "Der deutsche Jurist als Bürokrat – Zur Beziehung zwischen der sozialen Role des deutschen Juristen und der Entwicklung der staatlichen Bürokratie", in: *Soziologische Probleme juristischer Berufe*, ed. W. Kaupen, R. Werle, Göttingen 1974, p. 74.

47 B. Rüthers, "Recht und Juristen unter dem Sog und Druck wechselnder politicher Systeme", in: *125 Jahre Rechtsanwaltskammer Frankfurt am Main, Oberlandesgericht Frankfurt am Main, Rechtspflege*, Frankfurt am Main 2004, pp. 95-98.

attitude, sometimes referred to as "the sacrifice of one's own professional ethics,"[48] was unpopular and that resigning from a professional career according to the dictates of one's own conscience was significantly less frequent among lawyers than among officials working in administration[49].

The reason behind such attitudes of lawyers is to a considerable extent the fact that basic requirement set before them was the correct fulfilment of their professional roles and a too-far-reaching involvement could have been considered as exceeding their bounds. Once they recognized and acknowledged their roles, the German lawyers only reluctantly changed them. Thus, it is difficult to find in literature before 1960s a serious debate on legal ethics, or at least on lawyers' tasks in the changing world, that would be of culture-forming value. Therefore, lawyers in Germany are referred to as professionals conservative under all circumstances and conditions[50].

This effect is enhanced by the way these social roles are defined; the roles in their fundamental scope are established by the system or the legal order and they even may be *a priori* deduced from it[51]. On one hand, the lawyers' task is to always ascertain the content of the law and its subsequent application, which thus means translating evaluative judgements of the legislator into specific results in social and political realities, and in that sense the lawyers are always "in service" of every political power[52]. This, of course, exposes them to various hazards, beginning with being ideologised or indoctrinated, to simply putting their life in danger in the case of a change in the political system[53]. Particularly difficult dilemmas in this matter are posed before lawyers, who are assigned the role of justice administration organs (*Organe der Rechtspflege*) by the legal system, but who practise a free profession and are obliged to be loyal towards their clients[54]. However, it would be difficult to say of German lawyers that their main task was the close cooperation with the client in order to most fully realise his or her interests, as in the case of the American tradition of legal ethics, or independent and dignified protection of an individual's civil rights against the

---

48 *Ibidem*, p. 118.

49 K. Scheider, *Der deutsche Jurist...*, pp. 99-100.

50 R. Dahrendorf, "Zur Sozilogie der juristischen Berufe in Deutschland", *Anwaltsblatt* 1964, no. 14, p. 229.

51 *Ibidem*.

52 B. Rüthers , *Recht und Juristen…*, pp. 103-105.

53 *Ibidem*.

54 M. Lehmann, *Ethical Duties of Lawyers – Perspectives from the Continent*, XXIII World Congress of The International Association for Philosophy of Law and Social Philosophy (IVR) Kraków 2007, workshop *Legal Ethics: Its Horizon and Mandates*, copied materials, pp. 14-16. Cf. also B. Rüthers, *Recht und Juristen...*, pp. 117-120.

state as in the French tradition – even though this latter tradition had some influence on the German bar and free professions in general, especially with regard to such concepts as prestige and profession's dignity[55].

Another aspect of lawyers' social roles being determined by the system or legal order is the fact that positive law is considered a fundamental source of specific obligations. Therefore, reference to legal ethics expressed in terms of duties and virtues is rarely found[56], but reference to professional law or state's law (*Standesrecht*) is common[57]. Of course, aside from statutory regulations, these obligations consist of ethical codifications (*Berufsordnung, Richtlinien*) – whose legal status and the role in a legal system are not clear – together with unwritten or customary norms. However, all these sources are included as positive law[58]. In consequence, the interpretation and assessment of particular duties of lawyers are carried out from the point of view of their general role determined by the system or legal order concepts, which practically makes it impossible to go beyond the legislator's evaluative judgements and the service to the political power in solving specific problems.

This situation is explained by the fact that, contrary to German bureaucracy, which developed a significantly solid professional ethos versed towards virtues and values, legal professions in Germany have always been characterised by a kind of passivism[59]. In the case of bureaucracy the conflict between professional ethics and political power was possible, whereas lawyers usually remained loyal to the latter since they believed that only in this way they will be able to correctly fulfil their role determined by the law. Thus, what should be considered as characteristic of the German tradition of legal ethics is not only its being based on correct fulfilment of professional roles, but also that it obliges lawyers to comply with factors determining these roles, which results in the situation where lawyers' part in establishing their own obligation is limited.

55 E. Steindorff, *Freie Berufe – Stiefkinder der Rechtsordnung?*, Köln 1980, pp. 6-7.

56 Cf. for example F. Busse, "Anwaltsethik unter Geltung des neuen Berufsrecht", *Anwaltsblatt* 1998, no. 5, p. 231.

57 E. Steindorff, *Freie Berufe...*, pp. 11-16.

58 Though, there are different opinions, cf. E. Steindorff, *Freie Berufe...*, p. 15, and A. Brandstetter, *Der Erlaß von Berufsordnungen durch die Kammern der freien Berufe*, Berlin 1971, and H. Schippel, "Die allgemeinen Richtlinien für die Berufsausübung der Notare", *Deutsche Notar-Zeitschrift*, 1963, pp. 263-264.

59 K. Scheider, "Der deutsche Jurist...", pp. 69, 72, 102.

1.4. Transformations of legal ethics

1.4.1. Juridisation

The term "juridisation" in relation to professional ethics was first introduced in Polish literature in the context of dangers that this process poses to moral norms' functions, and referred to a situation in which, "abiding by ethical rules was increasingly fortified by the state's duress." This may also lead to the substitution of moral responsibility, in case of not observing these rules, with a legal one, which means abiding by the rules "in order to avoid negative consequences," and thus "out of purely legalistic motives."[60] Such attitude focuses only on one side of the process and, within it, on only one problem. Meanwhile, it seems that increasingly popular incorporation of professional ethics – including legal ethics – in broadly understood normative acts[61] has a more complex character. Nevertheless, I believe that is best to stay with the term "juridisation" as the most comprehensive one to distinguish two aspects in its sense, namely codification and legalisation.

1.4.1.1. Codification

Codification, in relation to legal ethics, is simply the formulation of codes of professional ethics, which are as far as possible not contradictory and complete bodies of ethical norms for each profession. In the case of lawyers, the beginnings of codification are usually traced back to a movement initiated in the United States as early as the end of the 19th century. Almost simultaneously the idea of forming codes of professional ethics appeared also in Europe, though, here, it had to wait considerably longer for its realisation. In recent years, thus conceived codification has become especially intensive in many various countries, also in those belonging to different legal cultures, and it encompasses many legal professions.

In 1887, in the American state of Alabama, lawyers associated in the local bar adopted the first *Code of Ethics*[62], which became the foundation for a

60 P. Rączka, *Nadzór nad samorządem zawodowym*, [*Control over Self-Governing Professional Organisation*], Toruń 1999, p. 73.

61 Broad (an act including abstract and general norms) and narrow (an act including legal norms) understanding of a normative act in the context of professional ethics was proposed by J. Stelmach, R. Sarkowicz, *Teoria prawa*, [*A Theory of Law*], Kraków 2001, p. 210.

62 On the breakthough role of this code and sometimes hilarious incidents connected to its formation cf. A. Marston, *Guiding the Profession...*

nationwide code called *Canons of Professional Ethics* formed by the *American Bar Association in* 1908. This code, as well as the following ones on the federal level, was not applied directly by lawyers, but required adopting by particular bars in each state. The bars were free to modify and even renounce these codes, which they often did. Such a model character of the codes found its expression in the name of the next one – *Model Code of Professional Responsibility* – which in 1969 replaced *Canons*. The situation was similar in the case of the most recent, but often modified, code, namely the *Model Rules of Professional Conduct* established in 1983. Thanks to such model codes established by the *American Bar Association,* legal ethics codification has gradually spread over the whole United States, and, despite some differences in particular states, similar standards are present in the whole country[63].

Apart from the United States, mainly in Europe, the representatives of the free legal professions – predominantly lawyers – were the ones who generally created first ethical codifications. Just to mention a few of such codifications let us recall the Austrian lawyers' code of 1951, the Japanese *Code of Ethics for Practicing Attorneys* of 1955, German lawyers' code of 1957, Icelandic *Codex Ethicus fyrir Lögmannfélag Islands* of 1960, Swedish *Code of Conduct for Members of the Swedish Bar Association* of 1971, or Swiss *Richtlinien SAV für die Pflichten – Codices der kantonalen Anwaltsverbände* of 1973.

A second wave of ethical codification began in the 1990s. Here, one may refer to the following codes as examples: Danish *Advokatsamfundets regler* of 1990, Dutch *Gedragsregels* of 1992, Latvian *Code of ethics of the Latvian Sworn Advocates* of 1993, Italian *Il Codice Deontologico Forense* of 1997, Estonian *Code of Conduct of the Estonian Bar Association* of 1998, Lithuanian *Code of Professional Ethics of Lawyers* and Hungarian *Szabályzata az ügyvédi hivatás etikai szabályairól és elvárásairól* of 1999, Slovenian *Code of Professional Conduct* of 2001, Scottish *Code of Conduct for Scottish Solicitors* and Norwegian *Rules of Conduct for Advocates* of 2002, and finally Slovak *Adwokatsky poriadak* of 2004[64].

---

63 Not only the content but also the character of these standards has evolved, which is discussed in the next point. An exhaustive presentation of the development of codification in the United States, including transformations involving their status, see Ch.W. Wolfram, "Toward a History of the Legalization of American Legal Ethics – I. Origins", *University of Chicago Law School Roundtable* 2001, no. 8; *idem*, "Toward a History of the Legalization of American Legal Ethics – II. The Modern Era", *Georgetown Journal of Legal Ethics* 2002, no. 15. In Polish literature, T. Stawecki, *Od perfekcjonizmu...*, pp. 133-139.

64 Enumeration mainly on the basis of a more detailed discussion in: M. Pieniążek, "Koncepcja etyki sytuacyjnej prawnika", ["A Conception of Situational Ethics of a

The same period witnesses the development of supranational and international codes. It encompasses the formation of, among other codes, *Code of Conduct for European Lawyers*, originally of 1988[65], *The International Association of Prosecutors' Standards of Professional Responsibility and Statement of the Essential Duties and Rights of Prosecutor* in 1999[66], and, in 2001, *Bangalore Principles of Judicial Conduct*[67].

In Poland, the first code of professional ethics for lawyers was *The Lawyer's Set of Principles and Dignities of the Profession* [*Zbiór Zasad i Godności Zawodu*] of 1961[68]. However, a dynamic development of legal ethical codifications occurred not before the last two decades, which established, *inter alia*, in 1987 the first *Principles of Ethics for the Legal Adviser Profession* [*Zasady Etyki Zawodu Radcy Prawnego*][69], in 1997 *Code of Professional Ethics for a Notary* [*Kodeks Etyki Zawodowej Notariusza*][70], in 2001 *Code of Professional Ethics for a Bailiff* [*Kodeks Etyki Zawodowej Komornika*][71], in 2002 *A Set of Ethical Principles for a Prosecutor* [*Zbiór Zasad Etycznych Prokuratora*] [72] and *A Set of Conduct Principles for Judges* [*Zbiór Zasad Postępowania Sędziów*] [73], and in 2003 *A Set of Principles of Professional Ethics for Judges* [*Zbiór Zasad Etyki Zawodowej Sędziów*][74].

Even this superficial overview of documents from the legal ethics field clearly indicates that codes of professional ethics are a basic form of expressing

---

Lawyer"], unpublished doctoral thesis, Kraków 2005, whose part was a basis for the publication of M. Pieniążek, *Etyka sytuacyjna prawnika*, [*Situational Ethics of a Lawyer*] Warsaw 2008.

65 CCBE plenary session resolution of 28th October 1988. Until the amendment of 28th November 1998 the code was entitled *Code of Conduct of Lawyers in the European Community*, it was then that the title was replaced with *Code of Conduct for Lawyers in the European Union*, and since the amendment of 19th May 2006 it is called *Code of Conduct for European Lawyers*. Cf. among others Ł. Bohdan, *Usługi prawnicze w Unii Europejskiej*,[*Legal Services in the European Union*], Kraków 2000, pp. 235-236, and R. Tokarczyk, *Etyka prawnicza*, [*Legal Ethics*], Warsaw 2005, p. 163.

66 IAP Executive Committee's resolution of 22nd April 1999.

67 Judicial Group on Strengthening Judicial Integrity's resolution of 2001. Eventually passed 25-26th November 2002.

68 Supreme Bar Council's resolution of 6-7th May 1961.

69 Legal Advisers National Congress' resolution of 1987.

70 National Council of the Notary of Poland's resolution no. 19/97 of 12th December 1997.

71 National Council of the Bailiffs of Poland's resolution of 26th June 2001.

72 National Congress of the Republic of Poland Prosecutors' Association's resolution of 25th May 2002.

73 Conference of Polish Judges Association Iustitia Delegates' resolution of 8th June 2002.

74 National Council of the Judiciary of Poland's resolution no. 16/2003 of 19th February 2003.

it nowadays, at least in regard to legal professions[75]. This fact is a source of many discussions and critical remarks, which most generally may be described as "an argument between the supporters of the so-called 'code-based ethics' and the supporters of 'codeless ethics'."[76] For instance, it is noted that, "since the times of Hippocrates doctors have multiplied codes not caring whether they are known nor accepted by patients and the public opinion. The codes have rarely referred to more general principles, and thus made tradition and doctor's opinions the highest authority. It seems that sometimes specific rules included in codes collide with, or even prevail over, more general norms. Abiding by them serves the interests of a professional group rather than the development of an impartial and a wide moral perspective."[77]

A relatively widespread and often cited reconstruction of this dispute has been provided by Magdalena Środa, who makes the following arguments against codification. Firstly, a code, "[...] is based on a presumption dangerous to morality, namely that the realm of values and duties may be transformed into an ordered and clear instruction of moral conduct. What flows from this is that a code of conduct reduces the problem of responsibility to abiding by norms. Here, the fulfilment of given duties, and not the reflection or the individual's conscience consideration, becomes the criterion of moral assessment." Secondly, "morality is something that is binding regardless of agreements and conventions. Professional ethics is connected with a convention, and even more significantly, with an agreement. In professional ethics the way of establishing its norms is suspicious. Who may decide about norms and goals of professional ethics [...]? All the interested? The representation? According to what criteria is it formed?" Thirdly, "[...] the need for the formulation of codes is of self-serving nature and arises in respect to those professions and public life institutions that are undergoing a crisis. Codes usually appear where simple honesty and personal morality are lacking."[78]

Similar arguments against codes as a means for regulating professional ethics or ethics in general were posed by Leszek Kołakowski. Firstly, he argued that a code bases on the assumption of moral rights and duties' symmetry. In other words, it assumes that duties contained in it may become the object of a

---

75 The following reflections to a great extent are repeating and developing the remarks included in P. Skuczyński, "Metoda i przedmiot etyki prawniczej", in: *Etyka zawodów prawniczych. Etyka prawnicza*, ed. H. Izdebski, P. Skuczyński, Warsaw 2006, pp. 59-62.

76 P. Łabieniec, "Etyka – Etyka zawodowa – Prawo (zarys problematyki)", ["Ethics–Professional Ethics–Law (the Outline of Issues)"], *Prokurator* 2002, no. 2, p. 22.

77 T.L. Beauchamp, J.F. Childress, *Zasady etyki medycznej*, [*Rules of Medical Ethics*], Warsaw 1996, p. 16.

78 M. Środa, Słowo wstępne. Biznes i cnoty, ["Preface. Business and Virtues"], in: J. Jackson, *Biznes i moralność*, Warsaw 1999, pp. XVI-XVIII.

claim. Whereas, the essence of morality is that one may require fulfilling moral duties only from oneself. Secondly, a code implies homogeneity of its decisions, and thus, a perfect hierarchy and consistency of moral norms. This in fact is a counterfactual assumption leading to apriorism, which in morality is unacceptable. Morality is something alive, full of conflicts and dilemmas that must be individually solved. Thirdly, an ethical code implies concordance of norms and moral judgements, which is also not true. For the subject of moral imperatives may often be deeds that are valued negatively, and inversely, deeds valued positively may be forbidden. Everything depends here on a particular situation, but codes exclude such type of valuation.[79]

The above remarks, which come down to pointing out deontologism, conventionalism and opportunism to codes of professional ethics' creators, together with dangers related to them, should certainly be taken into account. However, in response, one may formulate counterarguments showing certain one-sidedness of that severe criticism. First of all, it is to be noted that, "abiding by the code never absolves from individual responsibility but is helpful in articulating the criteria of this responsibility." Secondly, "professional ethics code very often contains the anti-pragmatic rule of honour (prestige, dignity). Thus, it is difficult to accuse it of 'self-interest', though undeniably to a significant extent it serves praxeological functions."[80] Thirdly, if one agrees with Jacek Hołówka that ethical norms may be a cause for human behaviour because of moral philosophy, collective conformism and social control[81], then codes of professional ethics may realise, or rather help realise, the two last functions. Fourthly, with several elementary requirements, which should be expected from a good code of professional ethics, being satisfied, one may dismiss the allegation of opportunism. Some classical propositions in this regard show that codes of conduct should concentrate on safeguarding the public interest, and the professional group's interest may not be its sole justification. The code's decisions should be of clearly obligatory nature and should form a basis for the enforcement of lawyers' professional duties. This is equal to saying that a code should in fact be a means of social control and not just a declaration or an appeal. Finally, codes of professional ethics should include only non-evident norms, not entrenched in common morality since repeating general moral rules is pointless[82].

---

79 L. Kołakowski, "Etyka bez kodeksu", ["Ethics Without a Code"], in: *Kultura i fetysze. Eseje*, Warsaw 2000, pp. 158-169.

80 M. Środa, "Słowo wstępne...", pp. XVI-XVIII.

81 J. Hołówka, *Etyka w działaniu,* [*Ethics in Action*], Warsaw 2001, p. 27.

82 R.T. De George, *Business Ethics*, New York-London 1990. Cf., among others, J. Stelmach, R. Sarkowicz, *Teoria...*, pp. 207-208; R. Sarkowicz, *Amerykańska...*,

On the basis of this discussion one may formulate two conclusions essential for further study. On one hand, it is to be marked that, "it is difficult to imagine deontology without clearly set principles,"[83] and these, at least in legal ethics, thanks to the codification process, are contained in codes of professional ethics. However, as it has been observed in the above discussion, no ethics can be reduced to a matter of duty. Therefore, it may be assumed that some part of professional ethics falls outside any codification attempts. On the other hand, "codes [...] should not simultaneously be a kind of 'legalisation of ethics'. Just the opposite, the point is that legal norms – including codes [...] – were rooted in a given community's systems of values."[84] This statement, also partially summing up the quarrel over codes of professional ethics, reveals some kind of particularistic character of this dispute, or rather accidental nature of codes of professional ethics existence. For it turns out that they may to a greater or lesser extent resemble law, and thus remain in different relation to ethics and to law as well. It also turns out that they are a historical product and so their status is not only unclear, but also it is not defined. This makes all generalisation and categorical valuations problematic.

In other words, not the existence of codes of professional ethics is dangerous, but reducing ethics to their regulations. Neither deontology, nor individuals' conduct may be rational or irrational only because of codes of professional ethics. Even if norms included in them perhaps may be reasons for practical reasoning, they are never the only reasons. For the present discussion it means, firstly, separating professional ethics problems from codes of professional ethics – this concerns theory and does not negate such relationship in practice – which process is taking place especially vividly nowadays. Secondly, the issue of codes should be considered in the context of their more or less legal character and in relation to law, and thus in the context of the second aspect of juridisation, namely of legalisation.

1.4.1.2. Legalisation

Apart from codification, one may also differentiate changes to the status of codes of professional ethics. Again, the changes are most visible in American

pp. 42-43; I. Bogucka, "Zagadnienia tworzenia i funkcjonowania etycznych standardów zawodów prawniczych", ["The Questions of Forming and Functioning of Legal Professions' Ethical Standards"], in: *Prawo a wartości. Księga jubileuszowa Profesora Józefa Nowackiego*, ed. I. Bogucka, Z. Tobor, Kraków 2003, pp. 12-16.

83 P. Łabieniec, *Etyka – Etyka zawodowa...*, p. 27.

84 W. Gasparski, Etyka biznesu – szkice do portretu, ["Business Ethics – a Portrayal Sketches"], in: *Etyka biznesu*, ed. J. Dietl, W. Gasparski, Warsaw 2002, p. 25.

legal ethics development, but undoubtedly also appear in other traditions of legal ethics. I assume that the very term "legalisation" in its fundamental sense means "legalise," and thus, it relates to legality of conduct or of state of things. Though, in the present study it is understood as a process of giving legal character to conduct norms or moral ideals and incorporating them in acts of gradually increasing rank. It may be said that legalisation in the sense accepted here is a process of transition from regulation measures typical of soft law to those typical of hard law, including statutes.

In the United States, starting with the first nationwide code of 1908, *Canons of Professional Ethics,* through *Model Code of Professional Responsibility* of 1969 up to *Model Rules of Professional Conduct* in 1983, the function as well as the terminology of the codes underwent a transformation each time. This is confirmed by the very names of the codes, in which terms *canons – code – rules*, as well as *ethics – responsibility – conduct*, changed respectively. Also the language used in them has become more technical and procedural and the withdrawal from ethical terminology more conspicuous. This avoidance of ethical terminology and its replacement with a professional one, having certain associations with professionalism, is to provide codifications with ideological neutrality.

With the language change, the content of the codes was getting closer to concrete and enforceable professional duties than to morality of aspiration referring to lofty ideals. Therefore, their function was gradually less of appealing or instructing, and more of regulating. And thus, while *Canons of Professional Conduct* of 1908 had unique characteristics of an appeal not fortified with the application of any kind of sanctions in a breach of norms case, the status of *Model Code of Professional Responsibility* of 1969 was more complicated. It consisted of three elements, "canons, ethical considerations and disciplinary rules."[85] Each canon had a corresponding ethical consideration as well as a disciplinary rule. The difference between those considerations and rules was primarily in the fact that breaching the latter resulted in disciplinary responsibility, whereas the former rather indicated aims and ideals which lawyers should pursue. As it is pointed out in literature, such structure of this code, both in philosophical and historical sense, is connected with the division into morality of duty and morality of aspiration – division as in the version of L.L. Fuller[86].

However, it was very soon decided that a complex structure of a code of professional ethics does not guarantee its sufficient effectiveness as far as ethical

85 R. Sarkowicz, *Amerykańska...*, p. 36.
86 T. Stawecki, *Etyka prawnicza a filozofia...*, pp. 146-147.

guidelines and disciplinary rules are concerned. For that reason, *Model Rules of Professional Conduct* of 1983 comprise only two elements: rules and commentaries, or guidelines that accompany the rules. To a great extent, these rules, have the character of professional duties, which are usually clear and precise. Corresponding comments, or guidelines, make it easier to remove any possible doubts by indicating the history of a rule formulation – including a discussion of preceding regulations – as well as by referring to the function of a given rule. This is why it may be said of the norms included in *Model Rules* that they are a kind of black letter rules of a few decades of achievements in the field of legal ethics, and thus their enforcement is possible just as of other legal rules. Naturally, one has to remember that the model character of the code requires a decision of a relevant state court or state legislature to make the norms directly binding, which, nevertheless, does not negatively affect the clarity as to which rules are in force.

As a result of this evolution, the status of codes of professional ethics in the United States is basically the same as of other legal acts. To American lawyers, "the codes of conduct are law or at least law-like, primarily because of their enforceability. They are the yardsticks by which grievance committees measure a lawyer's behavior, judges grant or deny motions, and juries accept or reject allegations of malpractice or breach of fiduciary duty,"[87] and so the norms in the codes are not only a material basis of disciplinary responsibility, but also of other kinds of legal responsibility. While to the European trained lawyers, especially those from the circle of the civil law culture, "the codes of conduct are general norms of professional behavior. The popular understanding is that the codes are less legalistic and less formal than their U.S counterparts."[88] Nevertheless, one has to remember that in some of the European countries their norms also belong to legal systems and as such are a basis for at least disciplinary or professional responsibility. This is significant because applying these sanctions, and thus enforcing the responsibility of – as it is usually accepted – a repressive type on the basis of acts not having legal character, is questionable in a society governed by the rule of law[89].

---

87 M.C. Daly, "The Dichotomy Between Standards and Rules: A New Way of Understanding the Differences in Perceptions of Lawyer Code of Conduct by U.S. and Foreign Lawyers", *Vanderbilt Journal of Transnational Law*, 1999, no. 32, p. 1122.

88 *Ibidem*.

89 On the sources of this dominating opinion and also on possible alternatives, cf. P. Skuczyński, "Granice odpowiedzialności dyscyplinarnej", ["Limits of Disciplinary Responsibility"], in: *Odpowiedzialność dyscyplinarna. Podstawy, procedura i orzecznictwo w sprawach studentów Uniwersytetu Warszawskiego 2000-2005*, ed. P. Skuczyński, P. Zawadzki, Warsaw 2008.

In this situation, non-contradiction of norms in the code with other legal norms should be provided for[90] since the existence of such contradictions may be a source of social tensions. The example of Polish problems with the status of codes of conduct that have occurred several times in recent years is symptomatic in this context. In legal professions the conflict was primarily about confidentiality. To a significant extent the conflict was prevented by reforming the criminal procedure, though, this has not headed off the tensions.[91] However, the conflict about medical ethics was more popular since the extent of controversial and at the same time socially important issues in this case was much greater[92]. The ruling of the Constitutional Tribunal on the discrepancy between acts and the Medical Code of Ethics is widely commented nowadays in the acute public discussion[93].

In order to recap[94], the Tribunal decided that the Medical Code of Ethics does not have the character of a legal act since, "[...] the norms included in the

90 The following reflections are partly a modified and supplemented version of the study by P. Skuczyński, "Metoda i przedmiot etyki prawniczej", in: *Etyka zawodów prawniczych. Etyka prawnicza*, ed. H. Izdebski, P. Skuczyński, Warsaw 2006, pp. 59-62, and P. Skuczyński, Soft law w perspektywie teorii prawa, ["Soft Law in Theory of Law Perspective"], in: *System prawny a porządek prawny*, ed. O. Bogucki, S. Czepita, Szczecin 2008, pp. 325-343.

91 See the Resolution of seven judges of the Supreme Court of 16th June 1994, I KZP 5/94, OSNK 1994 nr 7-8, poz. 41 [Criminal Law Chamber 1st Division - Legal Problems 5/94, Supreme Court's Judicial Decisions Criminal Law Chamber 1994, no. 7-8, item 41], and "Wokół tajemnicy adwokackiej – orzeczenia, uchwały i glosy", ["Around Legal Confidentiality – Rulings, Resolutions and Voices"], *Palestra* 1994, no. 7-8, and "Wystąpienia przed SN w sprawie tajemnicy zawodowej", ["Pleadings in the Supreme Court Concerning Professional Confidentionality"], *Palestra* 1994, no. 9-10. Current issues relating to the legal confidentiality in the context of the code of penal procedure of 1997 see M. Steinhagen, "Tajemnica zawodowa prawników: wyzwania i zagrożenia", ["Legal Confidentionality: Challenges and Hazards"], *Palestra* 2004, no. 5-6.

92 It covered, for instance, abortion and medical experiments. On one hand, legislation guaranteed access to the abortion procedure, and, on the other, Medical Code of Ethics forbade doctors to perform such procedures. Reference to the judicial decisions in relation to Medical Code of Ethics aims only at indicating problems connected with the status of professional ethics codes in general. I omit the question of possible similarities and differences between legal ethics and medical ethics. On this subject see M. Pieniążek, *Etyka sytuacyjna*..., p. 88 ff.

93 Constitutional Tribunal's ruling of 7th October 1992, U 1/92, OTK 1992, nr II, poz. 38, [U 1/92, Constitutional Tribunal's Jurisdiction 1992, no. II, item 38].

94 For a more comprehensive discussion of the decision as well as of the problems related to the argumentation included in it see P. Łabieniec, "O statusie etyki zawodowej i kodeksów etyki zawodowej", ["On the Status of Professional Ethics and of

code are of deontological nature and do not belong to the scope of state administration norms." The Tribunal accepted that norms of the Medical Code of Ethics clarify the rules authorizing its issuance, and decided to signalise to the Polish Parliament the contradiction between thus specified rules and acts of law. The idea of legal norms clarification by the code of conduct's norms did not win recognition even among members of the Tribunal's bench since four dissenting voices were declared; the thesis that the Medical Code of Ethics is a normative act, belongs to the legal system and as such falls under the Constitutional Tribunal's jurisdiction was justified in many different ways by them.

The argumentation behind the dissenting opinions was then recognized by jurisprudence, also taking the view of legal security and systemic approach[95], which is why it took hold in the attitude to codes of conduct in Poland. It was undermined by the change of constitutional status in 1997 and the closing of the sources of binding law catalogue since it was no longer possible to reasonably defend the view that codes of conduct are executory provisions. Probably this is why in the most recent adjudication of the Tribunal the construct of clarifying legal norms by codes of professional ethics has been upheld. Simultaneously, the Tribunal has expressed the view that these norms, "taken in isolation from appropriate acts belong [...] to a separate normative (deontological) order and acquire legal value in the field of the legally binding law [...] because of the acts."[96] In literature there have been other attempts made to describe the relation between legal norms and codes of professional ethics.

Firstly, it is sometimes recognized that codes of conduct are simply illegal nowadays. As one of the authors claims, "[...] constitutional norms today do not at all allow the possibility of a code functioning in the present form and rank ascribed to it."[97] One of the reasons for accepting this position is the fact that a code encroaches upon the field that is reserved for acts and really regulated by

Professional Ethics Codes"], in: *Etyka prawnicza. Stanowiska i perspektywy*, ed. H. Izdebski, P. Skuczyński, Warsaw 2008, pp. 45-55.

95 A. Wasilewski, "Aktualizacja porządku prawnego – potrzeby i rygory", ["Updating Legal Framework – Needs and Rigours"], *Państwo i Prawo* 1992, no. 5, pp. 11-13; F. Siemieński, "Jak daleko nam do państwa prawa? Pytania na marginesie postanowienia U. 1/92 Trybunału Konstytucyjnego", ["How Far Are We from the Rule of Law? Questions A Propos the Ruling Act 1/92 of the Constitutional Tribunal"], in: *Zagadnienia prawa konstytucyjnego. Księga pamiątkowa ku czci Profesora Tadeusza Szymczaka*, Łódź 1994, pp. 97-109.

96 Constitutional Court's Judgement of 23rd April 2008, SK 16/07, OTK-A 2008, nr 3, poz. 45 [Constitutional Complaints 16/07, Constitutional Tribunal's Decisions, A series - judgements and substantial decisions 2008, no. 3, item 45].

97 J. Wyrembak, "Kodeks etyki lekarskiej a system prawa", ["Medical Code of Ethics and the System of Law"] *Państwo i Prawo* 2003, no. 10, p. 44.

acts[98]. This solution makes any talk on self-regulation illusive and causes a resignation from the autonomy of a given social sub-system by leaving the whole decision on its functioning up to the legislative. It is worth emphasising that this perspective has been formulated on the occasion of another stormy discussion about the changes in the Medical Code of Ethics.

Secondly, one may try to defend the thesis that codes of conduct have the character of internal regulations for in their case the sources of law catalogue is open. This is advantageous since internal regulations must be issued on the basis of an act and in accordance with the legally binding law, thus legal security requirements are saved. However, it has to be noticed that this position harbours some serious dangers for this security. Constitution says that these so-called *interna* "are binding only for the organisational units that are subordinate to the organs issuing those acts."[99] One may have serious doubts whether the relationship between members and organs of a professional self-government constitutes organisational subordination since the role of the professional organisation is representing the interest of the professional practitioners and being responsible for maintaining control or oversight of the legitimate practice of the profession[100]. Even if one accepts that the professional association's goals entail such a relationship between its organs and members, then a question arises as to, "how much these goals differ from the goals of other kinds of self-governing bodies, of a local government for instance? ." This, naturally, would lead to absurd consequences.

On the basis of the above reconstruction of the Polish dispute over codes of professional ethics, it should be noted that in this discussion there are basically two perspectives present, which may be characterised as monistic and dualistic. Monism in this case should be understood as a view accepting the law to be the sole normative category that may regulate discussed issues. It does not, however, exclude the existence of other kinds of norms. However, if positive law orders to regulate, or regulates, a specific social sphere, then the other norms in this regard should be renounced. Every reference to norms other than the legal ones means their incorporation into the legal system. Formulation of a code of conduct and its application by public administration organs thus means legalisation of this ethics. Meanwhile, dualism, apart from the law, assumes the existence of another normative system, which is referred to as a realm of moral, ethical or deontological norms. This perspective, in regard to practical consequences, differs from monism – most generally speaking – because a

98 *Ibidem*, p. 41.

99 Art. 93 Paragraph 1 of the Constitution of the Republic of Poland.

100 Art. 17 Paragraph 1 of the Constitution of the Republic of Poland.

reference to other than legal norms does not result in losing their identity or incorporating them into the legal system. Instead of legalisation, it simply means the existence of specific functional relations[101]. In the mentioned rulings, by applying the original construct of clarifying legal norms with ethical norms, the Constitutional Tribunal took exactly such a position.

These positions may be translated into the discussion of deontology in yet another way. Namely, monists claim that accepting a specific code of conduct by a professional organisation is of constitutional nature and it establishes legal norms. While dualists take the view that this acceptance has a declaratory character in relation to ethical norms. My opinion is that both standpoints are fallacious and entail practical complications since both eliminate the code of conduct as a source of norms. First, because the positions lead to regarding codes as having no legal basis and, therefore, not binding if they do not belong to the sources of law catalogue. Second, because in case of including in it any content that is contradictory with an accepted morality conception – and experience shows that it is not easy to adopt one in human communities and then consequently apply it – a necessity of considering a code as an act that is contradictory to moral norms may arise. Thus, both views set for codes of conduct the requirements which codes, as a rule, cannot fulfil neither separately, nor simultaneously. Hence, it seems that one must search for some other solutions of codes of professional ethics' status. An attractive proposal in this regard seems taking some in-between position based on including the discussed acts in soft law.

In order to understand this position better, let us remark that negative aspects of legalisation in the sense accepted here also include the inadequacy of the method of regulation to its object since this process leads to a complete formalisation of professional duties, by the same rules as with other legal duties, and thus the principle: "Everything which is not forbidden or prescribed is allowed" is applied here. However, in regard to ethical conduct, which may be, for example, honest, reliable and dignified, it is difficult to foresee all possible situations that could infringe on these rules. Additionally, norms of this kind require special will of abidance by them on the part of the addressees, which – from the perspective of social psychology – needs identification with values at the core of these norms, and this is possible only in the case of a milieu consensus on the values by all those practising in a given profession. This requires in representatives of a profession the existence of a community of

101 For different kinds of relations between law and morality see H. Jankowski, *Prawo i moralność*, ["Law and morality"], Warsaw 1968; W. Lang, *Prawo i moralność*, Warsaw 1989.

values and not only a community of interests. The effectiveness of law as an instrument in formation of such a community and its ethical standards is thus clearly limited[102].

How, then, should the codes of professional ethics be viewed so that one could be able to accept that the method of regulation corresponds with its subject, which is the moral duties of lawyers? And how should one assess the legal ethics legalisation process? It seems that these duties are something between "law and conscience," and, hence, they have some legal as well as moral qualities. Since law in relation to an individual is an objective standard of behaviour and conscience is related to an individual, and thus is of a subjective nature, the codes of conduct in relation to law have subjective character, and in relation to conscience, objective. This is because codes' decisions are an expression of a community of values and a result of self-regulation process. Thus, the addressees of a code by assumption identify with its norms in a greater extent for they regard them as theirs, but simultaneously they lose all influence on their content and make them independent from their assessments.

This double nature of codes of conducts, on one hand, firms up behaviour standards that are rooted in each individual's sense of morality, and on the other, softens the legal norms. For this reason, it seems reasonable to include codes of conduct into soft law understood as a special type of social control which is characterised by pointing to its typical qualities such as specific way of its constitution in self-regulation forms, specificity of its application in non-formalised procedures and its relation with primarily soft sanctions, an example of which may be ailments of disciplinary nature[103]. Inclusion of codes of

102 H. Izdebski, "Granice prawa jako instrumentu kształtowania standardów zachowań w służbie publicznej", ["Limits of Law as a Means of Establishing Standards of Conduct in Public Service"], in: *Profesjonalizm w administracji publicznej*, ed. A. Dębicka, M. Dmochowski, B. Kudrycka, Białystok 2004.

103 For more on soft law see H. Izdebski, *Granice...*, p. 82 ff. and P. Skuczyński, *Soft law...*, with works cited there, especially F. Beveridge, S. Nott, *A Hard Look on the Soft Law,* in: *Lawmaking in the European Union*, ed. P. Craig, C. Harlow, London-Hague-Boston 1998; R. Bierzanek, "'Miękkie' prawo międzynarodowe", ["Soft International Law"] *Sprawy Międzynarodowe* 1987, no. 1; G.M. Borchardt, K.C. Wellens, "Soft Law in European Community Law", *European Law Review* 1989, no. 14; G. Falkner, *Neues Regieren und Soziales Europa. EU-Mindestregulierung und Soft Law in der Praxis*, Vienna, September 2004; H. Hildenberg, "A Fresh Look at Soft Law", *European Journal of International Law* 1999, no. 3; G.G. Howells, "'Soft law' in EC Consumer Law", in: *Lawmaking in the European Union*, ed. P. Craig, C. Harlow, London-Hague-Boston 1998; Ch. Inglese, "Soft Law?", *Polish Yearbook of International Law* 1993, no. XX, A. Jurcewicz, "Rola 'miękkiego prawa' w praktyce instytucjonalnej Wspólnoty Europejskiej", ["The Role of 'Soft Law' in Institutional Practice of the EC"],

professional ethics formulated by professional associations and self-governing professional organisations into the soft law instruments seems to probably solve many problems of the codes' status. Most generally speaking, it enables evaluating the codes' content both from the point of view of their compliance with legal as well as ethical norms. Thus, a professional association is neither granted the right or competence to form hard law, nor it is endowed with a patent for discovering ethical norms. For this reason, it is also possible to develop theories of professional ethics, including legal ethics, which will not reduce the range of professional duties only to those expressed in the codes' content.

1.4.2. Professionalisation

Professionalisation of legal ethics is even more complex than its juridisation. First, evidently, it is a result of a wider phenomenon, namely, the professionalisation of legal activity itself – of specific 'professionalising' it, which may be juxtaposed with amateur practising law as a subsidiary occupation. In this process the following aspects may be distinguished: standardisation, specialisation and commercialisation of legal practice, which must have affected legal ethics as well as ideas and norms that have evolved within its traditions. Secondly, professionalisation should be understood as a result of the influence of professionalism – a model of a characteristic way of life that is typical of a certain social group living in big cities, being hired and engaged in activities requiring high qualification. This model includes, *inter alia*, such important to legal ethics elements as continual improvement of qualifications and greatest reliability in performing duties. Therefore, it is a specific ideology of good practising of one's profession, deeply related with the previous bourgeois vision of good life through honest and hard work.

1.4.2.1. Profession's criteria

Learned and practised profession is one of the categories deciding on modern man's life in many aspects. It determines, partially at least, not only the way of spending one's work-time, but also the free-time, aspirations, interests and feelings. It influences the fulfilment of one's social roles and the place in the

---

in: *Implementacja prawa integracji europejskiej w krajowych porządkach prawnych*, ed. C. Mik, Toruń 1998; J. Marquier, *Soft Law: Das Beispiel des OSZE-Prozesses – Ein Beitrag zur völkerrechtlichen Rechtsquellenlehre*, Bonn 2004.

social structure[104]. How great this influence is remains debatable, though at least in one point there seems to be unanimity, namely that it is increasing, going far beyond economical relations and including other spheres, of custom and politics, for example[105]. The importance of professional ethics in the practice of many different professions may be taken as an argument for the thesis that this influence also occurs in the case of morality.

It is evident that there is no list of professions that is set in stone because of the continual process of some occupations undergoing professionalisation, while other deprofessionalise. In other cases still, an integration that joins different professions into one takes place. Transformations in this regard have become especially vivid in legal professions in European countries over the recent decades. For instance, in France, there was a significant simplification of legal professions' structure when the bar absorbed minor professions. This integration was a conscious and planned process that was possible to much extent because of the strength of the tradition of legal ethics of the French lawyers[106]. On the other hand, in Poland, a contrary process may be observed – the rise of new professions of increasingly specialised character. There are also some tendencies of professions becoming similar, at least in the scope of legal help they offer but, for a number of reasons, these tendencies do not result in their integration[107].

These processes concern not only legal professions, but also the entire professional structure, which is ever-changing because of it. Describing this structure and showing in it the place of legal professions, or professions that refer to professional ethics in general, seems necessary for several reasons. First of all, as far as professional ethics is concerned, an issue arises as to, "what is a profession and which of its elements enable rational discussion on ethics of a particular profession?" The essential thing is what elements of a profession affect the content of a particular professional ethics, and what makes it possible to speak of certain groups of ethics that cover different professions as, for instance, medical professions ethics or legal professions ethics. To answer these questions in the context of the present reflection, first, it has to be settled which aspects of professionalisation have influence on traditions of legal ethics, and which are irrelevant in this regard.

---

104 E. Łojko, "O roli zawodów prawniczych w dzisiejszym społeczeństwie", ["On the Role of Legal Professions in Modern Society"], *Palestra* 1997, no. 3-4, p. 52.

105 Cf. E. Łojko, *Role i zadania prawników w zmieniającym się społeczeństwie*, [*The Roles and Tasks of Lawyers in the Changing Society*], Warsaw 2005, p. 15.

106 J. Leubsdorf, *Man in His...*, p. 112 ff.

107 On the need of and obstacles in integration of Polish lawyers and legal advisers cf. Cz. Jaworski, "O integracji zawodów prawniczych i nie tylko", ["On Integration of Legal Professions and Not Only"], *Palestra* 1998, no. 9-10, pp. 120-127.

A relatively simple and simultaneously a very useful means of describing professional structure seems to be the ordering of professions contained within it. A scale of professions may be formed according to various criteria – formal education, income level or social prestige. It may be assumed that professions having their own professional ethics will rank the highest in virtually every classification. This is because the fact of having such ethics, directly or indirectly, translates into the functioning of the profession in society and into the possibility of its representatives gaining success. The legal professions belong to a wider group of such professions, though their status within its frame is not always the same. This variety within the framework of the professions themselves means that they take up not one definite place on this scale, but rather some range comprising the highest values[108]. Such a perspective allows constructing not only a model of legal professions' historical development, but also their models in particular modern societies. Hence, professionalisation is a process in which a given activity satisfies successive criteria of a profession and takes higher and higher places on a professions' scale. Discussing those criteria will simultaneously provide a presentation of key points closing succeeding phases of this process.

The first criterion of a profession is the identification of an occupation that is practised as a profession, which is to say specialisation. Such an occupation must, first of all, be clearly distinguishable from others, which naturally breeds questions on the differentiating criteria. In relation to legal professions, there are two types of occupational divisions on the basis of which one may reconstruct those criteria. On one hand, there is the division on lawyers that adjudicate, accuse, defend, represent, advise, negotiate, enforce and so on. The possibility to join some of these activities does not annul the division itself. On the other, one may speak of specialisation in regard to the scope of the cases in which these activities are being performed: for example, those relating to family law, labour law or patent law. The criterion here is the function and indispensable knowledge that make the basis of a legal specialisation[109]. It is noteworthy that a certain repeatability of an activity is a condition of thus understood specialisation – the condition that enables us to speak of them as an occupation. Formation of a group of such repeatable activities may be called standardisation, and it is worth stressing that their performance is a necessary condition to referring to a profession at all.

Another condition of a profession is commercialisation. Contrary to specialisation being a differentiating criterion of professions, commercialisation

108 W.E. Moore, *The Professions: Roles and Rules*, New York 1970, pp. 4-6.

109 *Ibidem*, p.36.

decides on the aspect in which all professions are the same. Commercialisation means that engaging in a specialised occupation is a basic source of income and maintenance for those who practise it, and, "though in objective dimension salaries differentiate people in the income structure (division into the rich and the poor), in the subjective dimension they unite them because of one main reason for undertaking professional activity, namely obtaining pay for one's work."[110] It must be noted that one of the most important problems of changes in legal activity and its ethical traditions arises in this place since commercialisation spoils the image of a lawyer as a profession representative who "is not thought of as engaged in the pursuit of his personal profit, but in performing service to his [...] clients, or to impersonal values [...]." This is why to some people, free professions are, "a mere survival of the medieval guilds. Some think that these spheres are becoming progressively commercialized, so that as distinctive structures, they will probably disappear."[111]

The third criterion of a profession is competence and organisation of the practised profession. This means first of all that there exist norms of performing a profession, observance of which may be required from the profession representatives. These norms are settled and enforced primarily within professional organisations by other members of the profession[112]. The most widespread form of such an organisation is a professional self-government, which performs its function fundamentally because of its powers to regulate the professional practice, grant admission to profession, and, by disciplinary responsibility, to expel those members who do not satisfy certain requirements. Effective care over the practice rests not only in the interest of clients or, more broadly, public interest, but also in best interest of the profession itself. Therefore, professional organisations are treated as entities expressing the interest of the profession. This is related to the risk of transforming such organisations into a kind of trade unions of free professions and two most important today reasons for that may be pointed out. On one hand, changes in the structure of clients seeking legal advice may be observed, namely clients are more often organised, conscious of their demands as well as of work standards that they expect, and a "business" type of relations more frequently determines norms of competence. On the other hand, it is noticed that bar examinations and licences lose significance as they are more rarely a confirmation of competence

110 E. Łojko, *Role i zadania...*, pp. 16-18; See also T. Parsons, "Spojrzenie socjologa na zawód prawnika", ["A Sociologist Looks at the Legal Profession"], in: *idem Szkice z teorii socjologicznej*, [*Essays in Sociological Theory*], Warsaw 1972, p. 476.

111 T. Parsons, "The Professions and Social Structure", in: *idem*, *Essays in Sociological Theory*, Glencoe 1954, p. 39 .

112 W.E. Moore, *The Professions...*, pp. 7-10.

in specialist fields which are in great demand but the lack of this confirmation is no obstacle to provide services[113]. Thus, commercialisation and specialisation influence the profession criteria considerably.

The fourth criterion of a profession is the appearance of professional training, which has various forms, and so may last shorter or longer, but in any case it covers three elements. First, its aim is the assimilation of some scope of theoretical, both specialist and general, knowledge by the learners. Secondly, training has, at least in some part, characteristics of an apprenticeship . This means that it helps the learners to acquire skills that will enable them to practise in a given profession. Thirdly, it is connected with professional socialisation, which means that it introduces its participants to the realm of values and norms of a particular profession and moulds their character and personal traits that are necessary to the professions. In the case of legal professions there are different models of such training, beginning with American law schools, ending with the European combination of university education and legal training[114]. The appearance of some new, though only subsidiary, forms of legal education such as clinical training – joining simultaneous acquisition of theoretical knowledge and practical skills, cooperation with clients and other lawyers and also *pro bono* activity – is noteworthy[115].

All these aspects of professional education are very significant and removing one of them may be dangerous from the perspective of the functioning of a profession. Especially worth stressing in the face of occasionally appearing postulates to make legal education more practical and to resign from – as it is emphasised by the supporters of such reforms – unnecessary and burdensome theoretical elements, is that the role of universities and of their curricula of legal education is more profound than it initially seems. For this role rests on taking in deposit what is "universal," both in regard to the whole culture and the profession as well. For this reason, on one hand, the tendency to culturally isolate lawyers may be fought thanks to the inclusion of legal professions in the so-called learned professions, in which starting specialist education requires having general education first[116]. On the other hand, due to combining research and didactics – which guarantees that trainees learn what the previous

113 *Ibidem*, pp. 64-65.

114 A presentation of these models and their convergences together with the critique of Polish legal education see F. Zoll, *Jaka szkoła prawa?*, [*What School of Law?*], Warsaw 2004.

115 See Ł. Bojarski, "Cele działania uniwersyteckich poradni prawnych", ["The Goals of Legal Clinics at the Universities"], in: *Studencka poradnia prawna. Idea-organizacja-metodologia,* Warsaw 2005, pp. 1-23.

116 W.E. Moore, *The Professions...*, p. 71.

generation has been taught and what is being required in bar examinations currently, as well as what is critical and postulatory in relation to practice – one may, on the scale of the entire professional community, keep the balance of conservatism and innovation[117].

The fifth criterion of a profession, orientation toward service, seems to justify the above claim even more strongly. Since the profession's task is to provide socially important services, and thus satisfy important social needs, then fulfilling this task will only be possible if the profession's representatives will comply with three groups of norms: competence, conscientiousness and trust[118]. The importance of professional competence is revealed especially in new and atypical situations, which require performing activities that go beyond not just a specialised branch but also beyond a standardised set of such activities. The problem known to lawyers under a recently popular term "hard cases" is an argument for general and theoretical professional education because only thanks to such a preparation, a professional is able to work out a set of activities that help solve new problems[119]. Whereas conscientiousness allows to go beyond competent behaviour standards in a similar way, especially when they are unclear or ambiguous. Such a situation often occurs in relation to the interpretation of codes of legal ethics, which of itself cannot envisage all the dilemmas appearing in professional practice. This means completing precise rules of conduct with a kind of virtues or attitudes which enable their interpretation and application.

A special place in this profession criterion belongs to trust[120]. Most generally speaking, trust is a factual relation, which may occur between individuals and groups of individuals. Its significance is marked by claiming that minimal trust between members of society is necessary for its existence at all, and the more trust there is between people, the better the society functions since costs related to the functioning of a system of protection, sanction and control are remove and social capital is created as a result[121]. The principle of trust is one of the most important legal ethics rules and a source of many other principles. Its great importance shows, at least indirectly, in the fact that Polish constitutional legislator decided in article 17 of the Constitution on legal

---

117 *Ibidem*, p. 74.

118 *Ibidem*, pp. 13-15.

119 *Ibidem*, p. 55.

120 Further development of these remarks, see. P. Skuczyński, "Zaufanie (lojalność)", ["Trust (Loyalty)"], in: *Etyka zawodów...*, ed. H. Izdebski, P. Skuczyński, pp. 98-105.

121 F. Fukuyama, *Zaufanie. Kapitał społeczny a droga do dobrobytu*, [*Trust. The Social Virtues and the Creation of Prosperity*], Warsaw-Wrocław 1997, chap. I.

protection of this trust by forming an institution of professions of public trust[122], which, naturally, does not cover legal professions only. Additionally, let us remark that in Polish legislation a notary is defined as a person of public trust[123].

The sixth and also the final criterion of a profession is professional independence, or autonomy, which may not only be variously referred to, but has several aspects, especially visible in the example of legal professions. Therefore, in the case of this criterion, one may speak of a "scale-in-a-scale" according to which professions can be arranged even if they have various degrees of independence[124]. Firstly, a profession's independence may be understood as self-regulation. Obviously, it is possible only with favourable institutional and political conditions in which a professional organisation has overwhelming influence on practice standards, professional education and it decides who will practise in the profession[125]. Essentially, in this case one may speak of autonomy of an organisation such as, for example, a professional self-government, whose formation is often regarded as the crowning achievement of professionalisation. Still, one has to remember that it is more appropriate to speak of self-regulation as a guarantee of a profession's independence, and not as of its essence[126].

Secondly, independence may be understood as the performance of work independently and on one's own account. In this aspect, independent lawyers are persons who decide about the conditions of their work: where, when and with

---

122 See classical presentations, P. Sarnecki, "Pojęcie zawodu zaufania publicznego (Art. 17 ust. 1 Konstytucji) na przykładzie adwokatury", ["The Concept of a Profession of Public Trust (Art. 17 Paragraph 1 of the Constitution) on the Example of the Bar"], in: *Konstytucja – wybory – parlament. Studia ofiarowane Z. Jaroszowi*, ed. L. Garlicki, Warsaw 2000, pp. 149-163; *idem* "Radca prawny jako zawód zaufania publicznego", ["Legal Adviser as a Profession of Public Trust"], *Radca Prawny* 2002, no. 4-5, pp. 22-29, and H. Izdebski, "Zawody prawnicze jako zawody zaufania publicznego", ["Legal Professions as Professions of Public Trust"], in: *Etyka zawodów...*, ed. H. Izdebski, P. Skuczyński, pp. 43-56.

123 Art. 2 Paragraph 1 of the Act of 14 February 1991 - Law on the notary (consolidated text in Dziennik Ustaw [Journal of Laws] of 2008 no. 189, item 1158 as amended.). *Code of Ethics for a Notary* develops this statutory term by proclaiming in Paragraph 10, that "a notary as a person of public trust is equipped by the state with defined administrative powers, he or she should care to keep balance in his or her activities between their public character and the free profession's status."

124 W.E. Moore, *The Professions...*, p. 16.

125 R.W. Gordon, "The Independence of Lawyers", *Boston University Law Review* 1988, no. 1, pp. 6-7.

126 J. Kurczewski, "Kształtowanie się profesji – perspektywa socjologa", ["The Formation of a Profession – a Sociologist's Perspective"] *Radca Prawny* 2002, no. 4-5, p. 13.

whom it is performed, but, fundamentally, what clients and what cases they accept, how much time they devote to them and according to what arrangements, in a contractual relationship, they are remunerated[127]. It seems that in reference to thus conceived independence one speaks of "free professions", which in Polish are identified with "professions." However, such a view raises doubts since in the context of the aforementioned variety of clients, and especially their institutionalisation, and segregating roles of a client and of a payer[128], lawyers are being more often permanently employed. Taking lawyers as an example, one may indicate persons practising as "in-house lawyers". In Poland, this concerns primarily legal advisers, who as the most numerous legal professional group have evolved from a group of lawyers practising exactly on this basis[129].

Thirdly, independence – and this is the aspect that links professions which are free in the above meaning with other professions – relates to the performance of professional activities itself, and so, for instance, to a legal opinion content or an issued ruling. Nevertheless, it should be noted that there are essential differences in particular legal professions' independence. This attribute seems to be ascribed primarily to judges, with regard to whom one speaks mainly of judicial independence. It means a right, and simultaneously a duty, to decide in a manner that is entirely free of external factors like some extralegal reasons – of course, provided that the law itself does not allow or forbid this. Since another principle of judicial ethics is impartiality, independence may be regarded as its condition[130].

It is difficult to perform such a theoretical operation in relation to legal professions representing a client, for example, to lawyers, because it seems that partiality is inscribed in their role. Despite this, independence of lawyers is treated as, "a special distinguishing mark in professional activity of a lawyer," or perhaps even as "a qualifier at a core of a lawyer's ethics." Independence is specially featured in the French tradition of legal ethics, where it means independence from public authorities, courts, legal opponents, other lawyers. It also means independence from clients because only when lawyers may

---

127 R.W. Gordon, *The independence...*, p. 8.

128 A classical example of a profession's deep transformations due to such changes is the rise of public health maintenance organisations, which have totally changed the image of the medical profession.

129 Cf. J. Kurczewski, "Kształtowanie...", p. 12.

130 Cf. Z. Tobor, T. Pietrzykowski, "Bezstronność jako pojęcie prawne", ["Impartiality as a Legal Concept"], in: *Prawo a wartości. Księga jubileuszowa Profesora Józefa Nowackiego*, ed. I. Bogucka, Z. Tobor, Kraków 2003, p. 280 ff.; M. Najda, T. Romer, "Etyka sędziowska", ["Judicial Ethics"], *Europejski Przegląd Sądowy* 2005, no. 3, p. 4.

formulate their opinions in an independent and unfettered way, they will be able to make the best decisions for the clients, and in some cases, also on their behalf. Some dangers for independence understood in such a way stem mainly from other profession criteria, especially from commercialisation. This is pointed out with a statement that, "a lawyer, when he resigns out of economical reasons from the right to refuse or to resign, loses a part of his or her soul, a great part of his or her identity and independence."[131]

It seems that legal professions have been satisfying the above profession criteria since a long time, and it may be assumed that they are a model case in this regard. However, as it has been indicated each of the criteria may be satisfied to a different degree and decide on a particular profession's place on a professional structure scale. Domination of one of them may lead to some disturbances in a profession's functioning, and it seems that recently specialisation and commercialisation have greatly intensified. These two cause confusion in such criteria as organisation, education and independence. Nowadays, keeping balance between all the profession criteria, and building on this basis a kind of identity of the whole profession as well as of its particular members, is mainly taking place within the framework of professionalism, which is a body of opinions or ideas on good professional practice.

1.4.2.2. Profession's mission

Professionalism as the idea of good professional practice is an attempt to reconcile all of the profession's criteria. However, professions always operate within a wider context, which – to a significant extent – determines what professionalism is in regard to particular professions. The context consists of the social structure, in which professions have more or less important functions to fulfil, as well as opinions and aspirations of the individuals involved in a profession. For this reason professionalism encompasses not only internal reconciliation of the profession's criteria, but also their harmonisation with social and individual context of professional practice, whereby this is basically the sole possible view since, "professionalism thereby forms a crucial link between the modern individual's struggle for fulfilling existence and the needs

---

131 Cz. Jaworski, "Niezależność i niezawisłość", ["Independence and Autonomy"] in: *Etyka zawodów...*, ed. H. Izdebski, P. Skuczyński, pp. 113-118. See also Cz. Jaworski, "Niezależność wykonywania zawodu adwokata w świetle regulacji prawnych europejskich i polskich", ["The Independence of a Lawyer's Practice in the Light of European and Polish Legal Regulations"], *Palestra* 1996, no. 7-8.

of the larger society, so that individual opportunity can serve the demands of interdependence."[132]

Then, one may say that good professional practice in the sense of professionalism does not only mean good in relation to expertise criteria, but also good of social and individual character. In other words, "a profession is 'in business' for the common good as well as for the good of its members, or it is not a profession."[133] Lack of balance in satisfying these different profession criteria leads to predominance of one of these goods – or interests – over and at the expense of other ones. Traditionally, this shift of the focal point in a profession is expressed in terms of a vocation, which unequivocally points to supraindividual goal of professional work, and of a career, which is connected with personal interest even if not simply egotistic[134]. What is usually meant when speaking of professionalism crisis is a vast historic transition in regard to motivation behind choosing a profession and various individual choices as well as preferences in the course of one's professional life, namely the transition from vocational thinking to career thinking.

The balance of these various criteria is typically referred to as "integrity". Due to the term's philosophical placement, it will be referred to later in the text. In this place it only needs to be recalled that it has several aspects[135]. First, it may be understood as moral integrity, which does not mean more than an obligation to keep moral consistence in judgements and actions. This is the postulate of applying the same standards in moral measurement to one's own and other people's deeds. A special form of thus understood moral integrity is consistence of thoughts, words and deeds, and so the avoidance of action that is only superficially driven by particular motives, whereas in reality these motives are totally different. There is a direct relationship between thus understood integrity and trust. For example, hiding one's intentions by a lawyer, on one hand, and assurances of care for client's interest on the other, do not promote mutual trust. Naturally, an opposite situation is also possible, namely when the client behaves disloyally towards the lawyer by breaching the moral integrity rule.

Secondly, professional integrity, which may be deduced from moral integrity, is at issue here. In a positive formula it is equal to saying that one is a representative of one's profession regardless of the role which one assumes at

---

132 W.A. Sullivan, *Work and Integrity. The Crisis and Promise of Professionalism in America*, New York 1995, pp. xvi-xvii.

133 *Ibidem*, p. 5.

134 *Ibidem*, p. 6.

135 See also P. Skuczyński, "Integralność", ["Integrity"] in: *Etyka zawodów...*, ed. H. Izdebski, P. Skuczyński, pp. 105-112.

the moment. In other words, one is a judge or a lawyer all the time, which translates into the possibility of assessing the lawyer's conduct according to the same criteria not only in his or her professional activity, but also in public and personal life. While, in a negative formula professional integrity means refraining from social conflict, especially from a conflict of roles or interests. Rules on avoiding these conflicts are usually included in codes of practice that are based on the general formula that one must not combine with a particular legal profession such activities which would affront that profession's dignity, diminish its esteem or limit its independence.

Thirdly, profession's integrity is the last but not the least aspect of the integrity principle. Most generally speaking, it is the translation of moral and professional integrity into duties of the whole professional community, which should apply homogeneous moral standards to all its members as well as in relations with society, to which it owes its special position and which has entrusted it with protection and decision about the goods that are most important to every human. A number of rules are employed to maintain professional integrity. Essentially, these are rules connected with identifying and sanctioning breaches of discipline. They are based on the assumption that only cooperation of the whole legal community may enable this identification and punishment of unethical actions, whereas not realising the integrity principle may undermine trust in the entire legal circle. In the countries where professional integrity principle is valued, particularly in the Anglo-Saxon countries, there is usually one organisation (corporation) of lawyers that – not necessarily obligatorily – associates all those practising in a profession. It does not mean that this organisation is not internally separated: basically, into those who practise as freelancers and those who practise as civil servants.

In each of its dimensions, integrity is connected with a relation of an individual to society, or simply, with a way that an individual functions in a society. In reference to this, it is noteworthy that, "an authentic profession can provide a strong sense of identity because, beyond providing a livelihood, it is a way of life with public value. It is the kind of thing one can build a life around,"[136] and, simultaneously, "neither economic incentives, nor technology, nor administrative control has proved an effective surrogate for the commitment to integrity evoked in the ideal of professionalism."[137] However, it is exactly under the influence of these factors that professionalism, and with it integrity as well as a type of identity or a way of life that is based on integrity, took various forms. It is particularly conspicuous in legal professions. Regardless of whether

136 W.A. Sullivan, *Work and Integrity…*, p. 6.
137 *Ibidem*, p. xvi.

one accepts the view that a lawyer should be especially engaged in his or her clients' cases and manifest in this regard a certain activism or the view that he or she should keep distance and reservation, the problem of the profession's integrity with extra-professional life – both internal and in relations with other people – will always arise[138].

Historically speaking, the first model of professionalism – including legal professionalism – is the one related to Protestantism. As it is known, thanks to the works of Max Weber, the Protestant ethos of work became the foundation of capitalism in its initial phase. This ethos comprised, among other things, such elements as "understanding of a profession as a vocation, respect for hard and assiduous work being a way of living, limiting consumption resulting from accepting asceticism as a value, subduing action to rational calculation, individualism and a sense of autonomy in [...] performed work."[139] In the case of the discussed professions the element of vocation, from which the term "profession" is derived, is especially important. Vocation signifies that a particular profession is chosen not only because of the necessity to earn one's living but that in some way one is being chosen by the profession[140]. Therefore, some thinkers, like for example Herbert Spencer, see the origins of a profession in a religious state and some others looking for professions' genealogy even mention shamans[141].

Legal professionalism in this shape has formed mainly in New England – dominated by Calvinism, having strong church and state institutions. Lawyers there, apart from theologians, constituted a group building the image of new society. Their function, described as a mission, was direct action for public interest by means of promoting justice[142]. As it has already been mentioned in the discussion on sources of the American tradition of legal ethics, the consequence of so defined function of lawyers was the so-called justice-centred model of professional practice, characterized by moralism, which in the case of attorneys meant that the boundaries of acceptable action for the client are set by

---

138 On the issue of involvement on the side of the client and the problem in relation to which the aforementioned dilemma is most widely known in Poland, namely the problem of the so-called mafia's lawyers, see P. Kruszyński, "Etyka adwokacka jako granica dopuszczalności działania obrońcy w procesie karnym", ["Lawyer's Ethics as the Action Admissibility Limit of a Lawyer in a Penal Procedure"], in: *Etyka prawnika. Etyka nauczyciela zawodu prawniczego*, ed. E. Łojko, Warsaw 2002.

139 K. Romaniszyn, *Rzecz o pracy i konsumpcji. Analiza antropologiczna*, [*On Work and Consumption. Anthropological Analysis*], Kraków 2007, p. 23.

140 W.A. Sullivan, *Work and Integrity...*, p. 12.

141 W.E. Moore, *The Professions...*, pp. 25-34.

142 W.A. Sullivan, *Work and Integrity...*, p. 32.

moral standards. Thus, accepting unjust cases or applying immoral methods, even if they seemed legal, was excluded. Hence, a professional lawyer should be independent, reliable, versatile and treat the commercial aspect of his or her work only as gratification being the effect of rightly performed vocation. It is also worth stressing that despite some connotations, contrary to the French legal ethics, it is hard to find such elements as the exclusive or aristocratic character of the bar in this perspective of professionalism, just as it is difficult to consider it a counterbalance for the state. Not heroic deeds but hard work was a way of action for lawyers of that time, whose income was not a matter of honour but a suitable pay for their work.

Another model of professionalism may also be most conveniently reconstructed on the example of American lawyers. Basically, it has appeared as a result of a crisis on the ruins of the previous model, which has been quite brutally destroyed by dynamic political, social and economic processes which essentially included the populist campaign of president Andrew Jackson, the American Civil War and the intensive industrialisation along with the accompanying changes in the social structure. The campaign, basing on extreme democratism, removed all inequalities that could pass for privileges, and also the important role of lawyers in the building of society, their self-governance etc. At the core of thus understood democratism was the lack of any limits on individual possibilities of economic development of a person[143]. This enabled rapid economic growth, which process – though hampered by the Civil War – since its ending even grew in intensity. A new corporational capitalism began to form.

Lawyers also participated in this unchecked activity, which gave rise to a new type of professionalism. They started to play an important social role again. They rebuilt their organisations but now perceived their profession in a totally different way and stressed the accents between its elements differently. Namely, strongly utilitarian thinking became dominant. It meant the justification of lawyers' position not with their direct activity for justice and public welfare but because this activity, as a whole, contributed to the nation's progress[144]. Limitations on the increase in commercialisation and specialisation disappeared since these two boosted the "efficiency" of legal work, especially in combination with new management techniques, and this, by its consequences and due to the functioning of Smith's "invisible hand of the market," increased the public welfare[145]. The focus was on clients; they were to be represented zealously and

143 *Ibidem*, pp. 36-37.

144 *Ibidem*, p. 37.

145 A.T. Kronman, "The Law as a Profession", in: *Ethics in Practice. Lawyers' Roles, Responsibilities, and Regulation*, ed. D.L. Rhode, New York 2000, p. 37, who considers this view of professionalism as dangerous.

their interests realised as far as possible for in this way a lawyer could contribute to the public welfare. In this type of professionalism, referred to as "liberal advocacy," loyalty within the framework of the adversary trial system provided for the most comprehensive realisation of justice by most complete presentation of arguments by both sides, most faithful ascertainment of truth and most broad protection of an individual's rights[146] and, simultaneously, guaranteed personal success owing to generous remuneration from clients for loyalty as well as to the sense of a well fulfilled duty.

However, this type of professionalism – widely spread even nowadays, though to much extent modified and dominated by its newer forms – the one most characteristic of the American tradition of legal ethics because of being based on loyalty and rules specifying it, seems not to fully realise the assumptions of integrity. Firstly, it is pointed out that this type of professionalism often makes lawyers become two-faced. Important figures are invoked as examples. For instance, David Dudley Field, the author of the first American *Code of Civil Procedure*, which to a great extent prevented dangers of exploiting loopholes and zealous advocacy excesses, which dangers Field himself had in great part introduced by representing *Erie Railroad* loyally and uncompromisingly for ample pay[147], or even Abraham Lincoln, who before showing concern for social egalitarianism and rights for the poor had made quite a fortune in representing *Illinois Central Railroad*[148].

It is even indicated that such an attitude is of a schizoid character and does not result in spontaneous growth in public welfare at all because, "having lawyers running around solving problems they helped to create seems a little wasteful."[149] Secondly, this type of a client-lawyer relation entails three negative phenomena: overrepresentation, which is overzealous representation and putting the client's interests above the public interest, underrepresentation, which is representation performed not enough conscientiously and putting the lawyer's interest before the client's interest, and finally, nonrepresentation, which simply means lack of representation and refers to a situation where potential clients do not get legal assistance they need. These phenomena concern different groups of entities, and the source of their diversity are, essentially, the financial possibilities of clients[150].

---

146 D.L. Rhode, "Institutionalizing Ethics", *Case Western Law Review* 1995, no. 44, pp. 668-673.

147 R.W. Gordon, "The Independence…", p. 23.

148 W.A. Sullivan, *Work and Integrity*…, p. 38.

149 R.W. Gordon, "The Independence…", p. 24.

150 D.L. Rhode, "Institutionalizing...", p. 666 ff.

The third kind of professionalism, most modern and simultaneously most debatable, relates to the rise of consumer capitalism. Within its framework, "it is hard and anachronistic to consider work [...] as a vocation and a way of life, respect the mutual loyalty rule and postpone consumption," thus, ethos of work erodes. In the social dimension, this manifests itself fundamentally in the predomination of consumerism of a hedonistic type, which leads to the instrumental treatment of work as a means of attaining pleasure. This type of professionalism does not change the professional structure directly, but it results in the formation of many new professions related to entertainment business or media, which affects the existing professions – for instance in the case of legal professions it means the appearance of new specialisations – and thus it may indirectly and to a significant degree influence the social structure[151].

Even deeper changes may be observed when one pays attention to individual problems. Namely, consequent separation of work and consumption spheres occurs here. Thus, whether the professional life is successful or not is determined not by the achievements at work but by their external manifestations of a material nature – that is the number and quality of consumer goods which one can afford on one's professional fee[152]. In this situation, "professional work loses its central position in individuals' lives to consumption. The essence of this change does not rely on radical shortening of work-time for consumption-time but on valuing work in relation to consumption. Work that is treated instrumentally – a means and a supplement necessary of financial reasons for consumption – loses its autotelic value." In combination with such phenomena as progressing specialisation, technicalisation and bureaucratisation of work, which result in reducing the extent of measures of an individual and his or her work and in alienation, this breeds the so-called identity crisis. Apart from one's social background, family and exactly professional work, human identity gains a new dimension – connected with consumption and formed for external benefit and not of oneself – and it becomes an identity just for show[153]. In comparison to the former types of professionalism, further disintegration takes place, and, "the tragedy of the times was that neither the romantic world of student rebellion nor the professional ethos of the technically oriented universities proved able to provide the needed imagination or commitment to invent the better form of life."[154]

---

151 K. Romaniszyn, *Rzecz o pracy...*, pp. 89-91, 145 and 151.

152 D. Bell, *Kulturowe sprzeczności kapitalizmu*, [*The Cultural Contradictions of Capitalism*], Warsaw 1998, p. 106. Cf. K. Romaniszyn, *Rzecz o pracy...*, p. 99, and W.A. Sullivan, *Work and Integrity...*, pp. 94 and 102.

153 K. Romaniszyn, *Rzecz o pracy...*, pp. 123-124; W.A. Sullivan, *Work and Integrity...*, pp. 94, 101, 106, 110 and 117.

154 W.A. Sullivan, *Work and Integrity...*, p. 118.

The appearance of a characteristic life stance known as the phenomenon of a yuppie in the Western countries in 1980s may be seen as such a failed attempt. Young urban professionals were 'discovered' by *Newsweek* in 1984 as something new in the local middle-class and their distinguishing trait was, "the apparent willingness [...] to subordinate all other life goals, including family and child rearing, to career success and consumption."[155] However, despite such dedication to work, unquestionability of orientation towards clients' welfare and loyalty to them – known from the previous type of professionalism – this style did not cover the existing integrity deficit. This was because corporations became increasingly dependent on their managers, clients on their lawyers etc. Concurrently, the priority of a career and consumption among young professionals caused the loss of trust in them. Thus, the result was, "an interdependence without mutual trust: the precondition for generalized hostility and fear."[156]

In regard to lawyers, this new and most modern type of professionalism emerges in several phenomena. First, the relation between the public, the client's and personal interest has changed. Exaggerating, one may say that the latter, understood in terms of a career and consumption, has become the most important and it sets bounds to realisation of the other two. Here, acting for the client's welfare boosts personal interest but the public interest does not motivate to anything at all. Naturally, it does not mean that public interest is not present in the set of declared values, but it seems that the basic form of its realisation is the famous 50 hours for the poor or other kinds of *pro bono* activity, which rarely constitute a part of lawyers' daily work[157].

Secondly, lawyers became objects of special interest to public opinion and figures in many forms of modern communication. Probably, one may even speak of specific genres, namely legal novel, legal film or legal jokes, which usually contrast a standard greedy cynic with a disquieting phenomenon of a lawyer in throes of a dilemma. Though this picture is nothing new in history, nowadays it seems to be a factor of public trust to legal professions as well as of self-identification of lawyers in the whole world.

---

155 *Ibidem*, p.122.

156 *Ibidem*.

157 The number of 50 hours is the effect of discussions and campaigns held in the U.S.A., in which an important element was the publication in 1987 by American Bar Association and American Medical Association of a common volume entitled *50 Hours for the Poor*. See W.A. Sullivan, *Work and Integrity...*, pp. 9-10. Cf., among others, D.L. Rhode, "Pro Bono in Principle and in Practice", *Journal of Legal Education* 2003, no. 53, p. 413 ff.; I.S. Russell, "The Lawyer as Public Citizen: Meeting the Pro Bono Challenge", *University of Memphis KC Law Review* 2003, no. 72, p. 439 ff.

Thirdly, lawyers' complicity in many scandals that got a lot of publicity, beginning with Watergate, ending with the bankruptcy of Enron. These examples have very suggestively shown that lawyers not only perform actions that are illegal but also contradictory to professional regulations, not to mention the mission or, simply, their officially declared function in society. If one assumes that it happens because of professionalism, even a misunderstood professionalism, then, naturally, a question arises, namely what is the attitude of legal ethics to thus perceived legal professionalism.

This relation may be viewed in three ways and each view may be related to one of the professionalism types mentioned before. First, professionalism requirements may be seen as a part of legal ethics, which would make ethical only this lawyer that has professional skills, or legal activity would be considered ethical only if it is professional at the same time. Hence, in this perspective, dilettantism in unethical. This view is supported by the fact that legal ethics has a far richer tradition, and the interest in it is significantly older than modern legal professions.

Secondly, it may be assumed that legal ethics is a part of professionalism concept, and that being professional or, simply, being a good lawyer is connected with complying with legal ethics requirements. Therefore, both sentences are true, "ethics is organically inscribed in profession [...], as well as technique [...] is organically inscribed in it," and a lawyer "not accepting ethical norms in his or her work is not a professional."[158] This position is endorsed by the fact that legal ethics' place in legal education is essentially determined by the need for professional training, and thus, at least in modern practice, professional thinking in a way precedes professional ethics and is a source of interest in it.

Thirdly, it may be held that the models of professionalism and professional ethics are relatively independent from each other and, "professional ethics is built on professional values"[159] This perspective should be related with clear separation, though not opposition, of professional skills and professional mission, or vocation, spheres. It means that particular professional activities may be assessed as professional and a lawyer as a professional irrespective of how the activities or the individual were measured from the point of view of professional ethics.

To solve this fundamental problem of longstanding evolution of legal professionalism – the problem that rests, in a way, on separation of the profession from professional ethics – and to restore integrity in lawyers, two

158 J. Pleszczyński, *Etyka dziennikarska*, [*Journalism Ethics*], Warsaw 2007, p. 29.
159 *Ibidem*.

kinds of strategies are being adopted. The first covers the attempts to define a new type of professionalism and a postulation to realise it usually by means of legal education. This is what Robert W. Gordon suggests by writing of the so-called purposive lawyer, who, in his opinion, "does not split public and private roles, but rather tries to unify them by seeking ways to harmonize the client's business plans with the purposes of the legal framework."[160] Naturally, such a lawyer can neither be fully independent nor completely loyal to the client. Nor can he or she be loyal to the "system", but will have to maintain a balance between those standpoints. However, because of this the lawyer can avoid the "schizoid" risk and finally discover a new form of the professional mission, which is being a kind of "a corporate conscience".

Another, more extensive proposition was formed by Anthony T. Kronman. He claims not only that legal professions differ from other professions because, "not every job is a profession. Not every job is a way of life,"[161] but also because practising in a legal profession is a form of life in the Wittgensteinian understanding, and, "a lawyer's sense of professional responsibility can no more be reduced to a knowledge of the rules of legal ethics than command of English can be reduced to a knowledge of the rules of English grammar."[162] This form, or a way of living, consists of four elements; each of them is a counterbalance for hazards of modern capitalism and the type of professionalism related to it. Among these elements is the orientation toward realising public welfare by lawyers, which is against the "privatization" of public life and domination of private interest. The second element is legal versatility manifesting itself in the capacities to handle many cases and advise in many matters, which is against the process of increasingly narrower "specialization". The third element is the typical of lawyers involvement of all emotional and intellectual capabilities in one's work, which is to act against "alienation". Finally, lawyers' deep-rootedness in tradition and related to it the accumulation of previous generations' experiences act against "forgetfulness" perceived as discontinuation and severance of ties with the past consequently leading also to the loss of care for the future[163].

The second strategy rests on the constatation that different types of professionalism – both the historical ones and those in the process of formation and only partly present in practice – are not mutually exclusive. On the contrary, they coexist in various configurations and accompany different forms of legal

---

160 R.W. Gordon, "The Independence...", p. 24.

161 A.T. Kronman, "The Law...", p. 31.

162 *Ibidem*, p. 30.

163 *Ibidem*, pp. 35-36.

practice. One type of professionalism is therefore present in lawyers specialising in family law who practise individually in small towns, while another type is present in lawyers defending in famous criminal cases and yet another type occurs in lawyers that work in big teams and who operate multimillion transactions[164]. Whereas in the case of only postulated kinds of professionalism, their strongholds may be found among lawyers working for non-profit organisations which give free legal advice or defend human rights.

It is observed that what differentiates those groups of lawyers is primarily their function. Most generally speaking, as Talcott Parsons points out, functions of lawyers mean that they have an "interstitial" position in social structure; because they are "integrated with the structure of political authority," and because they have – largely independent – trusteeship over the legal tradition, they are, "a 'secondary' line of defence against the disruptive consequences of [social] conflict" and act as kind of a "buffer between the legislature, the executive organ and the general public."[165] This does not exclude further differentiation of these functions since obviously some lawyers are more "integrated with political authority," and others are rather "the trustees of [legal] traditions." What seems crucial is that, in this view, performing functions by lawyers is possible after satisfying certain conditions. When looking for these conditions it must be recalled that, "[...] a profession is a cluster of "occupational' roles, that is roles in which the incumbents perform certain functions valued in the society[...],"[166] and thus with the term "occupational role" such search may be carried out.

Naturally, occupational roles are a part of a broader category of social roles. In the case of lawyers, the models of such roles are usually built in relation to, "values and norms forming a system of law, social expectations in regard to realisation of these values in the process of law functioning, and also expectations and requirements related to direct participation of lawyers in social interactions, and, essentially, in the most significant here, the interactions in a courtroom and decisions issued in the process of law application by the court."

164 About the clash of various forms of practice and related to them types of professionalism on the example of the Polish bar see K. Wierzbowski, "Jedna czy dwie adwokatury? Głos w sprawie przyszłości naszego zawodu", ["One or Two Bars? A Voice in Relation to the Future of Our Profession"] *Palestra* 2002, no. 3-4, pp. 57-65.

165 T. Parsons, "A Sociologist Looks at the Legal Profession", in *Essays in…*, pp. 375, 378, 379.

166 *Ibidem*, pp. 371-2.

Hence, primarily systemic, interactive and subjective factors are meant here[167]. In the context of the above drafted typology of professionalism it seems that what is at issue here is not only the legal but also economic framework – for example capitalism in its different phases – and a courtroom probably is a very characteristic place of social interaction between lawyers but its significance radically changes, which is expressed in a lapidary phrase that, "legal profession moved from the courtroom to the boardroom".

Of both legal norms as well as the requirements of codes of professional ethics one may say that they constitute legal professional roles in a normative sense, which correspond with the actual roles, though are not identical to them[168]. In this perspective the question of relations between professionalism and professional ethics, decided on the basis of occupational role in normative sense, would have to be decided within its bounds, and thus it would always concern a particular role and be internal to it. One has to keep in mind that thus understood role is only one of the factors forming professional role in its proper sense, which includes systemic, interactive and subjective factors. If it is assumed that the first ones are related to the requirements made by a society as such, and so with realising public interest, the second are connected with the pressure of clients demanding the realisation of their interests, and, finally, the third relate to the lawyer's interest itself, then, according to what has been already said, professionalism should integrate these spheres and indicate means of possibly peaceful realisation of them all. This means that professionalism has an internal character in relation to professional roles while still being very important as concerning all the other factors constituting a role. This cannot be said of professional ethics, which may be treated as internal only in constructions of normative models that correspond with particular roles. Therefore, contrary to professionalism, only in this second sense can it be the subject of interest to sociologists, which still, in opposition to professionalism, does not exhaust its issues.

1.4.3. Globalisation

Great complexity of the phenomenon of globalisation makes it difficult to define the term. Literature indicates many propositions in this respect. However, there is no agreement even in general elements of the definition and what, according

167 G. Skąpska, "Zawód prawnika czy społeczna rola?", ["Lawyer's Profession or a Social Role?"], in: G. Skąpska, J. Czapska, M. Kozłowska, *Społeczne role prawników (sędziów, prokuratorów, adwokatów),* Wrocław-Warszawa-Kraków-Gdańsk-Łódź 1989, p. 6.

168 *Ibidem*, p. 8.

to some authors, exhausts the globalisation description, to others, is only an aspect of the process. Hence, for the purposes of the analysis of globalisation in legal professions and legal ethics one has to adopt a broad meaning of the term according to which globalisation is, "a process of deepening of the worldwide relations in all aspects of modern political, social, economic and cultural life."[169] This will help avoid partial presentation of the phenomenon since in legal ethics it has both economic and political aspects – these aspects are related to the rise of global market and exchange, which possess their own continuously forming organisational and institutional framework that changes functions and the understanding of modern states and of the law being created by them – and also social and cultural aspects, which are connected with the creation of new forms of intercultural communication and social ties within the framework of global economy and its institutions.

1.4.3.1. Institutions of globalisation

Technological advancement certainly remains one of the sources of globalisation. On a global scale, it speeded up not only people's travels but, essentially, the flow of information. This means the advent of totally new freedom of mobility and new speed[170] in interhuman relations, and these two aspects are mentioned in the first place when characterising globalisation; its other qualities are treated as the consequences. Therefore, apart form this "time and space compression" globalisation consists of the "erosion of borders and removal of geographical barriers in the flow of goods, services, capital, investment, technology and information, spreading economic activity beyond borders, speeding up global interactions, intensifying international relations, deepening interdependence."[171] The economic aspect of globalisation seems crucial, though it remains multidimensional itself, which means that separating the consequences from the factors that drive economic transformations is simply impossible[172].

Many such dimensions are being identified. First, economic globalisation means an increase of the services sector that is not directly related to the production of material goods, which process is sometimes described as

169 B. Liberska, "Współczesne procesy globalizacji gospodarki światowej", ["Modern Processes of World Economy Globalisation"], in: *Globalizacja. Mechanizmy i wyzwania*, ed. B. Liberska, Warsaw 2002, p. 17.

170 See Z. Bauman, *Globalizacja*, [*Globalization*], Warsaw 2000, pp. 17-33.

171 B. Liberska, "Współczesne procesy...", p. 18.

172 P.H. Dembiński, "Globalizacja – wyzwanie i szansa", ["Globalisation – a Challenge and an Opportunity"], in: *Globalizacja,* ed. J. Klich, Kraków 2001, p. 21.

"dematerialisation." These services, at least to some extent – apart from the services related to consumption – are connected with increasingly greater complexity of global reality, which creates, "a more and more complicated formal-legal framework."[173] Services related to this framework, and legal services are certainly also to be included here, require a significant intellectual capital or, broadly speaking, human capital. On this basis, a new specialisation type arises, "traditional branches descend from the ladder of development to the less developed countries, whereas new branches, relying on intellectual capital, appear and ascend up the ladder to the most developed countries."[174]

Secondly, a considerably greater role is ascribed to financial institutions, in the interest of which, but also because of which, all barriers to the flow of capital are removed[175]. This in a large part determines the character of issues which in global reality are assigned to lawyers and simultaneously makes them a very important group from the perspective of the whole process. Thus, if, "there has been a transition to specialisation coming down to what is offered to global economy," then lawyers offer primarily an effective functioning of main mechanisms used for spreading globalisation[176]. Therefore, one may say that lawyers belong to the avant-garde of this process.

Thirdly, a very important dimension of globalisation is the creation of transnational corporations that, "perfectly mastered the art of arranging feedback mechanism all around the globe," and possess, "great skill in the acquiring, accumulation and use of knowledge for innovation."[177] Such corporations make the primary group of clients that specialised lawyers serve and are one of the organisation forms of legal work itself. It is to be retained that what concerns transnational corporations' position in regard to knowledge, applies also to law and legal firms, which also for this reason start to take special position in the legal community[178]. It is noteworthy that, as far as the role of transnational corporations in globalisation is concerned, a controversy persists, namely some

173 *Ibidem*.

174 W. Szymański, *Globalizacja. Wyzwania i zagrożenia*, [*Globalisation. Challenges and Risks*], Warszawa 2001, pp. 26-30.

175 P. H. Dembiński, "Globalizacja – wyzwanie…", pp. 22-24.

176 W. Szymański, *Globalizacja...*, pp. 29-31.

177 P.H. Dembiński, "Globalizacja – wyzwanie…", pp. 24-26.

178 See J. Leszczyński, "Dogmatyki prawnicze w dobie globalizacji", ["Legal Dogmatics in the Age of Globalisation"], in: *Filozofia prawa wobec globalizmu*, ed. J. Stelmach, Kraków 2003, p. 123, who indicated the role of great law firms' practice in the formation of new types of contracts such as leasing (which subsequently has been included to code regulations of the detailed part of obligations), franchising and factoring (which still fall into the category of innominate contracts).

people claim that the corporations are an answer to the problems of globalisation and can control the process, while others assert that they are a causative agent of both the process itself and of problems related to it. It seems that, all in all, corporations are both at the same time[179].

The very dispute, whether large corporations are able to control globalisation, is possible because of the certainty that institutions of a nation-state cannot fulfil this function. According to Zygmunt Bauman, who in his famous essay asserts that because of unlimited and unrestrained spread of the free market rules, especially because of the free flow of capital and financial means, the economy increasingly evades political control. Due to this, a traditional institution of political control, a nation-state, becomes disinherited, which means that it is deprived of an essential part of its governance that is based on ordering and controlling the economy and is left with only its narrowest scope – the policy towards territory and inhabitants.[180]

In this situation, globalisation has a significant dejuridisational potential, which not only means that in order to make their economies more competitive, nation-states deregulate whole spheres of social life, but also relates to the formation of law on the inter- and supranational levels – starting with technical norms, ending with the removal of barriers for free trade – which simultaneously equals standardisation of norms on the regional or even on global scale and deprives states of freedom in this regard at the same time. The latter consequence results in diminution of the number of regulations and the simplification of legal systems[181]. If, in the face of colonization of social life by the law this phenomenon is to be assessed positively, then one should not forget about the critical voices.

The perspectives of creating a global legal framework seem distant. The extrapolation of the existing tendencies may lead to the conclusion that such a system will not be associated with a nation-state or any world-state since, the replacement of weak territorial states with some kind of legislatory and political power of global reach would be noxious for the interests of the world markets. Bauman continues and writes that one may suppose that political fragmentation and economical globalisation are not mutually contradictory or at war with each other but remain close allies and co-conspirators.[182] For this reason a legal system of global reach will certainly have some special character because of the

179 W. Szymański, *Globalizacja...*, pp. 32-33.

180 Z. Bauman, *Globalizacja,* pp. 78-83.

181 J. Guść, K. Łokucijewski, "Globalizacja a jurydyzacja", ["Globalisation vs. Juridisation"], in: *Filozofia prawa wobec globalizmu*, ed. J. Stelmach, Kraków 2003, pp. 33-37.

182 Z. Bauman, *Globalizacja*, pp. 83-84.

departure from, as it seemed until now, a necessary or organic law-state relation. As it is pointed out in literature, such law would need to have the nature of one-sided regulation and this entails a deficit of democracy in its formation since nowadays only law making institutions of a nation-state have a democratic mandate.

If such law is not to be merely a series of, "acts of enforcing political and economic domination, then it must include the idea of the rule of law, which stands for equal standards for all participants of global exchange. It seems that in the current situation these standards may exist only as unilateral commitments taken on by global society out of respect for other exchange participants. [...] Settlements of this type may have only procedural and formal character binding, for the time being, on the basis of one-sided commitment adopted by global society, however without assuming the mutuality on the side of other participants of the global exchange. This would make it similar to an ethical system rather than legal."[183] It is also worth remarking that connecting the rule of law construction with the claim that there is no clear boundary between the law and other social norms[184] confirms another functional relation between law and morality: "in the densely populated world of human daily life, moral impulses need codes, laws, jurisdiction and institutions that install and monitor them all."[185]

Therefore, it is nothing unusual that especially lawyers from the common law culture, who over the last two decades have transferred the legal firm institution to the global scale, thrive in such an environment. Even though legal companies in the United States and the United Kingdom had existed much earlier[186], it was in relation to globalisation that they started their expansion in regard to transnational practice and quickly transformed from entities operating in one country into networks of global reach. It is worth emphasising that the very phenomenon of providing transnational legal services is nothing new and,

---

183 A. Bator, W. Gromski, S. Kaźmierczyk, A. Kozak, "Integracja i globalizacja z perspektywy filozofii prawa", ["Integration and Globalisation from the Perspective of Philosophy of Law"], in: *Filozofia prawa wobec globalizmu*, ed. J. Stelmach, Kraków 2003, p. 21.

184 H. Izdebski, *Fundamenty współczesnych państw*, [*The Foundations of Modern States*], Warsaw 2007, pp. 94-95.

185 Z. Bauman, "What Chance of Ethics in the Globalized World of Consumers?", in: *Does Ethics Have a Chance in a World of Consumers?*, Cambridge Massachusetts 2009, p. 45.

186 See B. Krzyżagórska, "Kilka uwag na temat amerykańskiej firmy prawniczej, cz. I", ["Some Remarks on the American Law Firm, Part I"], *Palestra* 1996, no. 1-2, and part II, *Palestra* 1996, no. 3-4.

in fact, is of trivial character[187]. What was characteristic of this phenomenon – and to much extent still is – is the fact that the number of foreign lawyers allowed to provide services in particular countries remains low, not exceeding a quarter of a percent. This is due to the high level of state "protectionism", which is very often stimulated by legal communities themselves, and to many obstacles in the access to legal professions – obstacles that comprise the requirements of not only having the knowledge of the law, but also of a given language and culture or obtaining a citizenship of a given country[188].

Despite little changes in this regard, legal firms managed successfully to expand globally mainly because of the significant increase in demand for transnational services. The expansion usually took two forms. Firstly, firms have decided to open offices in other countries out of necessity to control and supervise lawyers that represented their regular clients in those countries, on the firm's recommendation. Opening foreign branches by corporate clients brought the same consequences for the law firms. Secondly, in the period preceding the bankruptcy of Enron and the introduction of the ban on combining audit and legal counsel activities, legal firms carried out their expansion in the form of auditing networks – though it typically concerned minor companies and was not that significant as the first manner of expansion[189]. It appears that nowadays, apart from purely financial reasons, a greater role in deciding on the opening of a foreign office is ascribed to the prestige related to it, which not only translates into the satisfaction of the lawyers managing a particular firm, but also defines its position within increasingly conspicuous divisions of the legal community.

The aforementioned divisions concern not only the differentiation with regard to groups of clients served, categories of cases run and work organisation, and, eventually, to the adopted historical type of legal professionalism, but also to the scope of activity that from now on may be local or global. This in turn seems to increasingly determine the approach to professional practice standards including deontological ones. The first aspect of this phenomenon is the fact that legal firms with a global reach began to establish their own standards of legal activity also including standards related to ethical aspects of this work. These standards often take the form of a collection of rules of considerable length reaching the size of even several volumes. The collections mainly consist of norms of a technical-instructional character, and thus concern various aspects of work organisation starting with documents' storage and flow, ending with the dress-code and font type of letters issued. However, they also include norms that

187 R.L. Abel, "Transnational Law Practice", *Case Western Law Review* 1994, no. 44, p. 738.

188 *Ibidem*, pp. 739, and 750-762.

189 *Ibidem*, 743-748.

clearly relate to traditional scope of legal ethics, namely professional loyalty and reliability, financial settlements, avoidance of the conflict of interests, keeping professional secrets and *pro bono* activity[190].

Such collections are usually addressed to all employees of a given firm regardless of what kind of legal profession they practise, in what self-regulating professional organisation they associate or what code of professional ethics formally binds them. Admittedly, they often include a number of colliding principles allowing for settlement of the situations of convergence of various deontological norms that are appropriate for different lawyers working in a firm, but also allowing adjudication between these norms and the firm's standards. However, this may not affect the validity of the claim that globalisation for legal ethics means not only enhancement of juridisation but also significant complication of relations between legal ethics norms, which most generally may be described precisely as the convergence of deontological standards [191]. In this situation, it appears that solutions to the problems stemming from globalisation should also be searched on a global level, and thus, in relation to juridisation, the dejuridisational potential of globalisation should be exploited.

The second aspect of the influence of the global reach of legal firms on professional standards is exactly the creation of instruments serving to satisfy the needs of lawyers practising in a transnational manner and intensification of international contacts of the whole professional groups. The instruments may be discovered by analysing the efforts to create supranational codes of professional ethics. These codes, as for example the already discussed *The International Association of Prosecutors' Standards of Professional Responsibility and Statement of the Essential Duties and Rights of Prosecutor*, *Bangalore Principles of Judicial Conduct*, or essentially the *Code of Conduct for European Lawyers*, adopted by the Council of Bars and Law Societies of Europe (CCBE)[192], serve different functions in this matter, and so, particular norms or groups of norms of a given code may also be varied in this regard.

Firstly, norms of supranational codes may be a means of unifying national norms, and so their aim would be, to some degree, a replacement of local standards. Secondly, adopting norms of such codes may lead to harmonisation of national norms, and thus to realisation of common goals with respect to the

---

190 See T. Karaś, "Zasady obowiązujące w wybranych kancelariach prawnych działających w Polsce", ["Rules Valid in Chosen Law Firms in Poland"], in: *Etyka prawnicza…*, ed. H. Izdebski, P. Skuczyński, pp. 34-44.

191 H. Izdebski, "Zbieg standardów deontologii zawodowej", ["The Convergence of Professional Deontology Standards"], in: *Etyka prawnicza…*, ed. H. Izdebski, P. Skuczyński, p. 31.

192 See chapter 1.4.1.1.

specificity of national regulations. Thirdly, it may be about setting minimal standards which will satisfy the sense of security of lawyers acting globally. Fourthly, adopting norms of supranational deontology may result in creating collisional rules, which should be applied in case of the negative convergence of standards, namely in case of their conflict. Irrespective of which situation one deals with in relation to norms of the particular codes discussed here, the application of such instruments leads to the merging of local deontologies.

Nevertheless, one may speak of an opposite situation where adopting supranational standards is a result of a previous coming together of local codes. In this regard these codes are of a uniquely declaratory type and do not serve important practical functions. However, they are an unquestionable proof for globalisation of legal ethics. The origins of this process in this case remain the same as in a factual regulatory effort undertaken on the level of law firms or professional associations but the forms of the process are different. Here, most widely-spread is the inclusion of the requirements of transnational global practice in the phase of national standards' formation. So, for example in *Ethics 2000* project, within the framework of which significant changes have been made to *Model Rules of Professional Conduct*, the American Bar Association has carried out a series of consultations with CCBE representatives, which contributed to the creation of many international and interregional working groups for the purpose of constant discussion of problems that occur to lawyers in their work beyond the borders of the United States[193].

Hence, in the sphere of codes of professional ethics, globalisation is a conspicuous phenomenon, though assuming various forms and happening in various institutional frameworks. It still remains to be determined to what extent these changes exhaust the consequences of the discussed process for legal ethics and to what extent they reach deeper. It seems that carrying out debates that aim to settle common standards for lawyers belonging to not only different cultural circles, but also to different legal cultures, is in itself a new phenomenon that needs analysis especially from the perspective of conditions which participants of such discussions have to meet. It is unlikely that purely pragmatic reasons could decide the success of intercultural communication of lawyers on the subject of professional ethics standards, behind which stand different traditions of legal ethics[194].

---

193 L.S. Terry, "U.S. Legal Ethics: the Coming of Age of Global and Comparative Perspectives", *Washington University Global Studies Law Review* 2005, no. 4, p. 496 ff.

194 As an example of the beginning of the 1990s optimism based on the CCBE code' success and the belief in creating a universal professional ethics code through a compromise on rules see J. Toulmin, "A Worldwide Common Code of Professional

1.4.3.2. Intercultural communication

Literature indicates – and that is also a conclusion of the presented analysis of legal ethics' traditions – that an obstacle for globalisation of legal ethics standards is, *inter alia*, a varied approach to both codes of professional ethics – which resemble more or less hard law and that is why a greater or minor role is ascribed to their individual or corporate interpretation – but also to professional roles of lawyers. The latter is connected with the adoption of different types of professionalism and client-lawyer relation models[195]. Facing such intercultural communication differences, the best way of coping may be either technologisation – introducing procedures, or personalisation, that is, "a certain lack of technology being a systematic, enclosed within procedures, verified in its effectiveness system of action" – formation of a specific personality type able to reconcile contradictions, with imagination, aiming at self-realisation[196].

The first solution – the creation of new rules that give rise to a procedure of solving issues of intercultural communication in the context of formation and application of supranational deontological standards – only seems to aggravate the problem. One has to bear in mind not only the already mentioned dejuridisational potential of globalisation, but also that deregulation may be considered, along with technological advancement, as one of the elements of the globalisation genesis[197]. Therefore, it appears that if creation of common deontology is to fulfil its functions effectively, then it must encounter bounds behind which a sphere of "personal" intercultural communication should exist. In other words, of legal ethics globalisation one may say that, "globalisation of culture phenomena, typical of modern forms of technologically advanced civilisation, after a period of expansive standardisation have lead to the phase being its contradiction. They have revealed a great variety of cultures, the necessity of finding a form of their coexistence and, indirectly, the problem of

---

Ethics?", *Fordham International Law Journal* 1991-1992, no. 15, pp. 673-685. It seems that the optimism was groundless.

195 See also M.C. Daly, "The Cultural, Ethical, and Legal Challenges in Lawyering for a Global Organization. The Role of the General Counsel", *Emory Law Journal* 1997, no. 46, pp. 1068-1099.

196 L. Korporowicz, "Od konfliktu do spotkania kultur", ["From Conflict to the Intertwinement of Cultures"], in: *Komunikacja międzykulturowa. Zbliżenia i impresje*, ed. A. Kapciak, L. Korporowicz, A. Tyszka, Warsaw 1995, pp. 32-33.

197 U. Bernardi, "Globalizacja i kultury. Przeciw starym i nowym przesądom", ["Globalisation and Cultures. Against Old and New Superstitions"], *Społeczeństwo* 1998, no. 2, p. 275.

cultural identity of groups and individuals in the context of internationalised systems of social life and the increasing role of intercultural communication."[198]

Intercultural communication, both as a term and a modern field of knowledge, has been forming since 1950s. Nevertheless, it may be claimed that, "it owes its present popularity to changes in the ways of leading the economic life." On one hand, economic institutions of global reach, as organisations, give rise to their own subcultures. On the other, due to this process a culture of intercultural negotiations arises[199]. These two issues should be studied further. However, let us first remark that reflections on crossroads of cultures lead to the issue of the existence or creation of the so-called 'third culture', which usually is an effect of cultural differentiation processes, cultures' diffusion, acculturation, domination and the clash of cultures[200]. Still, its nature is debatable.

Firstly, it may be held that the 'third culture' is of an independent nature, though one may always identify cultures that are its source. In this sense one speaks of intercultural communication sphere, which is, "the functioning of supranational companies employing in many places of the world multinational teams of employees and creating their *own* culture that, despite the employees being rooted in separate national cultures, becomes their culture as of the company's employees."[201] However, in this view intercultural communication becomes something intracultural. This, of course, is not excluded in all cases, but does not provide the answer for the question about conditions of the company's culture formation, which may allow further communication between cultures.

Secondly, it may be assumed – like in the previous position – not only that cultures generally do not merge, and if they do, then only in exceptional cases – hence, a melting pot does not work here – but also it is only because of intercultural communication that the formation of the 'third culture' is possible. This is connected with rejecting – as inadequate – the communication models aimed at a synthesis and with focusing on models based on synergy. In the latter, "by allowing self-controlled processes there opens a possibility of a rise of 'intercultures', which in terms of quality really create something new."[202] Yet, a

198 L. Korporowicz, "Od konfliktu...", p. 39.

199 J. Mikułowski-Pomorski, *Komunikacja międzykulturowa. Wprowadzenie*, [*Intercultural Communication. An Introduction*], Kraków 1999, pp. 14-16, 19.

200 A. Kapciak, "Komunikacja międzykulturowa jako fenomen kultury współczesnej", ["Intercultural Communication as a Modern Culture Phenomenon"], in: *Komunikacja międzykulturowa. Zbliżenia i impresje*, ed. A. Kapciak, L. Korporowicz, A. Tyszka, Warsaw 1995, p. 183.

201 A. Kapciak, "Komunikacja międzykulturowa...", p.193.

202 J. Bolten, *Interkulturowa kompetencja*, [*Intercultural Competence*], Poznań 2006, pp. 112, 119-120.

problem arises, namely to what extent these spontaneous or self-controlled communication processes will really occur, and how to create favourable conditions for them. One of the answers of the proposition's supporters is the creation of meta-communication, which will be further discussed.

Thirdly and finally, one may speak not exactly of the global culture – even if one only means a subculture or interculture of global companies – but rather of "global ecumene." This is because culture's global character, actually, "is reduced to being only a way of organising variety," in which intercultural communication is a series of, "performed by individuals, acts of combining elements that come from different traditions – or different forms of living – and which in new situation of global society may temporarily be united in people's actions. However, they will never make some lasting whole."[203] This standpoint seems important because it exposes the individual, and thus passing, character of the 'third culture' and simultaneously underlines the role of tradition in its creation.

Therefore, it seems that two aspects of modern interest in intercultural communication – economic institutions of global reach and the culture of intercultural negotiations – in theoretical framework, but not in practical one, may play unequal roles. Thus, efficient functioning and development of a global company appears possible only because of creating and applying procedures and rules of its functioning. This is possible only within the framework of a certain culture, whose formation, in turn, requires rather de-formalised debates and negotiations based on particular standpoints of individuals distancing themselves from, though not cutting off, their own traditions. The latter may be named the culture of intercultural negotiations, in reference to which it has to be observed that it is a culture that conditions the creation of other cultures. Thus, the culture of intercultural negotiations is a culture in a different sense than the former and in its case one must speak of intercultural communication as of a communicational culture form, and so apply the view according to which the communication itself is a culture[204].

The very term communication in this context should be understood as a process in which people create a community by sharing significant meanings. This process, "should lead to a situation where people who participate in it have increasing trust in one another, where they better understand one another. If the desired level of trust based on understanding is attained, the exchange of signals between partners becomes reduced. People in a community understand one

203 M. Kempny, "Komunikacja międzykulturowa czy postkulturowa globalna ekumena", ["Intercultural Communication or Postcultural Global Ecumene"], in: *Komunikacja międzykulturowa. Zbliżenia i impresje*, ed. A. Kapciak, L. Korporowicz, A. Tyszka, Warsaw 1995, pp. 137-138.

204 A. Kapciak, "Komunikacja międzykulturowa...", p. 182.

another better and so they communicate less [...]."[205] Naturally, orientation toward community creation is not the only possible communication goal, which, consequently, determines strategy adopted for communication. From this perspective, one may distinguish three such strategies: code reproduction, which means defence and consolidation of the status of cultures that participate in communication; mutual acceptance of the code, which entails modification of cultures participating in communication through mutual adjustment in terms of functionality, and code transformation and creation, whose goal is integration and common development of communication participants[206].

Globalisation of legal ethics, at least as far as deontological standards are concerned, seems to be the process which may be impeded by adopting the first strategy – at least in relation to the entities applying it. However, the rareness of such an attitude will only lead to the exclusion and marginalisation of the traditions represented by them. For this reason more attention should be paid to the other two strategies: adaptational and integrational. Adaptation and integration are not goals that are mutually exclusive. Rather, the difference between them is in the level on which they occur; the former belongs to superficial structure, the latter to the deep. By viewing it in these terms, one may identify three fundamental differences in communication aiming only at mutual adjustment and at creating a community.

Firstly, in adaptational strategy, the interlocutor is regarded uniquely through conventionalised requirements of social roles. These requirements make communication meaningful, and not his or her intentions, which have this function in integrational strategy. Secondly, within the sphere of interpretations, in the case of the first strategy, one deals with signals, which may be ascribed a limited number of meanings. In the second, the carriers of meanings are symbols that are open to many interpretations, which enables holding a real discourse. Thirdly, both strategies engage and modify different parts of communication participants' personalities. The adaptational model reaches only to the sphere of changeable personality, and thus is formed to a great degree by social roles, including professional roles. Contrary to this, the integrational model – oriented toward community creation – requires involvement on the level of most stable personality traits that are least dependent on systemic-functional factors[207].

In the light of what has already been said – that culture of intercultural negotiations needs to distance itself from tradition, which may be attained by the orientation toward the building of a community, that engages deeper parts of

205 J. Mikułowski-Pomorski, *Komunikacja międzykulturowa...*, p. 7.

206 L. Korporowicz, "Od konfliktu...", pp. 34-36.

207 *Ibidem*, pp. 36-39.

personality than those formed by social roles – one may better understand the sense of tools – proposed in literature – of creating synergic communication. These tools rely on the adoption of three attitudes, which may be arranged by their importance and mutual relation. The first means is the distance of roles, which is the ability to look at one's social roles, including professional ones, in such a way that may be called reflective. This term in its fundamental, non-philosophical meaning stands for self-observation and self-control. The second tool of the discussed intercultural communication model is empathy, which through common emotions leads to the understanding of the interlocutor. The third and most refined tool is meta-communication, a kind of meta-discourse, in which one may discuss all misunderstandings occurring on the normal level as well as ways of solving and avoiding them in future[208].

Therefore, one may conclude that if a result of globalisation is to be development – also development of law in its new relation to the nation-state, new institutional context and over the boundaries of not only the circles of particular legal cultures, but also over these cultures – then lawyers participating in this process will have to not only go beyond their own deontological standards, but also beyond their own professional roles. This is why some authors go as far as to say that, "the reasons for development are not mechanically inscribed in having the resources, in the education level and the quality of the legal system. One may think that development has something in common with human *virtue* (...) Essentially, development process relies on making connections: with what is at our disposal (...) and links between people."[209] Without having to determine whether the category of virtue is really the best to apply in this context, it may certainly be stated that it is one of the possible views of personal ethics requirements, satisfaction of which will allow for the creation of the community of intercultural negotiations.

The awareness of these requirements in the context of lawyers appears important since before the intensification of globalisation processes and in accordance with critical assessment of them, the meeting places were a sphere in which norms were constituted, which was why justice arranged horizontally, it was administered in this way, and it consolidated the community formed by those who discussed it. Whereas a territory deprived of a public sphere gives little opportunity for beginning a discussion of norms, for a confrontation, for a clash and negotiation of values.[210] In such conditions the encounters of lawyers and their common work of global reach seem one of few sources of cultural

208 J. Bolten, *Interkulturowa kompetencja*, pp. 123-124.

209 S. Beretta, "Globalizacja i rozwój", *Społeczeństwo* 1998, no. 2, p. 272.

210 Z. Bauman, *Globalizacja*, s. 33.

phenomena that may start performing functions of a public sphere without territory. This translates into the rise of importance of lawyers and communication between them but also of values they share that would simultaneously be conditions of mutual trust between them. This, however, is, *par excellence*, a philosophical problem, though present also in the context of legal practice and education, which more often indicate the need for the return to ethical terminology in legal regulations and the need for training lawyers with high personal ethics as a condition of their participation in global legal relations.

1.4.5. Transformations of legal ethics: modernisation or Americanisation?

The relationship of tradition and modernity is one of the main and at the same time most complicated issues in social sciences[211]. The very description of what tradition and modernity are, defining them as scientifically useful terms, presents many theoretical difficulties. This is not only because of high level of their abstractness, but also because of the emotional charge related to them. It is difficult to imagine modern humanities free from valuation, but it is nevertheless important to distinguish descriptive and valuating elements of concepts and always use them consciously in one or the other meaning[212]. It has still to be remembered that using such concepts may have an ideological character, which, in consequence, gives also a political dimension to arguments about tradition and modernity. This essentially shows in the opposition of conservatism-modernity as a strategy of governance and of the functioning of social institutions.

This relation not necessarily has to be based on a dichotomic opposition and alternative as it was done in the 19th and in the beginning of 20th century by for example Tönnies with the use of *Gemeinschaft* and *Gesellschaft* categories[213] or by the supporters of the so-called detraditionalization and occidentalization. For it is also asserted that, "progress is only possible on the basis of the already existing tradition but that is open to change, and, inversely, tradition has always been established as a result of progress, which to us belongs to the past so distant that we often do not acknowledge it at all. Tradition is retained progress, progress is a

---

211 See the anthology of *Tradycja i nowoczesność*, [*Tradition and Modernity*], ed. J. Kurczewska, J. Szacki, Warsaw 1984, and particularly J. Szacki, "Wprowadzenie", ["Introduction"].

212 K. Pawłowski, *Tworzenie pojęć i definiowanie w naukach humanistycznych*, [*The Creation of Concepts and Defining in Humanities*], Warsaw 1978, pp. 6, 105-114.

213 On the significance of this view for professional ethics see the already quoted study H. Izdebski, "Granice..."

continued tradition."[214] However, nowadays, the dominant conceptions state that traditions and modernity are subjects of, "conscious selections, that try to minimise damages done by modernity to the way of life which they got used to. Anyway, it is not so much choosing between tradition and modernity as it is picking from both."[215] Such a perspective has some traits of post-modern eclecticism. Still, in reflections on legal ethics it presents many advantages.

Firstly, contemporary culture researchers connect modernist categories with the disintegration of various types of monisms: ontological, epistemological and methodological. As a result of this disintegration, naturalism associated with scientistic perspectives ceased to be dominant as the so-called scientific view and was replaced with culturalism linked to communication perspectives[216]. These perspectives give the advantage of facilitating the interpretation of modernity and its relations, namely they join the spheres of culture, society and personality in a way that does not confine theory to search the origins and explanations of modern rationalisation in Marxist and Weberian reductionism. Traditions and transformations of legal ethics seem to be based on various categories belonging to three spheres: duties, professional roles and virtues. Thus, in modernity it should be possible to connect them and build such a theory of legal ethics that would join all three traditions and simultaneously provide for its rationality.

Secondly, occasionally heard voices that modern transformations of legal ethics are essentially the domination of American tradition over its European counterparts may in such a perspective be relatively easily understood. If modernity combines primarily with free exchange and argumentation as well as with rational planning of collective problem solving, then in the American tradition of legal ethics counterparts may be easily found. On one hand, adversary trial system leaves a broad margin of freedom to lawyers who participate in the proceedings and assumes that even a brutal clash of opposing arguments leads to the fullest presentation of all circumstances of the case, revealing truth and making the best decision. On the other, continual debates on professional duties that are held within legal community as well as within the whole society allow a precise identification of legal practice problems and possible interests and also their regulation in compliance with a specified model. Though, it has to be remembered that these elements are also present – however to a lesser extent – in the continental traditions of legal ethics. Transformations of legal ethics – with different intensity – occur in each of its traditions and the expansion of the

214 C.F. von Weizsäcker, "O tradycji w filozofii", ["On Tradition in Philosophy"], in: *Jedność przyrody*, Warsaw 1978, p. 437.

215 J. Szacki, "Wprowadzenie", p. 12.

216 A. Mencwel, Trzy modernizmy, ["Three Modernisms"], in: idem, *Wyobraźnia antropologiczna*, Warsaw 2006, pp. 299-300.

American legal ethics is rather related to the changes in the world economy, in which the United States play the key role, and with the spread of their cultural models rather than with overcoming the French and German traditions.

Thirdly, as regards legal professions, the complex character of tradition-modernity opposition has revealed itself with all force in recent decades. It is worth noticing that this is not only a Polish problem, though our disputes about access to legal professions, disciplinary responsibility of lawyers or maximum fee levels are very intensive. More generally speaking, the disputes concern the role of the market, of self-regulating organisations and the state in the regulation of free legal professional practice. However, I believe that attempts at describing the disputes only in the categories of liberalism, communitarianism or statism have no positive influence on the development of the discussion in this matter[217]. A significantly more useful perspective seems to be employing the concepts of tradition and modernity. With these concepts one may define a framework in which appropriate reforms could be planned without annulling all of centuries-old achievements of legal professions – achievements that manifest exactly in traditions of legal ethics. Furthermore, with these concepts one may also set proper goals of these reforms so that development of legal professions keeps pace with social and especially economic development. Only within such framework mutual relations between the market, corporations and the state in regulation of such a complex and important sphere as functioning of free legal professions may be identified.

It is difficult do discuss in the present study the practical consequences in the scope of legal professions' structure that flow from the proposed theoretical way of reconciling traditions of legal ethics and the influences of modernity – consequences which would allow avoiding these difficulties and harsh political disputes. However, it appears that reaching to a tradition of legal ethics will help at least to mitigate them and facilitate sensible reforms that may enable keeping those elements from these traditions which are of value and, simultaneously, remove everything that today is an anachronism impeding development. The plan for theoretical combination of legal ethics' traditions with transformations that contribute to their modernisation may thus have practical consequences, namely balancing innovation and conservatism in legal professions.

---

217 See part of this dispute H. Izdebski, L. Morawski, "Dwugłos: Demokracja a przywileje korporacyjne", ["Divided Opinions: Democracy and Corporate Privileges"] *Państwo i Prawo* 2007, no. 6.

1.5. Legal ethics in Poland

There are two main reasons why legal ethics in Poland may be seen as very instructive from the perspective of legal ethics' theory. Firstly, the historical background makes it easy to identify influences of particular traditions of legal ethics and their modern transformations. Secondly, most recent Polish discussions on legal professions clearly show how problematic is the tradition-modernity relation and how much it translates into political disputes between conservative and radical positions. Therefore, it seems that even a brief characterisation of the most important qualities of legal ethics in Poland may prove the significance of legal ethics in general and, especially, of the theory presented in this work.

The most characteristic of legal ethics in Poland seem to be strong influences of the French tradition on the Polish bar, which date to the second half of the 18th century. The symbolic significance in this regard is related to the fact that one of the authors most often quoted by the Polish bar is Ferdinand Payen[218], president of the council of the Paris bar, whose works served as motto to the widely-known study in legal ethics[219]. Independence – typical of this tradition – inscribed perfectly in the context of the partitioned Poland as well as in that of the People's Republic of Poland, though for the greater part of the last two decades it had to be realised outside the self-regulating professional organisation. Because of this, the efforts to codify legal ethics undertaken by Polish lawyers as early as the 1880s[220] should be interpreted as attempts at integrating the profession upon the lack of other instruments to attain this. Especially intensive discussions in the Polish bar took place at the turn of the 1960s and they resulted not only in canon studies[221], but also in the first ethical code for lawyers, which was subsequently adopted by the Supreme Bar Council in 1961. The structure of the currently binding code of 1998 remains unchanged, though, naturally, many detailed decisions were adjusted to the new circumstances.

---

218 See chapter 1.3.1.

219 Z. Krzemiński, *Etyka adwokacka. Teksty, orzecznictwo, komentarz*, [*Lawyers' Ethics. Texts, Jurisdiction, Commentary*] Kraków 2003, p. 5. See also an in-depth presentation M. Materniak-Pawłowska, "Z polskich prac nad kodyfikacją zasad etyki adwokackiej", ["Of Polish Works on Lawyers' Ethics Rules Codification"] *Czasopismo Prawno-Historyczne* 2007, no. 2.

220 *Ibidem*, p. 18.

221 See, for instance, a series of articles by S. Janczewski, "Godność zawodu", ["Profession's Dignity"] *Palestra* 1959, no. 6, 7, 8, 9, 10, or W. Żywiecki, *Etyka adwokacka*, [*Lawyers' Ethics*], Warsaw 1970.

It is noteworthy that the debates on lawyers' ethic in Poland usually concern an array of virtues or even ethical ideals. These are primarily independence and professional dignity, which are typical of the French tradition of legal ethics, as well as related to them special responsibility and care for the profession's esteem. Also impartiality and disinterestedness appear in this catalogue and special place is given to the duty to keep professional secrets. It is said that practising in a legal profession requires, "possessing the essential moral virtue of legal professions, namely moral courage," which is particularly vital as regards the bar. The basic argument in this matter is that, "the cost of every convenient compromise and lack of courage on the side of a lawyer will be incurred by someone else."[222]

Slightly different approach is present among legal advisers – a much younger professional group and simultaneously more numerous than the bar. The beginnings of this community date to 1961, a time when lawyers formed their code of practice. It was then that with a Council of Ministers' resolution positions of legal advisers in national companies and similar entities were created[223]. Though, this move was not coincidental and it was a part of the wider context, namely of the fight for the bar's independence, for a long time it was believed that, "in this way only a certain professional specialisation of the bar was established."[224] The group of legal advisers to an increasing extent now resembled a professional group and after a couple of decades it created its own self-regulating professional organisation and codified its own professional ethics. What distinguishes Polish legal advisers from advocats is mainly the fact that the former cannot act as defenders in criminal cases but may provide legal services in labour relations and also advertise their legal services – the latter possibility, though limited, has been recently introduced[225].

All this results in a fact that though legal advisers also refer to such categories as independence and professional dignity, "the relationship of this

222 R. Łyczywek, "O etyce zawodów prawniczych", ["On Legal Professions' Ethics"], in: *Etyka zawodowa*, ed. A. Sarapata, Warsaw 1971, pp. 218-228.

223 See detailed discussion of the legal adviser profession's history E. Kwiatkowska-Falęcka, "Wykonywanie zawodu radcy prawnego na podstawie ustawy z 6 lipca 1982 roku o radcach prawnych", ["Practising as a Legal Adviser on the Basis of the Act of 6th July 1982 on Legal Advisers"], in: H. Izdebski, P. Skuczyński, *Etyka zawodów…*, p. 257 ff.

224 R. Łyczywek, "O etyce...", p. 245.

225 For many years there has been an on-going discussion on the possible merging of the two professions. The discussion seems particularly heated recently, see W.M. Jakubowski, "Adwokat i radca prawny – dwa różne zawody prawnicze", ["An Advocate and a Legal Adviser – Two Different Legal Professions"] *Palestra* 1997, no. 1-2, pp. 74-78.

profession to the professions of the administrative kind,"[226] which was being mentioned even several decades ago, left a lasting mark in legal advisers' ethics. Probably the German bureaucratic model has affected not only the understanding of legal ethics by the representatives of this profession employed directly in public authority organs and institutions, but also the entirety of the profession. Continually changing regulations concerning this profession as well as the group's functions and position in the system of legal advice and in the judiciary system, mean that the group's social roles have evolved significantly in a short period since its creation but simultaneously all the time remained a point of reference and a criterion of good professional practice. This is perhaps why legal advisers more quickly react to changes and social expectations and more easily than advocats introduce changes in such fields as admission to profession or advertisement of legal services.

The last two decades in legal ethics in Poland are full of significant influences of the American legal ethics. Due to considerable differences in cultures and legal systems these influences must remain limited and mainly concern lawyers practising according to most up-to-date models of professionalism in law firms and most frequently not belonging to the advocate or legal adviser professions. This process is related to the characteristic view of loyalty to the client and its limitations as well as with characteristic institutionalisation of professional duties, whose features have already been mentioned in the discussion of this tradition. However, it is worth noting that with the arrival of American law firms in Poland the attitude toward providing free legal services by lawyers has changed. Within the framework of *pro bono* programs in some companies a requirement has been established to work a defined number of hours for the benefit of poor clients. Programs serving highest efficiency and enforcement of this work have been launched. Special prizes have been awarded and even institutions that search for poor clients and prepare them and their cases for the contact with lawyers have appeared[227].

---

226 R. Łyczywek, "O etyce…", p. 245.

227 More on *pro bono* work as an issue in legal ethics and its institutionalisation R. Skowron, "Kultura pracy Pro Bono w Stanach Zjednoczonych", ["The Culture of *Pro Bono* Work in the United States"], *Państwo i Prawo* 2007, no. 3, and P. Skuczyński, "Praca pro bono a pomoc prawna i profesjonalizm prawniczy", ["*Pro bono* work *vs.* Legal Help and Legal Professionalism"], *Klinika. Czasopismo Fundacji Uniwersyteckich Poradni Prawnych* 2011, no. 11, pp. 19-27. The very term "*pro bono publico*", together with its shortened version "*pro bono*", are traditionally used to refer to work done by lawyers for the poor for the sake of the public interest, and it has to be distinguished from the term "*pro publico bono*", which is used in reference to any activity for the public welfare.

Transformations of legal ethics in Poland have also been very intensive over the last two decades. Development and mixing of different traditions of legal ethics make these transformations seem particularly deep and multidirectional. Essentially, legal ethics juridisation intensifies and that manifests itself not only in the creation of new codes of practice, among which one should name the aforementioned: *The Lawyer's Set of Principles and Dignities of the Profession* of 1961 and its last successor of 1998, *Principles of Ethics for the Legal Adviser Profession* of 1987 and their final successor – *Code of Professional Ethics for a Legal Adviser* of 2007, *Code of Professional Ethics for a Notary* of 1997, *Code of Professional Ethics for a Bailiff* of 2001, *A Set of Ethical Principles for a Prosecutor* of 2002 and *A Set of Conduct Principles for Judges* also of 2002 and *A Set of Principles of Professional Ethics for Judges* of 2003[228]. It is worth remarking that an increasing number of issues is regulated in normative acts belonging to the sources of the generally binding law and that the codes increasingly regulate and decreasingly appeal, which proves that the second aspect of juridisation occurs.

Professionalisation of legal ethics in Poland manifests itself primarily in the increasing specialisation and commercialisation of legal professions. Thus, there appear many new lawyers' professional roles, which are accompanied by new forms of training and organisation. Additionally, a dynamic development of market economy is associated with new forms of professionalism that treat the relations between its standards and traditional legal ethics as a practical problem. In the latter field there seem to be opposing opinions, namely the first stating that lawyers have some special public mission and that duties and ideals result from it and the second saying that simple reliability and honesty in business are enough to provide for lawyers' esteem in society and a high position in a social structure[229]. These discussions are mainly of journalistic and political character, and so they lack the kind of precision that is required in academic debates.

Also in that period, the forms of legal professional practice that are typical of globalisation, namely the international law firms, appeared in Poland. Foreign lawyers started to work in Poland and Polish lawyers began to occupy themselves with practice in foreign law or its fields that are most frequently globalised. The overlapping of these processes with the transformation of political structure together with the Europeanisation of the law is a source of continuous instability of the legal system and requires from lawyers the

228 For details of these codes see chapter 1.4.1.1.

229 The most recent empirical research in this matter is presented by E. Łojko, "O trudnościach wykonywania współcześnie zawodu prawnika", ["On Difficulties of Practising as a Lawyer in Modern Times"], in: *Prawo-władza-społeczeństwo-polityka. Księga jubileuszowa profesora Krzysztofa Pałeckiego*, Toruń 2006, pp. 268-272.

adaptation to different models of court proceedings and extra-court practice. Convergence of professional deontologies of advocates, legal advisers, foreign lawyers and lawyers not associated in any corporation – all practising in one law firm – is a daily occurrence, at least in major cities. Nothing surprising then that in the Polish context family law firms also form their own standards of lawyers' practice, in which issues that are typical of professional ethics are included[230].

Everything that has been said about legal ethics in Poland seems to be a source of a certain confusion that may be diagnosed as follows, "[...] the ethos of particular legal professions is abandoned. Not everything may be justified and explained with the so-called objective causes. Research workers have lost themselves in the conflict of roles of a scientist, an expert, an adviser and an advocate; advoocates and legal advisers [, who are] too one-sidedly oriented toward business turnover, lose from their sight other branches of law and [disregard] unprofitable forms of activity; the judges show the besieged fortress syndrome by concentrating on defence from external attacks and too rarely undertake the effort of ameliorating the situation from inside of the Palace of Justice."[231]

The breakdown of the homogeneous ethos of legal professions and the conflict of roles in many fields of practice must lead to searching answers to questions on the legal ethics' essence. Though referring to professional duties, professional roles or a catalogue of virtues cannot solve daily dilemmas and conflicts, discarding these traditional concepts of legal ethics could only deepen the vagueness of the situation. Therefore, it may be justly concluded that legal ethics' theory referring to all these concepts and traditions as their source may be of great practical importance provided that – directly or by means of carrying out further research – it will be useful in constructing new normative models of legal ethics that would include traditions as well as the challenges of modernity.

---

230 See T. Karaś, "Zasady obowiązujące…", pp. 33-44.

231 M. Safjan, *Rola prawnika we współczesnym świecie*, [*The Role of a Lawyer in the Modern World*], Lublin 2004, p. 34.

Chapter 2
Conceptions of legal ethics

2.1. Preliminary remarks

The existence of the phenomenon of legal ethics in the form of its traditions, which nowadays undergo comprehensive transformations, may be documented. That is the purpose of the first part of this study. However, in science and philosophy there are at least two types of essential disputes currently taking place about this issue. Firstly, one may point to a number of views on the character of legal ethics as an object of scientific inquiry, on research perspectives, and on the methodologies applied to such inquiries. These views usually take the form of more or less elaborate conceptions and theories, which, on one hand, apply a proper set of concepts, and, on the other, include some ontological and epistemological theses. Depending on how weak or strong the theses are, the approaches to legal ethics vary from perceiving its issues as marginal elements of the existing theories and sciences, to ascribing it a fully independent status within the framework of research disciplines. For this reason the disputes may be described as, to a large extent, relating to the cognitive value of the concept of legal ethics.

Secondly, and from a practical point of view, attitudes to legal ethics differ in assessment because the extent to which they are helpful in solving the real problems and moral dilemmas of lawyers is debatable. Thus, conceptions of legal ethics usually include ethical theses which take as a point of reference moral scepticism towards this concept. Depending on how weak or strong this scepticism is, the legal ethics may be perceived as destructive – used only for populist ends and devastating moral dictionary – or redundant – essentially, appearing in the moral dictionary as *superfluum*. Naturally, there are also non-sceptical approaches that assign to the concept of legal ethics some qualities of usefulness or even indispensability in solving practical problems. That is why these disputes may be seen as concerning, to a significant degree, the practical value of the concept of legal ethics.

Any presentation of conceptions of legal ethics which considers this duality should, by assumption, reveal the deficits of each perspective. These deficits may rest either on too a narrow view, which consequently leads to inadequacy, or on one-sidedness in the formulation of one's tasks, which results in limited explanatory and heuristic power. Also by assumption, every subsequent conception that is presented should be an answer to the deficits of the preceding one. It is necessary to make two reservations here. Firstly, on the basis of the dividing line between the main disputes regarding legal ethics, it is impossible to be wholly consistent in making a logical division that would enable unequivocal classification of each conception to a defined set. The following presentation is, therefore, only of a typology of conceptions of legal ethics. Furthermore, it is a typology within whose framework the differences between conceptions tend towards the quantitative, and the qualitative aspect has been covered with the division between empirical and analytical conceptions, on one side, and normative and critical conceptions on the other.

In accordance with its typological character, this presentation implies a certain kind of idealisation since conceptions of legal ethics falling into a given category are not always advanced enough and thus the analysis cannot base uniquely on one author's or a circle of a few authors' reflections. Works in this field are often of a contributory nature and fundamental theses and assumtions of particular conceptions must be reconstructed from the reflections on specific issues. The reason for this is the fact that, apart from in the United States and a few other countries which share the culture of common law, interest in legal ethics in academic circles is marginal, though increasing.[1] In the United States primarily, conceptions directly referring to their tradition of legal ethics emerge, and are broadly, though only locally, applied. Therefore, the present analysis is based, as far as possible, on works by Polish authors and their research practice, and secondarily refers to studies that originated in particular traditions of legal ethics.

The last remark that needs to be made concerns the starting point of our reflections. They do not inlcude conceptions which would be on the scale's extremes and which would deny the concept of legal ethics any cognitive as well as practical values. Such views, based on double scepticism, are excluded here, on one hand, for pragmatic reasons since it would not contribute significantly to our reflections as they are not represented in literature at all – which does not diminish the level of scepticism towards legal ethics – and on the other hand, for logical reasons, as they are based on a paradox, which resides in claiming a thesis of practical worthlessness of the concept of legal ethics while simulatneously denying any theoretical significance of this concept – and

1 See the example of arising interest in legal ethics in Canada, desribed in detail in: A.M. Dodek, "Canadian Legal Ethics: A Subject in Search of Scholarship", *University of Toronto Law Journal* 2000, no 1.

indirectly also of the first thesis. Thus, it seems that moral scepticism toward legal ethics must always be a consequence of some conception of legal ethics – even a minimalist one that refers only to the very usage of the term.

Ordering conceptions of legal ethics according to two criteria, namely their cognitive and practical values – with the assumption that every conception is a reaction to the imperfections of the preceding one – allows one to identify seven types in this regard. Within the framework of empirical and analytical conceptions these are legal ethics as the lawyer's ethos, as myth, as ideology and as professional deontology. Normative and critical conceptions comprise legal ethics as applied ethics, as the lawyer's situational ethics and as critical professional ethics, discussed further in this study.

2.2. Empirical and analytical conceptions

2.2.1. The lawyer's ethos and its forms

The first conception of legal ethics is a view referring to the category of ethos. According to the simplest definition, it encompasses, "the entirety of norms accepted and adopted by a social group, the spirit of a particular culture, [and] the pattern of processes and emotional behaviour that are typical of a group."[2] Already by this general description, one may point to the category's usefulness in discussing the legal ethics of various times and places. For instance, one may distinguish the ethos of the French lawyers of the 17th and 18th centuries or the ethos of Polish judges during the time of martial law. This category, of course, will not cover all contexts in which one speaks of legal ethics either in the form of traditions of the term's usage or of their modern transformations. The existence of the accepted and adopted norms and models is not a necessary condition for using the term "legal ethics"[3]. Thus, it seems that the very possibility of a normative conception of legal ethics must entail discarding the ethos view as too narrow.

A closer analysis of the conception of legal ethics as ethos will allow it to be proved that its inadequacy does not exclude using the term "ethos" in some broader views. The term may be applied as a means of theoretical combination of the two spheres in which legal ethics may be important, namely moral practice and ethical theory. This is possible because, according to an

2 Entry: "ethos" in: K. Olechnicki, P. Załęcki, *Słownik socjologiczny*, [*Dictionary of Sociology*], Toruń 1997, p. 57.

3 Cf. R. Sobański, "Uwagi o etyce zawodów prawniczych", [Remarks on Ethics of Legal Professions], *Palestra* 2003, no. 7-8, pp. 45-46.

encyclopedical descrpition, ethos is made of, "ideals, patterns of behaviour which are binding and realised in a certain community and also which are precisely defined and unequivocal. The distinctive mark and an advantage of the ethos idea is the fact that it refers to norms and values and also includes the rules of their specific and relatively unequivocal reference to social behaviour [...] Thus, ethos means enagagement in certain patterns of social behaviour. In those patterns values manifest and in this way they form daily life."[4] A few remarks must be made in relation to this.

Firstly, this description does not mean only that the existence of a specific ethos is an empirical question and requires detailed research, but also that its existence is of casual nature. Therefore, it is not true that in every group, for example, a professional group of lawyers, some ethos must always function, since there are periods in which such a situation exists and periods when it does not. Therefore, an ethos may arise, develop and break down in even a relatively short period of time, for example a single generation. This does not mean that with the breakdown of an ethos the ideas or norms related to it fall out of use, but that their relation with moral practice, which, for example, in a certain group may cease to be homogeneous or start to be negatively assessed, changes. This is why, when one of the authors reflecting on the varied level of political activism of courts in different countries remarks that, "it seems that [...] there exists something like the ethos of a judge, which in relation to a country's specific political and social situation encourages, or discourages, courts and tribunals from undertaking efforts for active creation of law and politics,"[5] he makes a counterfactual assumption.

Secondly, a tendency exists to apply the idea of ethos only in its positive connotation[6] and to reject the conceptions in which the idea would designate negative models in a certain group. Therefore, one rather cannot speak of a "thieves' ethos," of a "hooligans' ethos" or of "a Nazi judge's ethos" or "a Stalinist prosecutor's ethos" even though all of them are connected with the functioning of certain models. This does not exclude an examination of the problems occuring within these groups and at these times from a legal ethics perspective, at least concerning the categories known from its traditions and modern changes, for instance virtues and duties. Due to this, one may examine specific cases of lawyers' behaviour as well as generalised models of conduct regardless of whether they constitute an ethos or not. Hence, despite the fact that

4 T. Szawiel, "Etos", ["Ethos"], in: *Encyklopedia socjologii*, Warsaw 1998, vol. I, p. 202.

5 L. Morawski, "Czy sądy mogą się angażować politycznie?", ["Can Courts Engage Politically?"], in: *Państwo i Prawo* 2006, no 3, p. 10.

6 As for example: W. Świerzawski, *Etos prawnika*, [*The Ethos of a Lawyer*], Sandomierz 1996.

the concept is useful, it remains limited and related to the need for the creation of more adequate conceptions.

Thirdly, due to transformations of traditions of legal ethics, there is a question about the relation between an ethos, or particular forms of ethos, and the processes of social change. In this regard there are two possibilities referring to broader philosophical and sociological perspectives. On one hand, according to the Aristotelian usage of the concept, one may understand it as an element of a stable and rooted way of life. Thus, ethos is a static factor. On the other, in Weberian thought, ethos may be perceived as a factor in social change factor, and therefore dynamic. The influence of the Protestant ethos of work on the formation of capitalist economical relations is a classic example here. As regards traditions and transformations of legal ethics, neither of these perspectives can explain the relation of ethos to social change since it appears that there exists some special relationship in this matter. Namely, traditions of legal ethics, undergoing transformations, as well as the indicated characterisation of the ethos idea, are based on similar views: ethics resting on virtues in the first perspective, and professional roles resting on social structure in the second. This means that the conception of legal ethics as ethos may perform its tasks only within the framework of a certain tradition of legal ethics, and cannot neutrally describe relations between such traditions of legal ethics and their transformations.

Fourthly, the central idea of this conception is a model or an example. Naturally, one may ask, what this term stands for. On one hand, it may signify a certain regularity of behaviour, and so it may be purely descriptive. On the other, it may refer to some social expectations or demands, and so be a postulatory idea. However, it is noteworthy that in every case when we speak of a model as an element of ethos, it is connected with a specific individual. According to a widely-known approach, "a role-model to a certain individual or group is a human being that should be, or actually is, an object of aspiration for this individual or group."[7] According to another view, a role-model is, "a significant other, upon which an individual patterns his or her behaviour in a particular social role, including adopting appropriate similar attitudes. Role-models need not to be known personally to the individual: some people model their behaviour in particular roles on the real and legendary example provided by historical figures"[8].

7 M. Ossowska, "Pojęcie wzoru i pojęcie naśladownictwa", ["The Concept of a Model and Imitation"], in: *idem Ethos rycerski i jego odmiany*, Warsaw 2000, p. 11.

8 Entry: "Role-model" in: J. Scott and G. Marshall, *Dictionary of Sociology*, Oxford 2005.

This naturally breeds a number of questions that the conception of legal ethics as ethos cannot resolve. Among other issues, there arises the problem of mechanisms through which models of legal ethics could function. The fundamental concept in this matter is imitation, that is, "a tendency to imitate, to be guided by realized or unrealised conviction of some positive value of the imitated person."[9] However, this definition does not mention any imitation causes or reasons and is limited to a tautological claim that imitation is necessary for the role-model's existence, while at the same time the existence of a role-model is necessary for imitation. More elaborate conceptions of legal ethics usually employ these ideas but search for other ways of operationalising them as well as for completely different means of conceptualising legal ethics.

2.2.2. The myth of legal ethics

The conception of legal ethics as a mythology exceeds the idea of legal ethics as a model. The former, "is based on the assumption that, personality, both as a laywer and as a human being, is formed in part by reference to a collection of narrations typical of one's profession. Narrations about lawyers. Every social role, every profession has its own mythology and, just as fairy-tales teach children their roles and inscribe them in a scenario, professional mythologies teach one how to 'be', not how to 'perform', one's profession. 'Being' and not 'performing' the profession is at issue here. In essence, narrations about lawyers cannot teach one the law itself, how to bring a lawsuit or what advice to give to a client; instead, the narrations teach one how to be a lawyer."[10]

Legal ethics in this view assumes the concept of a model but also includes some other elements belonging to the myth idea. Firstly, a myth is contained in the form of a charcteristic narration. The Greek term *mythos* means a story, fiction or fairytale, which in the encyclopedical sense is, "a traditional narrative (anonymous) about final causes of things and the meaning of human life."[11] Secondly, myths come from the past and have a more stable character than models, which as a rule are subject to rapid disintegration and creation. Thirdly, myths have the capacity to convey various models, and so they can be

---

9 M. Ossowska, "Pojęcie wzoru...", p. 21.

10 S. Wojtczak, "Czy prawnikom potrzebna jest mitologia?", ["Do Lawyers Need Mythology?"], in: *Etyka, deontologia, prawo*, ed. P. Steczkowski, Rzeszów 2008, pp. 386-387.

11 H. Kiereś, "Mit", ["Myth"], in: *Powszechna encyklopedia filozofii*, vol. 7, Lublin 2006, pp. 279-290. Some further reflections on this perspective are based on the author's remarks.

interpreted in many different ways. It means that myths have a wider range and even in a situation where models disintegrate or compete, a group of people may still be joined by a common mythology. Fourthly, myths have a wider capacity to affect personality than models. This is because myths usually feature negative figures too, and so they operate with opposites, which are inaccessible to models. For this reason myths enable individual and collective identities to be built from their concepts[12].

Among the sources of modern legal mythology are mentioned historical legends of Roman or medieval lawyers. For instance, those relating to Emilio Papiniano, Saint Ivo of Kermartin (the patron of lawyers), or Saint Thomas More (patron of common law lawyers)[13]. Closer to modern times, one draws attention to lawyers' biographies, for instance, those assembled in whole catalogues[14]. However, it seems that nowadays the greatest role in this matter is played by non-literary narrative forms, primarily film and television. Essentially, legal film is meant here and, especially, predominating American productions and all kinds of TV series and reality shows. In the Anglo-Saxon countries, productions referring to lawyers are subjected to relatively systematic research, which suggests some remarks on the adequacy of the conception of legal ethics as myth.

On one side, legal films and television shows are problematic; since they are widely accessible on a global scale, they freely cross the bounds of legal cultures and traditions of legal ethics, and are perceived as neutral in this regard, though they are not in fact. On the other, because they usually show lawyers both as villains and heroes, they form a conviction in the average viewer that the legal system is based on the activity of a small number of heroic lawyers who fight and make sacrifices for justice, of which the system in itself is a contradiction[15]. However, this appears to contradict basic assumptions of modern legal training and legal practice, and here one of the fundamental difficulties of legal ethics as myth arises.

In order to understand the problem, let us recall that, "myth was historically the first way of capturing human experience and giving it the form of a useful world-view vision." Though, even in ancient times there was dispute about whether myth was only one of the literary genres or whether it had a cognitive value. One of the attempts to solve this dispute is the so-called aspect theory,

12 S. Wojtczak, *ibidem.*, pp. 387-389.

13 *Ibidem*, pp. 390-394.

14 See K. Pol, *Poczet prawników polskich*, [*The Catalogue of Polish Lawyers*], Warsaw 2000.

15 P. Robson, "Lawyers and The Legal System on TV: The British Experience", *International Journal of Law in Context* 2006, no. 4, pp. 333-359.

according to which one has to differentiate between theoretical (scientific) and practical (moral) cognition on one side and religious (prophetic, mystic) and poietic (creative) on the other. In this division myth falls into the latter category since it is inseparable from art, initially of oral character, then literature, and today cinema and television. Nevertheless, as a basis of social life, myth may function only in a situation where the distinction of cognition aspects would be unknown or unacknowldged.

Therefore, in modern societies, myths have an aspect of individual narrations, of metaphorical stories, rather than those that have the form of a rational plan. These "private mythologies" of modern man, "his dreams, reveries, fantasies, and so on – never rise to the ontological status of myths, precisely because they are not experienced by the whole man and therefore do not transform a particular situation into a situation that is paradigmatic."[16] Attempts at constructing modern mythologies are sometimes philosophically associated with a type of irrationalistic idealism which sees the causes of science's incapacity to form a world-view in dividing cognition on different aspects, and which advocates a second mythologisation not only through rejecting science and prophetic tradition but also through the return to those European roots that are, essentially, barbaric in character. In reference to legal ethics it entails a double hazard.

First, one has to bear in mind that the modern media, whose role in creating legal mythologies would be major – and thus cinema and television – have a far wider range of influence than does the legal community, both as creators and receivers. Therefore, contrary to theoretical or practical cognition, which in such a view would be subordinated to mythology, the scope of experience included in myths would be considerably limited. Secondly, in view of villains' domination, legal ethics would be not a mythology but rather a part of a myth in which the juridicised, professionalised and globalised form of legal ethics is an element of a system that is a negation of justice; namely, legal ethics would be a form of legal mendacity and hypocrisy. In this myth legal ethics allows lucrative activity at the expense of values, and as such is opposed to "true ethics" of lawyers fighting for justice. To recap, attempts at mythologisation in legal professions would probably lead to the creation of a negative myth of legal ethics instead of a positive body of legal ethics consisting of many different myths.

---

16 M. Eliade, *The Sacred and the Profane. The Nature of Religion*, New York 1987, p. 211.

2.2.3. Legal ethics as ideology

The interpertation of legal ethics in categories of ideology, which is a view close to mythology, refers to a characteristic way of the functioning of legal ethics in society. However, it has to be remarked that this view, in literature, is rather used as an instrument for analysis of specific problems in legal ethics, especially in the critique of dominating opinions and accepted deontological solutions[17], but it does not make an object of a coherent theoretical conception. However, due to the fact that this conception may not only be reconstructed from the works on detailed subjects, but also may be meaningfully conceived as an answer to deficits of the view of legal ethics as myth, its basic theses and assumptions should be presented. This is important also because in the typology of conceptions of legal ethics, the critique against that which refers to the category of ideology is a starting point for constructing the majority of the rest.

The very concept of ideology – despite its basis in Francis Bacon's concept of 'idols' – was used for the first time only at the end of the 18th century, by Destutt de Tracy, to name the "science of ideas", being a study of ideas, which was an element of the struggle against superstition – typical of the French Enlightenment – by means of constructing knowledge of sound foundations. The foundations were to be provided precisely by ideology, which would systematise the knowledge of ideas – understood, from the time of Descartes, in the categories of the subject's consciousness. The utopian nature of this project is one of several elements belonging to the modern concept of ideology, which – already during the French Revolution and in Napoleon's time – has been used in political arguments in a pejorative sense[18]. The evaluative use of this concept is typical not only of politcal disputes but also of a considerable part of theoretical perspectives.

The spread of the concept results first of all from the expansion of Marxism, which – thanks to the assumption of the social subjects' existence – significantly expanded the scope of the use of the consciousness concept and its ideas. One has to indicate the main qualities of ideology in this perspective, with the proviso that the view according to which the ideology's subject may be any social group, including for instance a professional group, is alien to Marxism, which held social class to be a fundamental unit in this matter. However, these qualities are present also in views with a critical attitude to Marxism, and also in

---

17 See, for example: C.A. Gear, "The Ideology of Domination: Barriers to Client Autonomy in Legal Ethics Scholarship", *Yale Law Journal*, 1998, no. 107.

18 H.-J. Lieber, *Ideologie. Eine historisch-systematische Einführung*, Padeborn-München-Wien-Zürich 1985, pp. 19-35. Also see part I as a discussion of the history of the concept to the Karl Mannheim's conception.

those analyses from the scope of legal ethics that more or less intuitively apply the concept of ideology. From many perspectives of which this concept is studied, the most helpful in these reflections seem to be the structural and functional approaches. The former search for ideology critera, whereas the latter examine its consequences for social life.

Social consciousness consists of elements of material character and those that exist only in human consciousness. Objectification of the latter, for instance, in scientific or literary works, is giving a form to social consciousness. Ideology is a specific form of social consciousness, in which, as a rule in an unconscious way, the interests of a social subject are expressed. The goal of the Marxist critique of ideology was to prove the ideological character of all forms of social consciousness, including itself, and on this basis to enable a fight for personal interest – a fight open and conscious to all sides of the social conflict, aided also by ideological instruments. Thus, for particular social groups, ideologies perform functions that mainly protect their own interests, but they can also integrate a group, inspire its members to action, and even program the collective activity of the group.

The problem of conscious and unconscious ideology became a basis for analyses, which, going beyond the Marxist view, may be directly referred to legal ethics as an ideology connected with the lawyers' group interest. First of all, it has to be observed that interests of various social groups, including professional ones, manifest in non-totalitarian systems, in other words, where there is a public debate, "in political discussion in modern democracies where ideas were more clearly representative of certain groups, the social and existential determination of thought became more easily visible."[19] Therefore, even though the age of ideology ended with the fall of totalitarian regimes[20], the liberal critique of these regimes which were based on the way of thinking typical of ideologists, the critique that is characterised by, among other things, a claim to, "present an invisible structure of the world, hidden beyond external chaos of events," obliteration of differences "between facts, values and emotions" and presenatation of a system relating to "all walks of life"[21], does not annul the concept itself as a means of analysing structures not connnected with the fight of great ideologies and their corresponding regimes.

---

19 K. Mannheim, *Ideology and Utopia, an Introduction to Sociology of Knowledge*, New York 1954, p. 35

20 See D. Bell, *The End of Ideology. On the Exhaustion of Political Ideas in the Fifties*, Cambridge-London 1988, particularly the epilogue.

21 P. Śpiewak, *Ideologie i obywatele*, [*Ideologies and Citizens*], Warsaw 1991, pp. 179-183.

In democratic debates, a manifestation of relations between consciousness and interest points to the historical or even situational character of ideology. On one hand, "morality and ethics themselves are conditioned by certain definite situations,"[22] on the other, "in certain situations the collective unconscious of certain groups obscures the real condition of society both to itself and to others and thereby stabilizes it."[23] This means that every ideology, even the one called "false consciousness", may arise and manifest itself only in relation to concrete historical situations, and may be evaluated only in relation to social structure, patterns of interests, or other elements of consciousness. More generally one may say that, "every point of view is particular to a social situation", which is why also legal ethics in every time and place may be taken as a more or less conscious manifestation of particular interests of a group of lawyers.[24]

This particular conception of ideology – as opposed to the total conception, which though historically stems from the former and simultaneously belongs to the philosophy of consciousness, to historicisation and class social movement[25]and which encompasses all statements of the subject and binds them structurally with group interests – may be characterised by enumerating its three basic qualities. Firstly, only parts of a given subject's statements, and only in relation to content, are ideology. Secondly, ideology occurs only on psychological level, and so is a kind of psychology of interests that employs the causality concept. Thirdly, it assumes that only individuals have consciousness, and thus group ideology may be inderstood only as a sum of ideologies within the framework of a certain group of individuals. "The particular conception of ideology therefore signifies a phenomenon intermediate between a simple lie at one pole, and an error, which is the result of a distorted and a faulty conceptual apparatus, at the other. It refers to a sphere of errors, psychological in nature, which, unlike deliberate deception, are not intentional, but follow inevitably and unwittingly from certain causal determinants"[26].

Legal ethics as ideology in this particular conception relies on a specific relationship of performed professional roles, interests motivating action, and of ways of experiencing the world. The relationship, if it functions as unconscious, leads to the creation of the "false consciousness"[27]. This poses for the ideological conception of legal ethics the following dilemma. On one side, the conception may aim at evaluating particular professions' ethics at a particular

22 K. Mannheim, *Ideology…*, p. 72.
23 *Ibidem*, p. 36.
24 *Ibidem*, p. 75.
25 *Ibidem*, pp. 57-62.
26 *Ibidem*, p. 54.
27 Cf. *ibidem*, pp. 36, 47.

time and place in regard to their degree of "falsity." As a criterion one has to assume that, "an ethical attitude is invalid if it is oriented with reference to norms, with which action in a given historical setting, even with the best of intentions, cannot comply. It is invalid then when the unethical action of the individual can no longer be conceived as due to his own personal transgression, but must be attributed rather to the compulsion of an erroneously founded set of moral axioms."[28] However, in this case the problem, how to provide for non-ideological character of this type of research and ensure that researchers themselves are not under an influence of "false consciousness", remains open.

On the other side, the ideological conception of legal ethics may aim at total de-ideologisation of legal professions' consciousness. This would solve the above-mentioned problem of research involvement but it would also have to be assumed that legal ethics has to start the process with itself. There have been formulated, or one may formulate, several conceptions of legal ethics, which, based on this assumption and relying on broader conceptions of knowledge-values relations, aim for study and practice in this matter that are free from ideological particularity. The first of them relates to the positivist and non-positivist models and focuses on professional deontology examination that is free from evaluation. The second is an attempt at applying general ethics' axiology and deontology to problems of legal ethics, and thus at ascribing it an essentially universal – though simultaneously applicative – character. The third refers to those conceptions of the sociology of knowledge that are directly against the ideology concept and that are based on a phenomenological view of knowledge and values. The fourth and the last from the discussed conceptions refers to the critically and reflectively oriented sociology of knowledge of Karl Mannheim, and to the elements of which were, in the later period, developed by represenatives of the Frankfurt School.

2.2.4. Professional deontology

Philosophical positivism is characterised by its four fundamental theses. Firstly, cognition cannot differentiate between phenomena and their hidden essences, namely hidden structures of being, and thus it may only concern what is available in experience (phenomenalism rule). Secondly, knowledge formulated in general terms in reality has its equivalents only in concrete objects, therefore, it rests only on generalisations (nominalism rule). Thirdly, all study must be devoid of valuation since evaluative judgements and normative utterances say

28 *Ibidem*, pp. 84-85.

nothing about reality but only about the subject that formulates them. Fourthly, scientific methods are basically similar in all sciences and knowledge has a homogeneous nature. Every assertion must be a part of the system[29]. Professional deontology seems to fulfil all these requirements and in relation to legal ethics this approach is especially popular because of the common assumptions with legal positivism.

The very term "deontology" (from the Greek word *deon* – duty, obligation) was first used by Jeremy Bentham to name a general science about morality that was to disregard evaluation and especially the categories of good and evil. Such an evaluative or imperative character of ethics was to reflect the fact that morality relies primarily on the sense of duty[30]. Nowadays, the term essentially refers to rules of professional conduct included in deontological collections formed by different professional groups, namely in codes of professional ethics. The increasing juridisation, regardless of the status that one ascribes to the codes[31], means that this phenomenon may be distinguished as an object of study. On one hand, the question on the methods of carrying out such study arises, and, on the other, whether the conception of legal ethics that aims at research uniquely in the field of professional deontology will be adequate and whether it will avoid the aforementioned risk of ideologisation.

The positivist assumptions of professional deontology define its methodology. Above all, professional deontology studies – as commonly available – the codes of professional ethics accepted by relevant self-governing organisations and associations. These documents are not treated as manifestations of any deep structures but simply as normative texts which do not correspond with any ideas or values. Therefore, the study of these codes should be separate from an evaluation of their content and by no means should it add anything to them. Methods applied in the research should be parallel to those in other sciences dealing with normative texts, essentially in legal dogmatics. Deontology as science should primarily interpret the codes' content giving special consideration to the history of the origin of particular rules, the disputes that resulted in relation to them and the disciplinary jurisdiction made on their basis. Secondly, deontology should systematise the codes' content, and thus primarily order them, remove contradictions and loopholes and – due to increasingly frequent situations of deontological standards' convergence – work

29 L. Kołakowski, *Filozofia pozytywistyczna. Od Hume'a do Koła Wiedeńskiego,* [*Positivist Philosophy from Hume to the Vienna Circle*], Warsaw 2003, p. 11 ff.

30 *Mały słownik etyczny,* [*Little Dictionary of Ethics*], ed. S. Jedynak, Bydgoszcz 1999, pp. 51-52.

31 See chapter 1.4.1.

out collisional rules. Thus understood, legal ethics will evolve organically to become part of the legal sciences.

The conception of legal ethics as professional deontology undoubtedly has many advantages, among which two seem to be of major importance. On one hand, it concentrates on what nowadays seems to be the most evident phenomenon and, simultaneously, a proof of legal ethics' existence, namely on codes of professional ethics. On the other, in a clear way, it defines the status of legal ethics within the framework of sciences division by classifying it as jurisprudence and including it in legal dogmatics, though it does not preclude possible problematization of a legal-theoretical character. However, drawbacks of this view, which seem similarly important, should be indicated. First of all, one may object that the conception does not acknowledge the fact that there are traditions of legal ethics which arise not from duties or professional rules but from virtues and social roles. Even if codes of professional ethics arise also in those traditions, that is even if they undergo juridisation, then simultaneously occurring processes of professionalisation and globalisation do not annul their achievements; just the opposite, because thanks to these traditions and their concepts, these transformations may be described.

An even more serious objection is based on the constatation that the conception of legal ethics as deontology, even if it does not directly entangle a researcher in ideological protection of lawyers' interests from the point of view of a professional group, it does so indirectly since in no way does it shield the codes themselves from manipulation, or from becoming instruments of lawyers' domination. The aforementioned criteria of good codes go beyond tasks of professional deontology, in the sense accepted here, and may at best be an argument for extending the discussed conception. Thus, basically, they mean this conception should be seen as inadequate. Supplementing it with some additional assumptions on codes of professional ethics' functions, for instance, regarding them as a means of social control over practice in legal professions and postulating the inclusion of public interest in codes' content seems to provide a point of reference against such legal ideologisation, though simultaneously it introduces evaluative elements, exceeds positivist assumptions and cannot be justified on the ground of jurisprudence alone.

However, the most serious charge that may be formed against the conception of legal ethics as professional deontology, and of which other objections may be entailed, is the assertion that legal ethics cannot be reduced to the content of codes of professional ethics. Even if legal ethics is perceived as duties that are a means of social control, one cannot forget that institutionalisation of ethics is highly problematic since it equals the resignation from universalism of ethical standards and this, "[...] questions the rationality of their presence in the system co-developed by legal sanctions and disciplinary responsibility. The position treating ethics only in descriptive categories holds that with the moment of institutionalisation it undergoes deconstruction."[32] Hence, professional deontology is not ethics at all, although this does not necessarily mean that it has to be rejected. The reasons for this may be provided only by this view's consequence in the form of cutting off from traditions of legal ethics. Only in the context of traditions may one understand the content of codes of professional ethics, especially of those that directly claim that they contain professional ethics' norms flowing from general ethical norms or related to them in some other way.

2.3. Normative and critical conceptions

2.3.1. Applied ethics

According to a popular approach, legal ethics is not professional deontology being a part of jurisprudence, but is, "a branch of ethics occupied with moral duties of people in professional relation to law through its formation, teaching and application. The character and aim of these duties endows them with some special subjective-objective dimension. It refers to every individual/group regardless of the criterion of performed function or role in a legal or related profession, represented interest, the form of the practised occupation or behaviour, and it also transfers itself into the sphere of private life."[33] This special dimension of lawyers' duties is an argument for distinguishing a branch of ethics referring to them. However, the term may be understood differently, which is why the distinction may be performed in different ways. Most frequently in such cases particular ethics, practical ethics or applied ethics are considered.

The division into general and particular ethics is typical of Christian ethics. The former comprises, "general moral rules of human conduct", while the latter, "particular normatives of human conduct." Although legal ethics could probably fall into the particular ethics' range of interest, the authors who base on the discussed division have not made this inclusion. Perhaps the reason for it is the fact that with further division of particular ethics into individual ethics and social ethics it is hard to unequivocally indicate to which part legal ethics could

32 Entry: "Etyka prawnicza," ["Legal ethics"], in: *Leksykon współczesnej teorii i filozofii prawa. 100 podstawowych pojęć*, [*Lexicon of Modern Theory and Philosophy of Law. 100 Fundamental Concepts*], ed. J. Zajadło, Warsaw 2007, p. 76.

33 *Ibidem*, pp. 72-73.

belong, and additionally its issues are, to a significant extent, covered by inquiries from the field of natural and positive law included in general ethics[34]. However, it appears that the division into general and particular ethics, and especially the subordination of one to the other, are reflected in the acceptance that legal ethics can be deduced from general ethics and of necessity does not contradict widely-held assumptions about general ethics. However, some serious alternatives to this view may be found.

Since the 1970s one may speak of a turn towards practical ethics, which took an imporatant position in academic ethics beside meta-ethics and normative ethics. Though the process of its formation has not yet been completed, one may distinguish several fundamental qualities of practical ethics. Firstly, it is composed of many sub-disciplines, among which the most developed are biomedical ethics and business ethics, but it is also indicated that legal ethics or journalism ethics as well as the ethics of other professions belong to them[35]. Secondly, though it attempts to consider moral intuitions in those fields, it is not merely a set of moral convictions, but also their critical analysis. Thirdly, by including empirical data, practical ethics is to a significant degree accordant with moral practice – its concepts become meaningful and it avoids a conservative image typical of traditional views. Finally, it approaches the ethical theory and moral practice relation in an innovative way[36].

The relationship between ethical theory and moral practice is an issue that in ethics is viewed from different perspectives. Practical ethics in this scope is sometimes opposed to applied ethics, understood as a discipline using reasonings composed of two premises out of which the first is an element of an ethical theory and the second is a particular situation's description. Contrary to this, practical ethics assumes that this relationship is more refined, since, on one hand, every ethical theory should include the critria of its statements' application, while, on the other, every practical consideration should be oriented toward theoretical thinking. For this reason the boundary between theory and practice may not be clear so it is rather an issue of quantity. From the point of view of the division of philosophy disciplines, meta-ethics, normative ethics and practical ethics should be viewed holistically as a network of interrelated statements[37].

---

34 Cf. for example: T. Ślipko, *Zarys etyki ogólnej*, [*An Outline of General Ethics*], Kraków 2004, pp. 37-38.

35 See R.A. Wasserstorm, *Lawyers as Professionals. Some Moral Issues,* in: *Applied Ethics. Critical Concepts in Philosophy*, ed. R. Chadwick, D. Schroeder, London and New York 2002, vol. 6, pp. 316-334.

36 *The Oxford Handbook of Practical Ethics*, ed. H. LaFollette, Oxford 2003, pp. 2-9.

37 *Ibidem*.

However, it has to be remarked that the identification of applied ethics with a deductive structure of moral reasonings would be too great an overimplification and in modern discussions the terms "applied ethics" and "practical ethics" are interchangeably used. However, undoubtedly one may speak of a dispute over the role of general theory in ethics. The anti-theoretical standpoint maintains that universal rules or principles formulated by theoreticians are too abstract and theories based on them are always reductionist. This leads to a deductive or syllogistic model, which under-acknowledges the situational character of morality. In its extreme interpretation this position results in rejection of any ethical theory. However, dominating, more moderate views aim at defining the qualities of a good theory within the framework of the aforementioned holistic character of its relation to practice. These qualities are primarily: the pluralism that links different traditional prespectives, a pro-discussion attitude, not resolving questions by deduction, awareness of one's own limitations – thus accepting that some problems cannot be solved, and openness to empirical issues[38].

Hence, however this discipline is named, applied ethics or practical ethics, it may be said that it is based not only on an innovative methodology and presentation of relations between various spheres of ethics, but it also redefines the very point of ethics. Thus, it is not only about merely constructing a theory, but about participation in a process of solving those social problems that have a moral dimension. This attitude assumes two important statements that are a source of many objections which may be formed against thus conceived applied ethics and which simultaneously cause the conception of legal ethics as a branch of ethics to become problematic since it requires the findings of various philosophical and scientific disciplines to be employed. The first of these statements claims that the social function of academic ethics should be perceived as performing tasks from the scope of expert evaluation and moral education, which means the necessity of institutionalising the very research. The other statement concerns morality itself, which is the object of such study and which, due to the spread of moral evaluations and education, must acquire a positive character and be included in the same institutional framework[39].

Institutionalisation of ethics in the form of morality experts and teachers' activities, dealing not with ethical theories but solving or helping to solve practical problems, seems to entangle the researchers in concrete systems of

---

38 T. Dare, "Applied Ethics, Challenges To", in: *Applied Ethics Critical Concepts in Philosophy*, ed. R.Chadwick, D. Schroeder, London and New York 2002, vol. 1, pp. 29-34.

39 K. Bayertz, *Self-Enlightenment of Applied-Ethics,* in: *ibidem*, pp. 39, 43.

interests and thus to increase the risk of ideologisation. It does not seem that the postulate of including interests of various positions in ethical debates could remove this risk[40]. Nor will the problem be solved merely by an obligation to neutrality and impartiality. This is because the knowledge from the ethical theory field is something generically different than the ability to solve practical problems. In other words, "intellectual virtue are not a sufficient condition of moral virtue." This means that preference of a particular practice in the course of creating a theory is possible – but so is the opposite situation, that is preference of particular theories in the attempts of solving practical problems[41]. One solution to this situation could be the acceptance that there exists a consensus as regards ethical theory and general moral rules, which would be an *a priori* exclusion of such preference. However, this would be an overtly counterfactual assumption.

The following critique by Alasdair MacIntyre is based on the assumption that arguments and discussions in applied ethics reflect the lack of consensus on the level of general moral rules and even if this discipline manages to work out an unanimous view, then it is a kind of social transaction aiming at conflict avoidance rather than an agreement on the moral rules[42]. The character of these general moral rules is of key importance for this critique. On one hand, one may assume that what is meant here are the rules functioning in social practice which have been formed and internalised there. In this case they may be studied only theoretically and there is no need to create additional, applied, ethics. Even if there the need to transfer these rules to another sphere of social life and extend their application to a new type of relations did arise, then this would also be a matter that one could perform in practice and only study the consequences in the framework of an ethical theory. However, the functioning of moral rules in this sense does not require the existence of such a theory; applying rules by a community does not require that it understands them, but presupposes the existence of a hierarchy of goods – the hierarchy corresponding with moral rules but not being their source. Consequently, solving practical problems may be performed only in the framework of agreement on rules, and while agreement cannot be neutral concerning a specific community's values, it can exist without any ethical theory[43].

---

40 *Ibidem*, p. 48.

41 D. MacNiven, "Practical Ethics. The Idea of a Moral Expert", in: *Applied Ethics…*, p. 197.

42 A. MacIntyre, "Does Applied Ethics Rest on a Mistake?", in: *ibidem*, pp. 230-231. See also P. Łuków, *Granice zgody: autonomia zasad i dobro pacjenta*, [*The Limits of Consent: The Autonomy of Rules and the Patient's Welfare*], Warsaw 2005, p. 82 and the following.

43 *Ibidem*, pp. 232-237.

On the other hand, one may hold that such rules have no moral aspect at all since it is essential to morality that it has universal character and is free from all evaluations depending on particular communities. In this perspective, both if there was an agreement on these rules and if there was not, one should practise applied ethics, which in the former situation would have a deductive structure and in the latter would reflect disputes on a general plane[44] and, basically, would bring nothing apart from institutionalisation of morality. If this perspective proves correct, and in modern societies it seems highly probable, then this is the only way for morality to function, despite all drawbacks related to reproducing the lack of moral agreement. Practising applied ethics does not necessarily need to be perceived as the protection of particular professional groups' interests – including lawyers primarily – but it also means discovering moral reflection which may in fact be considered as a new way of discussing old problems, and thus an attempt at continuing tradition in new cirumstances[45].

Though these attempts seem doomed to failure, it is noteworthy to identify two important elements that may help overcome the weak points of applied ethics. The first of them refers to the characterisation of spheres in which applied ethics occurs, namely the spheres in which the deficit of moral consensus is acutely felt. They are characterised, first, by the fact that they relate to the performance of standard actions of moral significance. Second, by the requirement of public trust, which may be provided for only through homogeneity of practice in the whole group. Third, due to the previous point a homogeneous type of study and education in this matter is necessary[46]. All these aspects appear in legal ethics and all these requirements should be satisfied by a conception of legal ethics. Whereas, the second element clearly shows that ethical theory should refer to moral practice, which means that thanks to it ethical theory will be able to perform falsification – in the Popperian sense – of own statements referring to the language of morality and to reasonings used in this theory[47]. As regards legal ethics this is primarily the language of professional ethics codes and of discussions related to them. Thus, legal ethics must draw on the achievements of professional deontology and social sciences.

44 *Ibidem*, p. 238.

45 *Ibidem*, p. 241.

46 *Ibidem*, pp. 241-242.

47 R. M. Hare, "Why do Applied Ethics?", in: *Applied...*, ed. R. Chadwick, D. Schroeder, vol. 1, pp. 263-264.

2.3.2. The situational ethics of a lawyer

A conception of legal ethics which tries to avoid all suspicions of particularity, both of itself and of its subject, rests on the assumption that there exists some objective realm of values. Because of this assumption all disputes on legal ethics may be settled and ideological manipulations with legal ethics exposed. Such a conception, which refers to the philosophical achievements of phenomenonology, has been recently developed in Poland as the situational ethics of a lawyer. It is based on three fundamental theses. Firstly, the best alternative to the code-based model of legal ethics is the view connected with the phenomenonological ethics of Max Scheler, Nicolai Hartmann and Józef Tischner, which refers to the intuition of values felt in situations of professional experience. Secondly, particular "corporations of legal professions" – but not the professional group of lawyers as a whole – have their own collective axiological consciousness being formed within the framework of a "community of communicative work." Thirdly, the ethics of medical professions and also business ethics are close to legal ethics in this view[48].

A more detailed characterisation of the situational ethics of a lawyer conception needs to refer to the phenomenological ethics' assumptions of the authors mentioned above. However, it has to be remarked that the assumptions are not convergent in all points, though in most cases they complement one another. First, there are differences in viewing the central category of this conception, namely values. According to Max Scheler they have informal, objective and intentional character, and thus they are intuitively felt in situations that compel an individual to give preference to one value over another. There are many groups of values, ranked in a hierarchy comprising values of the holy, of the spirit, life, pleasure and utility[49]. All values have not only obejctive but also absolute character since they are not experienced with senses or vitally as pleasure, for instance. Here, relativism is an effect of illusions.

From the point of view of legal ethics two consequnces of the above assumptions seem especially important. Firstly, the way of experiencing values by lawyers – and not only – is of fundamental importance to them as persons. This kind of personalism of the conception means that, "since a person is dynamic human *being*, then in the case of a judge, legal adviser or lawyer he or she continuously realises himself or herself under a considerable influence of

---

48 M. Pieniążek, "Fenomenologiczne podstawy etyki zawodowej prawnika", ["Phenomenological Bases of Professional Ethics of A Lawyer"], in: *Etyka prawnicza. Stanowiska i perspektywy*, ed. H. Izdebski, P. Skuczyński, Warsaw 2008, p. 58 ff.

49 M. Pieniążek, *Etyka sytuacyjna prawnika*, [*Situational Ethics of A Lawyer*], Warsaw 2008, pp. 118-119, 125 ff., 141, 146-147.

ethical-professional preferences made in concrete situations." Thus, legal ethics is a mode of being of a lawyer as a person. What also flows from this is a great significance of role-models, who, as expressions or concretisation of types of values, are an important element of one's ethical life. Hence, such role-models as a saint, a genius, a hero, the leading spirit of civilisation etc., exist as reflections of the groups of values. The question, in which group are the role-models of lawyers, is connected with the second major consequence of the discussed conception of legal ethics[50].

Namely, phenomenological ethics in this perspective is connected with a specific attitude to law. According to this attitude, analogically to values, there exists some objective legal order, in relation to which positive law realised by a legislator and by a judge is of a consecutive character. In other words, positive law does not constitute legal values. Therefore, observance of the legal order is an ethical requirement, which is typical of all legal professions. Naturally, this requirement is realised in each profession slightly differently since the functions of an advocate, a prosecutor or a judge vary, too. For this reason the requirement is met only by concerted and harmonious functioning – in the technical sense – of all professional roles of lawyers . In other words, one cannot build a single ethics of all legal professions because each type of ethics is based on different goods despite having common axiological grounds with other types. However, on the grounds of this perspective, actions peformed uniquely for "good's" or obligations' sake would in fact be based only on a desire to please oneself or others. Therefore, it is necessary to supplement and modify some of this perspective's assumptions[51].

Hence, the development of phenomenological ethics of values by Nicolai Hartmann rests on a different view of interrelations between values. According to him, there is no linear hierarchy of values because they are graded in regard to two qualities: their gravity and strength. An attempt at ordering them leads to the creation of a more complicated structure, represented by the so-called axiological square – patterened after the Aristotelian square of opposition – whose ends are determined by the gravest, the lightest, the strongest and the weakest values. Every individual is equipped with the axiological consciousness, whose scope is always limited only to a certain part of this structure because the source of this consciousness is intuitive cognition of values, which is situational in character and thus is related to the repeatability of certain situations and rare occurence of others in every man's life. A typical example of such a narrowed and changeable scope of axiological consciousness

---

50 *Ibidem*, pp. 125, 158-164.
51 *Ibidem*, pp. 138-139, 154-155, 167-170.

is professional ethics, including ethics of particular legal professions, which encompass only a certain "complex of values." It may be said that, "legal practice results (...) in the appearance in the axiological consciousness of a consistent complex of professionally relevant values."[52]

On these grounds one may say that the legal professions encompass more than one ethos, which change in time as do the situations in which representatives of certain professions happen to be. Most generally speaking, ethos is, "a definite structure of the collective preference of values that finds its expression in all spheres of life and culture." Thus understood, ethos does not differentiate the axiological consciousness into its professional and extra-professional part. Therefore, possible distinction between general and professional ethics can make only theoretical sense; the latter – as for example legal ethics – is not a deviation from or a modification of general ethics understood as common morality since there is no such common morality. Every field of axiological consciousness is an ethos, thus is of particularist nature and so is every morality. General ethics may only exist as a theory; for example, as the axiological square, thanks to which one may characterise, classify and evaluate any given ethos, including those of legal professions[53].

Within the axiological square's framework, any ethos of legal professions occupy, as a rule, the parts near the value of justice, which – as the strongest and most grave – determines one of the square's ends. The qualities of this value mean that, "the members of the indicated professions cannot expect a universal esteem when they show respect for their ethical-professional values, but certainly are condemned to universal protests in case of their violation." Thus, justice is a central value for legal professions. However, it has to be remarked that particular professions pursue or come close to other values. In the case of judges it is love and hence the similarity or proximity of judicial ethics to medical ethics. As regards lawyers and legal advisers the key value is profit, which locates ethics of these professions near business ethics. The source of continuous development of professional ethics is the existence of an "ideal ethos", which binds the representatives of particular professions to be guided by something more than basic values. This ethos is built on the most grave values and exceeds them[54].

The existence of the "ideal ethos" is possible through the existence of a professional organisation. Modern organisations, usually operating in the form of self-governments or professional associations, hold debates on the importance of professional ethics and formulate codes of professional ethics. This is

52 *Ibidem*, pp. 178-183, 197.
53 *Ibidem*, pp. 194-197, 200, 219-200.
54 *Ibidem*, pp. 180, 201-212.

possible because values may be the subjects not only of intuition of values occurring in concrete situations, but also of intellect and will, which draw on intuitive cognition. Their activity may give rise to "false consciousess", which is never caused by flaws of intuition. For this reason intuitive cognition of values should take central place also in the creation of the professional organisation model and it has to be accepted that, "the professional organisation community is a supraindividual whole expressing a universalising (within its frames) ethical-professional order." As such, a legal corporation is a corporation aggregate due to common axiological consciousness, community of ethical experience, unifying ethical-professional acts and independence of the corporation's being from the existence of its members[55].

The formation of legal corporation as a corporation aggregate having common axiological consciousness on the basis of intuition of values in the situations of professional experience raises questions on this process' character. Firstly, it has to be observed that the process is situational and not technological. Thus, treating all ethical debates and codes of professional ethics as means of shaping attitudes or of social control is a serious mistake. Since lawyers' work is connected with meeting other people and conversation, then one may associate it with fundamental assumptions of the philosophy of dialogue. In this perspective, "juridisation of legal ethics leads to its instrumentalisation," and therefore codes of professional ethics should not be a medium of dialogue forming the axiological consciousness of a corporation – they may be only an expression of professional ethics – but, according to Józef Tischner's conception, work itself should be this medium. Thus, the situations in which intuition of values operates are simultaneously the situations of communicating though work. This communication, because of the medium, is of an ethical nature and leads to the creation of the communicative community[56].

The conception of legal ethics as situational ethics is anti-code in character and aims at proving the inadequacy of the model of solving professional dilemmas based on codes of professional ethics. To a significantly greater extent, situational ethics is ethics of personality rather than ethics of conduct, and this is why it requires from lawyers, more so than an intellectual understanding of problems of legal ethics, the professional experience which enables intuitive cognition of a given profession's value and the formation of axiological consciousness, both in personal and corporational dimensions[57]. This

55 *Ibidem*, pp. 190-191, 229-230.

56 *Ibidem*, pp. 245-246, 250-251.

57 M. Pieniążek, "Koncepcja etyki sytuacyjnej prawnika", ["The Conception of the Situational Ethics of a Lawyer"], in: *Polska kultur prawna a proces integracji europejskiej*, ed. S. Wronkowska, Kraków 2005, pp. 256, 343-349.

conception is undoubtedly an original contribution to the development of legal ethics, also because it is a serious alternative to the widespread views of legal ethics as professional deontology and applied ethics. It reacts to their weak points in related to the risks of ideologisation and manipulation of legal ethics, though it is debatable whether it annuls this risk entirely. Nevertheless, this view has certain drawbacks as well.

Firstly, the presented conception is connected with a very articulate legal-philosophical position, in which the role of positive law is subordinated to the objectively existing legal order with its own axiology. Such a perspective was certainly inscribed in the so-called rebirth of law of nature after the Second World War but is difficult to reconcile with the positions dominating nowadays[58]. It also seems that a conception of legal ethics should be reconcilable with various perspectives or visions of law if it does not want to be merely a consequence of legal-philosophical assumptions, which, of course, does not preclude relativisation in this scope. Secondly, this conception, on one hand, asserts that it is impossible to create one, materially understood, system of legal ethics for all legal professions, while, on the other, it does not indicate limits of specialisation in this regard, and thus it does not consider the risk of narrowing the field of axiological consciousness of particular groups of lawyers ut to the moment when they are reduced to professional roles in a technical sense. This latter consequence would equal a secondary instrumentalisation of legal ethics. Thirdly, the conception ignores the problem of social control over lawyers. This makes legal ethics a subject of cognitive monopoly of individuals occupied with law since only they can find themselves in situations in which intuition of values of legal ethics is possible. However, this does not facilitate solving various disputes between lawyers and the rest of society, regarding the scope of their duties and rights. Fourthly, it makes further research problematic because it requires very strong epistemological and methodological assumptions, which impede its integration with previous research in the fields of social sciences, professional deontology or applied ethics[59].

---

58 M. Klatt, "Contemporary Legal Philosophy in Germany", *Archiv für Rechts- und Sozialphilosophie* 2007, no. 4, pp. 520-522, who the material ethics of values treats as a part of the post-war rebirth of law of nature.

59 See M. Pieniążek, "Kodeks czy wolny wybór? Koncepcja etyki sytuacyjnej adwokata na tle refleksji etyczno-zawodowej polskiej palestry",["A Code or Free Choice? The Conception of the Situational Ethics of a Lawyer in the Context of Ethical-Professional Reflections of the Polish Bar"], in: *Etyka. Deontologia. Prawo*, ed. P. Steczkowski, Rzeszów 2008, pp. 311-335.

2.3.3. Critical professional ethics

The most important conception of legal ethics refers to the critical theory perspective and to a great extent addresses the weak points of the preceding conceptions. Its goal is both de-mythologisation and de-ideologisation of legal ethics through opposing all kinds of superstition and false consciousness. Simultaneously, it tries to go beyond methodological limitations of phenomenological and positivist conceptions and accuses them of relations with objective reason and subjective reason as forms of rationality leading to dogmatism and instrumentalisation. This is possible by re-thinking the theory-practice relation, in which, through applying reflective self-examination, various interests reveal and, subsequently, may be discussed in an open debate. Thus understood critical theory is represented by many authors, whose views differ significantly and so the theory has passed through several phases in development of its theses. Presenting a critical conception of legal ethics requires a discussion of the most representative of these views.

It is noteworthy that it was Karl Mannheim who searched for a means of de-ideologising social sciences. He sought it in building a critically and reflectively oriented sociology of knowledge presupposing that, "every social science diagnosis is closely connected with the evaluations and unconscious orientations of the observer and that the critical self-clarification of the social sciences is intimately bound up with the critical self-clarification of our orientation in the everyday world." Simply put, the application of a general ethical theory was at issue here: a theory according to which, "In personal life, too, self-control and self-correction develop only when in our originally blind vital forward drive we come upon an obstacle which throws us back upon ourselves. In the course of this collision with other possible forms of existence, the peculiarity of our own mode of life becomes apparent to us. Even in our personal life we become masters of ourselves only when the unconscious motivations which formerly existed behind our backs suddenly come into our field of vision and thereby become accessible to conscious control. Man attains objectivity and aquires a self with refererence to his conception of his world not by giving up his will to action and holding his evaluations in abeyance but in confronting and examining himself. The criterion of such self-illumination is that not only the object but we ourselves fall squarely within our field of vision."[60]

These assumptions lead to the conclusion that, because of self-reflection, a thinker may become isolated from one's social status, which in turn would enable observation of social processes from outside – free from any interests resulting in the creation of ideological awareness. This view has not been

60 K. Mannheim, *Ideology…*, pp. 41-43.

accepted by the founders of the Frankfurt School. Though they agreed with the aims of ideology and social sciences critique, they claimed that individual reflection is not enough to attain these goals. Furthermore, they believed that the fundamental category that should undergo reflective procedures is reason, which expresses itself in historical ideas. Currently, the ruling form of reason is instrumental reason, which simultaneously is a subject of special critique because it considers usefulness as the sole criterion of reason without asking about the end to which the means are employed. Even if it does ask about the purposefulness of these means, it presupposes that they serve self-preservation of the subject. Concrete situations, the law, and traditions are treated only as conditioning; clearly put, being resonable in this view equals accepting the reality[61].

Numerous consequences flow from instrumental reason domination and they cast light on the issues of legal ethics. Firstly, Horkheimer asserts that because of this domination every sphere of culture maintains its independence in relation to general truth. The scheme of social division of work is automatically transferred to the life of spirit, and the parcelling out of culture into different spheres presupposes that general, universal truth is superseded by "formalized reason", which is thoroughly penetrated with relativism. Law and legal ethics, in relation to this, may be one of these spheres. In this parcelling out, legal ethics, as a sphere of practice and theory, will be characterised by separation typical of theory and practice; separation being the cause of instrumentalisation and ideologisation. This is because in the so-called practical world there is no place for truth, and thus it is split so that it resembles the practical world: natural sciences are characterised by the so-called objectivity but are devoid of human content; human sciences preserve human content but only as ideology, at the expense of truth[62].

Thus, from the outset, one must be aware that legal ethics, as theory and practice, is connected with certain different interests. General ambiguity of the idea of an interest is due to the fact that in a theoretical sense it means emancipation of reason from concrete social reality but also from itself and its products, while in a practical sense interests are various possible states of reality which are subjects of individuals' will[63]. In other words, in theoretical reason its interest serves validation of its principles, whereas in practical reason it is just the opposite, namely principles of reason serve validation of interests.

61 M. Horkheimer, *Krytyka instrumentalnego rozumu*, [*Critique of Instrumental Reason*], Warsaw 2007, p. 37, 42.

62 *Ibidem*, pp. 49, 95.

63 R. Bubner, "Was ist Kritische Theorie?", in: K.-O. Apel et al., *Hermeneutik und Ideologiekritik*, Frankfurt am Main 1973, pp. 185, 202-203.

Therefore, the concept of interest only reflects the division of reason but is incapable of overcoming this division. Mere awareness of the relationship with various interests is thus a necessary, though not a sufficient condition of such a theoretical view of legal ethics, which can free it from the ideologisation charge.

Secondly, in instrumental reason concepts were reduced to assemblies of qualities and became means. All other uses are treated as unjustified mythologisation or groundless metaphysical speculation. This pertains not only to the concept of legal ethics and its conceptions, but also, for example, to the related term "lawyer." Investing the term only with technical sense in order to define a certain professional group distinguished by education and occupation seems devoid of any reference to ethical content, which in traditions of legal ethics was associated with the term – whereas concepts are historical and so they should not be isolated from history. All philosophical, ethical and political ideas – having lost their connection with their historical source – easily become the seeds of new mythology. This is one of the reasons why the advancements of the Enlightenment at some phase turn into superstition and madness[64]. Therefore, the modern conception of legal ethics should refer to the tradition of legal ethics and include it in the creation of its new meaning. This does not mean to say that such a conception should not be useful; however, usefulness cannot be its unique content.

Thirdly, a critical conception of legal ethics should not only expose relationships of theory and interests as well as the historical character of its concepts, but should also critically examine itself. Since this theory aims at avoiding instrumentalisation of legal ethics, then it must assume that modernity, as a process connected with advancement of technique being the chief emanation of instrumental reason, cannot be revoked. Horkheimer writes that metaphysical therapies that want to revert the tides of history are tainted with pragmatism, which, allegedly, disgusts them. One cannot simply return to the traditions of legal ethics since this would be an instrumental treatment of them, and such an approach, as a remedy, would be doomed to failure. The only route between instrumental reason in its objectivist and subjectivist forms is criticism in the Kantian sense. Horkheimer explains that the task of critical reflection is not only to understand various facts in their historical development, but also to penetrate the very concept of a fact in its development and thus in its relativity. Hence, one should draw conclusions from the development of the legal ethics concept; even if it turned out that subjecting the concept to critique will lead to its complete relativisation, rejection or replacement with a more general conception. The thinker holds that truthfulness of thought to itself relies to a

64 M. Horkheimer, *Krytyka...*, pp. 51, 58, 164.

great extent on its ability to negate itself while still retaining – as an immanent moment of truth – the recollection of its genealogy[65].

What distinguishes traditional theories form the critical one is the ability to criticise and reject its own concepts. This distinction is present in Horkheimer[66] as well as in Jürgen Habermas[67]. The latter holds that though modern science and technique are ranged against ideologies, by treating the public sphere like an object – which is typical of instrumental rationality – and by destroying its communicative character, they become a substitute of old ideologies themselves[68]. The relationship between the sociology of knowledge of Karl Mannheim and the critical theory became clear in the 1970s when the Frankfurt School underwent a period of an intellectual and political separation or simply isolation. The common elements of these conceptions are: primarily, the critique of the social class concept, which was replaced with the opposition of the "lifeworld" (*Lebenswelt*) and the systems "colonizing" it; secondly, attempts to overcome ideology undestood as "false consciousness" or "disintegrated consciousness" (*fragmentierte Alltagsbewusstsein*) and reflectiveness and communication as means of synthesis[69]

Self-criticism of the concepts of reason is done through reflection. Thus, a critical conception of legal ethics must simultaneously be reflective. This means that theory must try to do away with the distinction between theory and practice, which is possible only when this theory is immanent, namely when it is a part of practice and even if it negates this practice. Reflective theory is thus self-critical in the scope of its social function. The basic category in this regard is such a combination of the theoretical and practical interest that the realisation of the latter – for example, in the form of the particularist interest of lawyers – will not preclude the realisation of the reason's interest; in other words, it will not preclude separation of concepts from this interest. Significantly, this means that the philosophical approach must of necessity be combined with practising social

---

65 *Ibidem*, pp. 85, 100, 163, 171.

66 *Ibidem*, p. 174, and *idem*, "Teoria tradycyjna a teoria krytyczna", ["Traditional Theory and Critical Theory"], *Colloquia Communia* 1983, no. 2, pp. 39-63.

67 Of many works on this subject see J. Habermas, "Interesy kontytuujące poznanie", ["Knowledge-Constitutive Interests"], *Colloquia Communia* 1985, no. 2, pp. 157-169, especially assigning technical interest to empirical-analytical sciences, practical interest to historical-hermeneutical sciences and emancipatory interest to critical sciences, which is also reflected in the divison into the spheres of pragmaticality, ethicality and morality, discussed in chapter 3 section 3.

68 G.C. Kinloch, *Ideology and Contemporary Sociological Theory*, Engelwood Cliffs 1981, pp. 5-6.

69 P.V. Zima, *Ideologie und Theorie. Eine Diskurskritik*, Tübingen 1989, pp. 89-99.

sciences and only mutual consideration of their results within the critical theory framework may provide for its reflective character. The critical theory must practise self-criticism totally; it must be reflective in each of its parts. It has to be remembered that critical theory is not self-contained since its critical goal is not directed at the critical theory itself but, essentially, at other theories, which it wants to de-ideologise. So critical theory co-exists only with them and protects the "lifeworld" (*Lebenswelt*) from them[70].

The concept of the "lifeworld", understood not only as a product of language-games, but also as a basic social phenomenon, was first used by Peter Winch. Thanks to this concept it is possible to avoid such a critical theory perspective which would entail an infinite process of reflection, whose subject would permanently be the theory-practice relations. This is because the "lifeworld" is based on a network of spontaneous communicative relations, and thus has an intersubjective character – contrary to reflection itself, being a theory making itself its own object (self-objectification and self-reference). Communicative rationality, which – and this flows from the essence of language – is immanent in relation to the "lifeworld", together with dialogue, as a fundamental form of both: communication and reflection, is the critical theory's validation[71]. In relation to the conception of legal ethics, the main problem resulting from this is contained within the question of whether legal ethics is one of such theories, or language-games, from which the "lifeworld" has to be protected by the means of the anti-ideological critical theory, or whether legal ethics has critical power, reflective character and is validated through its language analysis, and thus may effectively prove ideological character of competing theories.

One of the proposed answers to this question is the thesis that, "the discourse from which professional ethics emerges is a special case of practical discourse [...] specifity of professional ethics makes discourse, in which deontological rules are articulated, reveal some traits typical of legal discourse while still retaining ethical discourse character."[72] The discourse thus characterised has a specific audience (professional association), goal (determining professional deontology rules or deciding a particular case), and

70 M. Horkheimer, *Krytyka...*, p. 173; R. Bubner, *Was ist...*, pp. 161-164, 170-171, 182-183.

71 See: M. Zirk-Sadowski, "Dyskurs jako mowa regulowana wymogami moralnymi", ["Discourse as Speech Regulated by Moral Requirements"], in: *Prawo w zmieniającym się społeczeństwie,* ed. G. Skąpska et al., Kraków 1992, p. 193; R. Bubner, *Was ist...*, pp. 187-189.

72 P. Łabieniec, "Etyka zawodowa jako przypadek dyskursu praktycznego", ["Professional Ethics as a Case of Practical Discourse"], in: *Etyka. Deontologia. Prawo*, ed. P. Steczkowski, Rzeszów 2008, p. 255.

sorts of arguments (deontological, theological and consequentialist)[73]. The thesis on the special character of legal ethics discourse in relation to ethical discourse – a character which is, nevertheless, intermediate bewteen that of ethical and legal discourse – presumes that legal discourse is a special case of ethics discourse. The thesis is thus debatable and raises contentionsince it makes such a strong legal-philosophical presupposition. It is uncertain whether legal ethics will have the same status if one accepts that legal discourse is of exemplary character in relation to general discourse or if it is a completely different kind of social practice, namely the one rather destroying ("colonizing"), social communication[74].

Another proposition is to consider the discourse of legal ethics not as a special case, but as one exemplary of ethical discourse. Here, the fundamental thesis claims that some qualities of legal ethics, especially its procedural nature, may be useful in constructing general ethics. The thesis rests on several assumptions, primarily that if one understands general ethics not as customary but as reflective and critical morality, then it has to be observed that norms of legal ethics are formed through a specific procedure whose subject is the experience of lawyers – what they are and what they should be. This procedure consists of two phases: critically-reflective development of norms and studying their connection with a conception of being a lawyer. The latter is made of mutually adapted personality types and practised social roles. Lawyers are constructors of their own ethics and of themselves on the basis of social roles since by formulating conceptions of being a lawyer they choose bewteen various ethical views. This, basically, may be described as post-traditional thinking[75].

In this view, a reflective character of legal ethics discourse is provided by the attitude of lawyers to the performed professional roles. This attitude may be non-reflective (acceptance of the role's requirements), partially reflective (serching for the role's criteria), or reflective (searching for the criteria of a good fulfilment of the role's requirements). Only in the last case one deals with legal ethics. In this perspective, the criterion of reflectiveness is a kind of universalisation: one has to form one's professional role so that others could take one as an example, and so this way of forming one's role becomes universal. This forming of one's role may also include role-determining communities, and thus an active approach is acceptable as regards the formation of social culture and the place of lawyers within it. However, it seems that the level of this active

73 *Ibidem*, pp. 255-257.

74 For analysis of these possibilities see chapter 4, especially the discussion of Chaïm Perelman's thesis on an exemplary character of legal discourse.

75 V. Luizzi, *A Case for Legal Ethics. Legal Ethics as a Source for a Universal Ethic*, New York 1993, pp. 1, 8-9, 14-15.

approach should also be subject of the requirements of universalisation – specifically understood in this perspective. Most generally speaking, professional roles are equally an effect and a subject of a procedure typical of legal ethics. Simultaneously, they make a category occuring between norms of deontological nature and the ethical subject, and neither of these two concepts can be understood without the other[76].

It has to be mentioned that in the presented view the exemplary character of legal ethics is to a significant extent justified by the fact that legal ethics, contrary to general ethics, has for two decades continuously advanced because its juridicised form is the result of a defined procedure. Whether this holds true also for other fields of professional ethics is still to be resolved. This is probable if these other fields assume, first, that validation of rules, if it is not to be situational relativism, must refer to the whole practice, and thus it must subject them to the test of specifically understood universalisation; second, that there is no universal ethical subject but it is always a result of model-forming reflection on one's professional roles, or wider: social roles, and on their corresponding personality types[77]. Even though the perspective seems interesting and some of its elements may serve as a starting point for further reflections, both *implicite* and *explicite* it refers to arguments of pragmatic character. In this perspective, even generalisation of the reflective procedure of legal ethics cannot satisfy the requirements of the critical theory, and thus prevent parcelling out of culture and instrumental and ideological exploiting this part of it with which traditions of legal ethics are related.

---

76 *Ibidem*, pp. 110-115, 142-143, 157-158.

77 *Ibidem*, pp. 19-23, 25-26.

Chapter 3
Multi-dimensional theory of legal ethics

3.1. Preliminary remarks

In accordance with what was said at the outset of this work, when examining the relationship of legal ethics with the philosophy of morality, this chapter will attempt to determine whether the theory of legal ethics, and in particular, multi-dimensional theory – as proposed herein – is possible[1], i.e. whether it can be meaningfully considered, without exposing oneself to inconsistencies and antinomies. Of particular interest will be the conditions for the possibility of such a theory. These conditions can be determined only at a meta-theoretical level, which includes not only the possibility of this, but also other ethical theories relating to specific social or professional groups or to specific practices and behaviour. The conclusions of this part of the discussion can therefore be only of formal character and it is thus necessary to complement them in the next section which takes up the issues of the content of legal ethics theory, associated with philosophical-legal assumptions. The starting point for examining the meta-ethical issues of professional ethics consists of several assumptions.

Firstly, both the traditions of legal ethics as well as its modern transformations allow for a conclusion that this concept has three basic meanings: obligations, social roles and virtues. It may seem, accordingly, that the simplest way of proceeding would be to check whether legal ethics in each of these meanings can be reconciled with a general theory that applies to this concept, and thus whether deontic theory of legal ethics, social theory of legal ethics and virtue-based theory of legal ethics are possible. However, this proposal should be rejected due to the fact that the ethical theories which use the

---

1 Multidimensionality, both in ontological and methodological terms, is known in legal theory in Poland, mainly thanks to a lively discussion concerning the so-called planes of legal research, which took place in the late sixties. See, for example: A. Peczenik, "Płaszczyzny badania prawa" ["Planes of Legal Research"], *Państwo i Prawo* 1968, no. 2; K. Opałek, "Przedmiot prawoznawstwa a problem tzw. płaszczyzn prawa" ["The Subject of Jurisprudence and the Problem of the so-called Planes of Law"], *Państwo i Prawo* 1969, no. 6, and primarily J. Wróblewski, "Prawo i płaszczyzny jego badania" ["Law and the Planes of its Research"], *Państwo i Prawo* 1969, no. 6.

terms referring to only one of these concepts are radical, and therefore they are on the margins of ethical debate. The most significant theories – referring, among others, to Aristotle and Kant – although they consider virtues or obligations to be essential, also refer to other concepts discussed here, except that they differentiate them in terms of importance, namely they simply prioritise them. Therefore, the theory of legal ethics should make use of the ambiguity of its basic category by formulating a theoretical plane that corresponds to each of the meanings and it should be, as a whole, subject to analysis from meta-theoretical point of view.

Secondly, the requirement for the theory of legal ethics – resulting from the analysis of previous attempts to create such a conception – is to orient it critically, both toward practice and theory. It must be kept in mind that critical theory should, as a rule, fulfil its critical function both *vis-à-vis* other theoretical efforts as well as *vis-à-vis* itself. The first criterion can be met due to the instruments of analysis of such theories of legal ethics which could be described as formulated in the framework of normative ethics, which, according to the statements contained in this work, is only possible after adopting certain assumptions on the grounds of the philosophy of law. If the theory of legal ethics could be provided with such tools, then the critique of normative theories of legal ethics would indirectly turn out to be significant also for the philosophy of law itself. However, regarding the second criterion – namely that critical theory should be capable of self-criticism – the theory of legal ethics should be reflective, and thus it should apply such a procedure to its theses. If both these requirements are met, the proposed theory will avoid ideological entanglement in the ongoing disputes concerning the legal profession, without depriving it of its practical dimension.

Thirdly, the multi-dimensional and critical theory of legal ethics cannot be formulated and evaluated in isolation from contemporary meta-theoretical discussions. The latter are multi-layered, yet one can specify their primary axis, which is also of fundamental importance for the theory of legal ethics. What has already been noted was the dispute concerning the role of ethical theory, which should be considered in the context of the so-called validation crisis in ethics and the development of applied ethics. A similar line of division constitutes the basis of the controversy around the role of reason and tradition in ethics, which is particularly important for legal ethics because of its predominantly traditional character. A more precise determination of this dividing line is not easy, but neither, it seems, is it required for the analysis in question. It appears that both the extreme rationalist standpoint, seeking a "pure" theory of legal ethics, as well as opposing practical standpoints, aimed exclusively at practical issues, are impossible to defend, and certainly incompatible with the requirements of critical and reflective theory.

Fourthly, reflections on the theory of legal ethics should take into account the possible methodological consequences to which they may give rise. If the critical and multi-dimensional theory of legal ethics is to be the basis for further research, then its theses should be translated into methodological directives determined separately at each plane of the theory and partly performing its critical functions. What must remain an open question at this point is how these methods can be classified in terms of the division of science, and whether they constitute a homogeneous set that makes such a classification possible. The formulation of theory and methodology based on the latter will therefore not settle the question of whether legal ethics is a part of jurisprudence, or of the nature of its relation to general and specific legal sciences. Therefore, this issue will be addressed separately in the last part of this work.

3.2. Validation crisis in ethics

3.2.1. Two views of ethics

Validation crisis in ethics is a reflection of a broader philosophical dispute about the so-called ultimate justification (*Letztbegründung*), though two basic views of ethics are not a direct reflection of the standpoints presented in this dispute. These standpoints are associated primarily with the polemics that took place in the 1960s and 70s, between the representatives of critical rationalism and transcendental pragmatics, namely, above all, on one hand, between Karl Popper and Hans Albert and, on the other hand, between Karl-Otto Apel and Wolfgang Kuhlman. The subject of this controversy was mainly the place of the fallibilism principle, mainly in science, but also in other areas, including everyday, moral or religious thinking. The essence of the dispute is expressed in the evaluation of truth of the so-called Münchhausen Trilemma, under which any philosophical attempt at ultimate justification must end in three fallacies: the infinite regress of justifying (*regressus ad infinitum*), a logical vicious circle (*petito principii*), or arbitrary or dogmatic argumentation. Therefore, all judgements may be considered justified only in the sense that in a given historical moment no arguments were yet formulated to rebut them[2].

2 A broader presentation of the dispute on the ultimate justification (validation) and remarks on the Polish terminology in this area can be found in chap. IV in the book of B. Sierocka, *Krytyka i dyskurs. O transcendentalno-pragmatycznym uprawomocnieniu krytyki filozoficznej* [*Criticism and Discourse. On Transcendental-Pragmatic Validation of Philosophical Criticism*], Kraków 2003.

Within meta-ethics the dispute over an ultimate justification involves the validation of normative ethics by means of ethical theories. The crisis in this respect manifests itself in the rejection of the interrelation between ethical theories and ethical norms, and in the fact that the former mainly come down to the analysis of the language of morality, or that they are transformed into political theories. This was the fate of largely classical utilitarianism, which was transformed into emotivism on one hand and into political liberalism on the other. In this situation, the norms of conduct become the subject of interest to applied ethics, the starting point of which are moral practice and ethical theories that are applicable only in so far as they may be useful to clarify the specific norms, not their whole set or system. This understanding of applied ethics is based on the fallibilism principle, without seeking philosophical validation for ethical norms.

Therefore, attention needs to be paid to the modern trend of using the term "ethics" with predicates that refer it to a certain sphere of social life, such as speaking of "business ethics" or "media ethics", namely about "practical ethics, sometimes close to deontology", that is about an applied ethics, as defined in this study. It is "a new semantic tinge" which should not "overshadow the first and fundamental importance of ethics as metamorality and a founding doctrine" and therefore one should talk about ethics with two meanings: as a rational theory of the good, and as applied ethics, based on hypothetical imperatives[3]. According to the author, what is most important apart from the validation of ethics and making it a lodestar in the modern world, "is to raise a question about the consistency of applied ethics systems (...) Meta-ethics will ask about the meaning of these vague formulas which are a jumble of colloquial prejudice, deontology and expressions of good will."[4] Problems of validation and consistency of such ethics as legal ethics are therefore closely linked.

On this basis, meta-ethics offers two ways of dealing with the phenomenon of legal ethics, contemporarily occurring mainly in the juridisicised form of codes of professional ethics. Firstly, professional ethics is understood as, "a set of principles and norms that determine how, from a moral point of view, the representatives of a particular profession should behave. A logically structured set of norms of professional ethics is referred to as the 'deontological code' of a given profession. It is formed by the concretisation and detailing of general norms in society, adjusting them to the specifics of a given profession and enrichment of the rules related to the essence of professional activities."[5] In this

---

3 *J. Russ*, *Współczesna myśl etyczna* [*Modern Ethical Thought*], Warsaw 2006, pp. 8-9.

4 *Ibidem*, pp. 19-20.

5 *Mały słownik etyczny* [*Small Dictionary of Ethics*], ed. S. Jedynak, Bydgoszcz 1999, p. 82.

approach, the general ethical norms are the basis for formulating deontological norms and they derive validation from the latter. It should be noted that this adaptation to the specifics of a particular profession may be complex and involve the use of complex procedures. Thus, for example, "the solution of the ethics of consequence is the proposal of applying by lawyers a controlled approach method, taking into account many points of reference."[6] This is a procedure which can be defined as following from the ethics to deontology.

Secondly, one can assume the opposite standpoint, namely that it is deontology that should be the starting point from which one should aim at ethics. Yet such a standpoint is not identical to that of applied ethics, because, due to their uncertain status, one should ask, "whether it is about authentic forms of ethics, namely about reflective analyses of values, theoretical approaches concerning practice and norms of conduct" or rather about deontologies, in the case of which it should be kept in mind that from such deontologies to ethics – that is "from the empirical rules and obligations to a coherent and unified metamorality, based on the principles – it is a long way."[7] It seems that the objective of applied ethics is not a development of ethical theories in general and, therefore, also those which would be based on deontology and moral practice. This approach is much closer to the proposed critical legal ethics in a version that assumes that it has a mode character for the general ethics, yet it should be noted that the reference to principles of pragmatism and the criteria of good ethical theory directly connects it to fallibilism.

The basic problem of ethics relating to specific groups or practices is the status of broadly defined moral standards or requirements formulated by them, which is characterised by a permanent deficit of validation. If any such ethics, on one hand, repeals certain requirements of general ethics in relation to specific groups or practices whereas, on the other hand, it lays before them the special requirements, much more far-reaching, then we can say that it changes the general ethics[8]. Validation of these standards lies primarily in demonstrating the acceptable range and depth of these modifications. It should be noted that the decisive argument here is the very existence of certain social groups and the fact that the latter exercise their practices. It is difficult to think about media ethics without the existence of the media, about medical ethics without the existence of medicine, or about legal ethics without law and lawyers. Accordingly, the categories of social structure and social division of labour will necessarily

6 *Leksykon...*, ed. J. Zajadło, p. 76. See my proposal: P. Skuczyński, "Metoda i przedmiot etyki prawniczej" ["The Method and Subject of Legal Ethics"], in: *Etyka zawodów prawniczych...*, ed. H. Izdebski, P. Skuczyński.

7 J. Russ, *Współczesna...*, pp. 128-129.

8 M. Michalik, *Społeczne przesłanki...*, pp. 17-23.

appear both in the reasoning leading from ethics to deontology, as well the other way round.

The thesis of multi-dimensional legal ethics theory holds that three basic meanings of the term "legal ethics" correspond to the three planes of its theory, under which all further meanings contain the premises for the decisions taken at the lower plane, thus constituting the means of its validation. At the same time, it combines deontological, social and moral categories. The matter of reasoning which has as its subject norms and facts must raise considerable doubts, regardless of which of these are premises and which conclusions. Today, two great philosophical conceptions take this issue, trying to overcome the scepticism based on the construction of a naturalistic error. On one hand, there is the universal pragmatics of Jürgen Habermas and transcendental pragmatics of Karl-Otto Apel – both referring to Kantian rationalism – which profess the unity of theoretical and practical reason and provide reflective validation procedures. On the other hand, there is Alasdair MacIntyre's conception – based on the Aristotelian tradition and hence on ontological assumptions – whereby tradition that allows coherent and consistent resolution of moral issues due to the concepts of virtue and good life, constitutes the criterion of validity.

3.2.2. Practical rationality and the tradition

From the perspective of modernity, virtues and good life were political and social problems rather than philosophical ones, as practice showed that the diversity of visions with diverse religious and philosophical influences led to insurmountable conflicts. It has therefore become a priority to determine a way for peaceful coexistence and moral standards to which all rational individuals would agree. The basic category which was to help fulfil this task was freedom (autonomy). It should be noted, however, that liberalism in this respect has undergone a significant evolution, because, for example, whereas for John Stuart Mill liberalism was combined with utilitarianism in such a way that freedom provided the greatest amount of happiness, later approaches have increasingly drawn sharper distinctions between the ethical and political planes. Utilitarianism evolved in the direction of emotivism, which is no conception of human good life and happiness, and is not even a conception of conventional morality, since it came down to a set of perlocutionary expressions of individual moral convictions.

The opposition to the liberal standpoint is a postulated return to thinking in terms of community of citizens pursuing together the idea of a good life through civic virtues. The popular and influential works of Alasdair MacIntyre are a good example here[9], and their considerable advantage is that they do not introduce the historical and social character of morality. According to what has been said above, the author notes that the goal of liberalism was to provide opportunities to participate in political and economic life, based on reasonably validated rules, for all individuals regardless of their professed conception of the good life, and irrespective of the tradition from which these concepts are derived, unless of course it forces the rest of the community to change their conception. Under liberalism, solving moral problems becomes impossible, because there can be no understanding and agreement between the actors representing different traditions that would not lead to their renouncing their own beliefs. In this regard, "in respect of the ineradicability of disagreement so-called continental philosophy does not differ significantly from analitic philosophy" whereas "an interminability which was from the standpoint of an earlier liberalism a grave defect to be remedied as soon as possible has become, in the eyes of some liberals at least, a kind of virtue."[10]

Any attempts to create a language, and thus also theories unconnected with the tradition, are prone to cause very serious social problems. The author recognises the latter as a problem of "internationalized languages of modernity", which lies in the fact that one undertakes the interpretation which separates concepts from the historical and social context, and therefore from tradition itself. In this situation, the languages of tradition become collections similar to modern museums – "museums which in an important way have become the public buildings of this kind of educated modernity, just as the temple was for Periclean Athens or the cathedral for thirteenth-century France". This metaphor is to draw attention to this element of the condition of the inhabitants of large cities in the late twentieth century which is associated with the creation of a peculiar "rootless cosmopolitanism", more and more similar to the ideal use of "internationalized languages of modernity" and it is a clear trend toward the emancipation of the agents and their discussions from all particularities of the tradition[11].

In contrast to these languages, the prospect of tradition remains in opposition to the modern cosmopolitanism. The tradition in the philosophy of morality is as the paradigm is in the philosophy of science – a complex theoretical structure "operating" in real terms in solving problems, and thus it is a concept close to pragmatic trends – yet it is not the same. "A tradition is an

9 A. MacIntyre, *After Virtue. A Study in Moral Theory*, Notre Dame 1984; *idem*, *Whose Justice? Which Rationality?*, Notre Dame; *idem*, *Three Rival Versions of Moral Enquiry. The Gifford Lectures*, Notre Dame 1990.

10 A. MacIntyre, *Whose Justice? Which Rationality*, p. 335.

11 *Ibidem*, pp. 393-385.

argument extended through time," and its topicality is based on two types of discourses: the internal interpretative debates and conflicts with external criticisms. On one hand, what characterises tradition is that it is "more than a coherent movement of thought. It is such a movement in the course of which those engaging in that movement become aware of it and of its direction and in self-aware fashion attempt to engage in its debates and to carry its enquiries forward." Traditions are therefore not "wisdom without reflection," as Edmund Burke described them, but they have a reflective and hermeneutic structure, because the multiple critical reading of basic assumptions and theses allow continuation and development. The disintegration of historically founded certainties of tradition is a sign of its epistemological crisis[12].

On the other hand, "an ability to recognize when one's conceptual resources are inadequate in such an encounter or when one is unable to frame satisfactorily what others have to say to one in criticisms and rebuttal, and a sensitivity to the distortions which may arise in trying to capture within one's own framework theses originally at home in another are all essential to the growth of a tradition whose conflicts are of any complexity ore whose mutations involve transitions from one kind of social and cultural order to another and from one language to another." Accordingly, there are no rational criteria of proving the superiority of one tradition over another, and the reason is only an internal concept of each particular one. It does not mean, however, that the choice between different traditions must be irrational. Two major objections against such an approach to the relation between tradition and reason are referred to by the author as challenges, which are taken up in deliberations[13].

According to him these are, "relativistic challenge" which "rests upon a denial that rational debate between and rational choice among rival traditions is possible" and "perspectivistic challenge" which "puts in question possibility of making truth-claims from within any one tradition." The response to these extends to the very notion of tradition as a certain mental and conceptual structure based on internal criteria of rationality, which allows more or less serious moral problems to be solved. The choice of tradition must be based on which of them provides the system with the most consistent solutions and ensures these in the future. What must therefore be taken into account is whether the evaluated tradition is in the development phase, or whether it exhibits signs of crisis, and to what extent it is able in practice to generate a non-confrontational social order. According to the author, such tradition is the Aristotelian-Thomistic heritage, which is worth turning to, not for metaphysical

---

12 *Ibidem*, pp. 12, 326, 352-353.

13 *Ibidem*, p. 327.

reasons, but purely pragmatic ones. This heritage gives rise to a tradition which has proved that it is best able to solve moral problems. It is also consistent with the assumption that rationality is of internal character to the tradition which functions in a particular community, because "from Aristotelian (...) one cannot think for oneself if one thinks entirely by oneself (...), one become rational only by participation in the rational practice-based community."[14] It can be therefore said that, in a sense, the main thesis of the whole conception gains validation in the reflective procedure that overcomes the challenges of relativism and perspectivism.

With regard to the issue under consideration, this tradition has the advantage that it explicitly uses the concepts of virtue, in particular cardinal virtues and personality patterns that contain features essential to even being able to have virtues[15]. These virtues and abilities are necessary for the implementation of each practice, but they are necessary to varying degrees. Only continual, long-term refinement allows to attain practical knowledge of a benefit of a given practice in a particular situation. The benefits of various practices are therefore interdependent and they constitute the common good. Consequently, there is no opposition of morality and social structure: the fulfilment of social role guarantees good conduct and, in turn, good conduct shapes correct social structure. The norms of conduct are the consequences of such understood virtues, in both the ontological and epistemological senses. From the standpoint of legal ethics theory, the fact of adopting Alasdair MacIntyre's position – regardless of whether one regards Aristotelianism and virtue ethics as the best of traditions – would stand for the necessity to choose between them, and therefore reject others.

Even if it were only for that reason, an alternative position, approaching the relation of rationality and tradition considerably differently, should be analysed. As Alasdair MacIntyre holds in his critique of modernity, at the outset of the latter, Kant tried to create an ethical theory independent of the tradition. It is to him that modern attempts to continue the project of modern morality refer[16]. According to Max Horkheimer, "if the tradition – so often deprecated in recent scientific and political history – is now turned into the criterion of some ethical or religious truth, it discredits this truth and makes its reliability not less questionable than that of the principle which the latter would validate. At the times when the tradition could still provide a safeguard, belief in it stemmed from the belief in objective truth. Today, invoking the tradition seems to serve

14 *Ibidem*, pp. 352 and 396.
15 *Ibidem*, p. 127.
16 *Ibidem*, pp. 334-335.

only one function that remained from the old days: namely, it gives us to understand that the consensus, hiding behind this principle which one tries to re-legitimize, is – economically or politically – strong. (...) The fact that contemporarily we need to evoke tradition, provides just about the fact that it lost its power over men."[17]

In this perspective, it is not so much traditions that have the force of validating the principles of rationality and morality, but the opposite: their duration is only possible with consensus, the achievement of which is based on a rational basis. Philosophical explication of these principles is contemporarily undergoing the transformation associated with the replacement of the philosophy of consciousness with the philosophy of language and with a transition from the practical reason to communicative reason. "Communicative reason differs from practical reason first and foremost in that it is no longer ascribed to the individual actor or to a macrosubject at the level of the state or the whole of society. Rather, what makes communicative reason possible is the linguistic medium through which interactions are woven together and forms of life are structured."[18] In this perspective, reason is not directly practical, but its basic principles can occur only in the form of practical imperatives. Rationality is related to communication in the framework of discourses, which, thanks to the objectives of equality and lack of restraint, as well as compliance by their participants with the claim to subjective honesty, intersubjective correctness, and objective truth, validate the consensus reached within them as rational.

Therefore, as it seems, Habermas speaks of a post-traditional era in which traditions belong to the realm of ethicality, opposed, on one hand, to pragmatics and, on the other hand, to morality[19]. This triad refers directly to Kant's division between technology, pragmatics and ethics, in which only the latter is of universally normative character, while the other two are included in the hypothetical imperatives that bear the characteristics of the contingency inherent for reality[20]. Ethicality is therefore equivalent to the Kantian pragmatics and relates to a method for leading a good life and achieving happiness, whilst

---

17 M. Horkheimer, *Krytyka...*, pp. 60-61.

18 J. Habermas, *Between Facts and Norms. Contributions to a Discourse Theory of Law and Democracy*, Cambridge Massachusetts 1996, pp. 3-4.

19 *Ibidem*, pp. 151-168 and 308-314.

20 I. Kant, *Groundwork of the Metaphysics of Morals*, (trans. Mary Gregor), Cambridge 2006, pp. 27-35, [417-425]. All the references to Kant are cited after English translations of his works that I have access to. I use square brackets to additionally give page numbers of the Prussian Academy of the Sciences edition of Kant's work [*Kants Gesammelte Schriften herausgegeben von der Königlich Preußischen Akademie der Wissenschaften*], Berlin 1903-1911; Cf. O. Höffe, *Immanuel Kant*, Warsaw 2003, p. 171.

taking into account the personal conditions and social status of a given person, though not individualistically presented. In such a perspective, goods are relative, and if their acquisition is conditioned by certain virtues, then their choice is necessary only on account of these goods. Thus, it seems that even in a liberal democracy it is possible to formulate a catalogue of virtues, yet it has to be kept in mind that, "received practices and interpretations of ethical life were reduced to mere conventions and differentiated from conscientious decisions that passed through the filter of reflection and independent judgment."[21]

Such an understanding of post-traditional ethics may be characterised by noting its three aspects. Firstly, it stands for limiting the scope of ethics only to a certain sphere of life and the emergence of the norms of another type. On one hand, "what was considered 'ethics' since the time of Aristotle now assumed a new, subjectivistic sense. This was true of both individual life histories and of intersubjectively shared traditions and forms of life," whereas on the other hand, "legal and moral rules are *simultaneously* differentiated from traditional ethical life and appear *side by side* as two different but mutually complementary kinds of action norms." It can accordingly be stated that with the transition to post-traditional thinking, ethicality becomes something internal in relation to tradition and it is rational only insofar as this tradition is able to find its place among the rational discourses of modernity, i.e. moral and legal discourses that emerged, "from that encompassing societal ethos in which traditional law and a conventional ethic were still intertwined with each other."[22]

Secondly, individuals and communities make a conscious choice about the traditions which are hermeneutically handed down and maintained. Normativity of tradition is crucial only for people who have made such a choice and who make further interpretations of its heritage within community. This may of course also mean the selection and adoption of only part of the traditions or combining them with others, provided that such selectivity will not prejudice the existence of this new creation as a hermeneutic whole. Such a choice can neither be arbitrary, because the traditions or their post-traditional amalgams must function among reasonable legal and moral discourses. The latter thus form the framework within which individuals and communities can make their choices in the sphere of ethicality, adopting certain patterns and values of the good life. Any conception of professional ethics that derives from the tradition of the ethics of the profession concerned, must take into account that, on one hand, the operation of juridicised codes of professional ethics is subordinated to the form of rationality typical of law and, on the other hand, that the conception of good

21 J. Habermas, *Between Facts…*, p. 95.
22 *Ibidem*, pp. 96, 105, 106.

practice of profession and – more broadly – of the good life as a professional, must be subordinated to the requirements of rational morality.

Thirdly, in this context it should be noted that in modern societies, where strategic thinking is dominant, interactions of a legislative nature are free from the constraints of "traditional ethicality". This means that, "one no longer legitimates maxims, practices, and rules of action simply by calling attention to the contexts in which they were handed down." For the professional ethics, even if its traditions are still strong, it involves the necessity of validation outside the realm of ethicality, and therefore it raises the need for resorting to the rational morality – ie a morality based on a discourse principle. In light of this principle, it is essential to note the differentiation consisting in the fact that, "for self-interested actors, all situational features are transforme into facts they evaluate in the light of their own preferences, whereas actors oriented toward reaching understanding rely on a jointly negotiated understanding of the situation and interpret the relevant facts in the light of intersubjectively recognized validity claims." The speaker's performative orientation at the agreement, requires departing from the role of the observer and from being oriented only towards one's own success. Due to rational communication within discourses, strategic activities that implement the interests may be subordinated to the moral norms without the mediation of traditional ethicality, but of course it can also be done in this way[23].

Nonetheless, law is an even more efficient mechanism for the social functioning of morality based on communicative rationality than is tradition. It is not about a relation of subordinating law to rational morality, or about any form of inference. Rather, one deals here with functional relations, because morality in its post-traditional form is dependent on being complemented with positive law. Kantian opposition of morality and legality should therefore be understood not as a mutually limiting but as complementing one another. In particular, "the constitution of the legal form became necessary to offset deficits arising with the collapse of traditional ethical life. From that point on, an autonomous morality supported by reason alone is concerned only with correctjudgments. With the transition to a postconventional level of justification, moral consciousness detaches itself from customary practices, while the encompassing social ethos shrinks to mere convention, to habit and customary law."[24]

---

23 *Ibidem*, pp. 97 and 27. See also K.-O. Apel, "Szientistik, Hermeneutik, Ideologiekritik. Entwurf einer Wissenschaftslehre in erkenntnisanhropologischer Sicht", in: K.-O. Apel et. al., *Hermeneutik und Ideologiekritik*, Frankfurt am Main 1973, pp. 36-44; the author draws attention to a particular dimension of this problem in non-European cultures in which modernisation processes require even distancing oneself from one's own tradition.

24 *Ibidem*, p.113.

In this approach, codes of professional ethics of lawyers constitute the necessary complement of professional morality, regardless of the extent to which the traditions of legal ethics are still vivid, and the extent to which – as a result of transformations of ethics – they constitute the basis for isolating the spheres of juridicised deontology based on professional obligations, good professional life based on performing professional roles, and rational moral discourse that validates the basis of legal ethics. As to the latter, it should be noted that, "postconventional morality provides no more than a procedure for impartially judging disputed questions. It cannot pick out a catalog of duties or even designate a list of hierarchically ordered norms, but it expects subjects to form their own judgments,"[25] and for this reason, a multi-dimensional theory of legal ethics should take into account all the three abovementioned spheres as further planes of the procedures aiming at validation. Professional obligations must in fact be associated with the tasks that the representatives of legal professions have to face in a particular society. Yet, they cannot prevent the implementation of the individual or common conceptions of the good life, because they always govern interactive relations of a specific society and they require the existence of the community and – as the highest plane of professional ethics – a critical assessment of both of these conceptions, as well as social structure and the related deontology.

Validation may use different procedures: justification (understood as logical reasoning, for example, deductive or inductive), argumentation (understood as a discourse that meets certain conditions and leads to consensus) and reflection (interpreted as a self-reference or self-objectification). They are undoubtedly characterised by varying degrees of accuracy and certainty, and their use in legal ethics can take place at its various planes, which would be consistent with the classical Aristotelian and still frequently cited methodological postulate that the degree of formalisation of the theory depends on its subject and it is always smaller in the practical aspects than in other sciences. Therefore, the reflectivity as the most complicated and, at the same time, unreliable procedure, will primarily focus on the highest plane of the theory, which will entail a constant criticism of both the lower planes, as well as its own by means of the criticism of its applications on these lower planes.

---

25 *Ibidem*, p.114.

3.3. Three planes of ethical theory

3.3.1. The scope of the planes of ethical theory

Further clarification of the three planes of legal ethics theory poses some difficulties because the three basic meanings of legal ethics – responsibilities, professional roles and virtues – may correspond to the elements of two theoretical constructs in the light of the presented approach to post-traditional morality. On one hand, those spheres can be attributed to a division into social, moral and legal norms, yet, in accordance with what has been said, the first have contemporarily the nature of limited traditions, whereas the last two emerged in the era of modernity and they have post-traditional character so they functionally complement each other. On the other hand, however, one can refer to the Kantian distinction between technique, pragmatics and ethics, in which only the latter is universally normative, while the other two are included in the hypothetical imperatives that bear the characteristics of the contingency inherent for reality. This trichotomy can be better described as a distinction between the norms of skill, wisdom and morality[26].

In both these proposals, the fundamental role is played by consensus regarding norms, yet in the first one, it is regarded as a pragmatic category, whereas in the second, it has the character of idealising assumption. Therefore, according to the first proposal, legal norms are of the most objective character, whilst moral norms are most subjective. Such a gradation is based on the criterion of the attitude to individual autonomy, and the cause of diversity is, among others, the scope of consensus. This means that the broader the consensus achieved, the more rational the norms are and the more objective they are in relation to autonomous individuals. Legal norms as justified in terms of the broadest consensus as to the procedures and institutions, meet this criterion in the highest degree, whereas moral norms have only a claim to subjective validity. In this situation it is obvious that the autonomy of an individual is rather socially understood, namely unlike Kant[27], and therefore it may be in conflict with rationality. However, it seems that one does not take into account here the fact that the concept of consensus is also based on the autonomy of

26 I. Kant, *Groundwork...*, pp. 26-34 [415-425].

27 On the concept of autonomy and its relation to normativity and motives of conduct, see P. Łuków, "Kanta odkrycie normatywności" ["Kant's Discovery of Normativity"], in: *200 lat z filozofią Kanta*, ed. M. Potępa, Z. Zwoliński, Warsaw 2006, pp. 240-249.

individuals participating in the discourse and thus the whole normative sphere, irrespective of the scope of consensus, is of intersubjective character[28].

It is precisely the assumption of the second proposal, in which the conflict between rationality and autonomy are excluded with the fulfilment of the ideal conditions of communication. The autonomy of a social nature thus constitutes the result of a consensus as to the norms, and therefore it is of secondary character. The autonomy of the participants who achieve intersubjective agreement in the discourse is more primordial in relation to it and the scope of consensus underlying the division of norms into different types of such understood individuals should be adopted as a criterion. The basis of this criterion is a discourse principle, which states that, "just those action norms are valid to which all possibly affected persons could agree as participants in rational discourses", yet the ones who are "possibly affected" refer here to, "anyone whose interests are touched by the foreseeable consequences of a general practice regulated by the norms at issue." The expected scope of consensus results in diversifying the forms of arguments used in the discourses, and therefore the latter are divided into the pragmatic, ethical and moral ones, in which the principles of argumentation operationalise the discourse principle. Morality is based on universalisation principle, which means that its norms have the widest scope of consensus and are thus reasonably justified in the fullest sense of the word[29].

It should be noted that these proposals are diametrically opposite in terms of the conception of moral norms, and thus also the relation of law and morality, but they do not differ so much in relation to their other types. Therefore, further analysis may at least partly take both of them into account, yet the second one shall be deemed essential. A decisive argument in this regard seems to be the abovementioned thesis of the separation of the status of codes of professional ethics and the theory of legal ethics[30]. Although there arise demands that the codes of professional ethics should include exclusively professional duties, they often consist also of the determination of professional roles or catalogues of virtues and vice versa: duties often operate beyond the codes. Accordingly, the fact that should be taken into consideration is that contemporary juridisation of legal ethics causes that the typical situation is a legal or quasi-legal nature of professional deontology, yet one should not discern the necessity here and,

28 J-R. Sieckmann, "On The Tension Between Moral Autonomy and the Rational Justification of Norms", *Ratio Juris* 2003, no. 3, pp. 107-109, 114-118; *idem*, "The Concept of Autonomy", in: *Law and Legal Cultures in the 21th Century. Diversity and Unity*, ed. T. Gizbert-Studnicki, J. Stelmach, Warsaw 2007, pp. 150-151, 159-160.

29 J. Habermas, *Between...*, p. 107.

30 See chapter 1.4.1.

therefore, both this one, as well as other planes of legal ethics should be analysed in isolation from the degree of their juridisation.

3.3.2. Pragmaticality

The narrowest range of the participants in the discourse leading to a consensus is required in the case of pragmatic issues, since they relate only to persons who seek some measures to be implemented towards an already chosen goal. The principles of pragmaticality as rules of conduct are therefore binding only for those subjects who have already agreed as to the goal and they cease to be binding at the moment of withdrawal from the intention of its implementation. It can be thus stated that these are the norms of efficient operation, which derive their validity from the discourse, which is the study of empirical dependencies, whereas the choice of the goal of activity is, in principle, subject to a separate procedure. Turning to Kant, it can be recalled that, "all sciences have some practical part, consisting of problems [which suppose] that some end is possible for us and of imperatives as to how it can be attained. These can therefore be called, in general, imperatives of skill. Whether the end is rational and good is not at all the question here, but only what one must do in order to attain it."[31]

In the most modern approaches, this narrow interpretation of technique has been somewhat extended and according to Habermas, pragmatic issues also relate primarily to the choice of measures that lead to assumed goals. Yet, within this framework it is also possible to problematize mere goals and interests in light of preferred values. Pragmaticality thus includes technical and strategic directives, but, "ultimately, they borrow their validity from the empirical knowledge they take in," namely they take the form of conditional imperatives[32]. This means that the pragmatic issues may constitute the subject of norms of conduct only if there is already a consensus on values, which may become the criterion for the assessment of the principles of effective operation, objectives and interests from the perspective of the realisation of these values. It should be at the same time kept in mind that what is meant here is axiology in a weak terms, i.e. the values preferred by a particular community as part of its tradition recognised as a sphere of ethicality.

Legal ethics in the traditional sense of the term undoubtedly covers pragmatic issues in varying degrees, whereas the contemporary juridisation trends mean that it is sometimes even reduced to the so-called professional pragmatics. On one hand,

31 I. Kant, *Groundwork...*, p. 26 [4:415].
32 J. Habermas, *Between Facts...*, p.160.

as already mentioned, it would be a simplification to reduce the sphere of professional codes of ethics only to the norms of effective conduct, because they also include the formulation concerning professional roles, namely tasks, goals, values and interests deemed important in a given profession, and a number of principles of apragmatic character. On the other hand, however, what can be observed is the subordination of legal ethics to the requirements of professionalism, and thus treating it as a set of norms to achieve the objectives that are external to it. Such an approach covers all conclusions under which compliance with professional ethics is useful from the standpoint of conducted business[33].

The standpoint, presented in this dissertation, under which professionalism as a certain set of views on combining different social roles with a professional role and reconciling the different interests within a given profession is only possible due to ethical principles of integrity and trust *par excellence*, excludes the possibility of reducing legal ethics only to the pragmatic issues subordinate to professional values. Nevertheless, it does not mean that they do not play an increasingly significant role, and that ethical codes are not increasingly dominated by them. It does not happen, or it should not happen at the expense of the other planes of the theory of legal ethics, but as a result of their properties. The spheres of ethicality and morality as well as the discourses undertaken within them are not able to generate a catalogue of accurate professional obligations that could be subjected to juridisation. However, they may set goals and values that can be obtained by means of professional obligations, and they may restrict the freedom of participants in the discourses on pragmatic issues in the selection of these measures.

3.3.3. Ethicality

In the sphere of ethics there takes place determination of core values, which at the same time constitute the objectives of conduct around which human communities are being created, whether in the form of traditions inherited from the past, or modern forms of life selectively assimilating the elements of various traditions. In the language of classical ethical theories, the principal good in this area is always a good life or happiness of people. It should be noted, however, that just like pragmatic issues, the issues of aiming to provide the best life in community, at least so as to guarantee all people the opportunity to obtain differently understood happiness, do not yet belong to the realm of exclusively

33 See Cz. Porębski, *Czy etyka się opłaca? Zagadnienia etyki biznesu* [*Does Ethics Pay Off? The Issues on Business Ethics*], Kraków 1998.

rational morality. This is the case because, "only experience can teach what brings us joy" and the only method that can be used in the search for the principles of achieving the latter, is inductive generalisation rather than universalisation ((*principia generalia, non universalia*)[34].

In the theory of legal ethics, such an approach is close to the second of its planes, namely that where we can find constructed legal professional roles and ways to reconcile the roles and interests of a conflicting character. Finding that in the lawyer's work, the client's interest is the highest good, or that the judge should rule in accordance with his conscience, constitute the regulations of Kantian understanding of wisdom as the ability to develop such values and fundamental principles of conduct which will allow, on one hand, expectations to be met, and, on the other hand, to achieve personal satisfaction. There naturally arises the question about the status of ethicality understood in this way, whereas it is not so much about its relation to the realm of pragmaticality which is subordinate to it and conditioned by it, but more about the dependencies that connect it with the sphere of rational morality. This question also includes the problem of the degree to which a discourse of a certain professional group, for example, as a part of lawyers' self-governing council, concerning the purposes of a given profession, is able to independently validate the values and instrumental norms subordinated to the latter.

Even for Kant, the sphere of ethicality was to be subordinated to morality, both in the realm of the motivation of people who act, and in terms of validating norms. He argues that, "virtue as the condition is always the supreme good, because it has no further condition above it, whereas happiness is something that, although always agreeable to him who possesses it, is not by itself alone good absolutely and in every respect but always presupposes morally lawful conduct as [its] condition."[35] It should be noted that the interconnection between moral conduct and good life and a good work in profession, is not necessary in the case of the sphere of ethicality in the theory of legal ethics, and therefore a good work in a given profession is not a prerequisite for moral conduct, but the latter is only the condition of the former. It is therefore another reason why the traditional professional ethics cannot in itself legitimise professional duties, similarly as it cannot be done by a pragmatic approach both to the obligations themselves as well as to a tradition. In these areas it is possible to carry out only reflective procedures that control practical applications of rational morality.

---

34 I. Kant, *The Metaphysics of Morals*, Cambridge-New York-Melbourne 1991, p. 43, [215].

35 I. Kant, *Critique of Practical Reason*, Indianapolis-Cambridge 2002, p. 142, [111].

In other words, "the first of the two propositions, that the striving for happiness produces a basis for a virtuous attitude, is *false absolutely*; but the second, that a virtuous attitude necessarily produces happiness, is false *not absolutely* but only insofar as this attitude is regarded as the form of causality in the world of sense, and hence only if I assume the existence in that world to be the only kind of existence of a rational being, and therefore is false only *conditionally*."[36] However, if we considered the relationship between personal satisfaction and rational conduct from the standpoint of moral subjectivity, then moral conduct is always a source of some kind of sense of a well performed obligation, of course, always in so far as it has been subjected to appropriate consideration manifested in applying the authority of adjudicating which uses reflection as the basic tool. Therefore, "principles of the pursuit of happiness cannot possibly produce morality; and that, therefore, the *supreme* good (as the primary condition of the highest good) consists in morality, whereas happiness amounts indeed to the second element of the highest good, but in such a way that it is only the morally conditioned but yet necessary consequence of morality."[37]

With this in mind, the realm of ethicality is contemporarily defined as those discourses in which the community members, "in the face of important life issues, want to gain clarity about their shared form of life and about the ideals they feel should shape their common life [...] How we make our native traditions and forms of life our own by selectively developing them determines who we recognize ourselves to be in these cultural transmissions – who we are and would like to be as citizens." Thus, the ethical discourses combine the concepts of tradition, good life, community and its values. Therefore, reason and will mutually determine each other here within the framework of hermeneutic structure of obtaining self-understanding (self-agreement) within a given form of life and in this sense this approach is close to the understanding of the tradition in both Hans-Georg Gadamer and Alasdair MacIntyre. However, it definitely goes beyond it, recognising the possibility of exceeding the limits of tradition and its communities, and setting the primary role of rationality which allows for their external criticism[38].

One way to deal with ethical issues is – as it is called by Habermas – clinical advice, which is based on a reconstruction and critique of assimilated forms of life and traditions. Ethical discourses constitute their justification. Thus, they concern values which are formed by means of self-understanding within the

36 I. Kant, *Critique of Practical...*, p.146, [115].

37 *Ibidem*, p.151, [119].

38 J. Habermas, *Between Facts...*, pp. 160-161.

tradition[39]. As a result of the criticism of the tradition, the sphere of ethicality should not be disintegrated as a very important element of broadly understood sphere of intersubjective normativity. The fact that perhaps we deal with a transition from the traditional domination of the legal domination, should not obscure the circumstances that ethical issues constitute a major part of the broadly understood public sphere, which is the ground for the formation of the so-called communicative authority within the meaning of Hannah Arendt, and thus closer to the concept of *Gewalt* than *Macht*, and therefore not being directly owned by anyone[40]. In other words, ethical issues are closely linked with the problems of civil society, including its understanding, which derives from Hegel and which stands for a certain public sphere between purely political sphere and private sphere.

On one hand, in legal ethics, originating from pragmatic issues justified by the necessity of working well in a profession in order to achieve broader life objectives often leads to objections of lack of morality and ideological subordination to one's own interests. On the other hand, following from the sphere of morality in the direction of determining the professional communities their life goals and ideas of the good life, and leaving aside the pragmatic issues, can raise objections about moralizing. The goal of multi-dimensional and reflective theory of legal ethics is to resolve this problem in the vein of modernity by demonstrating the significance of the sphere of traditionally understood ethicality, due to which spontaneous public debate on issues of good performance in a given profession and its connection to civic conduct, may supplement pragmatic and moral discourses and thus secure legal ethics, on one hand, against cynical ideologisation and, on the other hand, against idealistic moralising[41].

3.3.4. Morality

Morality can be distinguished from other spheres of practical thinking in two respects. Firstly, in the area of the motives of conduct only if, "the idea of duty [...] is also the incentive to the action is called its morality."[42] What is therefore

39 *Ibidem*, pp.160-161.

40 *Ibidem*, pp. 147-149.

41 See O. O'Neill, "Kant: Rationality as Practical Reason", in: *The Oxford Handbook of Rationality*, ed. Alfred J. Mele, Piers Rawling, Oxford, 2004, for whom the presence of Kant's combination of all three spheres allows the very practical reason to avoid similar objections.

42 I. Kant, *The Metaphysics...*, p. 46 [219].

meant here is acting because of duty and not only in accordance with it, treating it as a means to achieve some goal, even as important as our own happiness. It does not naturally mean that a moral person cannot expect satisfaction from moral conduct, although it may have only a moral dimension, and relate to his sense of dignity, and this expectation can never relate to happiness understood empirically. Such expectation is not immoral because, "he must find himself under obligation to do his duty before he thinks that happiness will result from his observance of duty and without thinking of this [happiness]."[43]

Secondly, morality assumes the form the categorical imperative, as opposed to the conditional nature of pragmaticality and ethics. The obligation of basing one's conduct solely on such maxims in relation to which one may also want them to become a universal law, has undergone numerous reformulations with the transformation of the Kantian philosophy, but its normative and rigorous character has not changed. "A categorical (unconditional) imperative is one that represents an action as objectively necessary and makes it necessary not indirectly, through the representation of some *end* that can be attained by the action, but through the mere representation of this action itself (its form), and hence directly. No other practical doctrine can furnish instances of such imperatives than that which prescribes obligation (the doctrine of morals). All other imperatives are *technical* and are, one and all, conditional."[44]

Such an approach to morality constitutes a challenge for the theory of legal ethics, as well as for any theory of professional ethics. On one hand, it must refer to teleological categories because a professional activity always has the character of a practice focused on a certain goal, so it will consist of the principles that belong to the spheres of pragmaticality and ethicality, and without that it will not be a professional ethics at all. On the other hand, however, any such theory which does not take into account the sphere of morality, will be suspected of having common interests with the representatives of a given profession and will be unable to go beyond its own traditions. One way to solve this problem is to incorporate a universal morality to multi-dimensional theory of legal ethics and thus to relate teleological particularity and moral universality, yet the latter can be attempted with two methods because, "one can think of the relation of end to duty in two ways: one can begin with the end and seek out the *maxim* of actions in conformity with duty or, on the other hand, one can begin with the maxim of actions in conformity with duty and seek out the end that is also a duty."[45]

---

43 *Ibidem*, p.183 [377].

44 *Ibidem*, p. 49 [222].

45 *Ibidem*, p.187 [382].

The first path is followed by the theory of law within Kant's meaning, which leaves everyone just enough freedom in choosing their own goals, and which can be reconciled with the freedom of everyone else in the choice of his own goals. When implementing these rules into the field of the theory of legal ethics, the various legal professions would have as much freedom in the choice of the goal, both for the whole professional groups as well as for individual representatives, as not to undermine the foundations of a libertarian social order. However, it seems that the scope of this freedom would be differentiated due to the nature of the profession and the complexity of the factors determining its professional role. For example, legal advisors would have a much greater influence on their professional role and the choice of their goals and values than attorneys who act as defence lawyers, and the latter, in turn, would have a greater role than, for example, judges or prosecutors[46]. Such determination of limits may be very important, the more so due to the fact that any attempt of going beyond and changing such professional roles constitute activism. Nonetheless, there remains an open question of how to make that choice within freedom determined by law and how to distinguish permissible activism in the above sense from the one that constitutes an abuse.

These questions can be answered when we follow the second of the above paths, namely by searching for such goals, which may at the same time constitute a duty, following from the maxims of conduct. What is therefore meant here are such norms of conduct, under which one can act not only because of the sense of duty, but also due to the goal, which can be achieved by means of such norms. According to Kant, human goals, which also constitute duties, are, "*one's own perfection* and *the happiness of others*," but somewhat ironically, he adds that, "perfection and happiness cannot be interchanged here, so that *one's own happiness* and *the perfection of others* would be made ends that would be in themselves duties of the same person."[47] Such an approach can also be combined with communicative rationality, in view of which, normativity is of intersubjective nature, which means that the moral discourses, "aim at the impartial evaluation of action conflicts. In contrast to ethical deliberations, which are oriented to the *telos* of my/our own good (or not misspent) life, moral deliberations require a perspective freed of all egocentrism or ethnocentrism."[48]

---

46 Z. Cieślak, "Etyka urzędnika" ["Ethics of an Official"], in: *Etyka...*, ed. P. Steczkowski, Rzeszów 2008, pp. 32-38.

47 I. Kant, *The Metaphysics...*, p. 190 [385].

48 J. Habermas, *Between Facts...*, p. 97. Cf. A.M. Kaniowski, "Postawa krytyczna a etyka. Problem uniwersalizacji" ["Critical Attitude and Ethics. The Problem of Universalisation"], in: *Racjonalność współczesności. Między filozofią a socjologią*

In the case of moral justifications, the principle of discourse takes the form of the universalisation principle and such approach remains deontological, and as such excludes all teleology, and hence the reference to goods or interests that are worthy of preference, because those matters are the subject of pragmatic and ethical-political discourses. "With moral questions, humanity or a presupposed republic of world citizens constitutes the reference system for justifying regulations that lie in the equal interest of all. In principle, the decisive reasons must be acceptable to each and everyone. With ethical-political questions, the form of life of the political community that is 'in each case our own' constitutes the reference system for justifying decisions that are supposed to express an authentic, collective self-understanding. In principle, the decisive reasons must be acceptable to all members sharing 'our' traditions and strong evaluations."[49]

Transformation of a duty and the purpose of self-improvement and striving for the success of others in a spirit of rational communication, appears to be a method which will allow a multi-dimensional theory of legal ethics to be implemented in the sphere of morality, and, at the same time, it will provide it with a reflective and critical character. Both norms can be only intersubjectively implemented, namely in the framework of discourses, but in this approach they will stand for the efforts to make both oneself and others the best participants in the discourse. It can be stated that the above means adopting as one's goal the fullest possible realisation of the ideal conditions in which the communicative potential of the language could be realised to the fullest (the ideal speech situation). As a result, self-improvement and striving for other people's success will mean acting for the benefit of the full rationalisation – in communicative terms – of the practice in which one participates. It is obvious that such rationalisation will require an ongoing critical reference of the whole discourse taking place between its participants to oneself and referring its individual participants to the roles that they play in it. In this approach, both critical and reflective functions of legal ethics can be accomplished with the adoption of the principle of responsibility for the whole practice as its basis.

[*Rationality of Modernity. Between Philosophy and Sociology*], ed. H. Kozakiewicz, E. Mokrzycki, M. Siemek, Warsaw 1992, p. 85 ff.

49 *Ibidem*, p. 108.

3.4. The problem of universalisation of professional deontology standards

3.4.1. Universalisation and generalisation in ethics

As has been repeatedly stressed, the basic problem of legal ethics, understood as a professional ethics, is the status of the norms and ideals formulated by it. The essence of any professional ethics means that, on one hand, it repeals certain norms and ideals of general ethics in relation to specific professional groups. On the other hand, it also establishes specific norms and ideals concerning them. Therefore, it can be said that professional ethics modifies general ethics[50]. This popular approach involves the objection against professional ethics that its standards are not able to meet the test of differently understood principle of universalisation, which should be applied to any ethical judgements. The mere possibility of such judgements, and therefore of rational ethical discourse, has been based on this principle, at least since the time of its formulation by Kant, yet it should be noted that it has had many followers, who will be, at least partly, analysed at this point[51].

The classic Kantian formulation of the universalisation principle in the form of the categorical imperative has given rise to several similar proposals, while those associated with universal pragmatics have already been mentioned here. It should be noted, however, that just as the very difficulties arising from the universal character of morality constitute the modern heritage of practical philosophy, the possible ways to solve them also have their origin in the classical approaches. Firstly, one can refer to the aforementioned assumption that rational morality does not consist in developing a strict catalogue of duties, resembling a code of ethics, but it is only a certain adjudicating power, having as its objectives the maxims of conduct which are subject to a reasonable judgement. The codes of professional ethics should not, and may not include universal obligations and they can be at most the set of norms, which will be each time subject to a test of rationality.

50 M. Michalik, *Społeczne przesłanki...*, pp. 17-23.

51 Lawyers are primarily familiar with the proposals discussed in: R. Alexy, *Theorie der juristischen Argumentation. Die Theorie des rationalen Diskurses als Theorie der juristischen Begründung*, Frankfurt am Main 1992, in particular R. M. Hare, pp. 91-96, 107, 133; K. Baier, pp. 127-130; J. Habermas, pp. 150-151, 172; O. Schwemmer, pp.186-187 and Ch. Perelman, pp. 206, 215, 218. Cf. also T. Pietrzykowski, *Etyczne problemy prawa. Zarys wykładu*, [*Ethical Problems of Law. An Outline of a Lecture*], Katowice 2005, pp. 72-75.

Secondly, it still does not solve the problem that arises in a situation where the norms of the codes of professional ethics are not able to pass such test successfully, although from the viewpoint of pragmaticality and ethicality the action based on them would be most desirable. It should be noted that, according to multi-dimensional theory of legal ethics, presented in this dissertation, professional duties must be subordinate to the objectives and values of a given profession, which should be, in turn, subordinated to the principle of responsibility for the practice that one performs. In classical terms, the source of this principle, namely the duty of self-improvement and striving for the success of others, have the character of the so-called imperfect duties, and therefore they leave a wide leeway to the subject as far as the measures used in fulfilling them are concerned[52]. This would mean that professional duties need not be subject to universalisation in the same way as the so-called perfect duties, but they should meet the test, which consists in verifying the extent to which they implement the goals and values of a given profession and the extent to which they constitute the way to assume responsibility for the practice.

For a more thorough presentation of the problem, it is worth presenting another perspective, namely the achievements of analytic philosophy which, in terms of the universalisation in morality seems to be particularly interesting from the standpoint of professional ethics, since it usually constitutes attempts to combine continental idealist philosophy in the form of Kantianism with empirically-oriented Anglo-Saxon philosophy in the form of utilitarianism. The latter occurs naturally in many different forms, ranging from classical proposals of Jeremy Bentham and John Stuart Mill, through the intuitionism of Henry Sidgwick, to emotivism of Charles L. Stevenson. Contemporary utilitarianism of rules which uses universalisation principle – with its Kantian pedigree – is an attempt to stop this evolution of moral philosophy which degrades the very morality to the level of emotion, by means of appointing an instance of reason for intuitions, emotions, desires and interests of the actors, which exercises control over them. For legal ethics is all the more important that today its transformations have led to the fact that the starting point within it is usually the specific kind of interest treated as a value for constructing professional roles (expectations of its implementation) and the types of professionalism (balanced with other interests), whereas professional responsibilities are treated as indicators of the measures or restrictions on its implementation – determined in the field of pragmaticality.

---

52 D. Appelbaum, S.V. Lawton, *Ethics and the Professions*, Englewood Cliffs 1990, pp. 17-18.

One of the proposals for a rational approach to a complex social reality consisting of the expectations and interests is to develop a moral point of view. In this approach, moral reasoning constitutes the process of deliberation that leads to the best decision, namely that in which the best arguments weigh in favour. This requires rising above the level of interests, since "by 'the moral point of view' we *mean* a point of view which is a court of appeal for conflicts of interest. Hence it cannot [...] be identical with the point of view of self-interest."[53] The criteria for applying such point of view can be divided into formal and material and it is the exact order to be considered in the deliberations. The formal criteria include the requirements under which moral norms should be regarded as principles, rather than means to achieve goals and one should act on the principles applicable to everyone. The former requirement means that it is unacceptable to introduce undue exceptions in the practice of a given actor, the latter, on the other hand, means one cannot introduce such exceptions for certain groups of actors. The situation of meeting formal criteria can be called universalisation[54].

Substantive criteria of a moral point of view consist of three subsequent steps. First of all, it must be considered whether the discussed rule is good for all, which will probably not be applicable in case of conflict of interests. Therefore, it should be also checked whether it will be acceptable to all parties concerned and to this end one should be put in the role of each participant of the situation, which is the subject of deliberation (*reversibility*). Irrespective of the outcome of this test – resembling Rawls's veil of ignorance – there should be another performed under which one generalises a given action and examines the consequences of such a general practice. What is therefore being rejected are such rules, universal adherence to which would lead to undesirable consequences, with such character of this practice that anyone can without any special dedication join it. These three criteria that relate negatively or positively to empirical functioning of norms can be called generalisation[55].

---

53 K. Baier, *The Moral Point of View. A Rational Basis of Ethics*, New York 1958, p. 190.

54 *Ibidem*, pp. 191-200. Principles may not be therefore contradictory, yet Kurt Baier discusses three types of such contradictions, namely such which does not reach its goal, when it is applied by everyone (*self-frustrating*), the one that will not reach its goal if it is used explicitly (*self-defeating*), and one that is impossible to be morally assimilated (*morally impossible*). An example of the first norm is a rule under which "when you are in need, get help, but never help when someone asks you," an example of the second – "give a promise even if you never perform it, or you do not want to do it," and the third one "always claim falseness."

55 *Ibidem*, pp. 200-211. R. Alexy notes the similarity of the last of K. Baier's substantive criterion to the generalisation in terms of M. G. Singer, see R. Alexy, *Theorie der juristischen...*, pp. 129-130.

The differences between such understood universality and generalisation in ethics disappear in the later conception of Richard M. Hare, who also tried to avoid reducing the ways of moral thinking – derived from Jeremy Bentham and John Stuart Mill – merely to intuitionism. Therefore, in addition to intuitive plane of such type of thinking, where the actor is guided only by his own intuitively grounded moral preferences, he distinguishes the critical plane, which, thanks to the application of the universality method, allows him to resolve preference conflicts and a meta-ethical plane which, in turn, makes it possible to complement moral thinking by deliberating, "the meanings of the moral words and the logic of moral reasoning."[56] The multi-dimensional theory of legal ethics, presented in this dissertation, is based on another differentiation of the planes of ethical theory, because there is an assumption that each of them is critical, yet they differ in terms of their subject matter and methods of such criticism. It should be noted, however, that certain analogies can be drawn here, due to which formulating Hare's universalisation principle may be useful in the consideration on legal ethics.

First of all, in this conception, universalisation is not the same as generality, because the latter is, "the opposite of specificity, whereas universality is compatible with specificity, and means merely the logical property of being governed by a universal quantifier and not containing individual constants." Therefore it can be said that universalisation means that our ethical judgements have to contain the formulation "for every x,...," whereas x stands for a certain situation, that is why a universalised judgement will also cover all similar situations. It is worth adding, that, "these do not have to be *actual* situations; they can be precisely similar logically possible hypothetical situations."[57] According to the author, in contrast to the previously discussed approach, and in contrast to other analytical approaches, universalisation is of a one-step character and it does not need to be supplemented by differently defined generalisation. For in its method, it combines formal and substantive elements, due to which its mere application results in the fact that ethical judgements are imperatives, and thus it leads to prescriptivistic position and to the rejection of descriptivism[58].

Universalisation as a method consists in examining the situation from the viewpoint of each participant, and selecting these preferences that would be acceptable for anyone interested, irrespective of his or her role. It is therefore

56 R.M. Hare, *Moral Thinking. Its Levels, Methods and Points*, New York 1982, p. 41.

57 *Ibidem*, pp. 42.

58 *Ibidem*, p. 58. According to the author, the adoption of descriptivism must in practice lead to a morality of 'so what?'-type, namely to some form of cynicism which, incidentally, lawyers are being often accused of.

necessary to put oneself in each of these roles that occur in a given situation and assess whether from this point of view, moral preferences suggested by intuition are acceptable. Accordingly, one has to juxtapose many situations, but, "although the situations are different, they differ only in what *individuals* occupy the two roles; their *universal* properties are all the same." From the perspective of the individual, his own preferences become just as important as those of any other, and such research requires more of impartiality than altruistic sacrifice of one's own desires at the expense of others. What is methodologically important is, "how in principle unanimity can be reached by our method of reasoning, once each fully represents to himself the situation of the other. And there is in principle no difficulty in extending the method to multilateral cases; the difficulties are all practical ones of acquiring the necessary knowledge and correctly performing some very complex thought-processes."[59]

It seems that for legal ethics, universalisation that consists in considering the interests and preferences within the different roles is an interesting proposition. It means that, in order to determine whether we deal with a duty of conduct, one must first reconstruct the roles which actors perform in a given situation, *inter alia*, the roles of a defence lawyer, defendant, prosecutor, victim and judge in criminal proceedings, and then examine the candidates – suggested by intuition – for professional duties from the perspective of each of these roles. Hare discusses the objection against his version of critical utilitarianism consisting in that he ignores the special relationship of loyalty resulting from fulfilling specific roles. The reference is made here, among other things, to the bond between doctor and patient, as well as between teacher and student, but it seems obvious that these observations can be attributed also to the relationship between a lawyer and a client. Our intuitions associated with specific roles and to special relations of loyalty attributed to the latter, may be defended from the perspective of universalisation, "*in so far* as the intuitions are desirable ones […] as [they have] a high acceptance-utility. […] The best bet […] will be to cultivate them and follow them in all normal cases."[60]

The objection sometimes raised against such an approach is that the specific duties of loyalty are unitary, since our model lawyer should be loyal to his client and only to him, rather than to a broader category of clients in general. This individualisation of the relationships is to prove a non-universalisation of norms associated with them. However, this objection is based on a false identification of individual variables with individual constants, whereas in the example at hand we deal only with the names of the former (client, lawyer), not the latter kind. In

59 *Ibidem*, pp. 111.
60 *Ibidem*, p. 137.

addition, the author distinguishes between the normal principles, namely also minimal ones, which are the foundation of life in society and more difficult to meet, connected with vocation. Vocation is understood here in two ways: personal, close to the traditional teleological meaning and social one, on the basis of which such principles are binding,"[which] are desirable in those who occupy certain roles, or vocations in the professional sense, like that of doctor or lawyer or jobbing builder." Yet, these principles, "for some [..] will be pretty stringent; but others would be foolish to aspire to [them], because they will never bring it off."[61]

We should once more go back to already mentioned concepts of universalisation in the approaches that refer to communicative rationality. They have the advantage of treating all the norms – pragmatic, ethical and moral – as the spheres of a wider category of intersubjectivity, and thus the theory of legal ethics that takes it into account, will be able to be critical at each of its three planes – deontological, social, and moral. As already mentioned, moral issues are free from the teleological problems that are characteristic of pragmatic and ethical issues, because they are dealt with from a fully normative point of view. Thus, moral commands assume the form of unconditional imperatives, and therefore they are free from any subjective goals and preferences. "A norm is just only if all can will that it be obeyed by each in comparable situations." It does not mean that the starting point cannot be the preferences and the roles connected with them but, "the principle of universalisation compels the participants in discourse to examine contested norms in view of *foreseeably typical* cases, in order to determine whether the norms could meet with the considered agreement of all those affected."[62]

In this approach, discourse ethics is based on certain idealising assumptions expressed mainly in the form of the so-called claims to validity that every speaker must make in a discourse aimed at consensus. These are claims to objective truth, intersubjective correctness and subjective sincerity. However, while according to Habermas, they have the character of empirically verifiable assumptions, according to Karl-Otto Apel, they have only transcendental dimension. In the latter case, the universalisation principle is a part of the project of transformation of Kantianism, in which "the obvious fact of reason" which constitutes the primordial justification for this principle, by means of transcendental reflection having as its subject prepositional-performative nature of speech acts, is interpreted as a need for community of communication, in which not only the principle of universality and consensus (discourse ethics) are

61 *Ibidem*, p. 201.
62 J. Habermas, *Between Facts...*, p. 161-162.

valid, but also the imperative of the real application of the results and search for constructive solutions (responsibility ethics). The latter makes it necessary to criticise human institutions, including law and thus legal ethics, from the viewpoint of the principle of accountability as a historic, and therefore no longer transcendental version of discourse ethics[63].

3.4.2. 'Little' universalisation in deontology

The deontological plane of the theory of legal ethics contains criteria for designating professional duties of lawyers and the critical methodology of their research. According to what has been said so far, this criterion is not the text of the codes of professional ethics and other normative acts, although due to the modern changes of legal ethics, they – and only they – more frequently include the norms in question. However, this does not relieve lawyers who want to approach their duties rationally, or the public that criticises them or, finally, the researchers trying to be guided exclusively by cognitive interests, from taking an effort to separate those parts of the codes, which contain references to the social and moral plane of legal ethics, the search for professional duties outside codes and identify those parts of the latter which are of ideological character. The criterion proposed in this area, appropriate to the sphere of pragmaticality of practical reason, is to direct these obligations at the realisation of the basic objectives and values of a given legal profession.

Legal ethics, in the sense of deontology, thus refers to the duties imposed on lawyers due to their profession. Regardless of whether they have a written code of professional conduct, or are at the mercy of their own moral intuitions, in the work of each of them there are situations in which they must decide how they should proceed from a moral point of view. The starting point in such cases should always be a concrete or abstract dilemma resulting from the practice. For example, let us suppose that a lawyer dealing with criminal cases does not know what to do with the information provided by his client, relating to crimes committed by the latter. He asks the following question: should I disclose the circumstances that the client informed me about and thus provoke a situation in which justice may be done, or should I keep it to myself, adjusting it to my strategy of defence and thereby gain an advantage over the prosecutor?

63 K.-O. Apel, "Refleksja transcendentalno-pragmatyczna; główna perspektywa aktualnej transformacji filozofii Kanta" ["Transcendental-Pragmatic Reflection; Main Perspective of Current Transformation of Kant's Philosophy"], in: *200 lat z filozofią Kanta…*, ed. M. Potępa, Z. Zwoliński, Warsaw 2006, pp. 524-528.

Although the case does not appear to be obvious, a theorist is not exempt here from searching for a well-reasoned answer.

It is possible to formulate different rules, which will provide a solution to the above dilemma. It can be assumed with high probability that their different versions will be included in the code of professional ethics and in procedural rules, while another will be suggested by the public and economic interests of the lawyer himself, and yet another may be in line with his sense of fairness. It can be further assumed that the choice would include an absolute prohibition on disclosing the information obtained from the client, the duty of disclosure, if it is necessary for the benefit of the justice system, and the information cannot be otherwise obtained, permission to disclose due to the particularly revolting character of an act which the client is suspected of, or even permission to disclose the information because of a dispute on unfulfilled obligations between client and lawyer. The criterion for selecting one of the above solutions should pass a test about the extent to which each of these rules conforms to the objectives and values of the professional role of a defence lawyer in a given legal system and in a given society. This test should also take into account the universalisation principle but on account of the professional nature of the dilemma, it cannot be its simple application and it should take into consideration the profession which is practised by a given actor who faces the dilemma.

Firstly, it has to be determined which rule should be applied from a general moral point of view (this stage will be referred to as "large universalisation"). Secondly, one should determine whether the application of this rule would be compatible with the goals and values that are crucial for a given profession. Thirdly, if the result of the previous step is negative, then a general rule that could be reconciled with in a particular case with a given professional role, should be appropriate and to a necessary extent modified. Fourthly, the rule, established in the previous two steps, should be evaluated in terms of its universalisation within the scope of a professional role that is fulfilled, namely one should examine not so much whether it can be applied to everyone, but to anyone that has this role ("little universalisation"). Modifications of the rule obtained as a result of large universalisation and adapted to a particular dilemma, should be deepen until the criteria for a little universalisation are met[64].

In considering the above example, we can assume that the general moral rule is the duty to disclose any information in connection with the necessity of co-operation of all citizens in administrating justice. However, if the goal of a defence lawyer is to prevent clients against the indictment and conviction, and the interest of the client is considered a value, then such disclosure is out of question.

64 P. Skuczyński, "Wieloznaczność...", pp. 111-112.

Accordingly, maybe it would have been possible to rely on the recognition of lawyers and introducing here a peculiar conscience clause. This solution, however, as a uniform practice, would make it impossible to develop confidence between lawyer and client, since a potential client could never know whether a lawyer benefits from this clause or not and, therefore, to play safe, he probably would refrain from providing the lawyer with the information, without which the defence may not be effective. It is therefore necessary to deepen the modification of the general rule. Disclosure will probably also have to be excluded, at least in criminal cases, because of a dispute between lawyer and client, and the need for obtaining relevant evidence. The rule of professional secrecy is likely to be adopted in an absolute version or such which allows special exemption by the court or the client himself; it will depend on a closer characteristics of the role of defence lawyer than the one outlined here, and in particular on his relations with other participants in the trial[65].

The proposed way of reasoning, both in practice and in methodology, has the advantage that it is based on the specific presumption of rules resulting from general ethics. It also assumes that any moral practice deviating from these rules should be applied uniformly within the entire profession. In this way, the adopting premises that stem from a professional role in practical reasoning does not necessarily lead to extreme relativism and it minimises the possible tension that may arise between the representatives of a given profession and the public on this background, yet it certainly does not guarantee to remove it ultimately. At his point there arise two questions. Firstly, what is meant by, "premises arising from the professional role," that the above reasoning is based on and, secondly, whether it is possible to avoid the mentioned social tension which, in the case of legal professions, seems to be widespread. The answers to both these questions must be sought on the next levels of legal ethics.

3.5. Legal ethics in social structure

3.5.1. Professional roles of lawyers

A philosopher may claim that, "the judge must set the primary objective of his mission autonomously. He can decide to protect justice, defend the constitution and the dominant social order, or to stand for the law or civil rights and liberties [...]. Each judge is responsible for choosing the right way; therefore the concern may arise that even judges of equal integrity and competence might take

65 Cf. H. Gajewska-Kraczowska, *Tajemnica zawodowa* w: *Etyka zawodów…*, ed. H. Izdebski, P. Skuczyński, p.192 ff.

different decisions."[66] Even if this statement confirms neatly the significance of the human factor in all kinds of practice, including ones as significant ones as judicatory practice, it still awakes serious doubts, as it fails to explain why the judge chooses from a limited list of possible missions, which does not include more controversial proposals, such as implementing a worldwide vision, or moral rebirth of the national community. Moreover it does not indicate which criteria a judge, or in fact all legal professionals should follow, nor does it suggest if the choice may be evaluated from the rational point of view. Finally, it fails to establish limits to the pursuit of the chosen primary objective, i.e. the overriding purpose to which the entire legal practice of the judge serves as an instrument.

Lawyers tend to be cautious in stating this kind of dilemmas; the source of the cautiousness is in not only the moderation acquired during the professionalisation (i.e. professional socialisation) process, but also the awareness that the decision is not necessarily "autonomous"; first, because the unavoidability of the choice is questionable; second, even if so, the question remains if the nature of the choice is really individual, and if the decision has not been already made for them. In other words, the question arises if a general normative model of a professional role is necessary, and if so, then by whom it should be created: by individual lawyers, based on their moral and political views, by the legal milieu, or by the democratic society. In modern states it tends to be assumed that the model should be specified more or less precisely. The mission to create it is distributed among parliaments, local governments, and professional corporations, whereby it is assumed that democratic social participation in the process of creating the model guarantees that the legal professionals gain an opportunity, on par with other citizens, to affect the model, so that it considers their moral and political views[67].

According to the multi-dimensional legal ethics theory, the existence of professional roles of lawyers, constituting the primary category of the theory's social plane, allows to define professional obligations, as well as to establish the method of determining and criticising them. This is concordant with the previous literature, suggesting that professional ethics constitutes, "an attempt to present the social role of certain distinguished professions in moral categories. Hence, generally speaking, the character of all professional ethical norms would

---

66 J. Hołówka, "Dylematy moralne w zawodach prawniczych," ["Moral Dilemmas in Legal Professions"], in: *Etyka prawnika. Etyka nauczyciela zawodu prawniczego*, ed. E. Łojko, Warsaw 2006, p.14.

67 P. Skuczyński, "Powściągliwość sędziowska jako zasada etyki sędziowskiej", ["Judicial Cautiousness as a Principle of Judical Ethics"], in: *Dyskrecjonalność w prawie* [*Discretionality in law*], ed. T. Stawecki, W. Staśkiewicz, Warsaw 2010, pp. 290-301.

be hypothetical. They correspond with the teleological normative structure, according to the rule stating that 'if a profession is to perform its social function properly, its representatives should respect certain norms.' If a person decides to practice a particular profession, he or she must commit not only to the professional requirements, but also to its deontology. This approach eliminates a variety of philosophical barriers regarding the establishment of obligations or the extent to which the rules are binding."[68] With this approach, however, the issue remains open, as to instruments that enable critique of professional roles and the possibility of shaping those instruments by various groups of social stakeholders.

One solution could involve a reference to universal moral standards; nevertheless, as it was noted in the 1970s, due to the modern social pluralism and the fact that different moral systems are applied by different social groups nowadays, it is impossible to create a universal ethical system, which leads to serious ethical difficulties. There are attempts to overcome them, "by using, for the purposes of research into morality, the notion of social role in the normative meaning, as a set of postulates regarding an individual because of their social position. This provides an instrument to reconstruct the so called professional ethics, which may lead to creating moral codes of conduct for particular professional groups. This is only possible due to a long tradition of professional practice in the given area."[69] In other words, "creating a universal ethical system which would be non-contradictory, complete and including hierarchical norms is impossible within a morally pluralistic society. This does not imply rejecting all attempts of building moral systems; yet, the systems should only be created for well-defined social groups where formal relations are present."[70]

Professional roles are formed by a variety of functional, systemic and interactive factors, as it has been mentioned while reflecting on profession and professionalism. This means that the continuous, "processes of *social* differentiation necessitate a multiplication and variation of functionally specified tasks, social roles, and interest positions. On one hand, this allows communicative action to escape its narrowly circumscribed institutional boundaries for a wider range of opportunities. On the other hand, in a growing number of spheres social differentiation not only unshackles but requires the

---

68 H. Jankowski, "Kilka uwag na temat etyki zawodowej", ["A Few Remarks on Professional Ethics"], *Etyka* 1994, no. 27, p.182.

69 M. Zirk-Sadowski, "Postulat etyki bezkodeksowej a stosunek prawa do moralności", ["Postulate of Ethics Without a Code and the Relationship Between Law and Morality"], in: *Zeszyty Naukowe Uniwersytetu Łódzkiego* 1979, no. 25, p.21.

70 *Ibidem*, p. 23.

self-interested pursuit of one's own success."[71] Thus, the division into culture, society and personality, and, as a consequence, into respective processes of cultural reproduction, social integration an socialisation, observed in modern societies is only possible due to unrestricted and spontaneous communication, in which the processes occur through communicative actions. To put it differently, according to Talcott Parsons' concept of institutionalised individualism, "the development of ego-identities corresponds to the universalisation of law and morality, to the separation of *Sittlichkeit* into law and morality, and to the release of communicative action from normative contexts that become increasingly abstract."[72]

This problem may be interpreted as endangering the spontaneous social relations by the increasingly complicated social structure based on the division of tasks and functions. In addition, if morality is considered another part of the broad realm of communicative actions, capable of developing only in the form of an unrestricted discourse, which is capable of yielding universal results, then it should not astonish that professional ethics, understood as a set of rules justified and universalised only within certain roles, i.e. particular social structures, will be perceived as a dangerous phenomenon. In this respect, it seems a serious accusation that on one hand, "it is not a coincidence that the law of totalitarian states is extraordinarily rich in references to applied ethics," which implies, to put it more precisely, "a recourse of law to applied deontologies (both professional and others), as opposed to general ethics." On the other hand, "both concretisations and modifications are rather situational than professional. One should not tell lies; yet, lawyers are not obliged to reveal the truth about their clients, which does not follow from professional ethics but may derive from general obligation to help others."[73]

Nonetheless, it seems that the radicalism of both interpretations may be mitigated by the already mentioned elements of the two great concepts, which note that coexistence of the differentiating political structure with its complicated system of professional roles defined on the basis of function, and the universal moral sphere based on discourses meeting the criteria of communicatively rational actions is necessary. Hence, it is true that, "whoever desires to see the signs of mutual help in the society should be aware that it is hindered by the strict division of roles," because the roles, "are characterised [...] by expectations imposing special obligations on those who perform

71 J. Habermas, *Between Factss...*, p. 25

72 J. Habermas, *The Theory of Communicative Action*, vol. 2, *A Critique of Functionalist Reason,* Boston 1987, p. 288

73 J. Woleński, "Przeciw etyce zawodowej", ["Against Professional Ethics"], in: *Etyka* 1994, no. 27, pp. 185-186.

them."[74] The goal of the multi-dimensional theory of legal ethics is to reconcile both approaches, assuming that, "individual autonomy, sovereign balancing of opinions in case of conflicts, independent decision-taking" are very important; "nonetheless, the autonomy should be [...] limited in the area of professional practice" on the grounds of an additional risk resulting from the fact that professionals are entrusted with particular goods."[75]

The mutual relationship between instrumental rationality related to a broader notion of functional rationality, on which the structure of modern societies is based, with communicative rationality providing a base for modern morality has been traditionally decided upon by individual historic communities in the area of ethics. As this area has gradually divided into modern law and morality, it becomes necessary to redefine the relationship; whereby, seeking the solution should be conducted via rational arguments, without referring to various concepts of tradition, which are always accidental. One solution, regarding legal professions, although with a possible broader application, is proposed by the theses of the legal ethics theory's social plane. They concern, first, the special character of professional roles of lawyers, and second, arguments aimed at determining professional roles and their moral element. The theses lay premises to consider other ethical issues of the social plane, i.e. the principle of trust and the principle of integrity.

The thesis about the special character of professional roles of lawyers is based on the general assumption that social roles vary, depending on the extent of their differentiation. A role may be regarded as strongly differentiated, "if it requires unique principles, or if it requires its norms to be weighted more heavily than they would be against other principles in other contexts" In turn, poorly differentiated professional roles are those in which, “these features can be evaluated by applying in the usual way moral principles applicable elsewhere as well."[76] The strongest differentiation may be found in a non-professional and non-legal environment, i.e. within family, where the cited principle of helping others or taking care of relatives is regarded as a priority. Professional roles of lawyers, particularly that of a judge, belong to other roles with strongest differentiation.

The above mentioned quality of strongly differentiated professions, i.e. that professionals must regard the profession’s central goals and values as superior to the regular moral perception, is typical for judges, who, contrary to other

74 M. Ossowska, *Socjologia moralności. Zarys zagadnień*, [*Sociology of Morality. A Review of Topics*], Warsaw 2005, p. 66.

75 I. Lazari-Pawłowska, "Etyka zawodowa bez kodeksu", ["Professional Ethics Without a Code"], *Etyka* 1994, no. 27, p. 177.

76 A.H. Goldman, *The Moral Foundations of Professional Ethics*, Totowa 1982, pp. 2-5.

citizens, are morally obliged to obey the law and, consequently, to ignore their own moral beliefs when adjudicating a case, as it has been suggested in the literature. Although the statement above may seem controversial from the legal-philosophical point of view, if a general assumption is made that judges should display a special approach to the law, which distinguishes them from other citizens, and that they cannot consider their moral beliefs in legal discourses, then it can be claimed that the role of a judge is indeed strongly differentiated. The same could be claimed, although to a lesser extent, referring for instance to lawyers, who should be loyal and ignore their moral beliefs when serving clients, as required among others by the adversary trial system, by the prohibition of assuming the role of a judge or law, and by the lawyer's role to counterbalance the state justice and the investigation machine[77].

Naturally, within the structure of the multi-dimensional theory of legal ethics, the mere existence of a strongly differentiated professional role constitutes a premise for specifying its special obligations; yet, it cannot justify the special character of the role. Therefore, "this narrowing of moral focus must itself be justified in terms of deeper moral principles […] It cannot be a matter of mere preference on the part of professionals, if society is not to be justified in resisting it. Nor can it be a matter simply of moral division of labour, in which certain professions [...] take care of certain values." Therefore, to justify the differentiation of a particular profession, a reference must be made to its function, whereby to fully justify the strong differentiation of professional roles, their representatives should explicitly manifest their moral function in the society. It should be noted at this point that, as a consequence, professional values will dominate not only in the professional environment, but also in other contexts, which can lead to insensitivity to other values[78]. The problem will be dealt with by the principles determined within the social plane of the legal ethics theory, i.e. the principles of trust and integrity.

Hence, each legal profession has imminent central goals and values justifying its members' special obligations. Yet, even if assumed that the goals and values are of moral character, they cannot justify the strong differentiation, especially if it occurred by dividing a realm of values between individual professions. Nor can the special relationships between lawyers and their clients, which may be comparable to family ties, justify the differentiation of legal social roles. On the contrary, their special character derives from morality. Thus, the claim of a cited author that professional ethics consists of professional functions or roles, expressed in moral categories, is not true. On the contrary,

77 *Ibidem*, pp. 3, 34, 90, 106-112.
78 *Ibidem*, pp. 7, 18.

professional ethics introduces morality into the social structure and social division of labour. Rather than resembling family relationships, the premises of differentiation may be compared to the obligation of keeping promises, i.e. to a situation in which one must meet certain commitments as a principle, regardless personal beliefs or circumstances[79].

The second thesis of the legal ethics theory's social plane concerns arguments aimed at determining professional roles considering their moral element. These arguments could provide a moral basis of the legal ethics research. As it has been indicated, the criterion determining individual professional roles of lawyers, i.e. of legal professions, may be expressed based on systemic-functional and interactive factors. To simplify the argument, the latter will be ignored in the further discussion, which does not negate the practical significance of the interactive factors. Nonetheless, they are less tangible in academic terms. In this approach, professional roles are generally seen as social roles or patterns of conduct determined by the role an individual performs in a society or group[80]. Given the fact that individuals belong simultaneously to various groups and hold a number of social positions, it should be concluded that each person plays several roles, also conflicting ones, which is not insignificant, according to the theory of legal ethics.

Systemic-functional factors that define professional roles are of narrower extent than those regarding social roles in general; nevertheless, it has to be noted that professional roles become the principal roles, which increasingly determine people's lifestyles nowadays. Furthermore, the roles assigned to professions of public trust gain even more significance[81]. As it has been discussed, these professions are distinguished by a number of particular qualities, whereas professional roles as such are determined by two of them. First, professions involve activities performing particular social functions, which implies specialisation. In this respect, professions differ from one another. Second, the work (activity) performed provides the basic way of earning one's living, which in turn implies commercialisation. In this respect, all professions are alike[82].

Even if the essence of a professional role lies in a certain pattern of conduct, constituted by functional-systemic factors, in particular those related to specialisation and commercialisation of some activities, the question remains open as to how goals and values become premises for arguments regarding

79 *Ibidem*, pp. 21-22.

80 I. Lazari-Pawłowska, "Etyki zawodowe jako role społeczne", ["Professional Ethics as Social Roles"], in: *Etyka zawodowa*, ed. A. Sarapata, Warsaw 1971, p. 43.

81 E. Łojko, "Role i zadania...", p. 15.

82 *Ibidem*, pp. 16-17.

professional duties, and in what way the moral element, justifying their strong differentiation, is present. The pattern may be regarded, on one hand in a purely descriptive manner, as a regularity of conduct; on the other hand as a postulate, a certain social expectation or demand directed to the person performing a particular social role[83]. If the two aspects of the professional role differ profoundly, the significance of professional ethics is revealed, as it provides an instrument to criticise either professional practice or unjustified social expectations. Moreover, this implies that laymen should participate in debates regarding legal ethics, whereas the lack of experience or in-depth knowledge of legal practice should be balanced by an unbiased, so to say civic view[84].

Another problem necessitating a critical approach to professional roles and to the inclusion of a moral plane into the theory of legal ethics derives from the fact that in social reality entirely different, even contradictory, expectations or demands may be directed to individual professions. Whether we state that in such a situation there are two conflicting roles, or one which is characterised by an internal conflict, is of little importance as far as rational approach and research methodology of legal ethics are concerned. This is due to the fact that, apparently, in both cases two similar solutions tend to be offered, i.e. considering such internal or external contradiction normal or pursuing goals and values of the "properly understood" and "real" role of a particular profession[85].

From the legal ethics viewpoint, the first approach may be regarded as extremely relativistic. For instance, by referring to social expectations, it allows to approve of a judge's conduct, even if it betrays the role assigned conspicuously, such as judge's servility towards the political power or contributing by their adjudications to genocide. The latter approach may be considered absolutist, as it refers to a timeless and supracultural model. It raises, however, doubts, if such a model exists. First, it would be difficult to imagine, for instance, a model for patent agents or other highly specialised and relatively new professions. Second, even traditional and old professions do not necessarily have such a model. One example could be provided by the divergence between western and Asian models of a judge. While impartiality is virtually unquestioned in the European model, and any closer relationships to the interested parties would disqualify the judge, in Japan it is a common belief that disputes are best solved by a person who knows the parties[86].

83 I. Lazari-Pawłowska, "Etyki zawodowe…", p. 43.

84 A.H. Goldman, *The Moral Foundations…*, pp. 18-19.

85 I. Lazari-Pawłowska, "Etyki zawodowe…", pp. 56-58.

86 A. Aarnio, "Lawyers' Professional Ethics – Do They Exist?", *Ratio Juris* 2001, no. 1, pp. 2-4.

Therefore, it seems appropriate to take a via media, i.e. a moderately relativist approach based on distinguishing two elements of the professional role: the constant one, determined within the moral plane of the legal ethics theory, and the variable one, determined within the social plane. The constant element includes invariable obligations are related to all legal social roles, whereas the variable element refers to obligations depending on systemic-functional factors, which are typical of individual professions. The relationship between the two elements determines each legal profession's goals and values. It justifies strong differentiation of the professional role and special professional obligations. This is due to the fact that all legal professions must comply with particular prerequisites determining an inviolable sphere of goals and values of the "real" professional roles. Furthermore, with all professions, *differentia specifica* must be present, to determine obligations depending on social needs or on the organisation of justice in the given place and time.

Before specifying the relationship between the two elements of each legal professional role, it seems appropriate to make a reference to terminological issues which may provide an analytic confirmation of the legal ethics theory's social thesis. The accuracy of the terms "legal ethics" and "ethics of the legal professions" has been discussed, the first one referring to lawyers and the latter to legal professions. Therefore, the first approach tends to regard general moral principles binding all lawyers, whereas the latter concerns professional deontological norms. In order to relate, for critical purposes, morality and professional deontology via social plane of the legal ethics theory, we will further use the term "legal ethics", as it seems more accurate. For, if being a lawyer means meeting at least two criteria of the professional role's constant element, i.e. the person is capable of performing legal social functions of utmost moral significance, which unites all professional roles of lawyers. On the other hand, if being a professionally active lawyer means additionally meeting the variable element's criteria, then being a lawyer is a premise of being a professional lawyer. From the theoretical, and even more so critical, viewpoint, it seems adequate to consider both: premises and consequences, and not exclusively the latter.

Thus, the moral element is identical for all professional roles of lawyers, whereas there are several variable elements, depending on social expectations and solutions applied in a particular legal system. Naturally, the variable elements contradicting the moral constant must be considered invalid, whereas conflicts between individual variable elements are possible. A remarkable case to illustrate this is that of antagonistic legal roles, in particular, "the classic example and so to say symbol of defence and prosecution roles before court. It may justly be claimed that only by guaranteeing this antagonism the judiciary is capable of performing its inherent mission."[87] Hence, the moral plane of the legal ethics theory may criticise and control the duality by setting limits to the conduct of conflicted parties in order to avoid destructive actions, but also justifies it as a means of performing significant social functions present within goals and values of each legal profession.

Therefore, it may be concluded that the moral plane of legal ethics and, as mentioned before, its inherent principle of responsibility, allow not only critique of professional obligations and roles, but also their determination. Why social expectations should be considered and to what extent individual interests and expectations should be reconciled with performing a professional role as lawyer is the issue of trust and integrity principles. Both will be discussed subsequently, as a significant completion and consequence of the multi-dimensional legal ethics theory's social theses. Nonetheless, the principle of responsibility and its relation to other planes will be discussed in further sections, with the reservation that its status belongs still to the philosophy of morality, whereas its content is subject to legal-philosophical reflection.

3.5.2. Protecting and building trust

The social plane of the legal ethics theory should be also applied when addressing the question why social expectations must be respected when determining central goals and values of nearly all professional roles of lawyers. From the social science perspective, there are several dimensions of trust and several ways to understand it. First, it may be seen as a relationship between individuals and groups, and as such it occupies a significant position in the theories of rational choice. Second, it may be considered as cooperation of individuals which, "occurs when acting together, collectively, they aim at some common goal, which cannot be attained individually by each of them. In such situations the success of each depends on the actions taken by all others," which may be exemplified by any kind of team work. Third, it may be regarded as a personal tendency to place confidence in the environment perceived in this or that way. Last but not least, trust may be understood as a cultural rule, which, "is the property of social wholes rather than relationships or individuals," which may take various forms. According to the author, it may oblige individuals to manifest trust, such defence lawyers, or to elicit trust such as judges[88].

87 I. Lazari-Pawłowska, "Etyki zawodowe…", pp. 56-58.

88 P. Sztompka, *Trust. A Sociological Theory*, Cambridge 1999, pp. 62, 66.

In legal ethics, the principle of trust, regarded normatively, entails the obligation to protect relationships of trust, which first of all, involves individual obligation to care for the client's trust towards the lawyer. Secondly, it implies general obligation to care for social trust in lawyers and legal professions. The first refers to special relationships between lawyers and clients and the latter to non-individualised relationships. With regards to the first one, the principle of loyalty[89] may be applied, in which the lawyer protects the clients' trust by consistently assisting them in pursuing their interests. The principle of loyalty is the premise for several principles of legal ethics, most importantly for the protection of professional secret and avoiding conflicts of interests. Apart from editorial differences as to emphasising the significance of trust between the legal professionals and clients, Polish codes of legal ethics differ with regards to suggested consequences of losing trust. For the lawyer as advocate, the consequences include the obligation to terminate the legal representation, whereas for solicitors termination is allowed but not obligatory[90].

Acceptable scope of client's representation is subject to a number of limitations, primarily related to the second aspect of the principle of trust, i.e. protecting social confidence placed in lawyers and legal professions. If a lawyer representing his client fails to consider the perception of his role, i.e. integrity, conscientiousness, respecting public authorities and opponents, he undermines social confidence placed in the profession. Actions aimed solely at the client's interest and by no means at public good lead to serious dysfunctions of the given legal profession. Other lawyers' trust to a particular legal profession or to individual lawyers constitutes a significant element of social confidence in lawyers. The lack of a minimum of trust between a judge and a lawyer makes legal trial much more difficult and expensive. The lack of trust and communication between individual legal professions should be considered pathology, which may result from frequent and unpunished cases of breaking limits of acceptable scope of client's representation[91].

---

89 Polish examples show that this principle is problematic with regards to legal professions of public service, especially judges and prosecutors. With regards to notaries public and tax advisors, it applies to peer relationships, and for mediators it mainly entails symmetrical relationships with the party to the dispute. Consequently, the principle primarily applies to advocates and legal advisers' relationships with their clients.

90 *Zbiór zasad etyki adwokackiej i godności zawodu*, [*Code of Legal Ethics and Profesoional Dignity*], Article 51, and *Kodeks Etyki Radcy Prawnego* [*Legal Adviser's Code of Ethics*], Article 28, Paragraph 1.

91 These limits may be divided into several groups. They usually refer to the obligation to respect the law (the prohibition of legal assistance which could facilitate committing a crime or avoiding criminal responsibility for previous offences), the obligation to avoid

The aim of balancing general and individual aspects of trust toward lawyers is to build the culture of trust, where practising law would be easier and thus more effective, due to the fact that using costly substitutes of trust would not be necessary. Among typical examples of the latter are the faith in the providence or "the regression from the discourse of agency toward the discourse of fate," corruption, overgrowth of vigilance and control, excessive litigiousness, ghettoisation, paternalisation, or externalization, i.e. applying models drawn from other societies[92]. It seems that substituting trust to lawyers with other mechanisms is a frequent problem that is present in various forms and accompanied by specific tension between lawyers and the society nowadays. Ethical arguments regarding the conduct of lawyers tend to be cited in these cases, accompanied by the accusations of legal professions' moral crisis and by pushing limits of lawyers' independence back and forth. Traditionally, the response of legal ethics has involved establishing a condition for the existence of trust between lawyers and the society, i.e. that lawyers should not only be honest, but also perceived as such.

At this point, a classical and, irrespective of all associations it could elicit, topical question arises as to the relationship between trust and control. On one hand, "those living in a society with a relatively low level of respecting norms of this kind [regarding the need of trust – P.S.] lose awareness as to the benefits of respecting them [...]. Constant vigilance is tiresome and oppressive. At the level of states, it is reflected by exorbitant sums of money used for control activities."[93] On the other hand, "in the long run, all political problems are institutional problems, problems of the legal framework rather than of persons, and that progress towards more equality can be safeguarded only by the institutional control of power."[94] Seeking to solve this dilemma we should note that, contrary to traditional ethics, in some cases institutions cannot be trusted, even if in some situations they can. In other words, as a consequence of the world's complexity, trust has become unclear and has lost its normative

---

conflicts of interests regarding relationships with clients or other subjects, in particular courts and authorities, other lawyers, and other clients (the obligation of due respect towards courts, authorities and institutions, the obligation of telling the truth, in particular before court, the obligation of collaboration with other lawyers when representing one client, the obligation to communicate with the adverse party only through their lawyer, etc.), see P. Skuczyński, "Zaufanie...".

92 P. Sztompka, *Trust...*, pp. 116-118.

93 M. Ossowska, *Normy moralne. Próba systematyzacji,* [*Moral Norms. A Systematisation Attempt]*, Warsaw 1985, p. 113.

94 K.R. Popper, *Open Society and Its Enemies*, vol. 2, London 1945, p. 151.

character. Therefore, it cannot continue to serve as a universal moral principle, and the ethical tradition has moved closer to situational ethics[95].

In a general sense, the problem lies in the lack of a criterion to distinguish between good, reasonable, or simply rational trust from its contradiction. The criterion should serve not only as a premise for indicating cases subject to the principle of trust, understood as a principle targeted at professional lawyers and academics who study the extent of social expectations to be considered while building professional roles of lawyers. It should also serve citizens to help them determine whether they may trust particular groups of lawyers or entire legal professions or if they should employ additional mechanisms, such as institutional control. The search of this criterion within the critical theory unifies theoretical analyses and practical information gathering, which anyway should be deliberately closer related, in order to overcome the world's complexity and restore orientation as to who can be trusted, and how to act based on trust or lack thereof. Therefore, the individual must be able to assume that this task has already been partly completed by the appropriate social systems.

We have to observe, however, that trust, as a principle of professional ethics, differs from professional obligations in that it does not represent merely a means to an end. Nor does it constitute a forecast that may be used for calculations. Otherwise it would only be a functional equivalent of real trust. Trust occurs when basic orientation methods fail; thus, it may be concluded that, "trust is rational due to its function of increasing the potential complexity of systems." This refers to the notion of rationality, stating that rational things are those which enable a reasonable orientation of human activity in the external world, thus increasing human ability to comprehend and reduce complexity. Due to trust, social systems gain time, which allows critical work. At this point, the following relation should be noted: The more complex the system, the more trust it needs and the more distrust it provokes; which leads to the need of institutionalising control mechanisms. Therefore, trust tends to be replaced for instance with codes of truthfulness and legality, or science and law. Their advantage is that they are not subject to the rule which states that it is much easier to transform trust into distrust than vice versa[96].

The question remains open if this unavoidably implies the disintegration of traditional legal ethics into its juridised part, represented primarily by professional codes of conduct, and its theoretical part, i.e. reflective and critical study of all its planes. Yet, it emphasises the practical dimension of the research

---

95 N. Luhmann, *Vertrauen. Ein Mechanismus der Reduktion sozialer Komplaxität*, Stuttgart 2000, p. 113.

96 *Ibidem*, pp. 114-118.

in this area and allows a reference to the role of science in forming legal ethics, as indicated previously. It should be noted at this point that trust plays different roles inside and outside the system; hence the difference is defined by the boundaries of the system. The more trust within the system, the greater chance that it develops, i.e. the greater potential to balance the relationships with the environment, or to build trust. Thus, the critical and reflective approach to professional roles, with their respective professional obligations, is not deprived of external significance, even if it affects only internal trust building or if it may be understood only within the system. Hence, it seems a paradox that distrust may be used to build trust and because of their special tasks, some roles may be trusted as distrusting and they are entitled to distrust others, e.g. researchers or judges[97].

Whereas this argument answers the question of how the principle of trust should be interpreted nowadays as a legal ethics principle, how to build and restore trust, and how to evaluate the rationality of trust from the functional point of view, it fails to validate and establish limits to social expectations within the social plane of the legal ethics theory. Among others, this is due to the fact that the trust culture may be found in various social structures, e.g. in the world of organised crime, such as the mafia. However, despite high level of trust within those groups, the above mentioned external functions of trust are not present. While asking what good trust means we must, therefore reject the objective criterion of, "functionality and move the debate to another level, where we have to apply meta-judgements of non-objective, moral sort," thus "it is no longer a question of functionality for partners, or for groups to which they belong, but to the wider social system, the whole society." Hence, functional convergence inside and outside the system is necessary[98].

If, consequently, balancing the protection of individual and general trust with regards to legal professions is aimed at facilitating the practice and rendering it more efficacious, then social expectations which contribute to this end should be included in the goals and values of each profession. This method of determining legal roles will be rewarded twice; first, it will increase the profession's efficacy by the very fact of taking the expectations into consideration; second, it will enhance the potential or culture of trust, which will consequently simplify complex mechanisms of the professional practice. In other words, the more trust exists between lawyers and the society, the less complicated are the professional obligations and the less control is necessary, despite extending the scope of goals and values. Due to trust, if internal conflicts

97 *Ibidem*, pp. 120-124.
98 P. Sztompka, *Trust...*, pp. 114-116.

exist within a particular professional role, the resulting problems can be solved on a situational basis, i.e. on the grounds of power of judgement related to the moral plane of the legal ethics theory. It should be noted that, whereas the present reflection regards the entire social structures, it may also apply to particular aspects, such as specific professional activities[99].

Therefore, the moral principle of responsibility sets the limit to the inclusion of social expectations into professional roles of lawyers and to the protection of trust. The culture of trust, which is maintained due to the principle of trust, should facilitate responsible use of the critical and reflective approach to professional roles and obligations, as well as eliminate any action provoked exclusively by social pressure. Thus, the principle of responsibility at the same time validates and limits the above stated procedure used to determine professional roles of lawyers based on systemic-functional factors, including social expectations. Nonetheless, nowadays the source of trust does not lie in the traditional sense of ethical behaviour anymore, but in the organisation. In addition, responsibility tends to be understood as a structural premise for the culture of trust, or the existence of independent agencies and institutions which guarantee satisfying needs and meeting commitments met and which can be used by each person whose trust has been abused[100]. In further sections, the relationship between the two concepts of trust will be discussed.

3.5.3. The problem of good life and integrity

Before we pass onto the analysis of the moral plane of the legal ethics theory, we should discuss another significant principle of the social plane, i.e. the principle of integrity. Its value becomes transparent when various interests related to professional legal practice, especially public good, client's interest, and the very interest of the lawyer, contradict one another. The traditional legal ethics, in particular its part regarding a defence lawyer, which is better established than the judicial ethics, dealt with these issues by analysing them in terms of the ethics of good life. Hence, lawyers were assumed to compose a community where creation and practice of a range of virtues of various types is possible, such as e.g. in the 17th-century aristocratic France or the 18th-century protestant America. Thanks to this catalogue of virtues, the lawyer would be always able to issue a fair moral assessment of the client and his case. Moreover, it enables the judge to take the right decision about the extent to which

99 N. Luhmann, *Vertrauen...*, p. 123.

100 *Ibidem*, p. 125; P. Sztompka, *Trust...*

the assessment should affect the judge's involvement in the case, whereby the relation was typically inversely proportional, i.e. the more repulsive the act and the client himself, the less involved the judge is, with the extreme possibility of refusing to adjudicate on the case. This constitutes the premise of the social respect towards legal professions, based not only on the professional skills, remuneration, and social rank, but also on the moral qualities.

With the development of modern life and the breakdown of traditional values, the traditional model became obsolete and it has been replaced by legal professionalism of different kinds, although some of its elements are still present, especially within the European bar associations. In particular, procedural approaches have appeared, in which involvement and loyalty in the client's representation constitute the primary role of a lawyer, whereby the limits of representation are set by variable historic social factors, which gradually develop into an ample deontology. However, problems still arise regarding relationships of various interests and their balancing, which tend to be solved through attempts of reviving a tradition, especially the Aristotelian one. The question if it is possible to construct a modern concept of legal ethics, based on virtues and on the idea of good life, or if the same objectives may be accomplished through the integrity principle, may be seriously addressed only in the historical context. This results from the fact that analytical philosophy or, more generally, the philosophy after the linguistic turn, was not interested in the issue of good life. Nevertheless, with the turn to practicality in the 1970s and the transformation of the Kantian philosophy, questions regarding traditional perception of happiness have been returning, even if only in the form of post-metaphysical problems[101].

Therefore, according to the critical approach, it has been concluded that it is nonsense to call a particular lifestyle better or more authentic than another[102], and even if traditionally the model of a contemplative life, lived by philosophers regarded as the wisest of the wise, was seen as superior, the model was in fact possible only within a specific social structure. From the economical perspective, speculative thinking was a luxury good that, in a society governed by certain groups, could be afforded only by the social class which was free form hard compulsory work. Intellectuals, deriving from Plato and Aristotle, owe their existence and possibility to engage in speculative thinking to the system of government, from which they try to mentally emancipate

101 K. Konhardt, "Kant a odkryte dziś na nowo pytanie o 'dobre życie'", ["Kant and the Rediscovered Question: What is the 'Good Life'"], in: *200...*, ed. M. Potępa, Z. Zwoliński, p. 207.

102 M. Horkheimer, *Krytyka...*, p. 59.

themselves[103]. This serious accusation, clearly revealing the critical school's Marxist elements, besides rendering all attempts to see lawyers as philosophers problematic[104], suggests that the concepts of individual good life tend to be somehow related to the individual's social rank.

Therefore, the concepts will be based either on adapting to the requirements of the performed social roles, including professional roles, with the primary category being individual behaviour, which, "imposes adapting to the requirements that must be met to maintain the system," or on individuals subjecting their roles to particular interests, which means a cynical approach to the chief goals and values of the professional role[105]. Consequently, either individual identity or the society will be instrumentalised. The third way is provided by the attempt to combine social roles with the concept of good life in the critical and reflective approach, in particular via the multi-dimensional legal ethics theory and its integrity principle. Discussions regarding lawyers show that they not only should perform their role, but also engage their personality and use it to build their identity, whereas they must accept public morality, providing the basis for legal order, as their own. Moreover, professionalism, besides acting as an ideal model, constitutes a challenge to build individual identity based on the critical and reflective approach[106].

Strong differentiation of professional roles of lawyers, despite guaranteeing efficacy and a certain level of fulfilling social expectations, tends to be criticised, as it leads to perceiving lawyers as not being "good people". In this respect, two critical arguments appear in the literature. As follows from the first one, this approach leads to moral nonaccountability of lawyers, whereby professional ethics is subject to ideologisation. Second, the approach has been accused of provoking partiality, as it considers only the interests of one party to social relationships, i.e. the client. In general, this leads to the conclusion that "lawyering thus becomes more like a sport than a profession. All that counts is who wins so long as no rules of the game are broken."[107] Two solutions are suggested to escape the dangers of this approach, both assuming a concept of good life, which makes them subject to the previously mentioned accusations of

103 *Ibidem*, p. 116.

104 J. Zajadło, *Po co prawnikom filozofia prawa?*, [*Why do Lawyers Need Legal Philosophy?*], Warsaw 2008, particularly see chapter 1.

105 M. Horkheimer, *Krytyka...*, pp. 111 and 124.

106 F.C. DeCoste, "Towards a Comprehensive Theory of Professional Responsibility", *University of New Brunswick Law Journal,* 2001, no. 50, pp. 123-124.

107 S. Stier, "Legal Ethics: the Integrity Thesis", *Ohio State Law Review* 1991, no. 52, pp. 554-555, 573.

instrumentalisation and ideologisation on the grounds of failing to meet all criteria of a critical and reflective theory.

One of such proposals suggests establishing a thesis of integrity which states that "the capacity to apply moral principles fairly and honestly is founded on good character and is essential to being a good lawyer. The significance of good character is recognized by the professional standards in the good character requirement for admission to the bar. Thus, the good reader must first be a person of good character who is capable of interpreting the law of lawyering consistently with moral principles."[108] This notion of integrity leads to the conclusion that professional codes of ethics bind lawyers in a particular way, which is different from other citizens' relationship to the law. This is possible for two reasons: lawyers' economic monopoly on legal services, and their informed consent to perform this role and commit to its professional obligation[109]. In this approach, a universal moral attitude constitutes both the prerequisite to perform professional obligations in a responsible way, and the source of their particular character.

According to another proposal, where morality entails a constant reflection about one's own morality, in legal ethics this reflection regards the morality of another person. In other words, "legal ethics is thinking about my client's morals, but I am the one who is thinking"[110]; hence, the question is not what I should like for myself, but what I should like for others, in particular for my client. At least three answers are possible to this question: first, client's right conduct; second, client's freedom; third, client's good conduct. Yet, the first two suggestions will lead to one party, either the lawyer or the client, being dominated by the other, which implies treating them instrumentally, as a means to pursue one's own beliefs, and consequently it leads to the lack of integrity. Thus, we conclude that only by a common pursuit of good, the integrity of both parties may be respected, whereby this relationship, according to the Aristotelian tradition, is called friendship[111].

As it has already been mentioned, both concepts have the flaw of failing to respect the requirements of a critical and reflective theory, which is primarily evident in that they do not distinguish between the spheres of morality and ethicality, as well as in the attempts to reduce one of them to the other. The

108 *Ibidem*, p. 589. Perhaps these could be guidelines to interpet the term "impeccable character", present in the Polish legislation. See reference no. 22 in chapter 1.2.

109 *Ibidem*, pp. 591-592.

110 T.L. Shaffer, "Legal Ethics and the Good Client", *Catholic University Law Review* 1987, no. 36, p. 319.

111 *Ibidem*, p. 320. See also reference no. 40 in chapter 1.3.2 and the quoted literature on the lawyer-client relationship, described as "lawyer as a firiend".

concept assuming that being a good person is the condition of being a good lawyer uses the notion of a good person as a moral category, ignoring its obvious relationship to good life, which means that it belongs to the realm of ethicality. On the other hand, the concept assuming that the lawyer and client are friends in the Aristotelian sense, living good lives together, disregards the fact that relationships of this kind may be simply impossible in today's world, as various ideas of good life are incompatible and incongruous. The realm of traditional ethicality, which should guarantee integrity, has been in fact decomposed into law and moralities. Thus, if ethicality is to be functional, it must respect the latter.

To put more generally, "ethical questions regarding our own weal and woe arise in the context of a *particular* life history or a *unique* form of life. They are wedded to questions of identity: how we should understand ourselves, who we are and want to be;"[112] though, as such, they must respect the universal moral sphere. Consequently, ethicality is granted validation, whereas moral assessments, based on the self-knowledge, gain a motivating power. In order to answer the question more precisely, we should refer to Søren Kierkegaard, who was the first to propose the post-metaphysical notion of "ability to be oneself" and to distinguish between aesthetic and ethical approaches in response to the primary ethical question regarding successful and unsuccessful lives. Only the latter, ethical approach grants "continuity" and "transparency" to human life, as it consists of assuming responsibility for the world in a reflective and self-critical manner[113].

The search of modern legal professionalism, guaranteeing reconciliation of various interests, related to the professional role itself (client's interest), to the role of citizen (public interest) and to personal preference (lawyer's interest), within a particular society and its established roles, should also provide a concept of good life combining the ethics of responsibility with the ethics of authenticity, due to the critical and reflective approach. Therefore, ethics may assess the existential *modus* but it refrains from assessing specific *orientation* of individual projects and particular forms of life, thus responding to the requirements of the pluralism of views[114]. Naturally, the question must be asked, to what extent, according to the principle of integrity, public good and the very interest of lawyers should be included in the professional roles of lawyers, and to what extent the catalogue of each profession's goals, values, and

112 J. Habermas, "Are There Postmetaphysical Answers to the Question: What is the 'Good Life'?", in: *idem*, *The Future of Human Nature*, Cambridge 2003, p. 3.

113 *Ibidem*, pp. 13-14.

114 *Ibidem*, pp. 18-19.

respective professional obligations should be extended as a result of those interests. The answer will refer to the principle of responsibility again, precisely due to its relation to authenticity.

In order to better understand this relation, we should first of all remember that self-knowledge should not be taken for granted, and that being oneself is in fact an intersubjective issue, due to the fact that the "self-aware subjectivity and its identity" may appear and last only if placed in a communicative perspective. Subjectivity and identity are related genetically and functionally, whereby, "in this case, a particular role is assigned to the individual biography, always characterised by a certain standard with a unique structure deciding on experiences, beliefs and actions taken by the person, which are secondary to this structure." This constitutes a constant which protects the reflection from, "being dissolved in the stream of consciousness, adjourning itself constantly, and undetermined by the external objectivity." The identity involves not only a reflective approach to one's biography, but also perceiving it in a performative way and relating it to the validity claims, which grants it an intersubjective character[115].

If individual validity claims, i.e. claims of subjective honesty, intersubjective correctness and objective truthfulness, which regard the whole reflectively integrated biography, are met and recognised by other participants of the discourse, then we may talk about identity which meets the integrity criteria. Individual types of legal professionalism, regarded as ethical concepts of good life, may be seen as a generalisation of a group of similar biographies, due to the fact that they contain a particular individual structure standard deciding about experiences, beliefs and actions taken by the lawyers. A particular identity built on the basis of professionalism, just as any other identity, "results from development leading to a specific form of 'ethical' self-perception, which is revealed when auto-reflection is oriented towards a 'validity claim'. However, the ethicality of such, "self-understanding" requires a certain validation (the Kantian motif), which may only be guaranteed […]" by being rooted in the world of life, which enables "the process of its birth and growth."[116] Legal professionalism and its integrity principle constitute a method of conceptualising the legal professionals' world of life.

In other words, typical modern "worries": individualism (atomism), the primacy of instrumental reason, and the decline of political participation, mean a certain limitation of the moral horizon, due to a wrong interpretation of the

---

115 S. Dziamski, "Scjentystyczny neoracjonalizm 'etyki dialogu'" ["Scientist Neo-Rationalism of the 'Dialogue Ethics'"], in: *Dynamika praktyki moralnej i jej etyczne racjonalizacje*, ed. J. Wawrzyniak, Poznań 1999, pp. 37-41.

116 *Ibidem*, p. 40.

authenticity ideal, meaning self-fulfilment and being oneself. This ideal is related to the neutral liberalism, according to which, "a liberal society must be neutral on questions of what constitutes a good life". Hence, with regards to the ideal of authenticity, "critics of contemporary culture tend to disparage it as an ideal, even to confound it with a non-moral desire to do what one wants without interference. The defenders of this culture are pushed into inarticulacy about it by their own outlook."[117] Such opinions fail to consider the fact that, "this is not how things work with important issues, such as the definition of our identity. We define this always in dialogue with, sometimes in struggle against, the identities our significant others want to recognize in us," whereby, "the modes of contemporary culture that concentrate on self-fulfilment in opposition to the demands of society" are self-defeating[118].

Yet, contrary to traditional societies, where, "the background that made sense of what the person recognized as important was to a great extent determined by his or her place in society and whatever role or activities attached to this," even if, "the coming of a democratic society doesn't by itself do away with this, because people can still define themselves by their social roles," in fact nowadays, "what does decisively undermine this socially derived identification is the ideal of authenticity itself."[119] Thus, it may be concluded that the properly understood authenticity involves on one hand creativity, originality, and breaking limits, and on the other hand, opening to new horizons of meaning, and self-reference in the dialogue[120]. Hence, thanks to the principle of integrity, individuals pursuing the concept of a good life, i.e. authentic self-fulfillment, participate in the formation of professional roles, whereas in the past good life concepts and identities were formed by professional roles. The limit to this participation is set by the principle of responsibility, which also validates the principle of integrity as a principle of the legal ethics theory's social plane. The plane combines professional roles with the ideal of authenticity, due to the fact that authenticity, "indicates the way to a more self-responsible lifestyle" and "opens an age of responsibilization."[121]

---

117 Ch. Taylor, *The Ethics of Authenticity*, Cambridge Massachusetts and London 2003, pp. 17-21.

118 *Ibidem*, p. 33, 40.

119 *Ibidem*, p. 47.

120 The character of this self-reference is reflective, whereby the procedure should be differentiated with regards to form and substance: "Authenticity is clearly self-referential: this has to be my orientation. But this doesn't mean that on another level the content must be self-referential: that my goals must express or fulfil my desires or aspirations, as against something that stands beyond these." p. 82.

121 *Ibidem*, pp. 71-77.

3.6. Professional virtues and professional responsibility

3.6.1. The good of practice as the object of virtue

The moral plane of legal ethics theory is primarily concerned with the principle of responsibility, which, being justified in the reflective manner, both validates other planes and defines their scope. However, this is not the only way to regard morality within the multi-dimensional legal ethics theory. Another proposal could involve the classical catalogue of virtues. In fact, professional ethics tends to be described through the notion of virtue, by means of expressions such as "authorising the non-virtue"[122] or "regulated non-virtue."[123] Regardless of whether these are only rhetoric figures, and whether the notion of virtue, strongly related to the Aristotelian tradition, is obsolete and useless in terms of both theory and practice, there are several reasons to analyse it briefly from the perspective of legal ethics.

First, as has been repeatedly mentioned, the law and morality nowadays emerge from the realm of traditional ethicality. Responsibility, as the chief concept of both the theory of law and ethics theory, may correspond with the realm of virtue, its predecessor. This may certainly shed a new light on the principle itself and on the legal ethics theory, to which it is related. Second, some traditions of legal ethics, and the resulting codes of conduct, in particular with the European bars, are still based on the notion of virtue. Theoretically, this may be seen as a proof that the powerful realm of ethicality, which is rooted in the distinguished social status of legal professions, still exists. Yet, it should be noted that the realm of pure morality is seen as the self-fulfilment of individuals who form their identity in an intersubjective manner, through the good life concept, i.e. within the ethicality realm. Last but not least, it cannot be excluded that the development of various professional ethics will result in broadening the moral categories and bringing in new elements; hence the evolution of the ethics of virtue would be instructive.

The early example of ancient heroic societies shows, "first that all morality is always to some degree tied to the socially local and particular and that the aspirations of the morality of modernity to a universality freed from all particularity is an illusion; and secondly that there is no way to possess the virtues except as part of a tradition in which we inherit them and our

---

122 B. Skarga, "Usankcjonowanie niecnoty" ["Authorising the Non-Virtue"], *Etyka* 1994, no. 27, p. 169.

123 W. Pawlik, "Niecnota uregulowana", ["Regulated Non-Virtue"], *Etyka* 1994, no. 27, p. 171.

understanding of them." Despite containing a severe criticism of modernity and, consequently, of the legal ethics theory, which is presented in this study, the conclusion that, "the unity of the notion of an *aretē* resides [...] in the concept of that which enables a man to discharge his role"[124] is significant to this theory. Therefore, there is no tension between performing a social role effectively and the authentic self-realisation, because virtue means, "knowing how to act *both* efefctively in [one's] role *and* in a way which sustains rather than violates the overall order of things." In addition, "to do what my role requires, to do it well, deploying the skills necessary to discharge what someone in that role owes to the others, is to be *agathos*. *'Agathos'* comes to be translatable by 'good', and *'aretē'*, the corresponding noun, by 'excellence' or 'virtue.'"[125]

In the classical period of Athenian culture, "the conception of a virtue [becomes] strikingly detached from that of any *particular* social role." Thus, already then identity is not a simple consequence of the social role, whereas an individual, "transcends the limitations of social roles and is able to put those roles in question, but [...] remains accountable to the point of death and accountable precisely for the way" of handling oneself in conflicts[126]. Achieving excellence means not only conforming to the requirements of the role, but also acquiring personal qualities and skills by accompanying those more experienced, and it cannot be reduced to obeying the rules. Moreover, the good and development of the practice may require certain rules to be broken. At the same time, virtue may still exist only in a certain community, a form of life facilitating the use of each practice's goods and integrating them into a common good, whereas the process of developing and maintaining virtue was called politics. At this point we should specify what is meant by the good of the practice, given the fact that already in the classical period a distinction existed between the so-called good of effectiveness and good of excellence, as well as between external and internal goods related to various practices[127].

According to MacIntyre, goods which are internal to practices must be put in opposition to goods which are linked to practices in an external or casual way, such as money, power, or fame. The latter goods may be acquired, in some circumstances, due to succeeding in certain practices – proficiency in farming may sometimes lead to wealth; proficiency in chess-playing may render a person famous. Achieving these external goods requires specific skills, whereas

124 A. MacIntyre, *After Virtue...*, pp. 126-127.

125 A. MacIntyre, *Whose Justice...*, p. 15. See also an interesting analytical reflection on this issue: B. Williams, *Morality: Introduction to Ethics*, particularly chapters: "Good" and "Goodness and Roles".

126 A. MacIntyre, *After Virtue...*, pp. 132-133, 145.

127 A. MacIntyre, *Whose Justice...*, chapter 3.

achieving excellence and other goods internal to practices requires not only skills, but also virtues. Which virtues are necessary for which practices, depends to some extent on the kind of practice. What is however important, is the scope to which cardinal virtues – justice, including truthfulness, fortitude, including patience temperance, as well as the virtue of practical judgement called φρόνησις by Aristotle and *prudentia* by Aquinas- are necessary to achieving goods in absolutely every practice[128]. This understanding of virtues refers directly to the Aristotelian tradition, where the primary goods are those of excellence, or in other words, the goods internal to the practice.

As far as the notion of practice is concerned, it may only be understood through its internal goods, whereas internal goods of a particular practice may be defined exclusively in terms of this practice. Therefore, to identify and recognise them, it is necessary to engage in the practice. With regards to this understanding of practice, it should be noted that, "its goods can only be achieved by subordinating ourselves within the practice in our relationship to other practitioners. We have to learn to recognize what is due to whom; we have to be prepared to take whatever self-endangering risks are demanded along the way; and we have to listen carefully to what we are told about our own inadequacies and to reply with the same carefulness for the facts. In other words we have to accept as necessary components of any practice with internal goods and standards of excellence the virtues of justice, courage and honesty." It means that, "a virtue is an acquired human quality the possession and exercise of which tends to enable us to achieve those goods which are internal to practices and the lack of which effectively prevents us from achieving any such goods," and secondly, that every practice requires a certain kind of relationship between those who participate in it. Now the virtues are those goods by reference to which, whether we like it or not, we define our relationships to those other people with whom we share the kind of purposes and standards which inform practices."[129]

The relationship between tradition, practice, goods, and identity, suggested by MacIntyre, is based on the concept dating back to Ludwig Wittgenstein, which states that language and meaning are formed through social practice[130]. Thus, not institutions related to the practice, but the practice itself forms the language of morality, which describes its goods, perfection, and responsibility for morality. In

128 A. MacIntyre, *After Virtue...*, preface to the Polish edition: *Dziedzictwo cnoty. Studium z teorii moralności,* Warsaw 1996, p. 9.

129 A. MacIntyre, *After Virtue...*, p. 191.

130 A. Chmielewski, "MacIntyre a współczesna filozofia polityczna," ["MacIntyre and the Contemporary Political Philosophy"], in: A. MacIntyre, *Czyja sprawiedliwość? Jaka Racjonalność?*, [*Whose Justice? Which Rationality*], Warsaw 2007.

this respect, institutions are only concerned with external goods, such as achieving money or power, whereby they allow the existence of practices by conveying them. This is e.g. the case with the relationship of physics and university or medicine and hospitals, even if it is natural that some practices exist without a typical institutional environment. Furthermore, institutions provide a setting, where constant reflection on practice should take place, i.e. if, "an institution – a university, say, or a farm, or a hospital – is the bearer of a tradition of practice or practices, its common life will be partly, but in a centrally important way, constituted by a continuous argument as to what a university is and ought to be or what good farming is or what good medicine is."[131]

Thus, it seems that the author invokes the metaphysical notion of practice and institution when referring to the Aristotelian notion of virtues, which he considers primary. From the legal ethics perspective, the distinction is significant insofar as the search for a post-traditional and rational moral principle, which would validate the social and deontological planes of the theory, does not have to ignore traditional approaches. This is possible due to the fact that strong ontological premises related to the category of virtues may be replaced with a universal moral principle related to the power of judgement, which will remain in the same relationship to the legal practice and professional roles of lawyers as the notion of virtue. Its relationship to professional roles has already been discussed; hence, at this point we should analyse the relationship with legal practice, whereby we will refer again to the Aristotelian catalogue of virtues. Yet, this analysis may be still useful, also due to the fact that some legal professions continue to apply the ethics of virtues. A critical perspective of the responsibility principle and bringing the reflection on virtues to the social plane may only be beneficial.

Regarding virtue itself and its further connections with practices, "practices then might flourish in societies with very different codes; what they could not do is flourish in societies in which the virtues were not valued, although institutions and technical skills serving unified purposes might well continue to flourish." In order for the practices to exist and develop not only as techniques, the professionals must be virtuous. However, the reservation should be made that this does not apply to all of them, as it does not imply that e.g., "great violinists cannot be vicious or great chess-players mean-spirited. Where the virtues are required, the vices also may flourish. It is just that the vicious and mean-spirited necessarily rely on the virtues of others for the practices in which they engage to flourish and also deny themselves the experience of achieving those internal goods." Therefore, to avoid the situation where practices constitute solely a field of

131 A. MacIntyre, *After Virtue...*, p. 222.

competition, and to ensure their development not only in the technical sense, we must assume that development of virtue in terms of a better understanding of its internal goods is only possible through the perfection of professionals' virtue[132].

As already mentioned, the cardinal virtues of each practice are indispensable, i.e. justice, fortitude, temperance, and the most important, *fronēsis*, or particular practical intelligence, which enables obeying the rules. Seen as virtues necessary in legal practice, all of them seem very interesting; in particular the latter, which is regarded in the literature as the basic category of interpreting law and adjudicating in particular cases.[133] First and foremost, *fronēsis* is indispensable for judges, both for applying rules and dealing with loopholes, which does not mean that other professions can do without it. The special position of prudence in the sense of *fronēsis* is reflected by the fact that, "virtue is required if there is to be a right choice of actions, and it is *fronēsis* which issues in right action; so there is no *fronēsis* without *aretē*."[134]

It should, however, be noted that this notion has been subject to a considerable evolution. E.g. according to Aquinas, the virtue of *prudentia* is a premise for all other moral and intellectual virtues, whereas modern, Anglo-Saxon, meaning of prudence emerged in the 17th century, i.e., "ability to discern the most suitable, politic, or profitable course of action."[135]. Thus, a vast disparity exists between *fronēsis* and *prudence*, and respectively between rationality and reason. Hence, if the tradition of hermeneutics refers to the former, as the premise of its existence and development, it may be assumed that either jurisprudence is one of few practices which are still focused on internal goods, or this is not the case any more, due to the fact that, "it is within one specific kind of context that the intellectual and moral virtues of human beings characteristically have to be exercised and that apart from certain features of that kind of social context the concept of those virtues must for the most part lack application."[136] To solve this dilemma we may use the critical[137] and reflectively

---

132 *Ibidem*, p. 193.

133 See H.-G. Gadamer, *Truth and Method*, New York 2004, pp. 309 ff.

134 A. MacIntyre, *Whose Justice…*, pp. 97-98, 119.

135 *Ibidem*, pp. 196, 276.

136 *Ibidem*, p. 99; Cf. possibility of the so-called liberal virtues: R. Piekarski, "Cnoty polityczne a praworządność", ["Political Virtues and the Rule of Law"], in: *Etyka a praworządność i prawo*, ed. J. Pawlica, Kraków 1998, pp. 97-102.

137 Regarding Habermas's claim about the necessary complementation of the hermeneutical approach with critical reasoning, see M. Zirk-Sadowski, "Postmodernistyczna jurysprudencja?" ["Postmodern Jurisprudence?"], in: *Z zagadnień teorii i filozofii prawa. Ponowoczesność,* ed. M. Błachut, Wrocław 2007, p. 14.

validated standard conveyed by the responsibility principle, regarded as a principle of post-traditional and rational morality[138].

3.6.2. The good of practice as the object of responsibility

What is this constant element that allows people living in different eras, cultures, and legal orders, practising different professions, to be distinguished as lawyers? As it has been repeatedly mentioned in the multi-dimensional legal ethics theory, this element consists of the principle of responsibility, which enables the formation of professional roles of lawyers within specified limits, adding new goals and values, necessary in terms of trust to lawyers and their integrity, as well as the consequent definition of professional obligations through the procedure of little universalisation. A more precise description and validation of the principle of responsibility may be obtained from several perspectives, representing two major groups. The former refers to psychology, sociology, and anthropology, whereas the other, followed by the multi-dimensional legal ethics theory, deals with these questions from the perspective of various philosophical disciplines, in particular the philosophy of morality with regards to formal questions, and the philosophy of law with regards to substantial questions.

Regarding reflection within the former perspective, a starting point could be the previously discussed notion of "impeccable character", required from legal professionals. Devising a catalogue of mental qualities necessary to practise a legal profession and relating it to social expectations could be inspiring; yet it would entail a number of disadvantages. First of all, in the light of the assumptions of the above mentioned disciplines, in particular those regarding the evolving character of their subjects, the possibility of validating professional roles of lawyers as the source of professional obligations, seems problematic. This is due to the fact that these disciplines are usually based on functional-systemic factors; hence the moral element in all professions could only be general, but not universal. Thus, the very distinction between constant and variable elements would lose sense, as the entire model of a given professional role would be based on variable factors.

138 A similar discussion would be possible with regards to the other virtues, especially justice which has evolved in a similar way. See Ch. Perelman, *O sprawiedliwości* [*On Justice*], Warsaw 1959. Cf. P. Skuczyński, "Czy sprawiedliwość jest cnotą prawników?", ["Is Justice a Virtue of Lawyers?"], in: *Rozdroża sprawiedliwości we współczesnej myśli filozoficznoprawnej,* ed. B. Wojciechowski, M. J. Golecki, Toruń 2008.

Consequently, if this perspective was considered exclusive, the thesis stating the normative character of legal ethics would be difficult to defend, or at least the accusations of its extreme relativism would be difficult to refute. This is due to the fact that if one cannot name any rational limitations to goals and values of lawyers' professional roles, then, even provided the conditions of the little universalisation test with regards to professional obligations are met, excessive and unjustified inclusion of social expectations or interests of lawyers is possible, which means ideologisation understood in this or another way. This kind of danger may be avoided only through the critical theory of legal ethics, in particular through its moral plane, which entails the responsibility principle, and refers to the reflective validation procedure.

From this perspective, one cannot ignore the reservations related to unequal treatment based on personal qualities. Naturally, psychological tests tend to be used for recruitment purposes by various services; yet, their application should have a limited scope and firm grounds. It should be noted that to avoid certain negative psychological mechanisms, such as being guided by stereotypes and prejudice, or the so-called dispersion of responsibility, a model of judicial training is proposed, which emphasises, "on the one hand practical training supervised by a patron, and on the other hand working on one's personal development, aimed at acquiring 'self-knowledge' rater than 'knowledge in itself", which means a deeper understanding of one's values, one's professional style, and of oneself in relation to the part of social culture which concerns the notion of justice, law, and performing the judicial profession."[139] Hence, it may be claimed that even within the discussed perspective, assuming responsibility by lawyers is related to their reflective attitude.

Nonetheless, the philosophical perspective is not free of serious difficulties, either. It should be noted that the discussion regarding professional ethics reached a serious deadlock at a certain point. This is for instance reflected by the following remark: "If we assumed that this [ethics – P.S.] is the ontology of moral being, i.e. a kind of human knowledge which is based on the understanding of the essence of this being, its structure and transcendental conditions; thus, it is purely philosophical knowledge, then the so-called professional ethics, which should be rather called professional morality theory, is quite distant from it. Ethics as ontology, as eidetics, is neither normative, nor practistic, nor assessing. Yet, it remains the premise for all kinds of reflection on the moral nature of human behaviour."[140] Despite the earlier claim that legal ethics will never provide

139 T. Romer, M. Najda, *Etyka dla sędziów. Rozważania*, [*Judicial Ethics. Reflections*], Warsaw 2007, p. 132.

140 B. Skarga, "Podsumowanie" ["Recapitulation"], *in: Wokół etyki zawodowej. Dyskusja redakcyjna*, *Etyka* 1994, no. 27, pp. 204-205.

significant inspiration to the philosophy of morality in this sense but it may inspire the philosophy of law[141], the inclusion of the responsibility principle in the legal ethics theory gives way to multidirectional inspirations.

In the broadest sense, responsibility is a relationship which determines who is responsible, for what, and before whom; it determines normative consequences of fulfilling or breaching obligations[142]. One can be responsible before God, conscience, government, or before all people; whereby, from the moral point of view, the latter seems the most significant. It connects the issue of validation with the inherent universality of this sphere, because if moral responsibility is regarded as the obligation of all community members, the consequence is a universal obligation of justification in terms of the discourse ethics. Nevertheless, even in such a case, one must not forget about the ambiguity of the notion of morality, which means on one hand individual moral beliefs and individual ethos, and, on the other hand, socially institutionalised system of moral rules and principles. The relationship of the two meanings is immanently essential and functional, but, as a consequence, all moral theories are characterised with inherent tension between the requirements of moral autonomy and social coordination[143]. This tension is also present in the multi-dimensional legal ethics theory; however, it may be mitigated by means of the reflectively validated principle of responsibility.

To start with, "we always appear in a world which is a stage and are recognized according to the roles which our professions assign us, as physicians or lawyers [...], and so on," but our existence as moral beings starts before our social roles[144]. As far as professional ethics is concerned, in particular legal ethics, very often a phenomenon occurs, which was noticed by both Niccolò Machiavelli and Jean Jacques Rousseau, despite their different attitudes in this respect; namely the phenomenon in which living in a society and the consequent social roles necessitate the rejection of morality. Thus, unwillinness to make moral judgements arises in the society, behind which, "lurks the suspicion that no one is a free agent, and hence the doubt that anyone is responsible or could be expected to answer for what he has done." In particular, it is, "well-known that there exists hardly a walk of life in which you'll find people as wary and suspicious of moral standards, even ofe standards of justice, as in the legal profession."[145]

141 P. Skuczyński, "Wieloznaczność... " ["Ambiguity..."], p. 120.

142 O. Weinberger, "Moral zwischen Autonomie und Heteronomie", in: *Öffentliche oder private Moral? Vom Geltungsgrunde und der Legitimität des Rechts. Festschrift für Ernesto Garzón Valdés,* ed. W. Krawietz, G.H. von Wright, Berlin 1992, p. 252.

143 *Ibidem*, pp. 257-258.

144 H. Arendt, *Responsibility and Judgement*, New York 2003, p. 13.

145 *Ibidem,* pp. 19, 57.

Therefore, considerable tension exists between reflectively and socially validated moralities, the latter being related to professional roles. This tension results in the creation of professional ethics on one hand, and disciplinary mechanisms of responsibility on the other. The above mentioned connections between both types of responsibility have been changing over history, whereby their modern context seems significant insofar as the post-traditional morality, seeking to reduce the tension, must face specific problems of the contemporary times. First of all, it has been noted that morality tends to be regarded as a negative principle, i.e. one which excludes certain actions and imposes sanctions if one fails to comply with social and political systems that may even be brutal yet without requiring positive actions. Hence, people prefer to suffer rather than act, which is irresponsible from the perspective of the world[146]. Regarding lawyers who cannot accept the imposed requirements of professional roles, the fulfilment of which they consider irresponsible, this interpretation of responsibility principle offers them only one solution, i.e. withdrawing from the profession, thus in fact rejecting responsibility.

Whereas from the historic point of view, at the times when the representative type of the public sphere was dominant, lawyers bore responsibility due to representing an entity – justice, monarch, etc. "The staging of the publicity involved in representation was wedded to personal attributes such as insignia (badges and arms), dress (clothing and coiffure), demeanor (form of greeting and poise) and rhetoric (form of address and formal discourse in general) – in a word, to a strict code of 'noble' conduct."[147] To this day, the lawyer-client relationship is described with the term "representation", and a number of the above described rituals, such as gowns, wigs, or the famous image of Themis as a blindfolded woman with typical attributes, are present in the modern system of justice. Yet, this type of public sphere entails a purely social understanding of the responsibility principle.

In the formation process of the civil public sphere, "along with the apparatus of the modern state, a new stratum of 'bourgeois' people arose which occupied a central position within the 'public.' The officials of the rulers' administration were its core – mostly jurists (at least on the continent, where the technique of the received Roman law was adopted as an instrument for the rationalization of social organization)."[148] The institutional core of the civil society, which is related to this type of public sphere, is constituted by professional associations,

146 *Ibidem*.

147 J. Habermas, *Structural Transformation of the Public Sphere,* Cambridge Massachusetts 1993, p. 8.

148 *Ibidem*, p. 23.

naturally including the legal ones. In addition, responsible action means methodically taking a verifying perspective towards one's own action, a perspective of an expert, of the generalized self and one's own self simultaneously, thus determining the value of the action criteria in the substantial, social, and temporal terms[149]. Consequently, both meanings of moral responsibility emerge, which may be however reconciled by means of the critical discourses within the public sphere.

The modern disintegration of the civil public sphere in the above sense and the civil society crisis, noted since late 1800s, have several causes and symptoms. First of all, we should mention blurring the division between the state and society in welfare states, which entails the disintegration of privacy into family intimacy and the public sphere of work and profession. Other symptoms include shifting from the debate on literature to the consumption of cultural goods, and from journalism to the media industry, as well as reducing political behaviour to elections[150]. Consequently, society as regarded in the Hegelian terms is gradually engulfed by the state, and similarly social relations are colonised by the law. The techniques of regulation change, whereas, "The affairs requiring normative regulation now also comprise social conditions in the narrower sense; hence they are concrete, that is, they involve specific groups of persons and transitory situations."[151] This description seems to adequately describe the process of legal ethics juridisation, which implies the return to the dominance of responsibility in social terms. Yet, lawyers do not represent significant, e.g. social, entities any more; on the contrary, they are autonomous moral entities themselves.

Restoring the lawyers' lost position as civil society leaders is difficult, insofar as the chief values of professional roles usually consists in neutral and non-activist maintenance of the practice, which is based on social mechanisms of responsibility, formalised through mechanisms of legal responsibility, to which they are subject. From this perspective, therefore, all attempts to transform the notion of responsibility into a moral principle could be regarded as irresponsible. This deadlock may, and often does, create a sense of hopelessness and pessimism among lawyers, consequently leading either to withdrawal or cynicism. It is not surprising, given the fact that in this case authentic self-realisation, which always involves a sense of moral perfection, may occur outside professional life naturally only if it is possible to meet the requirements

149 C. Offe, "Bindung, Fessel, Bremse. Die Unübersichtlichkeit von Selbstbeschränkrugsforme", in: *Zwischenbetrachtungen. Im Prozeß der Aufklärung*, ed. A. Honneth, T. MacCarthy, C. Offe, A. Welmer, Frankfurt am Main 1989, p. 758.

150 J. Habermas, *Structural...*, chapters 5 and 6.

151 *Ibidem*, p. 178.

of the integrity principle within the social plane. Enabling it within the profession is another argument for the inclusion of the moral principle of responsibility in the multi-dimensional legal ethics theory.

Responsibility, even regarded solely as the issue of social courts, is characterised by a number of specific qualities in the modern world. First of all it should be noted that there are two basic premises for responsibility: the factual, or causal, and the moral one. They tend to be respectively referred to as "causing" and "answerability."[152] The dynamic technical progress and increasing interdependence result in the broadening of the former notion. Therefore, radical and, in a sense, utopian suggestions have arisen that the latter should also be extended to encompass the entire world and the future generations, for the sake of collective responsibility in the existential sense, thus eliminating environmental threats of the technological civilisation[153]. Nonetheless, this has been refuted by opponents who have claimed that considering the respective Kantian distinction between *causa naturalis* and *causa moralis*, the concept in which extending the former results in the extension of the latter, cannot be regarded as reasonable. Responsibility regarded as *causa moralis* must be individual, and as such it is subject to social differentiation as the so-called role-responsibility, whereby responsibility is reduced to duties related to his or her "distinctive place or office in a social organization" [154].

Even if from the analytical point of view, the above reasoning may lead to the conclusion that the essence of responsibility is unknown and only its conditions may be determined, the search for these conditions is extremely interesting. In fact, the notion of formalised legal responsibility, i.e. liability, entails the presupposition of the non-formalised notion of moral responsibility, i.e. accountability. It has been assumed that having realised this presupposition Kant included it in the notion of *imputatio* and in the broader approach to the relationship between law and morality[155]. Hence, in order to overcome the limitations of the analytical philosophy, it may be analysed through critical theories from the perspective of the transformation of Kantianism, in the light of the linguistic turn in philosophy and the respective communicative approaches.

---

152 W. Krawietz, "Moral versus Legal Responsibility? Different Motives and Models for Attributing Rights and Duties", in: *Öffentliche oder privat...*, ed. W. Krawietz, G.H. von Wright, Berlin 1992, p. 45.

153 H. Jonas, *The Imperative of Responsibility: In Search of Ethics for the Technological Age*, Chicago 1984; See also H. Jonas, "Teoria odpowiedzialności: pierwsze rozróżnienia", ["The Imperative of Responsibility: first distinctions"], *Znak* 1995, no. 10, pp. 74-84.

154 W. Krawietz, "Moral versus...", pp. 49-50.

155 *Ibidem*, p. 52-53.

The concept of transforming the Kantian philosophy is significant inasmuch as a number of modern problems genetically derive from the Enlightenment[156]. In particular this refers to the following paradox: never has ethics of responsibility and its inherent solidarity been so in demand, and at the same time never has such ethical crisis of validation occurred due to the fact that rationality has been monopolised by science. On one hand, ethics of responsibility is a Weberian notion which was subsequently applied by existentialism and situational ethics, in the sense of a responsible choice of values in the former case, and of one's own humanity in the latter. In this approach, the only limit to individual freedom is self-limiting, which cannot be rationally validated[157]. On the other hand, the critics of the Kantian approach, in particular Hegel, claimed that the entire structure of morality is based on the metaphysical "fact of reason" and as such it cannot answer radical critical questions: why be moral and why be rational?[158] According to Hegel, the only common ground of unlimited freedom and universal law is the sphere of ethicality – a specific social entity, which mediates the two categories, within the current development stage of the objective rationality[159].

However, according to Karl-Otto Apel, the fact of reason, "is not an empirical (or anthropological) fact, but a necessarily recognised, basic principle of ethics." It is a regulative principle and as such it cannot be fully realised; hence, no social entity, such as the structure of professional roles may constitute its source nor, consequently, a criterion of its action[160]. According to the author, between Scylla of existentialist freedom and Charybdis of solidarity forced by means of totalitarian methods, there is a third way which assumes validation of morality as the basic principle of reason. It may only be accomplished through reflection as a special procedure of self-reference, regarded, however, not as an act of consciousness, but as an act of communication. Using the issue of

156 Cf. A.M. Kaniowski, "Etyka a transcendentalizm w perspektywie kantowskiej i pragmatyczno-językowej", ["Ethics and Transcendentalism from the Kantian and Pragmatic-Linguistic Perspectives"], in: *Filozofia transcendentalna a dialektyka*, ed. M. Siemek, Warsaw 1994, p. 300 ff.

157 K.-O. Apel, "Die Konflikte unserer Zeit und das Erfordernis einer etisch-politischen Grundorientierung," in: *Idem*, *Diskurs und Verantwortung. Das Problem des Übergangs zur postkonventionellen Moral*, Frankfurt am Main 1988, pp. 16, 23. See also *idem*, "Uniwersalistyczna etyka współodpowiedzialności", [Universalistic Ethics of Co-Responsibility], *in: Idea etyczności globalnej*, ed. J. Sekuła, Siedlce 1999, p. 172 ff.

158 K.-O. Apel, "Der postkantische Universalismus in der Ethik im Lichte seiner aktuellen Mißverständnisse", in: *ibidem*, pp. 166, 173.

159 K.-O. Apel, "Kant, Hegel und das aktuelle Problem der normativen Grundlagen von Moral und Recht", in: *ibidem*, p. 83.

160 *Ibidem*, pp. 99-101.

knowledge as the starting point, the author claims that, on one hand, the objectivity of knowledge overlaps with freedom and responsibility[161]; however, on the other hand, the transcendental deduction of the cognition conditions is posterior, in terms of methodology, to the issue of pre-communicative validity of arguments[162].

This means that the principle of responsibility as a moral principle may only be validated through reflective research into argumentation processes. According to transcendental pragmatics, the arguers' statements always display a dichotomous, both performative and propositional, structure where the first element is pragmatic whereas the other is referential and semantic. Assigning values, such as true or false, to the latter is only possible due to the adequate performative approach both of the arguer and of other participants of communication who recognise the argument. Reflective research of such statements results in the conclusion that propositional and performative elements cannot be contradictory, which has been described by Jakko Hintikka as performative contradiction. Thus, one cannot say, 'I am not bound by the rules of argumentation,' without contradiction, because the performative element of this statement assumes the existence of the argumentation rules. In other words, one cannot reasonably argue against argumentation, disregarding its rules. Hence, rejecting these rules will only problematise, but not ultimately invalidate the rules[163].

Normative character of the validity criteria of argumentation means that reflection in transcendental pragmatics, unlike in the philosophy of consciousness, results in the unity of practical and theoretical reason, because the issue is not the transcendental unity of subject-object relationships (self-awareness and the awareness of objects), but the unity of several subjects of communication (intersubjectivity)[164]. This serves as foundation for Karl-Otto Apel's discourse ethics, which binds all participants of communication by means of inviolable presuppositions of their statements, comprised in four rules. First, if we really want to acquire knowledge or solve a problem, we should try to achieve it through rational argumentation. Second, we should then endeavour after a rational consensus on the solution. Third, every time the interests are contradictory, we should strive to reach a rational consensus between the stakeholders. Fourth, we

161 K.-O. Apel, "Die Konflikte...", pp. 30-34.

162 K.-O. Apel,, "Kant, Hegel...", p. 97.

163 B. Sierocka, *Krytyka...*, p. 75.

164 K.-O. Apel, "Kant, Hegel...", p. 98. See also K.-O. Apel, "Wspólnota komunikacyjna jako transcendentalne założenie nauk społecznych", ["Communication Community as Transcendental Premise of Social Science"], in: *Kultura współczesna. Teoria-Interpretacje-Krytyka*, ed. A. Zeidler-Janiszewska, Warsaw 1993, pp. 5-12.

must invariably endeavour to support the creation of the ideal communication community and to improve the conditions of its realisation[165].

Thus regarded and validated discourse ethics has a purely formal character and is not, "meant specifically for argumentative discourses, but it is ethics of loyal responsibility of those who are able to argue for others, with regards to all the problems that can only be subject to discourse." Consequently, it leaves specific values and norms to specific practical discourses[166]. Therefore, e.g. by indicating goals and values central to professional roles of lawyers as well as the respective professional obligations, the principles of the discourse ethics only determine inviolable formal limits of argumentation regarding these elements. Hence, the discourse ethics as such is dichotomous; the higher plane validates formal argumentation rules, and the lower includes practical discourses which validate material goals and values. As a result, it may annex the principles of other ethical theories, such as the utilitarian maximisation of certain interests, and at the same time respect the equality of all interests, which are regarded as participants of the discourse[167].

Based on the above discussion, we may claim that the mission of the modern philosophy of morality consists not so much "in suggesting norms adequate to specific situations, but rather in analysing normative conditions of the organisation of collective responsibility at various possible planes of the practical discourse,"[168] as endeavoured by the multi-dimensional legal ethics theory. However, to achieve it, the discourse ethics, as the ethics of responsibility, or the post-Kantian ethics of principles, must prove its post-metaphysical character, and thus solve the problem of its applicability. In fact, so far it has only partly succeeded in escaping the above charges[169]. With this end in view, the notion of communication community and the aforementioned distinction of its ideal and real types are analysed. Due to the fact that discourse ethics is universal, the consensus reached must also meet the criteria of the universalisation procedure. As described by Habermas, it is applied under

---

165 B. Sierocka, *Krytyka...*, pp. 5-12.

166 K.-O. Apel, "Kann der postkantische Standpunkt der Moralität noch einmal in substantielle Sittlichkeit ›aufgehoben‹ werden? Das geschichtsbezogene Anwendungsproblem der Diskursethik zwischen Utopie und Regression", in: *Diskurs...*, pp. 116-117, 120.

167 K.-O. Apel, "Diskursethik als Verantwortungsethik und das Problem der ökonomischen Rationalität, in: *Diskurs...*, pp. 271-273.

168 K.-O. Apel, "Verantwortung heute – nur noch Prinzip der Bewahrung und Selbstbeschränkung oder immer noch Befreiung und Verwilklichung von Humanität?", in: *Diskurs...*, p. 212.

169 K.-O. Apel, *Kann der postkantische...*, p. 110.

the assumption that the real communication community is the only existing, and the closer it is to the ideal communication, the more its participants may regard themselves as "the citizens of the world." Yet, it is taken into account that there are a number of deficits, such as those of trust or information; hence, a universal perspective itself cannot ensure the improved quality of communication.

Another mistake is made by supporters of the responsibility principle, such as Hans Jonas, with the concept of macro-responsibility, or Arnold Gehlen, with that of role-responsibility[170]. Hans Jonas cites the Aristotelian ontology; thus his ethics is not post-metaphysical and as such it may be criticised as invalid. Naturally, one may attempt to build ethical theories with Aristotelian spirit and at the same time rejecting the Aristotelian ontology, based solely on the social distinction between roles and *fronesis*. However, this is a dubious concept because first, it fails to solve validity problems, and second, as already indicated, responsibility reduced to social roles must be based on control mechanisms rather than on practical intelligence. Last but not least, a more general accusation regards the fact that responsibility reduced merely to the performed social role does not rank highest among possible stages of moral development, arranged in the order of evolution[171]. Thus, even if only for the reason that more advanced theories are conceivable, we should make an effort to develop them.

Lawrence Kohlberg's moral development theory distinguishes six stages thereof. They can be arranged in the following way: pre-conventional stages, where moral behaviour is driven by mechanisms such as mimetic imitation or naïve exchange; conventional, where behaviour results from role-taking, or from the position within the social structure and legalistic tendency to maintain law and order. Finally, with post-conventional stages, the chief motive consists in universal rights and maximising benefits; thus implying a moral, impartial perspective[172]. Therefore, the discussed theories are part of the conventional level, whereas the discourse ethics, which belongs to the realm of moral autonomy in the Kantian terms, certainly lies at the post-conventional level. It may also be noted that Habermas suggested that a seventh stage be distinguished, where universalisation is not a thought experiment but rather it means understanding and agreement of free individuals as members of the world society. Thus, this is still a kind of the power of judgment, and the concept was subsequently accepted by Kohlberg in his later studies[173].

---

170 *Ibidem*, p. 108.

171 K.-O. Apel, *Verantwortung heute...*, pp. 187-189.

172 K.-O. Apel, "Die tranzendentalpragmatische Begründung der Kommunikationsethik und das Problem der höchsten Stufe einer Entwicklungslogik des moralischen Bewußtseins", in: *Diskurs…*, pp. 317-328.

173 *Ibidem*, pp. 342-345.

According to Karl-Otto Apel, the principle of responsibility implies even deeper morality, which is however possible only under the assumption that the ideal communication community exists. At the seventh, highest, stage of moral development, individuals should pursue the ideal communication community constantly and progressively through the real communicative acts. It is their obligation derived from the responsibility principle, which links the power of judgement with the reality and historicity of the human condition[174]. The argumentation should distinguish the ideal and real communities, but at the same time, it should anticipate the former by the responsible support and correction of the latter[175]. Thus, the ideal communication community is a *sui generis* meta-institution or an *a priori* communicative entity, which legitimises real institutions. The relationship between the two manifests responsible support and development of the real community[176]. The distinction between these communities and their mediation through the principle of responsibility result in the need of taking any additional circumstances into account, such as deficits of trust or information, or at least assume or anticipate them, during universalization[177].

The principle of responsibility links not only the discourse ethics of the ideal communication community with discourses of the real community, but also two parts of ethics: A and B; whereby the former represents formal and reflectively validated discourse ethics, and the latter constitutes the normative ethics devised over history[178]. The responsibility principle validates and necessitates normative ethics insofar as it falls within the principle's limits. Due to the inclusion of the responsibility principle thus regarded, in its supreme, moral, plane, the multi-dimensional legal ethics theory meets the conditions of a critical and reflective theory. Specifically, it meets the criteria of the former by allowing the research into professional roles of lawyers, their professional obligations, and individual actions by controlling the degree to which they support and pursue the communication community, or in other words, the degree to which they render it

---

174 *Ibidem*, pp. 368-369. See also K.-O. Apel, "Etyka dyskursu jako etyka odpowiedzialności – postmetafizyczna transformacja etyki Kanta", ["Discourse Ethics as Ethics of Responsibility – Kantian Ethics Post-Metaphysical Transformation"], *Principia* 1992, no. 5, p. 16 ff.

175 K.-O. Apel, *Kann der postkantische...*, p. 141.

176 K.-O. Apel, "Die Konflikte...", pp. 37-39. See also *Idem*, "Das Apriori der Kommunikationsgemeinschaft und die Grundlagen der Ethik", in: *idem*, *Transformation der Philosophie, Band II, Das Apriori der Kommunikationsgemeinschaft*, Frankfurt am Main 1973, p. 358 ff.

177 K.-O. Apel, *Kann der postkantische....*, pp. 127-129.

178 *Ibidem*, pp. 141-143.

more rational. Regarding the criteria of the latter, the responsibility principle and the contents of other planes of the theory become validated through a reflective procedure; furthermore, critical research into professional roles and obligations of lawyers from the perspective of the responsibility principle implies also the research into practical effects of the theory itself, and consequently results in the development of its criteria.

It should also be noted that the strong distinction between the ethics of values and the deontological ethics becomes purely analytic due to the responsibility principle and its presence in all parts of normative ethics[179]. Thus, the distinction is significant only insofar as one needs to conceptualise this relationship. This is achieved by the multi-dimensional legal ethics theory by placing obligations in the pragmatic sphere, whereas goals and values in the ethical one. This is based on the generality level and the direction of the validation procedure. Yet, if an effort was made to devise a different approach, it would have to equally consider the responsibility principle as its moral basis. Therefore, legal ethics is the ethics of responsibility, whose subject is the good of the discourse itself and of the community where it takes place. Hence, participation in legal practice implies the assumption of responsibility for the practice, as well as the obligation to act for its good. At the same time, the rule of the responsibility for the discourse draws inviolable limits to activism and restraint, demanding activism when the discourse is endangered, in particular due to discrimination excluding some of its participants or their arguments; whereas in other cases restraint, conforming with social expectations, is required.

Concluding, we should ask whether lawyers' responsibly in the social sense, i.e. disciplinary responsibility as established in most contemporary countries including Poland, meets the requirements of the responsibility principle in the moral sense. This modern form of disciplinary responsibility assumes that the moral principle of responsibility should not be forced through sanctions; otherwise it loses its moral character. In addition, disciplinary sanctions should be reduced to stigmatising the violation of specific professional obligations, whereas their content should be determined by various discourses, thus considering other planes of the legal ethics theory; however, it is not subject to disciplinary discourses. Consequently, disciplinary responsibility must primarily perform repressive functions, thus providing simply a social control mechanism, balancing individual freedom and social protection, similar to penal

179 *Ibidem*, pp. 146-147.

responsibility[180]. The fact of being a moral entity is a source of e.g. freedom and intentionality of action, which not only may be used to verify the possibility of an action, but are also significant *per se*. Nevertheless, due to the ambiguity thereof, responsibility should rather be based on, "what a certain sort of agent did and how he did it then on the possibility of his having acted otherwise".[181]

This perspective tends to be criticised due to the fact that through the mechanism of disciplinary responsibility, "like criminal justice, the profession regulates wrongdoing but not competence. The punishment of wrongdoing does give the appearance of an attempt at self-regulation [...] however, the expectancy of regulation are somewhat higher. The profession must at least respond to this expectancy that the profession police itself," hence it is in fact able to assume responsibility, even if only for itself. The notion of responsibility should, therefore, be extended in order for its mechanisms to link their inputs and outputs, whereby, “the inputs are client complaints which are primarily concerned with performance-matters of competence, diligence, and applied skill. But the inputs are discounted because disciplinary agencies, and perhaps the profession as a whole, believe clients are unable to discern the proper or meaningful elements of practice of the law. Thus the outputs tend to presume that the complaints may rise only issues of lawyer misconduct or moral deviance."[182] In the absence of the extended disciplinary responsibility, significant elements of professionalism are doomed to extinction.

However, the above proposed extension must consider the special character of respective regulations, which necessitate the separation of the two initial adjudicative stages. The first one involves determining if the act is qualified as delinquency or disciplinary infraction, and the second requires and an adequate sanction to be imposed. The former is based on underdetermined notions, which refer to evaluation (professional dignity) or norms (ethical principles), whereas the latter is performed on a discretionary basis, which means two entirely different regulatory techniques. So elevated a level of freedom of disciplinary authorities should manifest a dichotomous function: first, to eliminate the abuse of disciplinary responsibility with regards to its subjects, and second, to eliminate its abuse with regards to the entire society. Both aspects may be found

180 See P. Skuczyński, "Granice...", and A. Bojańczyk, "Z problematyki relacji między odpowiedzialnością dyscyplinarną i karną", ["Problems of the Relationship of Disciplinary and Penal Responsibility"], (the example of legal professions disciplinary responsibility), *Państwo i Prawo* 2004, no. 9.

181 J.L. Mackie, "The Grounds of Responsibility", in: *Law, Morality and Society. Essays in Honour of H.L.A. Hart*, ed. P.M.S. Hacker, J. Raz, Oxford 1977, pp. 185-188.

182 A.I. Kaufman, *Problems in Professional Responsibility*, Boston-Toronto 1976, pp. 538, 542-544.

in the function which we call integrative. On the formal side, it consists in ensuring coherent practice of the given profession, whereby it should not be interpreted as a kind of mechanical and dehumanised unification of attitudes, which anyway would be unacceptable in a constitutional state[183].

It seems more appropriate to regard disciplinary responsibility as a limitation to diversity and arbitrariness of practicing legal professions and performing functions due to their goals and values. This may be achieved by using the multi-dimensional legal ethics theory to assess specific acts, which would involve not only verifying the violation of professional obligations presented by professional codes of ethics, but also subjecting them to procedures at all the theory planes, i.e. little universalisation test, considering the trust and integrity principles, as well as ultimate validation and critical verification through the responsibility principle in the moral sense. It should be noted that disciplinary authorities seem to be equipped with relatively mild measures, such as admonition, which is persuasive rather than repressive. An explicit use of these tools for the sake of integration and not repression may not only constitute a method of moving disciplinary mechanisms closer to the responsibility principle, but it may also be interpreted as a responsible approach to the professional association of lawyers with the respective institutions, which act as intermediaries in supporting and developing the legal practice.

3.7. Conclusions: multi-dimensional theory of legal ethics and methodology

The above presentation shows the multi-dimensional theory of legal ethics as a theory that, because it is formulated on the gounds of philosophy of morality, may be applied also to professional ethics outside the sphere of law. This theory, on one hand, based on the "legal ethics" term's ambiguity, does not try to remove it but tries to use in constructing the subject of legal ethics as composed of three planes – deontological, social and moral – corresponding with three basic senses of the term. On the other hand, multi-dimensional theory of legal ethics, by being guided by the requirements of a critical theory, views the relations between particular planes as reflective validation and critical limitation. On the highest plane, the theory is validated by reference to reflection as a procedure of transcendental pragmatics for validation of all normative ethics. Therefore, on the moral plane of legal ethics, the principle of lawyers' responsibility for law as social practice has been formed.

183 See broader on this issue: P. Skuczyński, "Granice...", pp. 19-20.

Legal ethics status in the multi-dimensional perspective may be described as professional ethics which rationally validates the professional duties of lawyers as well as goals and values of particular legal professional roles through reference to the universal power of judgement related to the moral principle of responsibility. Such a perspective agrees with classical views on professional ethics, which is usually defined as bodies of moral norms and values adjusting their universal moral standards to the specificity of a given profession. Assuming that the moral principle of responsibility for social practice, in which a given individual participates, is of universal nature, then multi-dimensional theory of legal ethics indicates the premises and means of this "adjustment", both on the plane of end and values central to each professional role, and also on the plane of specific professional duties. The theory, because of its reflective and critical structure, may validate and limit argumentation in this matter.

A multi-dimensional theory of legal ethics has the nature of a critical ethical theory, and thus it contains primarily theses from the scope of meta-ethics. Of course, by references to particular professional duties and some principles, especially the responsibility principle, some elements of descriptive and normative ethics also fall within the scope of the theory. However, these elements are auxiliary by nature, and serve one critical goal, namely the analysis and assessment of the language and argumentations referring to legal ethics. A theory thus formed undeniably has a general and formal character, and so it may be widely applied – not only to ethics of various legal professions but also, *mutatis mutandis*, to professional ethics of other professions. For it seems that the universality of the moral responsibility principle and of its relation to goals and values central to professional roles and duties enables one to speak of a wide range of a theory based on them. However, both in regards to ethics of legal professions and other professions, multi-dimensional theory may have various functions.

Firstly, as a critical analysis of the language and argumentations in legal ethics it may be applied in practice, and, according to assumptions of the critical theory, such an application will translate into advancement of theory as well as of practice. Thus, the multi-dimensional theory may be useful in for the resolution of each individual dilemma which a lawyer may encounter in his or her work as well as of problems before groups of lawyers – groups including lawyers collaborating on a particular case, running one law office or working in one law firm, but also entire legal professions and communities. By using the multi-dimensional theory of legal ethics one may search for solutions in particular cases, but also assess the content of codes of professional ethics, supplement them with new professional duties, or plan completely new acts in this regard. It appears that, because of this, multi-dimensional theory may be useful in resolving problems resulting from the convergence of professional deontology standards.

A multi-dimensional theory of legal ethics may also serve as an instrument of systematic study in this field. Without determining here what status this study would have, to what extent it should be distinguished in legal sciences as a separate discipline with its own research program, and the degree to which this program would be interdisciplinary, it has to be observed that the theory offers a methodology which allows formulation of particular ethics of legal professions. The methodology enables ordering and critical analysis of professional duties and of adjudication based on them, by referring to goals and values central to every legal professional role. This would mean that particular groups of duties may be related to professional roles, and these, in turn, serve the formation of professions as such. It seems noteworthy that these goals and values may be ordered according to values' categories, thus, for example, the principle of loyalty, as regards roles of the defence, means the client's interest is central, whereas the principle of impartiality contains central goals and values of judicial roles. Naturally, the study must include also the principle of responsibility.

Chapter 4
Legal ethics and some theoretical models of law

4.1. Preliminary remarks

On its highest plane, legal ethics is the ethics of responsibility. Because of this, the professional roles of lawyers may be validly formed on the basis of goals and values, which in turn provide a foundation for the formulation of professional duties. Due to reflective validity of the responsibility principle, its subject is the good of the argumentative discourse itself and of the community in which it is held. In consequence, mere participation in legal practice means taking responsibility for it and accepting the obligation of acting for its good. However, such a view raises some doubts, namely about the extent to which the concepts of discourse and community are connected with the concept of practice; thus firstly, does adoption of the responsibility principle validated in the aforementioned way exact simultaneous adoption of a defined conception of law, i.e. of some version of a discursive view? Secondly, do currently predominant views of law as practice include, more or less *implicite*, some legal ethics, and if they do then what is the relationship to the multi-dimensional theory of legal ethics, and can it be interpreted and systematically examined with its categories? It seems that the answer to the second question, being a more general one, will at the same time resolve the first problem from the scope of philosophy of law. Therefore, the search for this answer will be the focus of further discussion.

This of course requires the resolution of another issue – the extent to which law is practice, is a problem of philosophy of law. At the outset it has to be clearly remarked that the concept of practice in this context may most generally be understood in the categories of language-games, as a set of activities based on rules. In this sense, practice is neither an institution nor an individual's activity, but the "community which performs practice is in possession of it."[1] In further discussion, this understanding of practice will be termed 'broad', in contrast

1 M. Paździora, "Uprzywilejowanie praktyki, czyli o tzw. zwrocie praktycznym w teorii i jego konsekwencjach",["Practice Privilege: on the So-Called Practical Turn in Theory and Its Consequences"], in: *Z zagadnień teorii i filozofii prawa. Ponowoczesność*, ed. M. Błachut, Wrocław 2007, p. 189.

with narrow understanding, referring only to the practice of applying law. Further reflections should cover such theories formulated on the grounds of philosophy of law, which for historical reasons have at least a possibility to take a position on these assumptions, namely the theories that include the achievements of the linguistic turn in philosophy. This of course does not mean that it is necessary to cut oneself off from the sources of these theories; furthermore, it may even be said that to do so is inadvisable, since reaching for classical formulations of modern theories may bring the reflections closer to a more precise identification of the nature of the responsibility principle, namely, how to understand the good of law as practice in its broad sense, meaning its maintenance and advancement.

The search for the answers to the above questions within the framework of chosen legal-philosophical conceptions requires indicating the criteria of the choice, since a choice of "currently predominant" views is imprecise. It seems that the search should also cover theories' significance in academic discussions, but also their practical importance. However, if theory is a basis of practice in the narrow sense, then one may ask, how such theory-practice relations should be included in the present analysis, which has a limited aim. For it is possible to study only theory and accept practical significance uniquely as a criterion of choice, or to study theory through practice based on it. From the point of view of the critical theory the latter way is recommended. However, one should remember that the critical and reflective theory of legal ethics is not the critical theory of law, and its aim is not a critique of views which are based on assumptions other than those of the critical theory. Hence, the following presentation will concern theories themselves and not practices based upon them. Nevertheless, this simplification must be better justified and precede the choice of such theories. The issue will be discussed as a problem of the relations between paradigms of law and its theoretical models.

4.2. Paradigms of law and its theoretical models

As has been already mentioned, it has to be remembered that a multi-dimensional theory of legal ethics as critical theory does not make law its object. It is not a critical theory of law and as such it does not aim at any disputes with various views of law. However, in regard to the characteristic of the critical perspective, the theory-practice relation, in the framework of which continuous critique of practice based on theory satisfies the requirements of critical reflection of the theory itself, one cannot exclude the fact that extensive research may also lead to critical conclusions in relation to various perspectives of law.

However, this would always be an indirect critique resulting from the fact that legal practice, which is the subject of critique from the side of legal ethics theory, corresponds with legal-philosophical conceptions. If this study assumes that conceptions of philosophy of law will be compared rather than the practices related to them, then a question arises, namely what will be the range of the conclusions arising from the reflections based on such a perspective.? In other words, to what extent does the fact that a theory of legal ethics and a theory of law refer to the same practice enable a direct dialogue between the two? This is to say, to what extent does the concept of practice, which is an object of the responsibility principle, derive from the practice's own reconstruction of reality, and to what extent may it be taken directly from a general science of law?

One may search for the answers to these questions by referring to the paradigm of law concept. The very term "paradigm" in legal sciences breeds some reservations and it is observed that it acts as a kind of conceptual stop-gap, a term that is used until some more precise terms are formulated[2]. Therefore, in this context it has to be specified. From the perspective of the present reflections it seems that the best solution is to accept the classical understanding of the term, namely as a concept referring to basic structures of scientific thought. According to Thomas S. Kuhn, who popularised the term, it suggests that, "some accepted examples of actual scientific practice—examples which include law, theory, application, and instrumentation together— provide models from which spring particular coherent traditions of scientific research."[3] One may therefore say that a paradigm covers all that, in a given society and time, goes into the development of scientific thought and enables particular research problems (which the author calls puzzles) to be resolved. When a certain paradigm becomes ineffective, it undergoes a crisis, which may result in a scientific revolution and the establishment of a new paradigm[4].

Employing a thus understood paradigm concept to legal sciences, it is pointed out that, "a paradigm, as a pattern of thought, though it is a reflection of philosophical or theoretical theses, is formed in practice, in an unpredictable (contingent) melting pot of interactions,"[5] and as such is based on authority and

---

2 R. Sarkowicz, "Uwagi o współczesnej interpretacji prawniczej", ["Remarks on the Contemporary Legal Interpretation", in: *Polska kultura prawna a proces integracji europejskiej*, ed. S. Wronkowska, Kraków 2005, p. 17.

3 T.S. Kuhn, *The Structure…*, p. 10.

4 P. Skuczyński, *Czy sprawiedliwość…*, p. 292.

5 A. Sulikowski, *Współczesny paradygmat sądownictwa konstytucyjnego wobec kryzysu nowoczesności* [*The Contemporary Paradigm of the Constitutional Judiciary in Face of Modernity Crisis*], Wrocław 2008, p. 10.

social control. Because of this the problem of identity as the concordance of human actions and their image arises.[6] In the case of lawyers, this means that, "the sense of identity of an active lawyer with his theoretical representation is shaken when, according to legal theory, a lawyer should [...] be able to resolve a legal problem by referring to the rules of a legal method, while , in reality, he or she cannot fall back upon them." These are difficult cases, comparable to extreme cases of puzzle-solving being a test of the effectiveness of every paradigm, and which may lead to a paradigm's strengthening or crisis. In regard to lawyers it is added that, "ethical virtues of a legal community are the most important standard of practice."[7]

On this basis, reconstructions of law paradigms take place through the development of various kinds of theoretical models. A considerably widely-known proposition in this matter distinguishes the model of repressive law, which is based on a close relationship between law and obligation. In this model, a motive for obeying the law is solely the fear of the sanction. Second, the model of autonomous law is distinguished, in which legal order is not that much independent from state sanction, but it becomes a means – of equal rank – of directing society. Here, law does not serve politics any more, but limits it. Finally, the model of responsive law, which is flexible and takes into consideration social needs and expectations, is based on the significant involvement of society in the processes of making and applying law, and its effectiveness does not rely on obligation but on compromise and co-operation of state actors as well as public and private ones[8]. Another proposition is the distinction between three paradigms. First, the paradigm of the bourgeois formal law based on legal a person's autonomy and on mutuality in their relations. Second, a social-welfare paradigm of materialized law, which intrudes into that sphere of autonomy especially by providing provisions for its citizens. Third, the procedural law, aiming at institutionalising the public sphere and providing for fuller participation of citizens in making and applying law[9].

---

6 J. Leszczyński, *Problem tożsamości prawnika i jego alter ego w teorii prawa* [*The Problem of a Lawyer's Identity and His Alter Ego in the Theory of Law*], in: *Z zagadnień…*, ed. M. Błachut, pp. 159-160.

7 *Ibidem*, p. 166.

8 P. Nonet, P. Selznick, *Law and Society in Transition. Towards Responsive Law*, New York-Hagerstown-San Francisco-London 1978. Cf. E. Kustra, "Współczesne próby przezwyciężania antynomii pozytywizmu prawniczego oraz prawa natury w wyjaśnieniu idei prawa" ["Contemporary Attempts at Overcoming Antynomies of Legal Positivism and Law of Nature in Explaining the Idea of Law"], in: *Teoria prawa, filozofia prawa, współczesne prawo i prawoznawstwo*, Toruń 1998, pp. 111-121.

9 J. Habermas, *Between…*, chapter IX.

Thus, the relationship between legal theory and the practices of its making does not exhaust all the relations that are important from the point of view accepted here. Furthermore, the simple theory–practice scheme should be extended to a theory–practice–theoretical model, in which legal theory – for instance, legal positivism – becomes a basis for practice in the sense of the practices of applying law, and both of them constitute a paradigm of law, which may subsequently be described and criticised with some theoretical model. Such a view allows the inclusion of the broader context in which law functions, such as, for example, the image of society more or less *implicite* contained in a given legal order – the image created for the society's own use, or the image of lawyers themselves and their moral responsibility. In other words, "adopting this observer perspective discloses those connections that, latent for the participants themselves, functionally link a legal system with its social environment – and also link it through the image legal scholars have of their society,"[10] and, *mutatis mutandis*, also through the moral context.

Therefore, if legal ethics with the moral principle of responsibility uses the concept of practice in its broad sense, then this concept should cover not only the theory and practice of applying law that constitute its paradigm, but also its reconstruction with some theoretical models. Such a broad concept of legal practice as a subject of the responsibility principle has several advantages. First of all, it allows the concept of practice used by theory of legal ethics to be endowed with a reflective character. This, consequently, allows those paradigms of law which are coherent with the multi-dimensional theory of legal ethics to be distinguished from those that are not. Thus, it enables these paradigms to be studied in the light of the present work's assumptions without limiting the choice to paradigms related to the theories of law which already meet the requirements that are a basis of a multi-dimensional theory of legal ethics, and so do not demand of these theories a reflective and critical nature. This allows both disciplines of knowledge to keep their autonomous character, which, of course, does not preclude that all theses formulated on their grounds will be reconcilable.

Secondly, within these studies, the broad understanding of legal practice allows one to reach directly to various views on law with which particular legal paradigms are connected. The affirmation of the responsibility principle's coherence with these views will be a necessary though not a sufficient condition to claim that, in a given paradigm, lawyers are responsible for legal practice. This is to say that lawyers' responsibility for practice in the broad sense makes it necessary that specific views of law, or a "theoretical image" of their own

10 *Ibidem*, p. 388.

practice in the narrow sense, will not exclude such responsibility by the strength of their assumptions. Thus, the multi-dimensional theory of legal ethics will be irreconcilable with legal theories, which make lawyers nonaccountable, and, simultaneously, the theory enables this fact to be stated. However, only a study of complete paradigms with theoretical models, namely a reflection of legal ethics in the broad sense, could ascertain the extent to which, in a given paradigm, the responsibility principle is being realised by lawyers. Although the aim of the present reflections is narrower, it is at the same time primary to such ambitious projects.

Thirdly, it allows inclusion in the discipline of legal ethics the responsibility of legal science – both of dogmatists as well as theoreticians and legal philosophers[11] – for maintaining and advancing practice not only in the sense of description and critique of applying law, but also in the sense of revealing those broader contexts and latent assumptions inherent in the paradigm of law. On one hand, this means that one may speak of a kind of supplementary – moral – justification for those disciplines, a justification which, philosophically, expresses the aforementioned thesis of Harold J. Berman on the important role of legal science in modernity discourses' formation. On the other hand, this inclusion indicates a direction in which the search for means of resolving contradictions could go, namely contradictions which may occur between the results of research in the legal ethics and legal philosophy frameworks. However, it seems that this direction would rely less on a conflict between two theories that assume different perspectives, because as such it would be difficult to resolve, and more on creating such a discourse that would enable joint, interdisciplinary, research.

In relation to adopting the broad sense of the concept of practice, while simultaneously retaining the possibility of studying particular legal theories from the perspective of legal ethics, in the following turn three views chosen on the basis of the above criteria, namely legal positivism, juriscentric perspective and discursive conceptions, will be analysed. The choice, to a significant extent, though in a modified way, is based on two theses on the evolution trends of modern law. On one hand, Lech Morawski referred to them as "law as technique" and "law as discourse." Both trends are related to certain groups of philosophical and sociological conceptions. The view of law as technique is connected primarily with the critique of legal positivism, which was to be, "a modernist rationalisation of the positivist model of law." In this trend one may point to a number of conceptions formulated by such authors as Max Weber,

11 See U.H. Schneider, "O odpowiedzialności nauki prawa" ["On the Responsibility of the Science of Law"], *Kwartalnik Prawa Prywatnego* 1993, no. 2, p. 111 ff.

American legal realists in the manner of Oliver Holmes, social engineering supporters such as Roscoe Pound, or the creator of the scientific politics of law Leon Petrażycki[12]. Law as discourse is simultaneously an alternative to legal positivism and the whole trend viewing law as technique. The quoted author includes first of all the conceptions of law as an autopoietic system, by Günther Teubner, and the communicative conception of law by Jürgen Habermas, who both, "question the positivist model of law as well as the positivist conception of legal science."[13]

On the other hand, Artur Kozak, by setting himself an ambitious goal to exceed the limitations of both legal positivism as well as Ronald Dworkin's interpretivism, distinguishes three models of legal practice, which he views in a very similar way to the one presented in this work, namely, in connection with their paradigmatic character. These models are: classical, related to theories of natural law; modern, connected with legal positivism; and juriscentric, associated with interpretivism by including it into the "internal" structure thanks to which legal culture's entities in legal practice of this kind become real[14]. It has to be observed that in both theoretical propositions, the positivist model is considered an important point of reference, and therefore further analysis will start with this theory. Although the classical model will be disregarded mainly due to its historical character, this does not mean that comparing it with theory of legal ethics cannot be inspiring[15]. The analysis will also cover models that the authors indicate as contemporary alternatives to positivism, namely the juriscentric and discursive models.

Because of the impossibility of discussing all conceptions related to these particular models, and the limited aim of the present reflections, the propositions must be modified and appropriate representatives of each must be chosen. In the first case it will be legal positivism, a choice that can be supported by several arguments. First of all, because it is, "a starting point of practically all serious attempts at reforming the law in contemporary times," and it, "created foundations for contemporary science of law."[16] Therefore, its importance is beyond doubt, a point which is not diminished by the fact that this conception is

---

12 L. Morawski, *Główne problemy współczesnej filozofii prawa. Prawo w toku przemian* [*Main Problems of the Contemporary Legal Philosophy. Law under Transformation*], Warsaw 2000, pp. 40-42.

13 *Ibidem*, p. 41.

14 A. Kozak, *Granice...*, pp. 73-74.

15 See the attempt at such a comparison in: M.Szyszkowska, "Etyka sędziego w procesie stosowania prawa", ["The Ethics of a Judge in the Process of Applying Law"], *Gazeta Sądowa* 2000, no. 9, pp. 51-52.

16 L. Morawski, *Główne...*, p. 40.

severely criticised nowadays. Secondly, legal positivism is, for the whole area of 'law as technique', an undoubted point of reference and a kind of primary theory, presenting a thesis of the social nature of law which is sometimes undermined and interpreted from various perspectives. Thirdly, what is especially significant from the point of view of the critical theory of legal ethics is that legal positivism is a conception which constitutes a doctrine of modern practice and of legal science, and thus it is a theory which corresponds with practice in the narrower sense. Therefore, legal positivism may be studied as a theory connected with a defined paradigm of law.

In the second case, a certain aspect of the integral theory of law, which shares with the proper juriscentric model the thesis that law is an interpretive entity, will be presented. However, in the juriscentric model the thesis has a more philosophical and simultaneously a more radical form. In other words, the model presupposes that one has to go beyond an intuitive, not to say common sense, concept of interpretation of the integral theory of law by accepting the deeply philosophical conception of interpretation, which has clear ontological consequences[17]. Hence, in order to discuss the relationship of legal ethics with the juriscentric model, one has to briefly present the integral theory of law as the idea to which this model, more or less consciously, refers. Juriscentrism is important from the point of view of the theory of legal ethics because it discerns the problem of the subject of collective consciousness in the case of law and acknowledges the problem of a legal community group's distinction.

In the third case, discursive views will be presented as representative. First, because this work should analyse primarily legal-philosophical views and, from this perspective, treating law as one of social systems – an approach which may be and certainly is, philosophically, not neutral – is a thesis from the scope of sociology of law. Contrary to this approach, accepting that law is of discursive nature, is *par excellence* a legal-philosophical thesis. However, it has to be remarked that this argument refers only to the choice of the subject of further reflections and does not lead in any way to the conclusion that, extending the aim of the study, it should not be conducted also in such a direction. Secondly, the analysis of discursive views is definitely a broader task than analysing only the theory of law by Habermas. However, it seems that a group of conceptions claiming that one may speak of legal discourses which use specific legal arguments is representative of this current. The concept and requirements of communicative rationality in Habermas' perspective are important elements in the evolution of these conceptions. Nevertheless, for a more complete picture one must also consider previous threads and interpretations that are different

---

17 A. Kozak, *Granice…*, p. 18.

from the author's – especially considering that they are often better known on the ground of legal philosophy.

The study of certain groups of legal-philosophical conceptions corresponding to development trends of modern law from the point of view of consistency with multi-dimensional theory of legal ethics, which is based on the principle of responsibility, even in a version limited in scope only to the chosen criteria, still leaves open the issue of choosing subjects. Legal positivism, juriscentrism and discursive views have a rich literature, both belonging to these conceptions and critical of them. Therefore, because of the limited aim of the present reflections and accepting the perspective of the most important representatives of these currents, the reflections will be subordinated to basic theses in their most classic formulations. As far as legal positivism is concerned these will be the social thesis and the separability thesis as formulated by such authors as John Austin, Herbert L.A. Hart and Joseph Raz. In the case of juriscentrism, the integral theory of law by Ronald Dworkin, treated as an introduction, and the institutional perspective of Artur Kozak. In discursive views these will be the thesis on an exemplary character of legal discourse and the special case thesis. Here, the authors cited will primarily be Chaïm Perelman and Robert Alexy. However, it is important to remark that in legal positivism these theses are linked by conjunction, regardless of the power and consequences one ascribes to them, for instance in the dispute over the so-called inclusive positivism, whereas in discursive perspectives the theses are mutually exclusive.

4.3. Legal ethics and the positivist model

4.3.1. Legal ethics of classical legal positivism

Though the term "legal positivism" is often used as an invective, it certainly is one of most vital trends of legal-philosophical thought. This assertion of Herbert Hart brings consequences for the analysis of positivism from every perspective in general and from the perspective of theory of legal ethics in particular. If thus legal positivism is a vital current of legal philosophy, then the analysis should include the views of authors who originated it as well as more contemporary works. This means that it is difficult to understand contemporary legal positivism without making a reference to its historical formulations, which even today – though developed and modified – are contained in positivists' views. According to Hart, this is true essentially for the basic thesis of Jeremy Bentham and John Austin, which is developed in many different directions, namely the thesis, "on the separation of law as it is and law as it ought to be."[18]

The command or imperative theory of law by Austin rests on a thesis that the law is made of a sovereign's commands, backed with threats of sanction. However, it would be a mistake to reduce the theory to this claim. As a student of Bentham, Austin was primarily an utilitarian and, to him, maximising human happiness was an argument for separation of law and morality on the validation level and for this separation's practical consequences. On one hand, "there are therefore two dangers between which insistence on this distinction will help us to steer: the danger that law and its authority may be dissolved in man 's conceptions of what law ought to be and the danger that the existing law may supplant morality as a final test of conduct and so escape criticism." On the other hand, the possibility of criticism is associated with the thesis that not every law is of equal value.[19] Separation of good and bad law allows one to assume that it is possible to develop law. Naturally, this is not to say that law would have to be an object of lawyers' responsibility.

However, it seems that this issue has already been considered in classical English legal positivism, which points to the existence of a special category of subjects, namely officials. By officials one does not mean here employees of a bureaucratic system of public adminsitration, but rather the "officials of a legal system" or "legal officials". This group in later versions of positivism will be ascribed a special role in reference to the very concept of law validity. Though, in the position presented it is wholly connected with the power of a sovereign. However, in practical terms, "against accepted views, Austin sees the issue of previous elimination of law, even before its establishment. This duty rests on officials, who by being guided with the principle of utility must decide whether a given norm is beneficial to society or not [...] Austin gives very broad competence to those who carry out the commands of a sovereign, they have power to negate the sovereign's decisions."[20] Thus, one may say that from this perspective lawyers – provided that, at least to some extent, they may be identified with the group of officials – are not only responsible for the law but there is a procedure and the criteria indicated, which should guide them in this matter. Namely, they should do this "before introducing" particular rules and base on the utilitarian principle of maximising benefits.

18 H.L.A. Hart, "Positivism and the Separation of Law and Morals", in: *idem, Essays on Jurisprudence and Philosophy*, Oxford 1983, p. 51.

19 *Ibidem*, p. 54; see also J. Woleński, "O pozytywizmie prawniczym", ["On Legal Positivism"], in: *Etyka a praworządność i prawo*, ed. J. Pawlica, Kraków 1998, p. 15.

20 K. Dybowski, "Utylitarystyczna filozofia prawa Johna Austina" ["The Utilitarian Legal Philosophy of John Austin"], *Państwo i Prawo* 1992, no. 3, p. 70.

Nevertheless, some reservations must be made. Firstly, even if the principle of responsibility is mentioned, then it is rather understood as role-responsibility, thus one can be held responsible only for neglecting one's duties related to the role. This is important because, "an official cannot be absolved from liability for his or her actions because he or she should act in a maximally beneficial way for society even if the sovereign acts adversely."[21] Neither appeal to legal rules nor to one's power can be a reason for shirking from performing one's professional role. Though secondly, moral rules, by which officials should be guided, are not in this case a validation and simultaneously a limitation of goals and values central to these professional roles since every citizen – thus also every official – must define his or her position toward law or the situation. Thus, this is applying utilitarian morality within the framework of professional roles, and not the formation of those which would make those practising professional roles responsible for maintaining and developing the law as social practice.

Perhaps this difference on the surface is not great, but it may lead to serious consequences. Maintaining and developing the law will not always serve maximisation of social benefits, and inversely, realising social benefits may be destructive to the law. In case of this conflict, in Austin's view, law as practice should be developed only as much as it serves the utilitarian aims. For people performing legal roles this is the consequence of being a lawyer and a citizen simultaneously. As regards theory of legal ethics, civic conduct a lawyer means special responsibility for law itself and not using it for the realisation of other moral rules. It is not surprising in this context that together with the evolution of Utilitarianism and more frequent acceptance of non-cognitivism in morality by positivists, legal ethics was deprived of a moral plane. To what extent this opens a space for dialogue between morally validated theory of legal ethics and contemporary positivist views will be a subject of further reflections.

4.3.2. Legal ethics and theses of modern positivism

4.3.2.1. The social thesis

Modern positivism is characterised by two fundamental assertions, namely the social thesis and the separability thesis. Most generally speaking, the former claims that the source of law's normativity are social facts, while the latter holds that this normativity is in no necessary (conceptual) way dependent on morality. The relationships between these theses have been seen by various authors in two

21 *Ibidem*, p. 71; see also *idem*, *Johna Austina filozofia prawa* [*The Philosophy of Law of John Austin*], Toruń 1991, p. 87 ff.

ways. According to the first view, the separability thesis is a logical consequence of the social thesis, whereas in the second view – represented among others by Joseph Raz – such inference does not occur, and thus one may accept only one of them; however, to legal positivism both are constitutive, though the social thesis is cognitively more important[22]. Irrespective of which view is assumed, the discussion of legal positivism should start with the social thesis in the primary position, both in a logical and an epistemological sense.

The social thesis associates certain social facts with the formation of normativity of law, though they are not necessarily viewed as sources of legal norms. The cognition of those facts takes place through studying the use of language and especially of specific qualities of utterances related to law. On the basis of epistemology, assuming that the study of language may reveal something about society, the social thesis claims that, "the basic fact of this kind is the existence of some consistent practice of accepting and identifying certain norms as norms of the currently binding law – practice being only an expression of the accepted [...] convention."[23] This practice usually assumes that, "law is norms constituted or accepted by a competent regulatory authority according to a defined procedure." Thus understood, social thesis often derives the statement of, "law's superiority over any other normative orders." This position is sometimes criticised as being untrue because of, among other things, the development of international and corporate law, which fact proves that the law rather becomes a system of agreements rather than norms issued by an authority[24].

In order to better understand the nature of the social thesis and of the charges formed against it, one has to analyse closely the relation between concurrent practice of recognising laws as valid – a practice which is the source of the law's normativity – and between the authority of law, which is the expression of this normativity. This is primarily the issue of the nature of the rule of recognition, which among secondary rules of the legal system of Hart has a special place. On one hand, "its existence is a social fact, manifest in the normative behaviour of legal oficialls"[25] thus the rule of recognition exists as

22 T. Pietrzykowski, "'Miękki' pozytywizm i spór o regułę uznania" ["Soft Positivism and the Dispute about the Rule of Recognition"], in: *Studia z filozofii prawa*, ed. J. Stelmach, Kraków 2001, p. 100.

23 *Ibidem*, p. 99.

24 L. Morawski, "Pozytywizm 'twardy', pozytywizm 'miękki' i pozytywizm martwy" ["'Hard' Positivism, 'Soft' Positivism and Dead Positivism"], *Ius et Lex* 2003, no. 1, p. 326-331.

25 P.M.S. Hacker, "Hart's Philosphy of Law", in: *Law, Morality and Society. Essays in Honour of H.L.A. Hart*, ed. P.M.S. Hacker, J. Raz, Oxford 1977, p. 10.

a matter-of-fact. On the other, facing the uncertainty about the addressee of this rule, Joseph Raz makes a kind of interpretation on the basis of a statement that the conditions for the existence of social rules are practices of those people to whom these rules are addressed, and comes to a conclusion that the rule of recognition is addressed to the "officials of the legal system." The rule is not a "powerconferring rule" – this task belongs to the rules of adjudication and rules of change – but imposes an obligation on them, "to recognize and apply all and only all those laws satisfying certain criteria of validity spelled out in the rule."[26]

The above characterisation of Hart's rule of recognition shows the importance of the distinction of the legal officials or judicial officials group. Those "officials of the legal system" are a quite vaguely indicated group, which nevertheless is important since – at least in the above analysis – its practice is decisive for the content of the rule of recognition, and simultaneously this group is the rule's addressee. As regards this group, significantly from the perspective of legal ethics theory, Herbert Hart writes that one may demand the understanding of the law and its problems from „the officials or experts of the system; the courts, which are charged with the responsibility of determining what the law is, and the lawyers whom the ordinary citizen consults when he wants to know what it is."[27] However, the legal ethics perspective requires an answer to the questions of whether this group may be further characterised and whether it is possible to determine how much this is simply a group of lawyers that is a subject of the principle of responsibility, and whether this group may be ascribed moral responsibility for the law as social practice, and thus whether the status of this "may demand" is purely social and included in the scope of aims and values of legal professional roles or may be expressed in moral categories, too.

Analysing the first problem it has to be observed that the social thesis belongs to a certain view that is not the only possible one. For example, Raz discards from among many possibilities those that may be characterised as linguistic and legal ones, and chooses the institutional approach. Therefore, he indicates that, fundamental for positivism is: the moral thesis (connections between rules and values are a result of social circumstances), the semantic thesis (separation of legal and evaluative uses of concepts) and the most important the social thesis, from which, according to some interpretations, the former two derive. The author himself is of a different opinion in this respect, claiming that the social thesis is a kind of limitation; it reduces possible theoretical views of law to those which do not have to refer to moral philosophy and which presume the existence of value-free concepts used in law description and thus, according to such views, only

26 J. Raz, *The Authority of Law. Essays on Law and Morality*, New York 1979, pp. 92-93.
27 H. L. A. Hart, *The Concept of Law*, Oxford 1961, p. 59.

social facts are a necessary and sufficient condition to identify the content of the law.[28] The social thesis is associated with the test for existence and identity of a legal system, which comprises three elements: law's efficacy and its institutionality in the weak version, and, additionally, sources of the law in the strong version of this thesis.[29]

The social thesis in its strong version including the sources thesis is endorsed by an argument that refers to a important distinction from the perspective of legal ethics theory. Namely, in the characteristics of a judge one distinguishes two sorts – those which "reflecting his moral character," such as, "wisdom, moral sensibility, enlightened approach", and those which may be called "legal skills," such as, "knowledge of the law, [...] skill in interpreting laws," and their application. Only the second kind is constitutive for the judge's institution, while the first is only desirable, especially in a situation where one would assume that legal skills are important in the cases of normal application of the law and moral character is important in developing the law. However, it has to be emphasised that developing the law is understood here more in the sense of *Rechtsfortbildung* than developing the law as practice, as it is understood in the principle of responsibility in legal ethics theory[30]. In any case, the group of officials of a legal system from this perspective is made of judges applying the law.

This conclusion seems to be supported by further analyses, which state that the rule of recognition may be applied by everyone, while its addressees are only judicial officials, whom it invests with a responsibility to exercise their power through applying the law[31]. In the institutional view understood thus, primary in relation to a legal system are not the institutions establishing laws but the organs of its application, namely judicial organs. Raz seeks their identity not through searching for their social function but for their normative character. Precisely those norms of which this organs are composed are necessary in every legal system, and not the existence of its officials. Decisions of these organs are binding even if they are wrong but simultaneously they are under an obligation to apply the law[32]. From this perspective, all officials of a legal system are a group which does not actually apply law, but is obliged to apply it in executing its powers, which it exercises on the strength of rules constitutive to the institution of a judge.

---

28 J.Raz, *The Authority...*; see T. Kozłowski, "Społeczny pozytywizm Josepha Raza" ["Social Positivism of Joseph Raz"], *Studia Iuridica* 1998, no. 36, pp. 95-99.

29 J. Raz, *The Authority...*, pp. 45-49.

30 *Ibidem*.

31 P.M.S. Hacker, *Hart's Philosophy...*

32 J. Raz, *The Authority...*, pp. 108-113.

In the institutional view one has to distinguish rules of constitutive character from those of regulatory character. The former are crucial for the existence of institutions since they ascribe meaning to some kinds of conduct or allow speaking of them, in general, and their occurrence, and, "such forms of conduct are parts of some social practices and are possible only on grounds of a given social practice as a whole." Particular constitutive rules may perform different roles in forming of the practice: institutive (conditions of institutional facts formation), consequential (their normative consequences) and terminative (circumstances of fact extinction). Ontologically, institutions may be understood in abstract terms as a system of rules that are a basis of a given social practice, and factually as the practice corresponding with these rules[33]. Perceived in abstract terms, the group of judges, obliged to apply laws, is a product of law understood as a social practice and of the constitutive rules of the law. Neverthless, this group is not identical with a social group in which the existence of this practice manifests.

In other words, the criterion whether a legal system is in force or not, irrespectively of its content, always, "concerns the attitudes and responses of all or certain sections in the society to the legal system: Do they know it, do they respect it, obey it?, etc."[34] These groups cannot be identified with particular professional roles, which are determined by the legal system, though in reality they may be composed of the same persons. No necessity occurs here and this is only a matter of coincidence. This means that from the fact that judicial roles are necessary for the existence of a legal system, and every legal system must contain the duty – connected with these roles – of applying law, one cannot draw conclusions that there does not exist a wider group which knows laws, respects and obeys it – precisely this social fact endows the legal system as a whole with bindingness. Therefore, knowledge of the law, obedience and respect to it are the spheres in which one may search place for moral principle of responsibility of lawyers for law.

The epistemological conception of legal positivism in Hart's formulation relies on the distinction between internal and external point of view of rules. The external perspective is the one of the observer, the internal means that we accept a rule and perceive it as binding. Distinguishing law does not take place in a way of cognition parallel to natural obejcts but through language. According to Neil MacCormick, one has to distinguish the volitional and cognitive aspects of the

---

33 T. Gizbert Studnicki, "Ujęcie instytucjonalne w teorii prawa" [The Institutional View in the Theory of Law"], in: *Studia z filozofii prawa*, ed. J.Stelmach, Kraków 2001, pp. 129 and 131.

34 J. Raz, *The Authority...*, p. 103.

internal point of view. The former means emotional acceptance of a rule[35]. However, it is pointed out that the internal point of view may not only mean acceptance but also a critical attitude, and additionally, that the acceptance of every rule may result from common sense and not from any special rational or moral premises[36]. The cognitive internal point of view of the person uttering statements about rules may be associated with a certain attitude towards law, an attitude which may be described as critical-reflective. Such an attitude to rules, with simultaneous acceptance that they are valid, if genralised to the whole legal system, could be understood in practice as maintenance and development of the system, which is exactly the content of the principle of responsibility. Nevetheless, one must make a few reservations and comments.

Firstly, there appear propositions to distinguish, apart from the external and internal points of view, also such aspects of statements of law which are specific of special groups of lawyers. The staring point in this matter is the Kelsenian standard of "the legal man," assuming the existence of the basic norm. On the ground of this presupposition, positive law will have objective validity in his actions. Hans Kelsen does not distinguish on this plane between legal science and the application of law, and ascribes this assumption of the basic norm to both types of activity. Whereas, according to Joseph Raz legal science may only report the viewpoint of the legal man and not adopt it, while individuals applying law do it of necessity, but only to the extent to which they practise law. This distinction between professional and extra-professional points of view of law allows Raz to avoid the conclusion connected to the following dependence,"if a man were actually to adopt the point of view of the legal man he would have to adopt the law as his personal morality."[37] In conclusion the author by combining and modifying propositions of Herbert Hart and Hans Kelsen distinguishes three sorts of statements about the law and perspectives related with them.

The first kind are external statements – to which classic positivism was limited – which rely on stating some factual relationships related first of all to the law's efficacy, identify legal validity with factual presence of sanctions. The second kind is internal statements – uttered in most cases privately as well as in professional contexts by lawyers – which are applying the law or using it as a

35 M. Zirk-Sadowski, "Pozytywizm prawniczy a filozoficzna opozycja podmiotu i przedmiotu poznania",["Legal Positivism and Philosophical Opposition of the Subject and the Object of Cognition"], in: *Studia z filozofii prawa*, ed. J. Stelmach, Kraków 2001, p. 86. Cf. P. Kamela, *Prawo i moralność w koncepcjach H.L.A. Harta*, [*Law and Morality in the Conceptions of H.L.A. Hart*], Toruń 2008, p. 51 ff.

36 P.M.S. Hacker, *Hart's Philosophy*..., pp. 24-25.

37 J. Raz, *The Authority*..., pp. 140-142.

criterion to evaluate or criticise some behaviour. The latter statements are connected with endorsement of a given rule, though, naturally, they do not imply moral approval of it. The third kind of statements are detached statements about the law typically uttered in legal consultation by legal practitioners or by scholars in legal training. These statements rely on reporting to others the content of legal duties, however, without necessarily endorsing them. These statements thus do not have, "the same normative force of an ordinary legal statement."[38] Therefore, they are not accopanied by critical-reflective atitude, and so they are not oriented toward maintaining and developing the law.

Secondly, though the internal point of view does not mean that legal rules must become personal morality of judges, however the attitude to rules connected with viewpoint in this professional group is a necessary condition for a legal system existence. It is pointed out that the internal point of view does not have to include all rules of the system, and in the extreme case, it only has to include the rule of recognition[39]. It follows from this that, "since the so-called internal point of view decides on the distinction between a legal norm and a rule of etiquette, then the theory of society that this version of positivism builds for epistemological ends, is to a great extent a theory of a certain communicative community."[40] In this community, at least judges should know, what are the criteria of the law's validity, and thus, what is the law. Naturally, there is no reason to assert that this community should be limited only to judges or that such a situation actually takes place in contemporary societies.

Though, this raises a theortical problem of the relation between technocratic and always not numerous group of judges, whose cognitive attitude is versed towards interpreting rules in their internal aspect, who do understand the law, and between the majority of society, unacquainted with the content of the law. There have to exist mechanisms which will make individuals occupying positions from outside of the law abide by it. A classical solution in this respect are sanctions based on the state's constraint. This nevertheless breeds an important political problem since in such a situation this minority exercises significant and large power over the law, and thus also over citizens. This problem in many forms arises in modern countries relatively often, especially as a tension between lawyers and society. Usually, ethical arguments on lawyers' conduct are employed in such situations and they are blamed for the moral crisis of legal professions. A typical answer of lawyers for the problem is formulating a condition for existence of trust between lawyers and society. However, as it is

---

38 *Ibidem*, pp. 154-158; see also P.M.S. Hacker, *Hart's Philosophy...*, pp. 6-9.

39 P.M.S. Hacker, *Hart's Philosophy...*, p. 15.

40 M. Zirk-Sadowski, "Pozytywizm prawniczy...", p. 85.

indicated by multi-dimensional theory of legal ethics, the validation of this rule is the moral principle of responsibility.

Thus, the dispute for the rule over the legal text, though it may be viewed from the perspective of language theory or epistemology, has also an ethical aspect. In such a view, for example, interpretation rules have to be viewed as rules of political morality of judges, which is considered as something different and separate from professional ethics of judges. Political morality of judges, though it obliges them to maintain the democratic criterion of clarity in legal texts and in acts of law application, it simultaneously obliges them to show a critical and reflective attitude in relation to legal texts. Due to this attitude, all legal culture will become critical and reflective. This is the interpretation of the internal aspect of the rule and of the critical-reflective attitude as a moral duty[41]. Thus outlined, the distinction between political morality of judges and their professional ethics resembles the distinction between the moral plane of legal ethics and the other two planes – the distinction already discussed in the present work. However, it seems that in such a perspective a question arises about how this political morality of judges would be validated. If as a moral rule similar to the reflective principle of responsibility, then such a viewpoint would confirm that positivist theories and theories of legal ethics may complement each other.

However, if accepting political morality of judges as obliging judges to some attitude towards the law is a condition whose acceptance is necessary for constructing legal epistemology, then it seems that this exceeds the positivist view of law. Though legal positivism avoids formulation of clear philosophical positions in legal discourse, it rests on the Cartesian opposition of cognition subject and object[42]. Acceptance that morality of judges is a condition of knowledge, does not recognise this opposition and is closer to hermeneutical and communicative views since it is, "the hermeneutical critique of legal culture that allows to draft a communicative vision of the law and of legal culture, in which vision the law is not presented as a 'ready' object only to be recognised by by a lawyer, but as common meanings and symbols constituted in discourse. From this perspective, legal positivism and its accompanying presupposition of the legislator's rationality is one of legal discourse's forms, accepting which is not a necessary condition of knowing the law [...] A condition of proper cognition of the law by judges appears to be not only the institutional distinction of the justice system but also the ethical quality of judges."[43]

41 M. Zirk-Sadowski, "Epistemologia prawa a teorie wykładni", ["Epistemology of Law and Theories of Interpretation"], in: *Prawo-władza-społeczeństwo-polityka. Księga jubileuszowa profesora Krzysztofa Pałeckiego*, Toruń 2006, pp. 71-73.

42 M. Zirk-Sadowski, "Pozytywizm prawniczy...", pp. 84-85.

43 *Ibidem*, p. 95.

Thirdly, partly to recap, on one hand, it is to be noted that legal positivism in the form discussed does not command lawyers to accept any moral attitude, but only conceptually requires the critical-reflective attitude in judges. However, this is not a moral command. If any version of legal ethics is implied here, then it is one limited to professional roles of judges, in which, within the framework of practising their profession, the central value is the authority of law, which manifests in the statements of those who apply the law. Simultaneously, legal positivism is reconcilable with morally validated theory of legal ethics and its specific principle of responsibility. All in all, the principle of responsibility does not preclude that the whole community will be morally responsible for the law and that roles of lawyers other than those of a judicial professional nature will be constructed around values and aims validated by this principle. This is because the principle does not claim that existence of a responsible group of lawyers is necessary for the law, but it assumes that it is only necessary that a group of the law-applying judges exists. On the other hand, in order to accept that such complementing of one theory by another will not result in contradictions, it has to be examined whether the multi-dimensional theory of legal ethics does not conflict the second positivist thesis, namely the separability thesis.

4.3.2.2. The separability thesis

Most generally speaking, the separability thesis claims that, "law and morality are different normative systems. Validity of legal norms does not depend on their conformity with moral norms. In particular, no legal norm can lose its validity on the grounds of its being incorrect or unjust."[44] In most recent versions of positivism the separability thesis still holds that there is no necessary relationship between law and morality, but that legal norms may take moral criteria into account, and the rule of recognition especially may include these criteria[45]. The debate on validation revolves around the dispute over this issue. The dispute, nonetheless, does not exhaust problems that may be important from the point of view of theory of legal ethics. These problems are related to moral attitudes towards law, namely to obedience to law and moral duty of obedience and respect to law. The question of whether lawyers, from the persective of legal ethics, have some special duties in this scope, will be analysed in precisely this order.

44 L. Morawski, "Pozytywizm...", p. 326.
45 *Ibidem*, p. 338.

In recent years the the problem of law-morality relation appeared in the context of the so-called *torture memos*[46], which revealed connections between the old philosophical dispute and the classical problem of legal ethics, namley the client-lawyer relation. It appears that in the discussion about the extent to which legal advice should disregard morality, and to what extent it should be included in legal advice analogically to advice given between friends, some arguments characteristic of modern legal positivism are employed.[47] On one hand, the so-called standard defence of the authors of the abovementioned memos on torture's acceptability refers to the view of Raz, and thus it excludes a legal advisor from taking morality into account. This is because his or her task is only to report the content of the law, which, to the advice-receiver, excludes (is an eliminatvie argument) whole groups of possible reasons on which there is no consensus in society[48]. As it has been proven above, legal advice does not have the same normative power as an act of applying the law, and it is stated from a different point of view. Therefore it does not bind the receiver to obey. Nevertheless, it does not mean that legal advice may include reasons which judges, for example, shall not consider. It is the client who must decide whether any and if so what extra-legal reasons to accept.

On the other hand, even if one accepts that from these or any other reasons the person giving legal advice should assume that he or she is responsible for the authority of law in the same way as judges and other officials in power to whom the rule of recognition is addressed, then still, the advising person should act with restraint in including moral reasons in his or her advice. For if a judge has a special role, he is, "an element to much extent constituting the social aspect of law," therefore the judge, "must keep his neutrality towards values and maximally remove the influence of values from beyond a given legal system."[49] Thus, this position is specific to the so-called exclusive positivism, which excludes the incorporation of morality within a legal system mainly because the primary function of law is providing social order despite the lack of moral consensus. Such inclusion would prevent law from performing its fundamental fucntion.

Contrary to this view there lies the inclusive, or soft, positivism. In a nutshell, this view assumes that moral values may be incorporated into real legal

---

46 See J. Zajadło, "Prawo kontra etyka prawnicza" ["Law *versus* Legal Ethics"], in: *Fascynujące ścieżki filozofii prawa,* ed. J. Zajadło, Warsaw 2008, pp. 260-273.

47 B. Wendel, "Legal Ethics and the Separation of Law and Morals", *Cornell Law Review* 2005, no. 91, pp. 71-72.

48 *Ibidem*, pp. 86-98.

49 T. Kozłowski, "Społeczny...", p. 99.

systems as criteria of the law's validity.[50] Within the framework of this dispute between these two positivist currents there arise arguments referring to some statements of Hart, who, as it seems, agreed that the rule of recognition may encompass moral standards, not only performing negative (derogatory) function, but also a positive (validation) function. Nonetheless, he believed that the rule does not question the separability thesis as long as moral norms are not a criterion of validity of legal norms by force of themselves, i.e. *proprio vigore*, which seems to be excluded on the strength of the social character of the rule of recognition itself, "whose existence flows from its acceptance by judges and officials of state administration." Any possible inclusion of moral standards into the rule of recognition must therefore be logically preceded with acceptance, and thus inclusion without acceptance is excluded[51].

From the perspective of legal ethics and the related principle of responsibility, both positions seem to contain a common element which would allow one to search for the best solution. It has to be noted that in all cases there occurs a characteristic connection of different professional roles of lawyers, both judicial and consultative, with the functions of law itself. It may be said that, "if one of law's objectives is to enable citizens to act together, as a society, despite persistent moral conflict, then the duties of lawyers must be understood derivatively as furthering this end of law. Thus, insofar as lawyers interpret and apply the law to their clients' problems, they are required not to interfere with the law's capacity to coordinate activity."[52] The responsibility of lawyers will therefore be to care for the authority of law so that it can perform its function. The government lawyers' advice in the case of the 'torture memos' is faulty not because it does not consider the moral evil of tortures, but because it denies the authority of law and only in consequence does it underacknowledge the inclusion in a legal system of moral values that contradict permissibility of torture in any form[53].

However, if lawyers are responsible for maintaining and development of law as a social practice, then a question arises whether this is accompanied with the obligation to obey the law. Most generally speaking, even in a good society there is no general moral duty to obey the law, and there may exist a moral duty of disobedience which, according to the author, is natural since law cannot

50 T. Pietrzykowski, "'Miękki' pozytywizm...", p. 98.

51 A. Grabowski, "Zawartość reguły uznania w koncepcji H.L.A. Harta" ["The Content of the Rule of Recognition in the Conception of H.L.Hart"], in: *Prawo-władza-społeczeństwo-polityka. Księga jubileuszowa profesora Krzysztofa Pałeckiego*, Toruń 2006, pp. 132-134.

52 B. Wendel, *Legal ethics...*, pp. 105-106.

53 *Ibidem*, pp. 127-128.

"decree moral codes"[54]. It is noteworthy that such a statement may be a source of problems for legal ethics considering that contemporarily it exists in a juridicised form, and codes of professional ethics are more often not only soft but also hard law. Not settling whether this practice is 'decreeing moral codes,' namely whether it implies a moral obligation of obedience to decisions of these codes, it has to be assumed that in order to resolve this problem, one has to start with more a abstract issue of moral obedience to law in general. This problem is related to the question of the authority of law in its normative aspect.

The authority of law, according to Joseph Raz, does not rely on the existence of an additional reason for some kind of behaviour, but on revoking all other reasons, and settling in favour of a specific solution. Especially, if there are different, contradictory, moral reasons for some kind of behaviour, legal settlement in this matter will be a reason to exclude these moral reasons. Obviously, the rule of recognition contains a general criterion of distinguishing moral reasons from legal reasons, whereby it is important that the abovementioned revocation concerns only the epistemic and not the validation aspect of this rule. Law does not annihilate morality and the authority of law is only a reason for not being guided by morality in those situations that fall under legal regulation. The rule of recognition must therefore make a practical difference for the addressee and not put him in a position in which uniquely primary rules exist, which are often, to the addressee, contradictory reasons for some kind of behaviour[55].

As understood in this manner, authority of law has its origin in social facts resting on harmonious and conventional practice of law-applying organs, and not only it does need no moral validation, it also excludes it conceptually. Hence, there is no general moral obligation to obey the law. Nonetheless, it has to be noted that some people may and actually have moral reasons for such obedience. These specific moral reasons, which from the perspective of legal ethics are at least interesting, may have other sources. First of all, some individuals should obey the law out of moral reasons because they, "have such a position of pre-eminence in the community that their actions have profound influence on the attitudes and behaviour of many people." Another motive for the existence of these special reasons may be simply an undertaking to do so, as in the form of an oath of allegiance to a defined legal system or to a part of it, for instance to a constitution[56].

54 L. Morawski, "Pozytywizm...,", p. 341.
55 T. Pietrzykowski, "'Miękki' pozytywizm...", pp. 111-114.
56 J. Raz, *The Authority...*, pp. 237, 239.

It seems that such reasons should be considered individually, which means that they cannot be ascribed to the whole group of lawyers. Certainly, more often among them than in other social groups, such reasons will be present and taken into account, but no general obligation can be formed. An additional argument for its rejection may be the fact that, depending on the professional roles performed by lawyers, and the cases and branch of law they deal with, these reasons may be weaker or stronger. This may depend on how a given legal system is judged from the moral point of view, irrespective of which position one assumes in regard to morality. For even if one takes the cognitivist position and claims that rational moral judgements of law may be formed, then what flows from this is only that we accept, "that moral judgments are as rationally defensible as any other kind of judgments. What would follow from this as to the nature of the connection between law as it is and law as it ought to be? [...] The only difference which the acceptance of this view of the nature of moral judgments would make would be that the moral iniquity of such laws would be something that could be demonstrated."[57]

Therefore in legal ethics it is traditionally assumed that the obligation to obey the law is not a legal ethics rule, though, naturally, for a concrete breach one may be held diciplinarily responsible[58]. A special case in this matter is the responsibility for the breach of statutory norms and even the codes of professional ethics as containing legal rules. This responsibility is motivated by their incompatibility with the rules of legal ethics, especially with the moral principle of responsibility. Known from the adjudication, the ways of resolving these conflicts have been presented in the discussion of the juridisation processes of legal ethics; however, it is worth remarking upon the theoretical problems arising in this matter on the ground of legal positivism. It may be argued that the separability thesis leads to absurd situations – for example, a lawyer may face a dilemma where on one side there will be profound moral reasons for professional duties validated by the moral principle of responsibility and, on the other, duties that contadict them, contained for instance in an act and endorsed not only by the authority of law but also by validated with the same moral principle of responsibility obligation to mind this authority. This obligation creates a special moral reason for obedience to the law.

It does not seem that on the grounds of positivism it was possible to unequivocally settle such dilemmas, because the situation in which duties addressed to lawyers are contained in acts of law and codes of professional ethics would perfectly correspond with professional duties defined on the basis

57 H.L.A. Hart, "Positivism...", in: *idem*, p. 84.

58 H.S. Drinker, *Legal Ethics*, New York 1953, p. 22.

of the methodology of a multi-dimensional theory of legal ethics is probably impossible. Law formation in positivism is an answer to social needs and problems and occurs only after their conceptualisation. Legal duties therefore cannot provide for the realisation of ends and values that are central to legal professional roles, because these roles change more or less dynamically. The only way to avoid such conflicts is to provide appropriate procedures for including functional relations between law and morality, both on the law-making and law-applying stages. In the first case, this will manifest in paying continual attention to topicality of the codes of professional ethics and other normative acts that contain obligations addressed to lawyers. In the second, it will mean providing the institution of disciplinary responsibility with a possibility to modify the scope of professional responisbilities in relation to these included in those acts. Naturally, on both stages the intended result can be attained through a critical and reflective, and thus responsible, attitude towards laws on lawyers themselves.

Most generally speaking, it seems that the principle of responsibility from the perspective of the multi-dimensional theory of legal ethics may be reconciled with legal positivism as a theory indicating the sources of lawyers' power and describing on what this power rests. Thanks to these presuppositions, legal ethics may be a kind of theory of good exercise of this power. Thus, on the basis of the above analysis, one may draft an answer to the question: on what do law maintenance and development rely, which is the subject of the principle of responsibility. One should note the thesis – exposed especially in the so-called exclusive version of positivism – on the impossisbility of, "the existence of systems of law corresponding in a given time with the whole system of social problems."[59] The subject of responsibility in this view could be to make the legal system follow the social system, which gave rise to it, and precisely this strive for compatibility would be its maintenance and development. The adoption of inclusive version does not exclude such an interpretation but it certainly means another way of realising this responsibility on the plane of legal professional roles.

Irrespective of this, the conslusion should be upheld that obedience to law is not a general duty of legal ethics, but simultaneously it has to be added that it does not mean that people cannot or should not have some general moral attitude to law other than obedience. According to Joseph Raz such an attitude is respect, which signifies that law is always treated seriously and considered as a reason behind actions. Usually, in good and not unjust societies, respect for law combines with obedience, which is a normal situation. Nonetheless, this relation

59 T. Kozłowski, *Społeczny…*, p. 99.

is not based on any necessity[60]. In special cases one may respect law but not obey it and this attitude seems to be the constitutive element of civil disobedience. Still, from the perspective of legal ethics, the question of whether lawyers are obliged to give special respect to the law is more important.

The answer to this question should take into account the fact that respect for the law may be seen as a general duty of citizens, and because of that its special character for lawyers could rely on the following obligations. Firstly, it could entail a special obligation to obey the law, an obligation that is normally associated with respect. Nevertheless, this solution cannot refer to any premise not already indicated in discussion of the issue of obedience. For this reason, it may be assumed that whenever lawyers would have the special obligation of obedience, there would also occur the special obligation to respect the law; however, this latter duty will always be a result of factors related to the practised professional role and the content of a particular legal system. Secondly, it may be assumed that special respect for the law is itself a consequence of lawyers' responsibility for law as a social practice, though it seems that such reasoning is unjustified since respect for law does not seem to be directly indispensable in order to apply the principle of responsibility. It will be appropriate to accept that respect to law is indispensable in an indirect way, i.e. as a professional obligation connected with the principles of trust and integrity. Special respect for law manifesting itself in careful consideration of all arguments in in choosing particular action and in caring for its legality may build and save trust of citizens in lawyers, and being guided by this obligation in extra-professional life may protect the lawyer's identity from disintegration.

4.4. Legal ethics and the juriscentric model

4.4.1. Legal ethics and the theory of law as integrity

Legal positivism is subject to criticism from many sides, and attempts at going beyond its limitations lead to the rise of new theories that are applied in legal practice, which is why they may be jointly reconstructed as another theoretical model. An important trend of this critique has been established by the theory of law as integrity of Ronald Dworkin, whose legal philosophy is referred to as interpretivism. The thesis that law is an interpretive entity has been used also by positions relatively distant from Dworkin's point of view, and it has been given a more philosophical and radical form. Therefore, in order to discuss the relationships of legal ethics with the juriscentric model, one has to briefly

60 J. Raz, *The Authority…*, pp. 250, 260.

present this relation with the theory of law as integrity as a thought to which this model more or less consciously refers. The presentation will begin with a dilemma drafted when discussing the positivist separability thesis; the dilemma in which a lawyer has serious moral arguments for professional duties validated by moral principle of responsibility on one hand, and on the other, obligations – contained for example in an act – contradicting the first of duties. The second kind of obligations will be endorsed by the authority of law as well as the duty, validated by the same moral principle of responsibility, to care for this authority.

By analysing such dilemmas, some authors come to the conclusion that it is nothing unusual that legal ethics is such a complex discipline in which codes of professional ethics are only a part, and not even the most significant one. Therefore they should be treated as a kind of introduction to its proper subject, namely the principles of moral character. This is what may be called a "preface to ethics"[61]. However, in classical English positivism the distinction between law and morality and obedience to law has been suboridnated to the assumptions of the Utilitarian philosophy, whereas the resignation of positivism from the relationship with some moral conception leads to the opposition of law and morality and even to an antagonism between them. In connection with the thesis that judges are obliged to apply law and any possible disobedience in this regard would result in the legal system destruction, it must follow that in the positivist approach, legal ethics is reduced to amoral practice of professional roles and the principle of moral responsibility of lawyers can bind them as far as the law itself does not contain rules that are contradicting this principle. In other words, this argumentation in a situation of conflict ascribes to positivism a conclusion that as regards a judge, in a conflict between rules of professional ethics and legal rules, he or she will have to choose either amorality or questioning the legal system.

A proposed solution in such a situation is acceptance of Dworkin's conception and supplementing a legal system with rules which have the so-called institutional support and so which have been subject of previous decisions or occurred in the history of legislation. Among these rules also, the principles of legal ethics could be found. Their inclusion in the legal system would allow one to view the discussed dilemma not as an unsolvable law-morality conflict but as a collision within the legal framework[62]. Such a collision may be resolved within the legal framework more easily because in this view a significant role is ascribed to "adjudicative integrity", which, "instructs judges to identify legal

61 M. Strassberg, "Taking Ethics Seriously: Beyond Positivist Jurisprudence in Legal Ethics", *Iowa Law Review* 1995, no. 80, pp. 911, 915-917, 922-923.

62 *Ibidem*, pp. 929-930.

rights and duties, so far as possible, on the assumption that they were all created by a single author – the community personified – expressing a coherent conception of justice and fairness."[63] By adjudicating, judges contribute to a certain chain of adjudicatory statements, "a chain of novels," in whose framework they must give the best judgement which will integrate both the opinions on law included in adjudication of other judges as well as the personal conception of law of the adjudicating judge.

On this ground, moral rules of legal ethics may hold an appropriate position in adjudication on legal rules belonging to the domain of legal ethics as well as in the adjudication based on other rules of a legal system. This is why all collisions in which the subject could be, for instance, the principle of lawyers' responsibility for law may be removed by interpretivist methods. In this view the problem of possible disobedience to codes of professional ethics out of moral reasons related to principles of legal ethics is resolved since they will be a part of the law and both groups of norms will be considered by interpretation. Such a point of view is also advantageous because it does not mean that judges may freely include their moral convictions in judgements since their content must correspond with the rules. Simultaneously, integrity as an extra-adjudication rule makes all citizens responsible for society and its rules. Accordingly, integrity in adjudication is only a special case of integrity[64].

This reasoning requires a comment, not to the point of deciding whether possible conflicts between different norms belonging to the legal ethics domain because the juridisation processes are arguments for renouncing positivism and accepting Dworkin's critique, nor about whether these problems may be resolved by adopting the inclusive version of positivism. Nonetheless, it has to be noted that though interpretivism based on adjudciative integrity could be an answer to possible dilemmas connected with obedience to legal rules in conflict with norms of legal ethics, it gives rise to other theoretical problems which are related to its fundamental assumptions. First of all, it is noteworthy that in this conception the principle of responsibility for maintaining and developing law could be taken as one of the legal system's rules that are institutionally supported; but in every legal system this is an empirical matter. Thus, one can imagine systems in which this principle will not be taken into consideration at all, or it will be regarded as secondary and inferior to other principles in situations of collision.

In these circumstances, it seems hard to treat the principle of responsibility simultaneously as, on one hand, reflectively validated and morally validating the

---

63 R. Dworkin, *Law's Empire*, Cambridge Massachussets and London 1986, p. 225.

64 M. Strassberg, "Taking...", pp. 935-938, 950.

ends and values of legal professional roles and obliging to maintain and develop law as social practice regardless of the legal system in which particular lawyers work and, on the other hand, as an internal rule of this system, which, as are all its rules, is subject to limitations and institutional support. Naturally, there is no obstacle to accepting that in this situation two principles of responsibility are obejctively binding, namely in the sense of moral and legal principles. However, this neither solves the problem of obedience to law nor does it seem particularly in accordance with Dworkin's thought. Hence, it seems that, on the level of normative structure of society, the multi-dimensional theory of legal ethics and the discussed conception contain contradictory assumptions, since the former presupposes at least a conceptual possibility that moral norms may be distinguished, though it does not contain any statements on the relation of these moral norms to law. Interpretivism makes such a distinction problematic.

However, it may also be assumed that the principle of responsibility is not one of the legal system's rules, but rather a consequence or an interpretation of the integrity principle in Dworkin's view. This would invert the hierarchy adopted in the multi-dimensional theory of legal ethics, which seems understandable due to the fact that Dworkin's interpretivism is, "an individualistic theory, in which a decision is not a result of a moral consensus of a certain community,"[65] whereas a multi-dimensional theory of legal ethics, by validating its statements, refers directly to critical and reflective procedures that are typical of communicative views. In the first perspective, lawyers, by contributing their concepts of justice and correctness to the discourse, must standardise them with other people's opinions which are expressed in the legal system's rules, as required by integrity, and this, in consequence, makes them responsible. In the second perspective, it is responsibility that conditions the existence of the discourse in which the conceptions of justice and correctness are being formed with respect to integrity.

Therefore, the interpretation of the principle of responsibility specific of positivist view cannot retain its validity; the interpretation according to which the object of responsibility would be to make the legal system constantly follow the social system, which gave rise to this legal system, and this strive for compatibility would be its maintenance and development. In interpretivism, censorious toward positivism, by including rules in the legal system, this compatibility is already assumed, which is why it is difficult to speak here of its development or maintenance. Nevertheless, it seems that, in this view, providing normative integrity of society, and thus providing and increasing the coherence of various conceptions of justice and correctness within one legal framework,

65 M. Zirk-Sadowski, "Pozytywizm prawniczy...", p. 93.

could be accepted as the subject of responsibility in the sense of a moral principle.

To provide integrity thus understood, it requires the realisation of adjudicative integrity and belongs to law-applying. However, in especially hard cases, the effort which a lawyer should make to make a correct judgement will be "Herculean", namely superhuman[66]. The lawyer's responsibility is to undertake this effort, to include the widest scope of viewpoints on justice and correctness expressed in principles, and to choose the solution which will best realise this integrity, and there is always one such a solution. Accordingly, this solution will not only be based on the best premises, but it will also be most valuable from the perspective of a given political community. Therefore, lawapplying is is not only a legal but also moral obligation of judges[67]. Pursuing the ideal of applying law in a way that integrates political community, together with the obligation to constant development of law understood in this way and of one's abilities to attain the greatest skill in this development, is close to the perspective of multi-dimensional theory of legal ethics and invests the principle of responsibility with content.

4.4.2. Legal ethics in institutional reality

The theory corresponding to the juriscentric model sets an ambitious aim to exceed the bounds of legal positivism as well as of Dworkin's interpretivism. On one hand, it rests on the assumption that one may distinguish three models of legal practice: the classical, related to natural law theories, modern associated with legal positivism, and juriscentric, connected with interpretivism by including it into its "internal" structure, which is why entities of legal culture become real in legal practice of this type. Thus, the juriscentric model answers all deficiencies of positivism even in its institutional view[68]. On the other hand, it simultaneously assumes that one has to go beyond the intuitive, not to say common sense, concept of interpretation in Dworkin by accepting a deeply philosophical conception of interpretation with clear ontological consequences[69].

Legal positivism in the institutional view claims that, in rational actions, social values are realised, and thus actions may be rationalised by referring to social practice. Therefore, certain collective consciousness in which norm-

66 The figure of Hercules was characterised in: R. Dworkin, *Taking Rights Seriously*, Cambridge Massachusets 1977, pp. 105-130.

67 See T. Stawecki, "Etyka prawnicza...", p. 155.

68 A. Kozak, *Granice*..., p. 73-74.

69 *Ibidem*, p. 18.

formation processes occur is assumed, and this position may be described as noncognitivism holding that vaules are of intersubjective and subjective nature[70]. Juriscentrism notices essentially the problem of the subject of this collective consciousness in the case of law. By continuing Hart's thought, it also notes the problem of distinguishing the group of the system officials and their realtionship to the rule of recognition, and it takes David Lyons' position in claiming that this group is made by the whole legal community. However, it claims that referring only to social practice cannot legitimise the power of lawyers over the law, which power, by the assumed position, becomes an unlimited discretionary power. This results in scepticism and distrust towards law both in societies and in the very community of lawyers[71].

These phenomena may be prevented by accepting the perspective of interpretivism in viewing institutions, but in accepting this perspective not as a theory of law-applying, but as a philosophical standpoint being the source of views developed in various philosophical currents over the last two centuries, and being composed of two statements common to all these views. First, according to this view, cognition is not passive or contemplative in nature but active; it is a kind of action and knowledge is practice. Second, specific of Cartesianism the cognition subject-object opposition is repealed, and subjectivity constitutes in cognitive activity[72]. All knowledge, both of the world and the subject, is therefore always an interpretation from a certain point of view, wheras in contemporary world this viewpoint is formed by institutions. Participation in the system of some institution always equals adopting some local perspective contained in the knowledge about this institution, which means that this knowledge is its cultural foundation, and that the perspective becomes etnocentrism. Thanks to this knowledge, "we may speak of the existence around this institution of its specific realm of meanings, which explains not only this institution but also the whole reality. This realm constitutes not only the reality of of institutions in a given form, but also the reality of the world from the perspective specific of this institution."[73]

The task, or program, of radical interpretivism, which consistently realises the "anti-Cartesian revolution," is to report the cultural character of the institution and realities and subjectivities related to it. In relation to law, "in this

---

70 M. Smolak, *Prawo, fakt, instytucja. Koncepcje teoretycznoprawne Prawniczego Pozytywizmu Instytucjonalnego* [*Law, Fact, Institution. Legal-Theoretical Conceptions of Legal Posivism*], Poznań 1998, p. 13-18.

71 A. Kozak, *Granice...*, pp. 158-159.

72 *Ibidem*, pp. 23-24.

73 A. Kozak, "Trzy modele praktyki prawniczej" ["Three Models of Legal Practice"], in: *Studia z filozofii prawa* 2, ed. J. Stelmach, Kraków 2003, p. 145.

role, it [radical interpretivism – P.S.] has to 'validate' reality of the intra-institutional reality in which a lawyer acts and which – because of this validation – may oppose the lawyer's possible will."[74] Since institutions make a reality based on cultural foundations, and law is an institution, then law can exist only as long as the reality it creates is based on legal culture. Juriscentrism, in other words etnocentrism, of lawyers means accepting by them legal culture as a foundation of reality in which they act. Because of this, their practice will simultaneously be legitimised and limited by this culture. Thus, the juriscentric model limits the discretionary power of lawyers in a significantly more mature way than, for example, legal formalism, which eventually appears to be incompatible with basic assumptions of legal positivism and the rule of law[75].

Legitimisation and limitation of lawyers' power by legal culture, which thanks to interpretivism in the institutional view creates a kind of reality, is possible because the postulate of juriscentrism means basing legal thought on thus created autonomic and non-casual foundation of institutional reality." From the perspective of theory of legal ethics it seems important that in relation to this one may state that, "the moral dimension is given to this postulate by often expressed view about the legitimisation crisis of the whole legal ethics." This crisis is related to the loss of social trust to law as a discipline that is understood only to lawyers and to the loss of trust of lawyers themselves because of scepticism accompanying this practice[76]. Since the postulate has its moral dimension, one may accept the inertpretation that lawyers are morally obliged to adopt the juriscentric attitude; as a result, law as social pracitce will regain trust and be legitimised, and legal discretionary power will be limted.

Nevertheless, it has to be observed that, "any attempts at legitimisation of legal practice by invoking the ethos, or rather defined moral qualities of lawyers, is doomed to failure especially in a situation where media scrupulously draw attention to any signs of crisis regarding this ethos. The only way to validate law and legal prcatice in the eyes of the public (and lawyers themselves, who are increasingly better aware in how inconvenient situation they are) leads through validation of institutions in which lawyers act."[77] Thus, if lawyers are to be morally obliged to adopt the juriscentric perspective, then this fact can by no means substitute the validation of institutions itself. Such statement does not seem to contradict the multi-dimensional theory of legal ethics, which reflectively validates only the principle of responsibility and lower planes of

74 A. Kozak, *Granice…*, p. 155.

75 M. Matczak, *Summa Iniuria. O błędzie formalizmu w stosowaniu prawa* [*On the Formalism Fallacy in Law Application*], Warsaw 2007, p. 207.

76 A. Kozak, *Granice…*, p. 162.

77 *Ibidem*, p. 166.

legal ethics and not law as prcatice, whose validation is the task – if at all is a task – of legal theory and philosophy. The responsibility of lawyers would rely on maintaining and developing legal culture being a foundation of law as institution, and thus on performing self-limitation of its discretionary power.

The acceptance of the above interpretation breeds a certain difficulty to juriscentrism, namely validation of law as institution requires accepting some culture and its values. On one hand, the conclusion that a lawyer is obliged to accept this perspective and in this way limit his or her power seems invalid since this obligation rests on the lawyer only after he or she accepts this perspective. On the other hand, when after the lawyer adopts this perspective, "acting within the institutional structures of law deprives him of power over his own conduct by forcing his to make defined decisions even if he is personally unwilling to make them."[78] In such a situation, it is relatively easy to question the practical dimension of juriscentrism since its acceptance becomes very unlikely: it does not formulate any premises that would be motivating enough to accept it, and even if it had already been accepted, there are no premises to authentically remain in it. consequently, it seems that either juriscentrism will require from lawyers the acceptance of its perspective as a personal morality – however, in this way it will incur difficulties similar to already mentioned by discussing legal positivism – or it will adopt moral premises that are external to legal culture.

The principle of responsibility thus becomes not only a possible addition to the juriscentric perspective, but also its indispensable supplement. Agreeing that lawyers are responsible for law – just as any other professional group practising in a social sense – makes a moral premise to accept legal culture as an intra-institutional reality and, according to its requirements, to limit one's power. Of course, this does not mean that without accepting this responsibility law as an institution will not exist and that the juriscentric point of view will not be adopted by lawyers; nevertheless it will always be a casual matter. In conflict situations when a lawyer will not be convinced of the correctness of the action required by an institution, the principle of responsibility will allow him or her to maintain subjective honesty, in other words, to avoid manipulating the values of legal culture, which essentially would be an implicit or explicit abandonment of the juriscentric perspective, provided that procedures of critical and reflective formation of legal professional roles and duties, and thus of validated with the principle of responsibility and lower planes of legal ethics, will become will part of these institutions.

78 *Ibidem*, p. 169.

4.5. Legal ethics and the discursive model

4.5.1. Topical-rhetorical conceptions

4.5.1.1. Exemplary character of legal discourse

The problem of a specific perspective adopted by lawyers has been analysed also from viewpoints other than the juriscentric one. The problem has been examined by the whole current of thought that ascribes law not only a systemic but also discursive character. This current comprises not only theories that refer directly to the practice of law applying and use a number of examples taken from adjudication, but also to those which are based on the concept of rationality, understood in many ways. To begin with, two remarks have to be made due to this diversity. Firstly, despite this diversity, the theories may be discussed jointly since discursiveness of law is a central thesis in all of them, and the conceptions of authors such as Chaïm Perelman and Robert Alexy are typically presented together[79]. Secondly, the whole current has deep connections with practice as evidenced not only by the fact that the works on this matter are full of references to adjudication, but also by the observation that a contemporary lawyer should be creative and not reactive, should indicate ways of development and risks connected with various decisions, demostrate the initiative in searching for new forms of action, and primarily, should be open in communication[80].

All this means that one may speak of a theoretical discursive model which satisfies the selection criteria of legal-philosophical conceptions for purposes of the present discussion. It must also be noted that the development chronology of this model begins with topical-rhetorical views that try to significantly transform legal methodology by making a broad reference to ancient thought. To a great extent, thanks to the fruifulness of these attempts, one may build argumentation theories referring to the achievements of universal pragmatics. The topical-rhetorical conceptions originated in reaction to the domination of formal logic. Within the framework of this reaction, in the 1950s, research was initiated on the so-called informal logic focusing on the reality of argumentation processes. By this, the research reached for the approach which several dozen years before had been applied by Friedrich Frege in studying the language of mathematics. The main figures of this movement were Stephen Toulmin and Chaïm Perelman.

79 See M. Zirk-Sadowski, *Wprowadzenie do filozofii prawa*, [*An Introduction to the Philosophy of Law*], Kraków 2000, pp. 111-130, who in philosophy of law describes it as an argumentative-discursive view and broadly includes universal pragmatics.

80 J. Jabłońska-Bonca, *Prawnik a sztuka negocjacji i retoryki*, [*A Lawyer and the Art of Negotiation and Rhetoric*], Warsaw 2002, p. 13.

While the former concentrated on moral argumentation, the latter looked at the legal one and therefore one should here refer to him[81].

As has been mentioned, the contemporary interest in rhetorics is a result of failed attempts at building a formal logic of evaluative judgements, and refers to the ancient view on this discipline as a techique of contructing a persuasive speech indispensable in decision making. In classical rhetorics, persuasion means are divided into arguments in a strict sense (*logos*), those referring to the orator's authority or credibility (*etos*) and the emotions of the audience (*patos*)[82]. In each of these types, argumentation differs from formal proving by the ambiguity of the natural language used in the former as well as the status of premises. The aim of argumentation is not so much to draw consequences from premises but to evoke or reinforce the audience's endorsement for certain theses on the basis of convictions already accepted by them[83]. The concepts of argument and audience, characteristic for the topical-rhetorical conceptions, thus refer to the pragmatic aspect of language. Most generally speaking, one may say that rhetorics tries to persuade by means of discourse[84].

Argumentative discourse, in the division for system-thinking and problem-thinking, falls into the second category since it is oriented towards decision-making. This distinction corresponds with a typology of reasonings that are used in both types of thinking. This typology indicates that the deductive model corresponds with the system-perspective, wheras the topical model corresponds to the problem-perspective[85]. Therefore, it may be said of argumentation that it refers not as much to truth as to conviction, and so to obtaining the assent of the audience to the thesis presented by the orator. This adherence does not have to be of intellectual nature, but it is often connected with inciting to action or creating dispositions for it[86]. Hence, some people claim that Perelman's conception, "clearly refers to psychological aspects of persuasion, and

81 K. Szymanek, "Perswazja, argumentacja, słaby argument, mocny argument", ["Persuasion,Argumentation, Weak Argument, Strong Argument"], in: *Studia z filozofii prawa 2,* ed. J. Stelmach, Kraków 2003, p. 42. Other authors and works worth mentioning in this development phase of that current are: Th. Viehweg, *Topik und Jurisprudenz*, 1953, G. Struck, *Topische Jurisprudenz*, Frankfurt am Main 1971.

82 W. Cyrul, "Topika i prawo (Krytyczna analiza topicznej wizji dyskursu prawnego)", ["Topics and Law (A Critical Analysis of a Topical Vision of Legal Discourse"], *Państwo i Prawo* 2004, no. 6, p. 48.

83 Ch. Perelman, *Imperium retoryki. Retoryka i argumentacja,* [*The Realm of Rhetoric. Rhetoric and Argumentation*], Warsaw 2004, pp. 6, 22

84 Ch. Perelman, *Logika prawnicza. Nowa retoryka,* [*Legal Reasoning. The New Rhetoric*], Warsaw 1984, p. 145.

85 W. Cyrul, "Topika i prawo...", p. 50.

86 Ch. Perelman, *Logika*.., p. 147; *ibidem*, *Imperium*..., p. 25.

concentrates less on the problem of truth and false of an utterance."[87] Though it tries to introduce additional, apart from efficacy, criteria of good argumentation, the fact is that this conception lacks *a priori* criteria of reasonableness, and if it was deprived of, "a dialectical attitude, it could not define clear criteria of division between rational or reasonable justification and efficacious persuasion."[88]

The dialectical foundation of the discussed view reaches to the ancient perspective, in which dialectical reasonings present arguments whose end is convincing or persuading and their value is measured on the ground of whether they can change the opinion of a person to whom they are addressed. The new rhetorics, sometimes called new dialectic, contrary to the ancient one, is addressed to all kinds of audiences, including specialists. The aim of argumentation is to transfer the endorsement of the premises given by the audience to the conclusion proposed by the orator. For this reason, one has always to conform to the audience by choosing for one's speech such premises that are accepted by the audience so that the premises may be convincing. On this basis it may be asserted that the audience is the entirety of those individuals whom the orator wants to influence with the argumentation. This is to say that the audience is not the entirety of those who listen to the discourse but a group of individuals whom the orator wants to convince[89]. The division between the universal and particular audience as well as the disticntion of the abovementioned specialists is of key importance from the perspective of distinguishing a legal discourse.

As it has already been said, in every argumentation it is assumed that the audience accepts some statements, holds some presumptions and on the basis of their scope one may distinguish various sorts of audiences. The universal audience consists of all rationally thinking individuals and, apart from opinions which may be ascribed to any rational individual, their convictions do not form any particular premises to which the orator should conform. On the contrary, the particular audience has somepeculiar convictions exceeding those accepted with common sense. It may be stated that conforming to the audience does not relate only to linguistic issues. Mere understanding of the orator is not enough for the audience to accept the proposed statements. The orator has also to use the opinions accepted by a given audience as premises behind his or her arguments. The difference between persuading and convincing rests on the fact that the former is an argumnentation addressed to the particular audience, whereas the latter to the univesal audience. The speech will be convincing as long as its

87 J. Jabłońska-Bonca, *Prawnik a...*, p. 50.

88 W. Cyrul, "Topika i prawo...", pp. 51, 53.

89 Ch. Perelman, *Logika..*, pp. 34,166; *ibidem.*, *Imperium...*, pp. 6, 14-15, 17, 27, 36.

premises and arguments are acceptable by all the members of the universal audience, namely as long as they may be subjected to univesalisation[90].

The legal discourse has a special place in this context. Already Aristotle distinguished three genres of rhetoric: deliberative, forensic, epideictic – whose end was not making a decison but making an oratory exercise. Nowadays, it may be said that, *prima facie*, the audience of legal argumentation is determined by premises in the form of legal norms making up the legal system of a given country. Legal topics, which from the discursive point of view are specific arguments of legal discourse, confirm this thesis. Though, "the concept of particular kinds of topos functioning within a specific field is compatible with the role of acts, judicial law and legal dogmatics in legal discourse, [...] these kinds of topos should be viewed as the sources from which we draw to advance understanding through the knowledge of the subject."[91] In other words, evidently legal norms are premises of legal argumentations but it is not perfectly clear whether legal discourse refers to law because of this specificity or whether it is specific because it refers to law[92].

If one begins with the statement that the new rhetoric is a study of discursive techniques which aim at establishing or reinforcing the endorsement of statements proposed to a certain audience, and that these statements are formulated in a specific language of a cultural – and sometimes professional – community, in a language created in culture history and discipline development, then it seems that existence of a professional group of lawyers may be an argument that legal discourse is always addressed to the particular audience, composed of lawyers, who, thanks to the understanding of the argumentation subject, are susceptible for convincing with legal topics. Neverthless, it has to be retained that, firstly, *loci communes* remain in the same relation to the non-specialised reflection as *loci specificii* in relation to the particular discipline, and thus legal discourse is composed not only of typically legal arguments. Secondly, legal disputes – in contrast with for example philosophical reflections – are limited in time and have a defined audience because of legal norms regulating time frames and jurisdictions. Therefore, one has to take the position that legal discourse, and especially judicial decisions, should satisfy three different audiences, namely: every litigant party, lawyers, and finally public opinion[93].

---

90 Ch. Perelman, *Logika*.., p. 149; *ibidem*, *Imperium*…, p. 31.
91 W. Cyrul, "Topika i prawo…", p. 54.
92 Ch. Perelman, *Logika*.., p. 150.
93 *Ibidem*, pp. 156, 160, 167, 227.

Thus, as regards legal discourse, it cannot be said that arguments are addressed only to one type of audience, though in different concrete discourses this address may be more or less to one particular type of them. The litigant parties may be veiwed as a typical particular audience, and public opinion as a representative of the universal audience. In this context, a professional group of lawyers appears to be a kind of specialist audience. The admission to the latter audience has the character of a sort of initiation, and introducing young individuals to the community allows to suppose that they have learned its habits and distinction and especially a common language and all the concepts to which it refers. Since lawyers cannot address their arguments uniquely to other lawyers, that is to say to other participants of a social practice, but should also try to convince those to whom the law is applied as well as those who from the perspective of reasonableness observe this practice, then this also means the superiority of legal thought over philospical one. According to Perelman, this superiority rests on the circumstance that the latter may be satisfied with general and abstract formulas, whereas the former must overcome difficulties arising with their application.[94]

Thus, it may be said that the existence of a professional group of lawyers as the specialist audience allows both applicative-persuasive elements as well as reasonable-convincing ones to be combined in legal argumentation. However, it should be emphasised that this complexity of requirements towards a legal discourse – complexity which stems from the complexity of audiences to which the argumentation is addressed – historically, has become a reason for establishing informal argumentations which, according to Perelman, may have to other types of discourse, and especially to philosophical reflections, an exemplary character. Since attempts to construct formal logic of values lead to scepticism towards them, a necessity arises to work out such a theory of rhetoric which would broaden the concept of rationality so that it encompasses also informal argumentation. What may be helpful in this attempt – specific of our age – is the centuries long experience of lawyers, who managed to work out a theory of rational law, a subject of consensus of a certain organised community[95]. It seems that here one may refer to the ideas of Harold J. Berman on the role of legal discourse in formation of the philosophical and scientific European thought, yet nonetheless it has to be remembered that in the discursive perspective the key role belongs not to the doctrinal discourse but to the judicial one, which has exemplary character, though it is more than the former addressed to the particular audience,

94 *Ibidem*, pp. 151, 163.

95 Ch. Perelman, *Imperium...*, p. 179.

and thus it focuses more on efficacy and not validity of arguments. Because it is more limited, it is simultaneously more exemplary[96].

4.5.1.2. Legal ethics as the limit of argumentation

The relation of the multi-dimensional theory of legal ethics to the discursive model, in which legal argumentation is viewed as exemplary due to the specificity and complexity of the audience that it has to convince, is an important issue because if the thesis of the exemplary character of legal discourse is correct, then it may be held that this is a historical result of the principle of responsibility. Thus, since traditional professional legal roles and professional duties related to them were subordinated to the principle of lawyers' responsibility for maintaining and developing law, then developing the specialist audience and argumentation techniques that are subordinated to informal reason – techniques which may serve as an example for other discourses – may be regarded as a great success of lawyers and their professional ethics. However, in order to determine whether this praise is deserved, one has to study how much legal ethics in this view may influence the choice of arguments in legal discourse, both from the perspective of viewing some of these arguments as inadmissible and from the perspective of selection criteria of the best arguments.

First of all, according to Perelman, it has to be noted that whoever argues and tries to influence the audience through discourse, is not just carrying out abstract logical operations, but cannot avoid making choices. Because of their disputable character, legal argumentations cannot be regarded as correct in isolation from those people who participate in the dispute, and the entity responsible for making a decision in legal matters, namely a legislator, judge or official, should take responsibility for this decision. Personal involvement is unavoidable irrespective of a possible justification of the position he or she has taken[97]. Thus, it seems that already in the beginning it may be observed that the principle of responsibility is a significant element in the discursive model. Naturally, in accordance with the theses of the multi-dimensional theory of legal ethics, the principle of responsibility will mean something else for each professional role. Similarly, as in the case of other theoretical models of law, a special role is played by judges in the discursive view, though argumentation held by the defence is also significant.

96 K. Kukuryk, "Retoryka prawnicza a orzecznictwo sądowe", ["Legal Rhetorics and Jurisdiction"], in: *Polska kultura prawna a proces integracji europejskiej*, ed. S. Wronkowska, pp. 377-378.

97 Ch. Perelman, *Logika...*, pp. 35-36, 165.

An important observation also from the perspective of theory of legal ethics is the contemporary rise of the importance of judcial roles. This observation reaches to various traditions of legal ethics formed in relation to such professional legal roles as defender or legal counsellor. The metaphor of transformation from the state of laws (*Gesetzesstaat*) to the state of judges (*Richterstaat*) is related to the fact that there arises a reborn conception of legal and especially judicial argumentation, which in the second half of the 20th century seems to predominate in Western Europe. This is because discursive theories shift the discussion focus to judicial judgements' justification, which nowadays is considered a foundation of a good system of justice. The very requirement of preparing statements of reasons for the decisions dates to the 13th century but it was very limited and soon disappeared, while its contemporary genesis may be found in the time of the French Revolution. Because of this requirement different importance is beginning to be assigned also to arguments not belonging to the formal justification but related to the credibility and authority of the judge, namely the ethos of a judge. This tendency is revealed, for example, in the obligation to exclude a judge from a deciding a case whenever he or she knows the grounds for this exclusion[98].

Within the audiences to which a statement of reasons is addressed, lawyers are an important group, and the justification should aim at making the decision acceptable to lawyers, especially in higher instances. Since every decision may serve as precedent in future, one should prove that it may fulfil its role by smoothly including itself in the collective work, namely adjudication. As regards judges, the principle of responsibility thus means maintaining and developing law through providing justification for decisions so that this decision inscribes in the entirety of practice and is convincing to other lawyers. In other words, a responsible judge, when seeking a justification of the decision, feels at ease only when this justification continues and supplements a series of decisions, when it is incorporated into the legal order formed by precedents[99]. Selecting the best argumentation to convince lawyers and continuing the adjudication lines, in this view are not legal ethics duties *par excellence*, but duties which in the case of judicial roles should be related to them. This means, among other things, that reaching to unconvincing argumentation, ignoring legal audiences by negligent statements of reason for decisions, or disrespecting achievements in adjudication may be considered not only ineffective but also irresponsible.

According to Perelman, in contrast to judges, lawyers' roles rely on employing – within the bounds set by professional deontology – all the means that

98 *Ibidem*, pp. 102-103, 203-205, 210.
99 *Ibidem*, pp. 37, 214.

allow one to conduct a defended thesis, provided that the case is not a lost one and the lawyer does not play for time. In order to perform this task responsibly, every bar has its own traditions in deontology. They may differ in details but in general outline they aim at a situation where a laywer is not impeded in the proper fulfilment of his or her task, and also he or she does not become an accomplice of those whom he defends. Numerous limitations in client represenation have alerady been mentioned, but in this place it has to be remarked that legal ethics limits also the acceptable scope of argumentation. It does so in various ways, such as forbidding the lawyer to deceive the judge or to lie. Nevertheless, the lawyer is not obliged nor entitled to disclose anything that comes from confidential confessions of clients[100]. It may be said that the principle of responsibility contained in the aims and values of legal roles of defence, on one hand, limits lawyers' argumentation by excluding arguments which could be effective and convincing but do not serve realisation of tasks of defence.

On the other hand, the realisation of these tasks with the use of argumentation is limited by the responsibility for the whole legal practice, which is why manipulation is excluded. Unacceptability of deceiving or misleading the audience has already been indicated, but it has to be noted that what a lawyer tries to obtain with his or her speech is precisely to convince the judge. However, it is obvious that in the light of the abovementioned consequences of the principle of responsibility, in the case of judges the most convincing to them will be the arguments contained in the hitherto practice of law applying, namely in adjudication. It seems that in the case of lawyers the principle of responsibility does not bind them to fully consider the achievements of adjudication nor to contribute with their argumentation to the adjudication lines, especially when it does not agree with what client wants. A possible retort anticipating arguments that may be posed by other participants of the process and anticipating adjudication which may be indicated as a basis of a decision contradictory with the ends of the defence, is not a lawyer's obligation. Though, a lawyer should consider in every case whether these may be the most responsible actions. Accordingly, in such a situation, a lawyer should try to change tendencies in adjudication by reasoning on its basis, exploiting its weaknesses and inconsistencies and in this way realise the principle of responsibility[101].

To recap, one may attempt to give a general description of relations between the thesis on the exemplary character of legal discourse and the limitations of legal argumentation which are due to lawyers' responsibility for maintaining and

100 *Ibidem*, p. 209.
101 *Ibidem*, pp. 211, 228.

developing law as practice. First af all, it may be observed that law develops through sustained satisfaction of two requirements. The first, of systemic nature, is reduced to working out a coherent legal system. The second, of pragmatic nature, relies on searching solutions that are acceptable because the community regards them as just and correct. The responsibility for this development means for each legal professional role something different, but most grave in this scope is the responsibility resting on judges. It is also worth mentioning the role of legal science, which nowadays is not a major one, and, to Perelman, resembles in some way the role of lawyers, though the authority ascribed to the doctrine stems partially from the fact that it is treated not as a defence of private interests of clients, but as an advocate of general interest, of common good and rightness[102].

Disregarding the question of which legal professional roles in the discursive view are more or less responsible for law as social practice, it has to be remarked that legal logic, especially judicial, eventually appears to be a reasoning dependable on the way in which legislators and judges regard their tasks and on their opinions on law and its functioning in society[103]. The main thesis of the multi-dimensional theory of legal ethics is removing the arbitrariness from comprehending tasks of various legal professions and making them critically and reflectively subordinated to the responsibility for law. The principle of responsibility also plays another function, namely by reference to law as social practice it serves as a theoretical link between goals and values of particular legal professions and those opinions of lawyers on law and its functioning in society. Legal ethics is not applied philosophy of law, however without basing on its achievements it would certainly be incomplete.

4.5.2. Procedural conceptions

4.5.2.1. Special character of legal discourse

Nowadays, it is regarded that the most important among discursive perspectives – aside from topical-rhetorical conceptions – are those which from the position of theory accept as the central thesis that legal discourse has a procedual character[104]. These conceptions usually refer to argumentative philosophies,

---

102 *Ibidem*, pp. 213, 227.

103 *Ibidem*, p. 232.

104 J. Stelmach, B. Brożek, *Metody prawnicze. Logika, analiza, argumentacja, hermeneutyka*, [*Legal Methods. Logic, Analysis, Argumentation, Hermeneutics*], Kraków 2004, p. 181.

which base on theories of rationality understood one way or another, and especially on communicative rationality in the meaning of universal pragmatics of Habermas. Nonetheless, it is noteworthy that, in methodological sense, argumentation as such is located betwen "hard" analysis and logic and "soft" hermeneutics, but having the widest scope of all of them, it often refers to the other ones. Therefore, primarily the ancient hermeneutics was closely related to various argumentative philosophies, but despite distinction of these two disciplines over the last two centuries, their relationships remain strong, which naturally cannot be of no influence on our reflections[105]. Legal interpretation understood hermeneutically is often a part of legal discourses, a fact included by discursive conceptions – by some of them at least.

In recent decades, the most popular procedural view of legal discourse has been the conception of Robert Alexy, who reaches to analytical philosophy as well as to Kant and Habermas. Especially important is the latter inspiration since it is connected with viewing discourse as a process of rational communication, in which a consensus is reached whereby its criterion is truth – in the case of theoretical discourses – and correctness – in practical discourses[106]. One of the arguments for the thesis that legal discourse is a special case of general practical discourse is precisely that all propositions of conclusions of such discourse as well as decisions contained in judicial statements must advance the claim to correctness if they do not want to fall into performative contradiction. This thesis provides grounds to pose before legal discourse and its participants the requirements included in general practical discourse standards. This, from the perspective of multi-dimensional theory of legal ethics, is significant because it raises question, in what mutual relation are legal ethics and the legal discourse ethics.

The thesis that legal discourse is a special case of general practical discourse (*Sonderfallthese*), is ambiguous and problematic. Alexy offers three possible interpretations of it; but still, only one is perceived as correct by him. Firstly, the special case thesis may be understood as *Sekundaritätthese*, which is the thesis on superficiality of legal discourse – practical discourse is always a real ground for decision, which thus is made as if independently from and previously to justifying it with legal argumentation. Secondly, *Additionsthese*, is also a possible interpretation. This thesis claims complementarity of general practical discourse, which is applicable only in those cases in which legal arguments have exhausted their possibilities and did not come to a settlement. According to Alexy, the two interpretations should be discarded because, on one hand, they

105 *Ibidem*, pp. 157-160.
106 *Ibidem*, pp. 171-172.

deprive settlements of real legitimacy by basing them on general reflections, and thus essentially depriving them value of legal safety, and, on the other, legal discourse in these interpretations does not have to meet the requirements of discourse ethics since it is not necessary to provide for correctness of the settlement, and thus the settlement may in consequence be deprived of correctness by inconlusiveness of general discourse[107]. In other words, legal discourse cannot serve only the application of settlements of moral nature even though law and morality are conceptually related.

The third, and simultaneously held as correct, interpretation of the special case thesis is *Integrationsthese*, the integrality of discourse thesis, which refers to a situation where in every phase of reasoning, legal and general arguments should correlate[108]. However, the thesis in this form is still a subject of wide criticism of its justification as well as consequences. As regards reasons for which one should accept the special case thesis, Alexy points to the three most important. Firstly, he asserts that legal discourse concerns practical matters because legal issues have a simultaneously practical nature. Secondly, legal discourse is based on the claim to correctness otherwise it would be performatvely contradictory. Thirdly, it is limited in subject to the currently binding law, which allows one to avoid vagueness and inconclusiveness of general practical discourse[109]. It has to be added that the first two arguments justify why legal discourse is a case of general disocurse wheras the last argument explains why it has a special character[110]. Some reservations may be formulated in reference to all arguments, however, essentially the first two will be discussed.

The fewest controversies are connected with the question of whether legal issues are practical ones, though even this sometimes ignites disputes on specific forms of legal discourse. For whereas judicial discourse, as a rule, is oriented towards settling practical issues, it is not that obvious in the case of legal science disourse. Alexy himself claims that dogmatic discourse is a pure legal discourse because it is non-institutionalised, hence it is as practical as discourses *par excellence* applicative[111]. Most generally, one may only say that the tasks of dogmatics, namely analysing, organising legal concepts and applying these

107 R. Alexy, *Theorie...*, p. 38. See also *idem*, "The Special Case Thesis", *Ratio Juris* 1999, no. 4, pp. 374-384.

108 R. Alexy, *Theorie...*, p. 38.

109 *Ibidem*, p. 263.

110 A. Grabowski, "Dyskurs prawniczy jako przypadek szczególny ogólnego dyskursu praktycznego", ["Legal Discourse as a Special Case of General Practical Discourse"], in: *Studia z filozofii prawa 2*, ed. J. Stelmach, Kraków 2003, p. 48.

111 *Ibidem*, p. 51.

analyses in concrete cases[112], make dogmatics – just like judicial discourses – deal with practical issues. From the perspective of theory of legal ethics, an important conclusion in this regard is the statement that discourse ethics concerns lawyers participating not only in processes of law applying but also of its study, which statement corresponds with the role of legal science and its institutions in legal community, as it has already been signalled several times.

More reservations are formed in relation to the argument from the claim to correctness (*Anschpruch auf Richtigkeit*), which is essentially based on reference to the transcendental-pragmatic concept of performative contradiction, though naturally it has to be remarked that Alexy's use of this category neither implies the acceptance of other assumptions of discourse ethics and the responsibility ethics in the perspective of Apel, nor the consequent application of universal pragmatics of Habermas. The very claim to correctness in legal discourse derives from necessity of avoiding performative contradiction and does not mean that normative utterance contained in a proposition or a statement is rational, but that it may be rationally justified within a legal framework[113]. This is significant because if every judgement raises the claim to correctness, it simultaneously refers to the correctness criteria – the general practical discourse rules in general, and to legal norms of a given legal system in particular. In his later works, Alexy distinguishes two aspects of the claim: the one concerning general practical correctness, and thus referring to law itself, and the one within a legal system, thus referring to a particular system's law applying[114].

According to some critics, the transcendental-pragmatic argument fails because in order to validate any rationality concept, at least to a non-contradictory one, there must already operate some concept of rationality. Therefore in view of the critics, it would be sufficient and advisable to adopt Popperian rationalism, which refers to a certain kind of existential choice and irrational faith in reason. An even greater problem is the nature of the very claim, which implies justifiability in the meaning of practical reason, and this leads to the universalisation requirements. However, it is observed that another possible interpretation of practical reason is the one in instrumental categories, which are not subject to universalisation, and thus legal discourse would not be a special case of the general discourse. In consequence, reference to the claim to correctness can justify neither the content of rules of reason, namely its discursive character in general, nor the general discourse rules which would be applicable in legal discourse in particular[115].

112 R. Alexy, *Theorie...*, p. 311.

113 *Ibidem*, pp. 264-267.

114 A. Grabowski, "Dyskurs prawniczy...", p. 54.

115 B. Brożek, *Rationality and Discourse. Towards a Normative Model of Applaying Law*, Warsaw 2007, pp. 41-42, 78-79, 175-176. See R. Alexy, *Theorie...*, pp. 230-231.

Analysing this critique closer, it has primarily to be noted that rejecting the justification of the claim to correctness by refering to the performative contradiction concept because the concept already presupposed some idea of rationality, is characteristic of the already presented dispute around the issues of ultimate validation. It seems that the difficulty mentioned here is based on not considering such an interpretation of the performative contradiction which holds that in order to accept some criteria of rationality, one already has to use some, but, similarly, that in order to discard some concept of rationality, one also has to already use one. In other words, one should agree with the thesis that any discussion of rationality already refers to its criteria. This is why any statement of this kind of necessity refers to its basic version included in the concept of perfomative contradiction. It simultaneously ascribes raising the claim to correctness by those who defend as well as those who criticise the rationality concept.

Reflective validation of validity claims of all statements and, consequently, also of the claim to correctness in legal discourse, is what distinguishes the discursive model from the positivist one – referring to social practice – or the juriscentric one – referring to the culture established within institutions. This validation refers to the structure of argument as a speech act, which is a basic unit of problematising all acts of communication. Thus, the concept of communicative rationality is primary to instrumental rationality. Therefore, the interpretation of the concept of practical reason, to which the claim to correctness refers, as intrumental reason is a misunderstanding since discourse always rests on communication. Hence, one speaks of the claim to correctness and not to efficacy because efficacy is not an argumentative concept, which of course does not preclude it from becoming an object of discourse. This often occurs in legal discourse when in a statement of reasons to a decision instrumental issues are taken into account out of the intention to make it effective. Nevertheless, one cannot draw from it a conclusion that efficacy is equal to or competing with the correctness criterion of practical rationality, which exists in the form of the claim.

Apart from the claim to correctness, in discursive theory there appear also other kinds of claims referring to functional analysis of speech acts. In this regard, one has to mention primarily the thesis of Habermasa, according to whom rational consensus is possible as long as discourse creates conditions of mutual recognition by its participants of three claims of their statements, namely to subjective honesty, to intersubjective correctness and to objective truthfulness. Though from the perspective of legal decision the most important is correctness, the judgement which would contradict the judge's conscience or which would infringe establishment of facts, has to be considered faulty. It may be said, of course, that these elements are not part of legal reasoning but of a more broadly understood process of law applying. Nevertheless, both discourse rules as well as their possible institutionalisation in the form of legal procedure should enable advancing and admitting these claims by their participants.

Habermas, when characterising the discursive view of Alexy, observes that starting with analysis of procedural conditions of rational discourses in general and proceding to conditions of legal discourses, Alexy introduces universalisation in Kantian sense, which is why the correctness of judicial decisions is ultimately measured by whether they meet the communicative requirements of argumentation. The proposition to build the discurisve theory of law on discourse ethics is to Habermas problematic since the special case thesis falls if one treats seriously this already mentioned parallel formation and distinction of law and morality. Therefore, it is better to assume that moral as well as legal discourses are separate realisations of the discourse rule. They refer to binding law by nature and so the problems of dual character of the claim to correctness, i.e. to what extent it concerns legitimacy of the decisions and to what extent of the norms applied, do not arise. Also, moral issues will appear in the dicourse only with regard to legal norms, and an acknowledged claim to correctness will mean that the decision meets the requirements of argumentative discourse only on the grounds of a particular legal system[116].

Such an interpretation is not far from what is proposed by Alexy because it is often claimed when accepting the special case thesis that legal discourse is a special case not that much of the general discourse but rather of moral or ethical one. Whereas Alexy, consistently, "identifies practical discourse neither with moral discourse nor with ethical one, and even emphasises [...] that the special case thesis, if referred only to moral discourse and not to general practical one, is false."[117] However, the problem is that general discourse does not exist at all because there is no possibility of its application. Only particular argumentative discourses, inlcuding legal discourse, may be applied. Hence, the special case thesis in the understanding of Alexy as well as the thesis on the exemplary case in the meaning of Perelman, should be rejected, and one should simply assert that legal discourse is only one of argumentative discourse cases[118]. It seems that the interpretation of general discourse as an abstract discourse rule corresponds well with these views.

116 J. Habermas, *Between...* p. 229.

117 A. Grabowski, "Dyskurs prawniczy...", p. 47.

118 J. Stelmach, *Kodeks argumentacyjny dla prawników*, [*An Argumentative Code for Lawyers*], Kraków 2003, pp. 26-31.

Simultaneously, this discourse rule requires that legal discourse is organised in such a way that it is possible to advance all sorts of validity claims by discourse participants. Naturally, this does not mean that every participant is obliged to search for a correct settlement as legal discourse is not a moral one. Because of that some typical forms of legal discourse institutionalisations in the form of legal procedures become understandable; especially the division of professional roles, in which participants functionally share the task of such formulation of arguments and suggestions of settlements which acknowledges validity claims. However, it has to be remembered that only the course of the process is at issue here, while the judicial discourse itself, relying on considering all arguments and making a decision, is freed from all external influences and takes place outside the procedure[119]. Legal argumentative discourse therefore must fulfil all the requirements related to validity claims – primarily to the claim to correctness – irrespective of whether it occurs within the procedure stipulated by the law or outside this procedure.

If one wanted to build on this ground a legal discourse ethics, then its status as the set of discourse criteria stemming from the claim to correctness will cause that, "an argumentative discourse that is not compatible with rules guaranteeing 'ethical miniumum' may not be held at all and its results may not be accepted." In this view, efficacy as a criterion of good communication, "cannot be superior and autonomic in relation to the correctness and rationality criteria," therefore the view excludes eristic, and rhetoric is treated rather as a technical skill.[120] Specific 'ethical axioms' are the following rules of discourse ethics: (1) allowing for holding a discourse in the case of disputable uncertainties, (2) commanding to hold a discourse with one's conviction of the arguments' correctness (moral conviction is at issue here), (3) commanding truthfulness, (4) commanding taking previous establishment of facts into account, (5) commanding including universally accepted practices and rules, (6) commanding respecting rules of freedom and equality (limited, for example, by the requirement of competence and knowledge of the discourse subject matter), (7) commanding aiming at resolution of a difficult case (it excludes obstruction by the use of eristic or rhetoric), and (8) commanding applying rules of linguistic communication[121].

Applying all these rules of discourse ethics could be perceived as particularisation of the principle of responsibility. For if this principle obliges one to maintain and develop law as practice, and if this practice is of discursive

---

119 J. Habermas, *Between...*, pp. 230-231.

120 J. Stelmach, "Etyka dyskursu prawniczego", ["Ethics of A Legal Discourse"], in: *Prawo a wartości. Księga jubileuszowa Profesora Józefa Nowackiego*, ed. I. Bogucka, Z. Tobor, Kraków 2003, pp. 261-263.

121 *Ibidem*, pp. 264-268.

nature, then the better discourse requirements will be satisfied, and the better this task will be accomplished. Interestingly, the principle of responsibility as the obligation to realise discourse ethics was viewed by Apel himself, though, naturally, the disputability of such application is shown by the very discussion on the special case thesis. Its ambiguity and various critiques indicate that the criterion of applying discourse ethics to legal discourse is first of all accepting that it is a discourse at all. Such a statement may have different status from the methodological perspective, i.e. it may be treated as empirical constatation of a fact or a description of a certain relation between two types of theory. However, as it has been shown in the presented discussion, in each of these perspectives serious difficulties occur.

However, on the basis of the same discussion it may be asserted that the methodological status of the special case thesis is not descriptive nor empirical but normative, and, "according to this interpretation, the special case thesis is a postulate, expressed in the form of a definition, to treat (or interpret) legal discourse as a special case of general practical discourse. The nature of this postulate is considerably complex because it seems to be addressed to all participants of legal discourse (i.e. to the legislator, judges, parties in judicial proceedings) and also to scientists analysing this discourse. Depending on the context, especially the one of the possible receiver of the postulate, it may be ascribed ideological, moral or methodological character."[122] It seems that accepting this interpretation and recognising that in reference to lawyers this postulate has moral aspect may constitute the content of the principle of responsibility. According to this interpretation, the lawyers' responsibility is realising discourse ethics in legal discourses, but not because these have such character *ex definitione*, but because the lawyers should treat it like that.

4.5.2.2. Legal ethics as a condition of argumentation

Accepting that moral responsibility of lawyers means that they should treat law as discursive practice and realise discourse ethics in it is in this situation, analytically speaking, a condition of rational argumentation. However, the multi-dimensional theory of legal ethics claims something more than that, namely that the principle of responsibility validates the whole structure of legal ethics composed of, apart from the moral, also social and deontological planes. Therefore, it should be studied in what relation legal ethics and the legal discourse ethics are in other spheres, especially in view that different positions appear on this matter. On one hand, there appears scepticism towards legal

122 A. Grabowski, "Dyskurs prawniczy...", p. 61.

ethics, based on the statement that discourse ethics and legal ethics, though both are built in relation to the principle of responsibility, contradict each other. On the other, there are viewpoints according to which legal ethics, provided that it is not reduced only to professional deontology, is crucial from the perspective of legal discourse ethics.

The first position is represented primarily be Aulis Aarnio, who claims not only that legal ethics is redundant, but also that it may even be dangerous as it threatens legal settlements' rationality and correctness, which may be attained simply by complying with ethics of discourse as such. He also asserts that such principles as, for instance, protection of professional confidentiality or the conflict of interests are parts of the institution and not norms of legal ethics, and are regulated in a more varied way. Therefore, the one thing all lawyers have in common is educaction and all their professional roles differ greatly. Not without irony he adds that that sanctions for breaching legal ethics duties are illusion – even exclusion from the profession is not very severe because such a person will always find a way to stay in business. Then he goes on to more philosophical sophisticated reflections, but to simplify it he examines only the problem of judicial ethics, whereby as ethics he means more qualities and attitudes rather than actions to which one refers the concept of morality. In this context he points to such phenomena behind popularity of judicial ethics as increasingly closer relationships of law and morality in many areas of law (criminal, family, etc.), more frequent questions about legitimisation, the crisis of authorities, democratisation of the judiciary relying on increase in openness and not representativeness, and a general decrease in credibility of state institutions, including courts[123].

All attempts at rebuilding the credibility of courts – which was undermined in the result of these processes – inscribe in a certain theoretical model consisting of three elements. First, uncertainty or law's vagueness and the facts of a case causes the rise of discretionary power. Second, the obligation to adjudicate in every case determines using this power. Third, the attempts are also influenced by social expectations of providing the widest legal protection. These three elements of a judge's situation define his or her social responsibility. Therefore, to satisfy this responsibility requirement, judges cannot be arbitrary; their judgements must be predictable, and this may only be provided for by their rationality. A settlement in adjudication will be rational when it meets not only the standards of legality, but also of correctness, which is a matter of social acceptability. The acceptability is attained not by comparing substantive

123 A. Aarnio, "Lawyers' Professional Ethics…", pp. 2-4.

standards of correctness, but by discourse, in procedural sense, which fulfils the requirements of discourse ethics[124].

The fundamental requirement of procedurally oriented discourse ethics in this perspective is justification of its own statements, and so, in the discussed case, of judicial adjudication. From this position, it is exactly a good justification of legal decisions that may, significantly more effectively than judicial ethics in the sense of ethical quality or a catalogue of virtues, restore trust in courts. Additionally, requirement of justification has a universal aspect and there is no need to formulate some special obligations addressed uniquely to judges. Moreover, any special requirements of necessity contradict universal standards or at least undermine them[125]. It seems that this conclusion is too far-reaching; just as, from the fact that all people are bound by the same, in content, standard of honesty, it does not flow that it has the same status in relation to all, similarly, from the fact that all people are morally responsible for their practices to the same extent does not mean that all practices are socially of equal importance. The significance of lawyers' responsibility for law is connected with the fact that as a rule, performing legal roles is related to exercising power, and to the question, "how to exercise it", legal ethics gives a more precise answer than does discourse ethics.

Taking this cirumstance into consideration, Marek Zirk-Sadowski envisages a different role for legal ethics in his discursive view emphasising the importance of legal hermeneutics. The view is an answer to the crisis of the judiciary – understood in the way described above – but simultaneously it is directed at the positivist model, and draws on legal and cultural achievements of European integration. Most generally speaking, every discourse requires understanding as well as communication. Hermeneutics and argumentation presuppose some ethical requirements, but still, the hermeneutical vision must be complemented with critical attitude that is specific of communicative rationality. Thanks to this attitude one may state whether, on the grounds of a particular tradition, there occurs a real consensus on its content or not. Hermeneutical deepening of the understanding of legal ethics and simultaneous critical attitde to it are correlated with its role in legal epistemology, which most concisely is expressed in a popular saying that, "only an honest lawyer can know (understand) law."[126] It may be added that honesty entails incessant reflection on what it means to be honest.

---

124 *Ibidem*, pp. 5-8.

125 *Ibidem*, p. 9.

126 M. Zirk-Sadowski, *Prawo a uczestniczenie w kulturze*, [*Law and Participation in Culture*], Łódź 1998, pp. 57-70, 80. See also *idem*, *Rozumienie ocen w języku prawnym*, [*The Understanding of Evaluations in the Legal Language*], Łódź 1984, especially part 3.

Among the proposed ways of overcoming the crisis of the judiciary, apart from organisational actions, it is necessary to, "restore the prestige to rules of professional ethics and to the sense of responsibility for law itself" among lawyers[127]. Speaking more precisely, this sense of responsibility may be viewed as the moral principle of responsibility because the problem of contemporary jurisdiction is that society expects greater responsibility of lawyers for law, and particularly, "greater activity of courts in correcting bad law in the process of law applying." Thus, lawyers should maintain and develop law, nonetheless, it has to be noted that those lawyers who have been raised in radical positivism rarely manifest such attitude and regard it as a noxious activism. Positivism thus allows them to maintain in relation to law uniquely a cognitive, and not moral, attitude, but its criticism leads to the conclusion that it is based on, "false conception of law cognition, in which professional ethics of lawyers does not play any significant role" and is essentially reduced to norms contained in various normative acts[128].

Social and deontological planes of legal ethics, as validated and limited by the moral principle of responsibility, from this perspective, may play an important role since the procedural model – in this view, strongly connected with legal hermeneutics – combines with the necessity of meeting the discourse ethics requirements, which make its outcome rational and acceptable. In other words, "the cognition of law is done [...] through communicative actions, in which the rationality criteria contain [...] ethical requirements," and, "in the case of legal discourse a considerable proportion of these requirements is defined by legal ethics." This is a consequence of the special case thesis in the interpretation of integrity of general legal discourse with general practical discourse, which means that the former is a 'superstructure' on the latter. From thus perceived relation of the two discourses it flows that aims and values of legal professional roles and professional duties of legal ethics are a particularisation of discourse ethics[129]. If one adds that the special case thesis may be treated as a moral postulate addressed to lawyers, then their responsibility will be not only maintaining and developing law as practice, but also of legal ethics so that it enabled them to realise this task.

The additional dimension of such strong consideration of legal ethics in the functioning of courts and of the related theoretical model will be development and integration of legal culture. Professional participation of lawyers in culture is

127 M. Zirk-Sadowski, "Uczestniczenie prawników w kulturze",["The Participation of Lawyers in Culture"], *Państwo i Prawo* 2002, no. 9, p. 3.

128 *Ibidem*, pp. 6, 12-18.

129 M. Zirk-Sadowski, *Prawo a...*, pp. 8-80; in: *idem*,"Uczestniczenie"..., p. 13.

associated with performing some defined functions reserved for them, among which one may distinguish enforcement, mediation and legal counselling. The latter may be regarded as, "a conventional moment of the rise of professional legal practice." Legal ethics in the multi-dimensional view will enable lawyers of all professional roles – not only the judicial ones – to accept responsibility for law, and by this, to fully participate in culture. This is especially important from the persective of European integration, which also in its legal aspect has a strongly cultural character. Furthermore, in the scale of the whole continent one may speak of the formation of the European law practice, which needs harmonisation of, among other things, education and deontology. Within its framework, "legal professions are equipped with professional ethics with which the course of legal practice is evaulated. The content of these ethics is connected with legal rationality since it decides on the choice of arguments in legal discourse."[130]

Finally, it is worth adding that legal ethics in the proposed view may perform similar functions in the discursive model based on the procedural perspective directed against some statements of the integral theory of law. Habermas rejects Dworkin's conception because his formulations, "presuppose that the judge is exceptionally qualified, both by reason of her professional knowledge and skills and thanks to her personal virtues, to act as the citizens' *representative* in securing the integrity of the legal community." The judge is a representative of integrity not of the community itself, but to it. this theory based on, "the ideal personality of a judge who is distinguished by her virtue and her privileged access to the truth." should be replaced with wider participation of society[131]. In organising this participation an important role should be played by lawyers, and their responsibility for maintaining and developing law by realising discourse ethics will rely on enabling the society to participate in legal discourses freely and on equal terms.

Extending social participation in legal discourses, or more broadly, in legal culture, is possible because of adequate formation of social and deontological planes of legal ethics. Habermas suggests that a lawyer, "Hercules could conceive himself as a member of the interpretation community of legal experts; his interpretations would then have to follow standards recognized in the profession […] *Professionally proven standards* are meant to guarantee the objectivity of the judgment and its openness to intersubjective review." It has to be noted that in this view the range of legal ethics would be extended so that it encompasses the standards of statutory interpretation, but simultaneously standards of practising in a profession are validated here only by "traditions of a

---

130 M. Zirk-Sadowski, *Prawo a…*, pp. 36, 109, 123-125.

131 J. Habermas, *Between…*, pp. 224-225.

culture of experts." This is a drawback since, "From the observer's perspective, however, such standards are no more than a self-legitimating code of professional ethics. Even within the same legal culture, various subcultures oppose one another over the choice of the right standards. In any event, from an internal perspective, the mere fact that a hardly homogeneous professional class legitimates itself is not sufficient to demonstrate the validity (*gultig*) of the very procedural principles that ground validity within the system (*geltungsbegrundenden*)."[132] Therefore, a discursive model of law is needed, of which in my belief, a critical and reflective legal ethics based on the principle of responsibility is an important element.

4.6. Conclusion: morality of law and morality of lawyers

Summarising this part, it has to be stressed that on the grounds of legal philosophy it has been studied here whether the conceptions – selected on the basis of their practical importance – constituting the positivist, juriscentric and discursive models, *explicite* or *implicite* – contain any conceptions of legal ethics and what relation they have to the multi-dimensional theory of legal ethics. Accordingly, on the basis of each of the presented views, conclusions on the content of the principle of lawyers' responsibility for law – meaning that lawyers should maintain and develop it – have been formed. In the positivist model the conclusion holds that the object of the lawyers' responsibility is to make the legal system constantly follow the social one, which has brought it into being, and this strive for compatibility is the maintenance and development of law.

In the juriscentric model the lawyers' responsibility relies on making a herculean effort in order to include the widest range of viewpoints expressed in principles concerning justice and correctness and on choosing the solution which realises this integrality best. There is always only one such a solution. Therefore, at issue is the aspiration to the ideal of applying law in a way that intergrates political community and the obligation to constantly develop law and one's skills in order to attain the greatest proficiency in this development. Lawyers' responsibility could also rely on maintaining and developing legal culture, which is a foundation of law as institution, and thus on self-limiting their discretionary power.

In the discursive model, as regards judges, the principle of responsibility means maintaining and developing law through justifying their decisions so that

132 *Ibidem*, p. 225.

they inscribe into the entirety of practice and are convincing to other lawyers. While in a different view, the responsibility for maintaining and developing law by realising discourse ethics relies on enbaling society to participate in legal discourse on free and equal terms.

This analysis seems to show some evolution of legal-philospohical conceptions, and throws light both on contemporary interest in legal ethics as well as on the perspectives of its development. For it has to be noted that moral reflections are present in philosophy of law in three different modes. Firstly, they are present as a point of reference for evaluation of legal norms in relation to which they are an external standard. Such a program of "external morality of law" is realised, for example, by ethics of law (*Rechtsethik*) as a search for good law by referring legal norms to substantial moral norms. Secondly, also "internal morality of law" seems to be equally popular. It searches formal standards that would be *ex definitione* connected with law; standards which set the criteria of bounds of law as well as of good law. Both trends have a firm status in legal sciences[133].

Nevertheless, if the presented reflections have some cognitive value and indeed one may speak of law paradigm transformations, to much extent consisting of the fact that, "legal, community standards of evaluation no longer serve integration around the employer but around certain soial roles which a lawyer has to fulfil,"[134] then perhaps it is appropriate to analyse the chances of the third view which will not refer to externally or internally understood morality of law itself but to morality of lawyers, who maintain and develop it as practice. In this view it has to be remembered that in the cultural perspective one may pose a question, "can law do without the lawyer, and precisely without the legal community." The response seems to confirm, at least in reference to contemporary law, the necessity of the legal community's existence. This community may be integrated by standards contributing to its pragmatics of professional conduct. This pragmatics has to be understood as universal legal pragmatics referring to discourse ethics[135]. Maybe the multi-dimensional theory of legal ethics indicates how this pragmatics could be designed.

133 See: M. Safjan, *Wyzwania dla państwa prawa*, [*Challenges to A Law-Governed State*], Warsaw 2007, p. 22 ff., p. 58 ff. and p. 195 ff.

134 A. Bator, "Wspólnota kulturowa jako element integracji prawa",["Cultural Community as an Element of Integration of Law"], in: *Z zagadnień teorii i filozofii prawa. W poszukiwaniu podstaw prawa*, ed. A. Sulikowski, Wrocław 2006, p. 12.

135 *Ibidem*, pp. 18-20.

Chapter 5
Legal ethics among legal sciences

The multi-dimensional theory of legal ethics, presented in the previous chapters, is an attempt at creating a perspective that would correspond with contemporary transformations of the traditions of legal ethics and simultaneously that would enable modern and critical studies in this discipline to be carried out. However in order to conduct such studies, a theory is not enough, even if it offered appropriate methodology and defined the status of its own premises and statement. For it has to be remarked that systematic research requires additional directives heuristic in nature, which may steer often dipersed efforts of scientists. Typically, such directives are formulated on the ground of particular scientific disciplines, which, in reference to legal ethics, must raise two serious questions. Firstly, whether it has a research program that is precise enough to distinguish legal ethics from other disciplines being part of broadly understood legal sciences. Secondly, whether the multi-dimensional character of legal ethics and the methodological compexity related to it do not obstruct such a distinction or do not make legal ethics a field of knowledge of special status.

5.1. Research program of legal ethics

Legal ethics, both in its traditional versions as well as from the perspectives of modern and critical theory, concerns phenomena occurring in legal practice. Therefore, one may accept the assumption, without the need of justification, that if legal ethics may be regarded as a discipline of knowledge – as it is by the multi-dimensional theory of legal ethics – then within the framework of sciences' division, the place of legal ethics is among legal sciences. This is not impeded by accepting that its highest plane is of moral character, and thus it belongs to philosophy, because also for the philosophical disciplines whose subjects are related to law there is a place among legal sciences. However, to specify the status of legal ethics on the ground of jurisprudence, one has to draw attention not only to the way of justifying the statements of legal ethics (the context of justifcation), but primarily to the way of setting directions of systematic research (the context of discovery). It seems that accepting the methodology of research programs in the understanding of Lakatos as the criteria of evaluation of heuresis proposed by the multi-dimensional theory of legal ethics is justified for the following reasons.

Firstly, this perspective is critical towards justificationism, according to which whether a particular theoretical proposition is true rests on its justification. According to Imre Lakatos, justificationism 'spreads between two polar opposites', and sooner or later must lead to acceptance of one of the positions, which are described as scepticism and dogmatism[1]. In contrast to Popper's falsificationism, Lakatos proposes its sophisticated version, which, "replaces the concept of *theory* as the basic concept of the logic of discovery by the concept of *series of theories*. [...] But the members of such series of theories are usually connected by a remarkable *continuity* which welds them into *research programmes*. This continuity reminiscent of Kuhnian 'normal science' – plays a vital role in the history of science."[2] Thus, it may be said that the multi-dimensional theory of legal ethics is based on a view similar to that of methodology of research programmes, namely on a historical nature of knowledge.

Secondly, in opposition to Kuhn, he claims that this continuity of science is not of psychological or sociological character, but normative, and this distinguishes "mature" disciplines from "immature." It may be said that, "Mature science consists of research programmes in which not only novel facts but, in an important sense, also novel auxiliary theories, are anticipated; mature science – unlike pedestrian trial-and-error – has' heuristic power'." Contrary to this, "immature" science consists of, " a mere patched up pattern of trial and error" since all research directions are set by anomalies arising on the ground of accepted theories – anomalies, being phenomena unexplained by such theories[3]. According to Lakatos, a scientist should be guided by methodological rules of a research program and, "It is primarily the positive heuristic of his programme, not the anomalies, which dictate the choice of his problems."[4] The multi-dimensional theory of legal ethics contains methodological rules concerning directions of research on the social and deontological planes of legal ethics. Thus, the theory has a heuristic power and the development of legal ethics may happen on its grounds, and not only in reference to it.

---

1 I. Lakatos, "Newton's Effect on Scientific Standards", in: *idem*, *The Methodology of Scientific Research Programmes. Phliosophical Papers,* Vol I, Cambridge 1978, pp. 193-195.

2 I. Lakatos, "Falsification and the Methodology of Scientific Research Programmes", in: *idem*, *The Methodology*..., pp. 46-47.

3 *Ibidem*, pp. 87-88.

4 I. Lakatos, "History of Science and Its Rational Reconstructions", in: *idem*, *The Methodology*..., p. 194.

Thirdly, the historical character of science and normative character of research programs enable one to speak of progress in science. Progress is not meant in cumulative categories but critical ones. Lakatos remarks that, "Criticism is not a Popperian quick kill, by refutation. Important criticism is always constructive: there is no refutation without a better theory," which becomes evident in the light of the Hegelian inspirations of the author. The more critical of one another that research programs are, the more progressive they will be. However, it has to be noted that some programs may prove progressive, while others may degenerate and it is a matter of a scientist's honesty to report it straight to the public. Nevertheless, it is not dishonest to cling to a program which undergoes troubles, or to try to defend it and change it into a progressive one[5]. In other words, mature science in its research programs includes the requirement of constant development, and this is close to the formulations of the multi-dimensional theory of legal ethics as a critical and reflective theory.

If therefore it is justified to apply the methodology of research programs to the attempt at distinguishing legal ethics as a scientific discipline, then it should also be emphasised that methodology is based on the distinction within every research program between negative and positive heuristic. The former contains a methodological rule prohibiting the program's "hard core", which is irrefutable because its change would mean "problem shift", namely a modification of the very grounds of the program, and such modification would be tantamount to its abandonment. Contrary to that, the framework of positive heuristic commands that problem shifts which serve development of the "protective belt" of the program containing hypotheses auxiliary to the "hard core" are performed. This part of the research program also includes hints and suggestions about how to perform these shifts so that they may be viewed as developing the program and as the subsequent steps of its realisation. Lakatos frames it, "Positive heuristic is [...] more flexible than negative heuristic,"[6] therefore it seems that characterisation of legal ethics as a discipline should be based on determining its 'less soft' part, namely the issues belonging to its "hard core".

The presentation of a multi-dimensional theory of legal ethics required multiple discussion of the range of issues belonging to its study. Thus, here it need only be stated that these issues are slightly different for each of the planes. On the deontological plane, the problems include the critique of professional duties that occur in the practice of lawyers from the perspective of aims and values of particular professional roles. Whereas on the social plane, the range

---

5 I. Lakatos, "Introduction: Science and Pseudoscience", in: *idem*, *The Methodology...*, p 6.

6 I. Lakatos, "Falsification and the Methodology...", p. 52.

includes the critique of thee aims and values also from the position of the principle of responsibility and the principle of trust and of integrity. On the moral plane, the problems concern reflective study of lawyers' responsibility for law as social practice, maintenance and development. It seems that abandoning any of these ranges would be such a problem shift that would result in a loss of identity of legal ethics and abandonment of its research program in this view.

For if problems of legal ethics were reduced to professional duties, or rules of professional practice, then such a study may be conducted within the framework of dogmatic sciences. However, typically the study is divided between a number of various disciplines; to refer to just one example, one may indicate that the duties related to the role of a criminal lawyer or prosecutor or a legal agent in civil proceedings are subjects of interest to science of procedural law, just like duties connected with debt proceedings. Whereas notarial deeds, and it seems that also legal counselling, fall within the range of interest of private law. In turn, administrative law dogmatics within the framework of study on professional self-governing organisations concentrates primarily on lawyers' duties in this scope. It is significant that the so-called organs or corporations of legal protection are an attempt at unifying all these elements. However, this is rather a didactic subject, which has not developed its research program, and, historically, its issues have been transferred to procedural law's dogmatics[7].

Also reducing the reflections from the range of legal ethics to aims and values central to particular legal professional roles or professions leads to including its elements in research programs of other disciplines and makes it lose its identity. For if these aims and values are taken in legal sense, thus as directly included or reconstructed from the content on legal acts, then the study of them may be successfully conducted within the framework of particular legal dogmatics, though, naturally, the integration of its findings will require an interdisciplinary dialogue between them. However, if it is assumed that the concepts of professional roles and of a profession itself have social character, then the reflections on aims and values central to each of them could not be detached from research from the scope of social sciences, and especially from sociology of law. On the social plane of legal ethics also systemic, functional and interactive factors should be considered, as well as – on the basis of the principles of trust and integrity – the social expectations of the whole society and of lawyers themselves towards their professional roles. If these issues were detached from other planes of legal ethics, this program could be described merely as a sociology of legal professions, and such a discipline cannot be identified with legal ethics.

---

7 See *Organy i korporacje ochrony prawa*, [*Organs or Corporations of Legal Protection*], ed. S. Sagan, Warsaw 2001.

There is also a position according to which, "legal ethics, as an autonomic scientific discipline, is a philosophical reflection on the morality of practice of people practising in legal professions." As such, legal ehics has been distinguished from general moral philosophy, despite on-going disputes over its autonomy. The subject of legal ethics is complex and it cannot, "be reduced only to a scientific discipline or only to a subject in academic education, or to norms of professional practice. Legal ethics is all that in a way as an expression of collective efforts to define the meaning of morally good legal practice indicating paths of simultaneous personal moral satisfaction of a lawyer and social respect for him or her."[8] Ethics of particular legal professions – for instance, a judge's ethics – though it is described as a part of legal ethics, is an adjustment of, "more general norms of legal ethics to more specific situations associated with this profession," and thus it concerns only the normative aspect and, it seems, is not recognised as a scientific or didactic sub-discipline[9].

The abovementioned perspective, though it declares the autonomy of legal ethics as a discipline and sees the need of its distinction from general spheres containing theses on all legal professions or all lawyers and from more specific ones including the specificity of particular professions, ascribes the whole undertaking a philosophical character. If legal ethics according to the drafted proposition is, "a philosophical reflection on the morality of practice," then what is the status of such reflection among research disciplines? For it may be accepted that although thus understood legal ethics has been distinguished from ethics as such, then it does not necessarily have autonomous status, but is a part of the broadly understood general science of law. The fact that the methodological character of general science of law is ambiguous and that disputes arise between proponents of theory of law on one side and philosophy of law on the other does not have to be an obstacle here since the legal character of many concepts of legal ethics with its general importance to the legal system makes a simultaneous theoretical and philosophical study of them advisable.

Despite many differences between theory of law and philosophy of law, it is indicated that studies of the first type, "do not show any methodological prevalence over classical philosophical reflections on law," and, "general science of law is essentially philosophical in nature."[10] In relation to this view, the standpoint that general sciences of law should be regarded as a pluralist

---

8 R. Tokarczyk, "Przedmiot etyki prawniczej" ["The Subject of Legal Ethics"], in: *Państwo, prawo, myśl prawnicza*, Lublin 2003, pp. 285-287, 297.

9 R. Tokarczyk, "Kształtowanie przedmiotu etyki sędziego" ["Formation of the Subject of Judicial Ethics"], *Państwo i Prawo* 2004, no. 7, p. 15.

10 P. Kamela, "Teoria prawa a filozofia prawa" ["Theory of Law and Philosophy of Law"], *Kwartalnik Prawa Publicznego* 2006, no. 4, pp. 217-218.

discipline described as philosophy of law in a broad sense[11] or just as theory and philosophy of law is considerably widely represented. Thus understood, the field of knowledge, by exceeding limitations typical to traditional research disciplines, is not so much inter-disciplinary in character, but rather post-disciplinary, and thus ascribes itself into a typically post-modern attempt to construct a holistic views[12]. It seems that legal ethics perceived as 'philosophical reflection' may be practised within the framework of a theory and philosophy of law thus understood as a sphere of research that is very close to – though in subject matter and methodology distinct from – the traditionally understood theory of law and philosophy of law. It is advisable also because the moral plane of legal ethics, though distinguished on the grounds of philosophy of morality, employs legal-philosophical concepts.

To summarise, it may be said that in order to speak of legal ethics as a distinct discipline among legal sciences, it has to be programmatically multi-dimensional – otherwise it will be exposed to problem shifts, which enable some of its spheres to be included in other scientific disciplines. Naturally, this does not mean that the multi-dimensional theory of legal ethics is the only acceptable, but, according to the methodology of research programs, one should consistently conduct research on all planes of legal ethics and in this way aim at working out better theories. Such a view simultaneously realises the postulates of critical and reflective theory. It is worth adding that, though, according to Lakatos, science as such is not socially responsible, and even though he does not share the view, which he ascribes to leftist thinkers, that due to some civilisation risks some type of research – as, for example, in nuclear physics or genetics – should be forbidden, this does not mean that scientists, as citizens, are not responsible for the way in which their research findings and science as a whole are used. Still, these are two different problems[13] and this chapter – together with the normative command to develop research program – resembles the reconstruction of ethics of science based on the principle of responsibility described in the present work in relation to legal ethics.

---

11 T. Stawecki, "Filozofia prawa a teoria prawa: spór nierozstrzygalny czy pozorny?" ["Philosophy of Law versus Theory of Law: An Unsolvable or a Superficial Dispute"], *Studia Iuridica* 2006, no. 45, pp. 217-220.

12 H. Izdebski, *Elementy teorii i filozofii prawa*, [*Elements of Theory and Philosophy of Law*], Warsaw 2008, p. 51. Cf. J. Stelmach, "Ponowoczesna filozofia prawa", ["Postmodern Philosophy of Law"], in: *Studia z filozofii prawa 2*, ed. J. Stelmach, Kraków, 2003, pp. 15-21.

13 I. Lakatos, "The Social Responsibility of Science", in: *Mathematics, Science and Epistemology. Philosophical Papers,* vol. 2, ed. J. Worrall and G. Currie, Cambridge 1997, pp. 256-259.

5.2. Interdisciplinarity of legal ethics

The research program of legal ethics rests on the assumption of its multi-dimensionality. This means not only that legal ethics joins many traditions, which is typical of modernity, but also means the acceptance that the very phenomenon is complex. Therefore it is possible to carry out research on the particular planes from various perspectives and with various methods, which nevertheless – as I have tried to show – cannot lead to satisfying results, and so it is necessary to distinguish legal ethics as a discipline integrating them all by the use of methodology proposed by the multi-dimensional theory of legal ethics. However, one may ask to what extent a discipline distinguished in this way will be specific in regard to its methodology and subject matter, and to what extent it will only be an interdisciplinary undertaking in which its distinction will be justified only by the fact that it organises scientific work. Taking into account that interdisciplinarity is first of all a matter of researchers' orientation, the answer seems to be a gradable matter and a lot depends on how practice is being formed in this regard[14].

It has to be remarked that literature distinguishes horizontal interdisciplinarity – described as proper interdisciplinarity – which concerns integration of many scientific disciplines having common ground, for example, a common subject studied from different perspectives, and vertical interdisciplinarity, in which more specific disciplines integrate with the more general ones, or the entirety of science with general ideas. The difference between these types of interdisciplinarity relies primarily on the fact that in the second case, ideas or principles are postulated before research is carried out, whereas in the first case they result from research activity. This means that a premise of proper interdisciplinarity is the lack of prerequisites which would basically rely on the necessity of accepting the theses of one discipline by other ones[15]. In reference to legal ethics one may speak of two kinds of interdisciplinarity only in a limited way.

Vertical interdisciplinarity of legal ethics is connected with its multi-dimensional structure, in which the principle of responsibility, common to all professions, integrates the ethics of particular legal professions; ethics, which differ in aims and values central to each professional role and in professional duties. Though it would be difficult to speak of lawyers ethics, judicial ethics, notarial ethics or bailiffs' ethics as separate disciplines which require to be integrated through a more general legal ethics, however they may be

14 H. Parthey, K. Schreiber, "Voraussetzungen und Formen interdisziplinärer Forschung", in: *Interdisziplinarität in der Forschung. Analysen und Fallstudien*, ed. H. Parthey, K. Schreiber, Berlin 1983, p. 304.

15 *Ibidem*, p. 305.

distinguished as some sub-disciplines which need such integration. Therefore, as it has been emphasised, there is a point in distinction between legal ethics and the ethics of legal professions since the latter is – in a way resembling the vertical interdisciplinarity – a part of the first and remains determined by it as regards basic rules and methods. Naturally, one can speak here more of a kind of resemblance or figurative interdisciplinarity, rather that of actual research carried out between scientific disciplines.

However, also from the multi-dimensional structure of legal ethics one may draw the conclusion that it, at least to some extent, is interdisciplinary in character in the horizontal sense. For if reflections belonging to the particular planes – deontological, social and moral – may be, and actually until now in majority have been, carried out within the framework of dogmatic, sociological and philosophical disciplines, then their integration by research from the range of legal ethics may be treated as interdisciplinarity. Undoubtedly, legal ethics in the perspective of multi-dimensional theory of legal ethics and the research program proposed by it draws on the achievements of these disciplines and uses these to formulate its own conclusions. This is possible thanks to its own methodology, which allows to conduct systematic research. This is why one may speak of the interdisciplinarity of legal ethics only in a weak sense. This of course does not mean that co-operation with other disciplines is of little importance; just the opposite, the co-operation is all the more important, the more legal ethics uses the findings and the more it can be helpful in understanding and setting directions for research.

Among the conditions behind such co-operation of an interdisciplinary character, one usually cites some basic ones of a primarily social nature. Firstly, all disciplines participating in interdisciplinary programs must be sufficiently developed, i.e. have their own research programs and identity. Secondly, there must be some communicative possibilities between the representatives of particular co-operating disciplines. Thirdly, an interdisciplinary program must be attractive for all the engaged disciplines, i.e., for example, be socially significant and enforceable[16]. It seems that the multi-dimensional theory of legal ethics showed that social significance and the perspectives of realisation of the research program in this scope allow for hope that an interdisciplinary program will prove attractive enough to draw the attention of scholars from various disciplines and to integrate the efforts which have been scattered until now. Thus, it may be concluded that although legal ethics is not interdisciplinary in the full sense of this word, interdisciplinarity plays an essential role in the study of legal ethics and simultaneously does not prevent its distinction as an autonoumous discipline among legal sciences.

---

16 *Ibidem*, p. 306.

Conclusion

The aim of the present work was to examine the status of legal ethics on the grounds of various philosophical disciplines and from the point of view of methodology. This was reflected in distinguishing several parts of the refelctions. Partial conclusions from each chapter contribute to the conclusions of the whole research and allow these to be reformulated as the recapitular thesis. This final thesis claims that legal ethics is a discipline of knowledge concerning deontological, social and moral aspects of practising in legal professions – a discipline with a critical task – and reflective examination of both the content and the relationships between these aspects, which are planes of the multi-dimensional theory of legal ethics. This examination is performed with methodology of an interdisciplinary character, utilising methods that are specific to legal dogmatics, social sciences, the philosophy of morality and the philosophy of law. The multi-dimensional theory of legal ethics is central to reinforcing and explaining this thesis. The theory may be interpreted as a theory of good practice in legal professions as well as a scientific program for researching standards accepted within its framework.

The first chapter of the present work, examined three traditions of legal ethics – the French, the American and the German, alongside their contemporary transformations – juridisation, professionalisation and globalisation. This exmination leads to the conclusion that the concept of legal ethics is used to denote three main meanings – professional duties, professional roles and personal virtues. The co-appearance of these three meanings in many discussions on legal ethics is connected with the existence of such countries as Poland, where influences of all the three traditions are strong, and with the modernising processes, which change the role of tradition in performing legal professions.

The second chapter classifies and critically presents a number of conceptions of legal ethics that were formulated in science. Within the framework of empirical and analytical conceptions these are: the conception of legal ethics as the ethos of a lawyer, as myth, as ideology and as professional deontology. Whereas the normative and critical conceptions include applied ethics, situational ethics of a lawyer and critical professional ethics, the latter being further developed in this study.

The third part presents the multi-dimensional theory of legal ethics as a theory which, because it has been formulated on the grounds of philosophy of morality, may be applied also in professional ethics other than legal. This theory, on one hand, asserts the ambiguity of the concept of legal ethics, and does not try to remove this ambguity but to use it in construction of a subject of legal ethics. This subject is composed of three planes – deontological, social and moral – which correspond with three basic meanings of the concept. On the other hand, the theory is guided by the critical theory's requirements and it views the relations between particular planes as reflective validation and critical limitation. On the highest plane, the theory is validated by reference to reflection as a procedure provided for by transcendental pragmatics in validation of any normative ethics. Therefore, on the moral plane of legal ethics, the principle of lawyers' responsibility for law as social practice has been formulated.

The fourth part analyses, on the grounds of philosophy of law, whether the selected conceptions – chosen on the basis of their practical importance – which make the positivist, juriscentric and discursive models, *explicite* or *implicite* contain any conceptions of legal ethics and what is their relation to the multi-dimensional theory of legal ethics. On the basis of each of the views presented conclusions referring to the content of the principle of lawyers' responsibility for law have been drawn. The principle indicates that they should maintain and develop law. In the positivist model the conclusion is that the subject of lawyers' responsibility is to make the legal system continually follow the social one, which brought it into existence, and this aspiration to compatibility would be its maintenance and development.

In the juriscentric model the lawyers' responsibility rests on making a Herculean effort to include the widest possible scope of viewpoints on justice and correctness expressed in principles, and on choosing a solution which will realise this integrity best. There is always only one such a solution. Thus, this is aspiring to an ideal of applying law in a way that integrates political community and an obligation to advance continuously law in this direction and to develop one's skills to gain the greatest mastery in this process. The responsibility of lawyers could also rely on maintaining and developing legal culture, which is a foundation of law as institution and, in this way, on performing self-limitation of one's discretionary power.

In the discursive model, in the case of judges, the principle of responsibility means maintaining and developing law through justifying decisions so that they inscribe in the entirety of practice and are convincing to other lawyers. In another perspective, the responsibility for maintaining and developing law through realising discourse ethics rests on enabling the society to participate in legal discourses freely and on equal terms.

Finally, the fifth part raises the issue of the status of legal ethics as a scientific discipline which not only has its theory, but may also be practised in a systematic way. It has been ascertained that one may speak of legal ethics as a separate discipline among legal sciences provided that it is by assumption multi-dimensional – otherwise it will be exposed to problem shifts, which may cause some of its spheres to be included into other fields of knowledge. This does not mean that the multi-dimensional theory of legal ethics is the only acceptable theory, but, according to the methodology of research programs, one should consistently carry out research on all the planes of legal ethics and in this way aim at working out better theories. It may be said that although legal ethics is not interdisciplinary in the full sense of this word, interdisciplinarity plays an important role in its research.

Works Cited

Aarnio A., "Lawyers' Professional Ethics – Do They Exist?", *Ratio Juris* 2001, no. 1.

Abel R.L., "Transnational Law Practice," *Case Western Law Review* 1994, no. 44.

Alexy R., *Theorie der juristischen Argumentation. Die Theorie des rationalen Diskurses als Theorie der juristischen Begründung*, Frankfurt am Main 1992.

Alexy R., "The Special Case Thesis", *Ratio Juris* 1999, no. 4.

Andrews C.R., "Standards of Conduct for Lawyers: An 800-Year Evolution", *Southern Methodist University Law Review* 57, Fall 2004.

Apel K.-O., "Szientistik, Hermeneutik, Ideologiekritik. Entwurf einer Wissenschaftslehre in erkenntnisanhropologischer Sicht", in: K.-O. Apel et al., *Hermeneutik und Ideologiekritik*, Frankfurt am Main 1973.

Apel K.-O., "Das Apriori der Kommunikationsgemeinschaft und die Grundlagen der Ethik", in: *idem*, *Transformation der Philosophie, Band II, Das Apriori der Kommunikationsgemeinschaft*, Frankfurt am Main 1973.

Apel K.-O., "Die Konflikte unserer Zeit und das Erfordernis einer etisch-politischen Grundorientierung", in: *idem*, *Diskurs und Verantwortung. Das Problem des Übergangs zur postkonventionellen Moral*, Frankfurt am Main 1988.

Apel K.-O., "Kant, Hegel und das aktuelle Problem der normativen Grundlagen von Moral und Recht", in: *idem*, *Diskurs und Verantwortung. Das Problem des Übergangs zur postkonventionellen Moral*, Frankfurt am Main 1988.

Apel K.-O., "Kann der postkantische Standpunkt der Moralität noch einmal in substantielle Sittlichkeit ›aufgehoben‹ werden? Das geschichtsbezogene Anwendungsproblem der Diskursethik zwischen Utopie und Regression", in: *idem*, *Diskurs und Verantwortung. Das Problem des Übergangs zur postkonventionellen Moral*, Frankfurt am Main 1988.

Apel K.-O., "Der postkantische Universalismus in der Ethik im Lichte seiner aktuellen Mißverständnisse", in: *idem*, *Diskurs und Verantwortung. Das Problem des Übergangs zur postkonventionellen Moral*, Frankfurt am Main 1988.

Apel K.-O., "Verantwortung heute – nur noch Prinzip der Bewahrung und Selbstbeschränkung oder immer noch Befreiung und Verwilklichung von Humanität?", in: *idem*, *Diskurs und Verantwortung. Das Problem des Übergangs zur postkonventionellen Moral*, Frankfurt am Main 1988.

Apel K.-O., "Dikursethik als Verantwortungsethik und das Problem der ökonomischen Rationalität", in: *idem*, *Diskurs und Verantwortung. Das Problem des Übergangs zur postkonventionellen Moral*, Frankfurt am Main 1988.

Apel K.-O., "Die tranzendentalpragmatische Begründung der Kommunikationsethik und das Problem der höchsten Stufe einer Entwicklungslogik des moralischen Bewußtseins", in: *idem*, *Diskurs und Verantwortung. Das Problem des Übergangs zur postkonventionellen Moral*, Frankfurt am Main 1988.

Apel K.-O., "Etyka dyskursu jako etyka odpowiedzialności – postmetafizyczna transformacja etyki Kanta" ["Discourse Ethics as Ethics of Responsibility – Post-Metaphysical Transformation of Kantian Ethics"], *Principia* 1992, no. 5.

Apel K.-O., "Wspólnota komunikacyjna jako transcendentalne założenie nauk społecznych", ["Communication Community as a Transcendental Assumption of Social Sciences"], in: A. Zeidler-Janiszewska, *Kultura współczesna. Teoria-Interpretacje-Krytyka*, Warsaw 1993.

Apel K.-O., "Uniwersalistyczna etyka współodpowiedzialności", ["Universalistic Ethics of Co-Responsibility"], in: *Idea etyczności globalnej*, ed. J. Sekuła, Siedlce 1999.

Apel K.-O., "Refleksja transcendentalno-pragmatyczna; główna perspektywa aktualnej transformacji filozofii Kanta", ["Transcendental-Pragmatic Reflection; The Main Perspective of the Current Transformation of Kant's Philosophy"], in: *200 lat z filozofią Kanta*, ed. M. Potępa, Z. Zwoliński, Warsaw 2006.

Appelbaum D., Lawton S.V., *Ethics and the Professions*, Englewood Cliffs 1990.

Arendt H., *Responsibility and Judgement*, New York 2003.

Baier K., *The Moral Point of View. A Rational Basis of Ethics*, New York 1958.

Barton B.H., "The ABA, the Rules, and Professionalism: the Mechanics of Self-Defeat and a Call for a Return to the Ethical, Moral, and Practical Approach of the Canons", *North Carolina Law Review* 2005, no. 83.

Bator A., "Wspólnota kulturowa jako element integracji prawa",["Cultural Community as an Element of Integration of Law"], in: *Z zagadnień teorii i filozofii prawa. W poszukiwaniu podstaw prawa*, ed. A. Sulikowski, Wrocław 2006.

Bator A., Gromski W., Kaźmierczyk S., Kozak A., "Integracja i globalizacja z perspektywy filozofii prawa", ["Integration and Globalisation from the Perspective of Philosophy of Law"], in: *Filozofia prawa wobec globalizmu*, ed. J. Stelmach, Kraków 2003.

Bauman Z., *Globalizacja*, Warsaw 2000.

Bauman Z., "What Chance of Ethics in the Globalized World of Consumers?", in: *Does Ethics Have a Chance in a World of Consumers?*, Cambridge Massahusetts and London, 2009.

Bayertz K., *Self-Enlightenment of Applied-Ethics,* in: ed. R. Chadwick, D. Schroeder *Applied Ethics. Critical Concepts in Philosophy*, London and New York 2002, vol.1.

Beauchamp T.L., Childress J.F., *Zasady etyki medycznej*, Warsaw 1996.

Bell D., *The End of Ideology. On the Exhaustion of Political Ideas in the Fifties*, Cambridge-London 1988.

Bell D., *Kulturowe sprzeczności kapitalizmu*, Warsaw 1998.

Berman H.J., *Law and Fevolution: the Formation of the Western Legal Tradition*, Cambridge Massachusetts and London 1983.

Bernardi U., "Globalizacja i kultury. Przeciw starym i nowym przesądom", ["Globalisation and Cultures. Against Old and New Superstitions"], *Społeczeństwo* 1998, no. 2.

Beretta S., "Globalizacja i rozwój" ["Globalisation and Development"], *Społeczeństwo* 1998, no. 2.

Beveridge F., Nott S., "A Hard Look on the Soft Law", in: *Lawmaking in the European Union*, ed. P. Craig, C. Harlow, London-Hague-Boston 1998.

Bierzanek R., "'Miękkie' prawo międzynarodowe", ["Soft International Law"], *Sprawy Międzynarodowe* 1987, no.1.

Bogucka I., "Zagadnienia tworzenia i funkcjonowania etycznych standardów zawodów prawniczych", ["The Questions of Forming and Functioning of Legal Professions' Ethical Standards"], in: *Prawo a wartości. Księga jubileuszowa Profesora Józefa Nowackiego*, ed. I. Bogucka, Z. Tobor, Kraków 2003.

Bohdan Ł., *Usługi prawnicze w Unii Europejskiej,*[*Legal Services in the European Union*], Kraków 2000.

Bojarski Ł., "Cele działania uniwersyteckich poradni prawnych", ["The Goals of Legal Clinics at the Universities"], in: *Studencka poradnia prawna. Idea-organizacja-metodologia,* Warsaw 2005.

Bojańczyk A., "Z problematyki relacji między odpowiedzialnością dyscyplinarną i karną," ["Problems of the Relationship of Disciplinary and Penal Responsibility"], *Państwo i Prawo* 2004, no. 9.

Bolten J., *Interkulturowa kompetencja*, [*Intercultural Competence*], Poznań 2006.

Borchardt G.M., Wellens K.C., "Soft Law in European Community Law", *European Law Review* 1989, no.14.

Brandstetter A., *Der Erlaß von Berufsordnungen durch die Kammern der freien Berufe*, Berlin 1971.

Brandt R.B., *Etyka. Zagadnienia etyki normatywnej i metaetyki*, [*Ethics. The Issues of Normative Ethics and Meta-Ethics*], Warsaw 1996.

Brożek B., *Rationality and Discourse. Towards a Normative Model of Applaying Law*, Warsaw 2007.

Bubner R., "Was ist Kritische Theorie?", in: K.-O. Apel et al., *Hermeneutik und Ideologiekritik*, Frankfurt am Main 1973.

Busse F., "Anwaltsethik unter Geltung des neuen Berufsrecht", *Anwaltsblatt* 1998, no. 5.

Chmielewski A., "Filozofia moralności Alasdaira MacIntyre'a" ["The Philosophy of Morality of Alasdair MacIntyre"], in: A. MacIntyre, *Dziedzictwo cnoty. Studium z teorii moralności*, Warsaw 1996.

Chmielewski A., "MacIntyre a współczesna filozofia polityczna" ["MacIntyre and the Contemporary Political Philosophy"], in: A. MacIntyre, *Czyja sprawiedliwość? Jaka racjonalność?*, Warsaw 2007.

Cieślak Z., "Etyka urzędnika" ["Ethics of an Official"], in: *Etyka-deontologia-prawo*, ed. P. Steczkowski, Rzeszów 2008.

Conrad H., *Deutsche Rechtsgeschichte, Band II, Neuzeit bis 1806,* Karlsruhe 1966.

Cicero, *O prawach*, [De Legibus], Kęty 1999.

Cyrul W., "Topika i prawo (Krytyczna analiza topicznej wizji dyskursu prawnego)", ["Topics and Law (A Critical Analysis of a Topical Vision of Legal Discourse"], *Państwo i Prawo* 2004, no. 6.

Dahrendorf R., "Zur Sozilogie der juristischen Berufe in Deutschland", *Anwaltsblatt* 1964, no. 14.

Daly M.C., "The Cultural, Ethical, and Legal Challenges in Lawyering for a Global Organization. The Role of the General Counsel", *Emory Law Journal* 1997, no. 46.

Daly M.C., "The Dichotomy Between Standards and Rules: A New Way of Understanding the Differences in Perceptions of Lawyer Code of Conduct by U.S. and Foreign Lawyers", *Vanderbilt Journal of Transnational Law* 1999, no. 32.

Dare T., "Applied Ethics, Challenges To", in: *Applied Ethics. Critical Concepts in Philosophy*, vol.1, ed. R. Chadwick, D. Schroeder, London and New York 2002.

Dawson J.P., *The Oracles of the Law*, Ann Arbor 1968.

DeCoste F.C., "Towards a Comprehensive Theory of Professional Responsibility", *University of New Brunswick Law Journal* 2001, no. 50.

De George R.T., *Business Ethics*, New York-London 1990.

Dembiński P.H., "Globalizacja – wyzwanie i szansa", ["Globalisation – a Challenge and an Opportunity"], in: *Globalizacja,* ed. J. Klich, Kraków 2001.

Dodek A.M., "Canadian Legal Ethics: A Subject in Search of Scholarship", *University of Toronto Law Journal* 2000, no. 1.

Drinker H.S., *Legal Ethics*, New York 1953.

Dworkin R., *Taking Rights Seriously*, Cambridge Massachusets 1977.

Dworkin R., *Law's Empire*, Cambridge Massachusets and London 1986.

Dybowski K., *Johna Austina filozofia prawa,* [*The Philosophy of Law of John Austin*], Toruń 1991.

Dybowski K., "Utylitarystyczna filozofia prawa Johna Austina" ["The Utilitarian Philosophy of Law of John Austin"] *Państwo i Prawo* 1992, no. 3.

Dziamski S., "Scjentystyczny neoracjonalizm 'etyki dialogu'" ["Scientist Neo-Rationalism of the 'Dialogue Ethics'"], in: *Dynamika praktyki moralnej i jej etyczne racjonalizacje*, ed. J. Wawrzyniak, Poznań 1999.

Eliade M., *The Sacred and the Profane. The Nature of Religion*, New York 1987.

Falkner G., *Neues Regieren und Soziales Europa. EU-Mindestregulierung und Soft Law in der Praxis*, Vienna, September 2004.

Fukuyama F., *Zaufanie. Kapitał społeczny a droga do dobrobytu*, [*Trust. The Social Virtues and the Creation of Prosperity*], Warsaw-Wrocław 1997.

Gadamer H.-G., *Truth and Method*, trans. J. Weinsheimer, D.G. Marshall, New York 2004.

Gajewska-Kraczowska H., "Tajemnica zawodowa", ["Professional Confidentiality"], in: *Etyka zawodów prawniczych. Etyka prawnicza*, ed. H. Izdebski, P. Skuczyński, Warsaw 2006.

Gasparski W., "Etyka biznesu – szkice do portretu", ["Business Ethics – a Portrayal Sketches"], in: *Etyka biznesu*, ed. J. Dietl, W. Gasparski, Warsaw 2002.

Gear C.A., "The Ideology of Domination: Barriers to Client Autonomy in Legal Ethics Scholarship", *Yale Law Journal* 1998, no. 107.

Gizbert-Studnicki T., Ujęcie instytucjonalne w teorii prawa" [The Institutional View in the Theory of Law"], in: *Studia z filozofii prawa*, ed. J. Stelmach, Kraków 2001.

Goldman A.H., *The Moral Foundations of Professional Ethics,* Totowa 1982.

Gordon R.W., "The independence of lawyers", *Boston University Law Review* 1988, no. 1.
Grabowski A., "Dyskurs prawniczy jako przypadek szczególny ogólnego dyskursu praktycznego", ["Legal Discourse as a Special Case of General Practical Discourse"], in: *Studia z filozofii prawa 2,* ed. J. Stelmach, Kraków 2003.
Grabowski A., "Zawartość reguły uznania w koncepcji H.L.A. Harta" ["The Content of the Rule of Recognition in the Conception of H.L. Hart"], in: *Prawo-władza-społeczeństwo-polityka. Księga jubileuszowa profesora Krzysztofa Pałeckiego*, Toruń 2006.
Guść J., Łokucijewski K., "Globalizacja a jurydyzacja", ["Globalisation *vs.* Juridisation"], in: *Filozofia prawa wobec globalizmu*, ed. J. Stelmach, Kraków 2003.
Habermas J., "Interesy konstytuujące poznanie", ["Cognition-Constituting Interests"], *Colloquia Communia* 1985, no. 2.
Habermas J., *Theory of Communicative Action vol. 2, A Critique of Functionalist Reason,* Boston 1987.
Habermas J., "Are There Postmetaphysical Answers to the Question: What is the 'Good Life'?", in: *idem*, *The Future of Human Nature*, Cambridge 2003.
Habermas J., *Between Facts and Norms. Contributions to a Discourse Theory of Law and Democracy*, Cambridge Massachusetts 1996.
Habermas J., *Structural Transformation of the Public Sphere,* Cambridge Massachusetts 1993.
Hacker P.M.S., "Hart's Philosphy of Law", in: *Law, Morality and Society. Essays in Honour of H.L.A. Hart*, ed. P.M.S. Hacker, J. Raz, Oxford 1977.
Hare R.M., *Moral Thinking. Its Levels, Methods and Points*, New York 1982
Hare R.M., "Why do Applied Ethics?", in: *Applied Ethics. Critical Concepts in Philosophy*, ed. R. Chadwick, D. Schroeder, London and New York 2002, vol.1.
Hart H.L.A., *The Concept of Law*, Oxford-New York 1994.
Hart H.L.A., "Positivism and the Separation of Law and Morals", in: *idem*, *Essays in Jurisprudence and Philosophy*, Oxford 1983.
Hildenberg H., "A fresh look at soft law", *European Journal of International Law* 1999, no. 3.
Hoeflich M.H., "Legal ethics in the nineteenth century: The 'other tradition'", *University of Kansas Law Review, Special Issue on Professional Responsibility* 1999, no. 47.
Holly G., *Geschichte der Ehrengerichtsbarkeit der deutschen Rechtsanwälte,* Frankfurt am Main-Bern-New York-Paris 1989.
Hołówka J., *Etyka w działaniu*, [*Ethics in Action*], Warsaw 2001.

Hołówka J., "Dylematy moralne w zawodach prawniczych," ["Moral Dilemmas in Legal Professions"], in: *Etyka prawnika. Etyka nauczyciela zawodu prawniczego*, ed. E. Łojko, Warsaw 2006.

Horkheimer M., "Teoria tradycyjna a teoria krytyczna", ["Traditional Theory vs. Critical Theory"], *Colloquia Communia* 1983, no. 2.

Horkheimer M., *Krytyka instrumentalnego rozumu*, [*Critique of Instrumental Reason*], Warsaw 2007.

Howells G.G., "'Soft Law'" in EC Consumer Law", in: *Lawmaking in the European Union*, ed. P. Craig, C. Harlow, London-Hague-Boston 1998.

Höffe O., *Immanuel Kant*, Warsaw 2003.

Inglese Ch., "Soft law?", *Polish Yearbook of International Law* 1993, no. XX.

Izdebski H., "Granice prawa jako instrumentu kształtowania standardów zachowań w służbie publicznej", ["Limits of Law as a Means of Establishing Standards of Conduct in Public Service"], in: *Profesjonalizm w administracji publicznej*, ed. A. Dębicka, M. Dmochowski, B. Kudrycka, Białystok 2004.

Izdebski H., "Zawody prawnicze jako zawody zaufania publicznego", ["Legal Professions as Professions of Public Trust"], in: *Etyka zawodów prawniczych. Etyka prawnicza*, ed. H. Izdebski, P. Skuczyński, Warsaw 2006.

Izdebski H., *Fundamenty współczesnych państw*, [*The Foundations of Modern States*], Warsaw 2007.

Izdebski H., "Zbieg standardów deontologii zawodowej", ["The Convergence of Professional Deontology Standards"], in: *Etyka prawnicza. Stanowiska i perspektywy*, ed. H. Izdebski, P. Skuczyński, Warsaw 2008.

Izdebski H., *Elementy teorii i filozofii prawa*, [*Elements of Theory and Philosophy of Law*], Warsaw 2008.

Izdebski H., Morawski L., "Dwugłos: Demokracja a przywileje korporacyjne", ["Divided Opinions: Democracy and Corporate Privileges"] *Państwo i Prawo* 2007, no. 6.

Jakubowski W.M., "Adwokat i radca prawny – dwa różne zawody prawnicze", ["An Advocate and a Legal Adviser – Two Different Legal Professions"], *Palestra* 1997, no. 1-2.

Janczewski S., "Godność zawodu",["Profession's Dignity"] *Palestra* 1959, no. 6, 7, 8, 9 , 10.

Jankowski H., *Prawo i moralność*, ["Law and Morality"], Warsaw 1968.

Jankowski H., "Kilka uwag na temat etyki zawodowej", ["A Few Remarks on Professional Ethics"], *Etyka* 1994, no. 27.

Jaworski Cz., "O integracji zawodów prawniczych i nie tylko", ["On Integration of Legal Professions and Not Only"], *Palestra* 1998, no. 9-10.

Jaworski Cz., "Niezależność i niezawisłość", ["Independence and Autonomy"], in: *Etyka zawodów prawniczych. Etyka prawnicza*, ed. H. Izdebski, P. Skuczyński, Warsaw 2006.
Jaworski Cz., "Niezależność wykonywania zawodu adwokata w świetle regulacji prawnych europejskich i polskich", ["The Independence of a Lawyer's Practice in the Light of European and Polish Legal Regulations"], *Palestra* 1996, no. 7-8.
Jedynak S. ed., *Mały słownik etyczny* [*Little Dictionary of Ethics*], Bydgoszcz 1999.
Jonas H., "Teoria odpowiedzialności: pierwsze rozróżnienia" [The Theory of Responsibility: The First Distinctions"], *Znak* 1995, no.10.
Jonas H., *The Imperative of Responsibility: In Search of Ethics for the Technological Age*, Chicago 1984.
Jurcewicz A., "Rola 'miękkiego prawa' w praktyce instytucjonalnej Wspólnoty Europejskiej", ["The Role of 'Soft Law' in Institutional Practice of the EC"], in: *Implementacja prawa integracji europejskiej w krajowych porządkach prawnych*, ed. C. Mik, Toruń 1998.
Jurzyk M., "Wybrane zagadnienia kolizji interesów w amerykańskiej praktyce prawniczej", ["Selected Issues on Conflict of Interests in the American Legal Practice"], *Radca Prawny* 2002, no. 3.
Kaniowski A.M., "Postawa krytyczna a etyka. Problem uniwersalizacji" ["Critical Attitude and Ethics. The Problem of Universalisation"], in: *Racjonalność współczesności. Między filozofią a socjologią* [*Rationality of Modernity. Between Philosophy and Sociology*], ed. H. Kozakiewicz, E. Mokrzycki, M. Siemek, Warsaw 1992.
Kaniowski A.M., "Etyka a transcendentalizm w perspektywie kantowskiej i pragmatyczno-językowej", ["Ethics and Transcendentalism from the Kantian and Pragmatic-Linguistic Perspectives"], in: *Filozofia transcendentalna a dialektyka*, ed. M. Siemek, Warsaw 1994.
Kant I., *Groundwork of the Metaphysic of Morals*, Cambridge 2006.
Kant I., *Critique of Practical Reason*, Indianapolis-Cambridge 2002.
Kant I., *The Metaphysics of Morals*, Cambridge-New York-Melbourne 1991.
Kamela P., "Teoria prawa a filozofia prawa" ["Theory of Law and Philosophy of Law"], *Kwartalnik Prawa Publicznego* 2006, no. 4.
Kamela P., *Prawo i moralność w koncepcjach H.L.A. Harta*, [*Law and Morality in the Conceptions of H.L.A.Hart*], Toruń 2008.
Kapciak A., "Komunikacja międzykulturowa jako fenomen kultury współczesnej", ["Intercultural Communication as a Phenomen of Contemporary Culture"], in: *Komunikacja międzykulturowa. Zbliżenia i impresje*, ed. A. Kapciak, L. Korporowicz, A. Tyszka, Warsaw 1995.

Karaś T., "Zasady obowiązujące w wybranych kancelariach prawnych działających w Polsce", ["Rules Valid in Chosen Law Firms in Poland"], in: *Etyka prawnicza. Stanowiska i perspektywy*, ed. H. Izdebski, P. Skuczyński, Warsaw 2008.

Kaufman A.I., *Problems in Professional Responsibility*, Boston-Toronto 1976.

Kempny M., "Komunikacja międzykulturowa czy postkulturowa globalna ekumena", ["Intercultural Communication or Postcultural Global Ecumene"], in: *Komunikacja międzykulturowa. Zbliżenia i impresje*, ed. A. Kapciak, L. Korporowicz, A. Tyszka, Warsaw 1995.

Kiereś H., "Mit",["Myth"], in: *Powszechna encyklopedia filozofii*, vol. 7, Lublin 2006.

Kinloch G.C., *Ideology and Contemporary Sociological Theory*, Engelwood Cliffs 1981.

Kojder A., "Etyka – przedmiot i stanowiska", ["Ethics – The Subject and Views"], in: *Etyka zawodów prawniczych. Etyka prawnicza*, ed. H. Izdebski, P. Skuczyński, Warsaw 2006.

Klatt M., "Contemporary Legal Philosophy in Germany", *Archiv für Rechts- und Sozialphilosophie* 2007, no. 4.

Kołakowski L., "Etyka bez kodeksu", ["Ethics Without a Code"], in: *Kultura i fetysze. Eseje*, Warsaw 2000.

Kołakowski L., *Filozofia pozytywistyczna. Od Hume'a do Koła Wiedeńskiego*, [*Positivist Philosophy from Hume to the Vienna Circle*], Warsaw 2003.

Konhardt K., "Kant a odkryte dziś na nowo pytanie o 'dobre życie'", ["Kant and the Rediscovered Question: What is the 'Good Life'"], in: *200 lat z filozofią Kanta*, ed. M. Potępa, Z. Zwoliński, Warsaw 2006.

Korporowicz L., "Od konfliktu do spotkania kultur", ["From Conflict to the Intertwinement of Cultures"], in: *Komunikacja międzykulturowa. Zbliżenia i impresje*, ed. A. Kapciak, L. Korporowicz, A. Tyszka, Warsaw 1995.

Kozak A., *Granice prawniczej władzy dyskrecjonalnej* [*Borders of Legal Discretionary Power*], Wrocław 2002.

Kozak A., "Trzy modele praktyki prawniczej" ["Three Models of Legal Practice"], in: *Studia z filozofii prawa* 2, ed. J. Stelmach, Kraków 2003.

Kozłowski T.,"Społeczny pozytywizm Josepha Raza" ["Social Positivism of Joseph Raz"], *Studia Iuridica* 1998, no. 36.

Krawietz W., "Moral versus Legal Responsibility? Different Motives and Models for Attributing Rights and Duties", in: *Öffentliche oder private Moral? Vom Geltungsgrunde und der Legitimität des Rechts. Festschrift für Ernesto Garzón Valdés*, ed. W. Krawietz, G.H. von Wright, Berlin 1992.

Kronman A.T., "The Law as a Profession", in: *Ethics in Practice. Lawyers' Roles, Responsibilities, and Regulation*, ed. D.L. Rhode, New York 2000.

Kruszyński P., "Etyka adwokacka jako granica dopuszczalności działania obrońcy w procesie karnym", ["Lawyer's Ethics as the Action Admissibility Limit of a Lawyer in a Penal Procedure"], in: *Etyka prawnika. Etyka nauczyciela zawodu prawniczego*, ed. E. Łojko, Warsaw 2002.

Krzemiński Z., *Etyka adwokacka. Teksty, orzecznictwo, komentarz*, [*Lawyers' Ethics. Texts, Jurisdiction, Commentary*], Kraków 2003.

Krzyżagórska B., "Kilka uwag na temat amerykańskiej firmy prawniczej, cz. I", ["Some Remarks on the American Law Firm, Part I"], *Palestra* 1996, no. 1-2.

Krzyżagórska B., "Kilka uwag na temat amerykańskiej firmy prawniczej, cz. II", ["Some Remarks on the American Law Firm, Part II"], *Palestra* 1996, no. 3-4.

Kuhn T.S., "The Structure of Scientific Revolutions", in: *International Encyclopedia of Unified Science*, vol. 2, no. 2, London, 1970.

Kukuryk K., "Retoryka prawnicza a orzecznictwo sądowe" ["Legal Rhetorics and Jurisdiction"], in: *Polska kultura prawna a proces integracji europejskiej*, ed. S. Wronkowska, Kraków 2005

Kurczewska J., Szacki J. ed., *Tradycja i nowoczesność*, [*Tradition and Modernity*], Warsaw 1984.

Kurczewski J., "Kształtowanie się profesji – perspektywa socjologa", ["The Formation of a Profession – a Sociologist's Perspective"] *Radca Prawny* 2002, no. 4-5.

Kustra E., "Współczesne próby przezwyciężania antynomii pozytywizmu prawniczego oraz prawa natury w wyjaśnieniu idei prawa" ["Contemporary Attempts at Overcoming Antynomies of Legal Positivism and Law of Nature in Explaining the Idea of Law"], in: *Teoria prawa, filozofia prawa, współczesne prawo i prawoznawstwo*, Toruń 1998.

Kwiatkowska-Falęcka E., "Wykonywanie zawodu radcy prawnego na podstawie ustawy z 6 lipca 1982 roku o radcach prawnych", ["Practising as a Legal Adviser on the Basis of the Act of 6th July 1982 on Legal Advisers"], in: *Etyka zawodów prawniczych. Etyka prawnicza*, ed. H. Izdebski, P. Skuczyński, Warsaw 2006.

LaFollette H. ed., *The Oxford Handbook of Practical Ethics*, Oxford 2003.

Lakatos I., "Newton's Effect on Scientific Standards", in: *idem*, *The Methodology of Scientific Research Programmes. Phliosophical Papers*, vol. I, Cambridge 1978.

Lakatos I., "Falsification and the Methodology of Scientific Research Programmes", in: *idem*, *The Methodology of Scientific Research Programmes. Phliosophical Papers*, vol. I, Cambridge 1978.

Lakatos I., "History of Science and its Rational Reconstructions", in: *idem The Methodology of Scientific Research Programmes. Phliosophical Papers*, vol. I, Cambridge 1978.

Lakatos I., "Science and Pseudoscience", in: *idem, The Methodology of Scientific Research Programmes. Phliosophical Papers*, vol. I, Cambridge 1978.

Lakatos I., "The Social Responsibility of Science", in: *Mathematics, Science and Epistemology. Philosophical Papers*, vol. II, Cambridge 1997.

Lang W., *Prawo i moralność*, [*Law and Morality*], Warsaw 1989.

Laskowski M., "Ustawowe pojęcie 'nieskazitelność charakteru'", ["Statutory Term 'Character Impeccability'"], *Prokuratura i Prawo* 2008, no. 6.

Lazari-Pawłowska I., "Etyki zawodowe jako role społeczne", ["Professional Ethics as Social Roles"], in: *Etyka zawodowa*, ed. A. Sarapata, Warsaw 1971.

Lazari-Pawłowska I., "Etyka zawodowa bez kodeksu", ["Professional Ethics Without a Code""], *Etyka* 1994, no. 27.

Lehmann M., *Ethical Duties of Lawyers – Perspectives from the Continent*, XXIII World Congress of The International Association for Philosophy of Law and Social Philosophy (IVR) Kraków 2007, workshop *Legal Ethics: Its Horizon and Mandates*, copied material.

Leszczyński J., "Dogmatyki prawnicze w dobie globalizacji", ["Legal Dogmatics in the Age of Globalisation"], in: *Filozofia prawa wobec globalizmu*, ed. J. Stelmach, Kraków 2003.

Leszczyński J., "Problem tożsamosci prawnika i jego alter ego w teorii prawa" ["The Problem of a Lawyer's Identity and His Alter Ego in Theory of Law"], in: *Z zagadnień teorii i filozofii prawa. Ponowoczesność*, ed. M. Błachut, Wrocław 2007.

Leubsdorf J., *Man in His Original Dignity. Legal Ethics in France*, Aldershot-Burlington USA-Singapore-Sydney 2001.

Leubsdorf J., "On the History of French Legal Ethics", *University of Chicago Law School Roundtable* 2001, no. 8.

Liberska B., "Współczesne procesy globalizacji gospodarki światowej", ["Modern Processes of World Economy Globalisation"], in: *Globalizacja. Mechanizmy i wyzwania*, ed. B. Liberska, Warsaw 2002.

Lieber H.-J., *Ideologie. Eine historisch-systematische Einführung*, Padeborn-München-Wien-Zürich 1985.

Luhmann N., *Vertrauen. Ein Mechanismus der Reduktion sozialer Komplaxität*, Stuttgart 2000.

Luizzi V., *A Case For Legal Ethics. Legal Ethics as a Source for a Universal Ethic*, New York 1993.

Łabieniec P., "Etyka – Etyka zawodowa – Prawo (zarys problematyki)", ["Ethics–Professional Ethics–Law (the Outline of Issues)"], *Prokurator* 2002, no. 2.

Łabieniec P., "O statusie etyki zawodowej i kodeksów etyki zawodowej", ["On the Status of Professional Ethics and of the Codes of Professional Ethics"], in: *Etyka prawnicza. Stanowiska i perspektywy*, ed. H. Izdebski, P. Skuczyński, Warsaw 2008.

Łabieniec P., "Etyka zawodowa jako przypadek dyskursu praktycznego", ["Professional Ethics as a Case of Practical Discourse"], in: *Etyka. Deontologia. Prawo*, ed. P. Steczkowski, Rzeszów 2008.

Łojko E., "O roli zawodów prawniczych w dzisiejszym społeczeństwie", ["On the Role of Legal Professions in Modern Society"], *Palestra* 1997, no. 3-4.

Łojko E., *Role i zadania prawników w zmieniającym się społeczeństwie*, [*The Roles and Tasks of Lawyers in the Changing Society*], Warsaw 2005.

Łojko E., "O trudnościach wykonywania współcześnie zawodu prawnika", ["On Difficulties of Practising as a Lawyer in Modern Times"], in: *Prawo-władza-społeczeństwo-polityka. Księga jubileuszowa profesora Krzysztofa Pałeckiego*, Toruń 2006.

Łuków P., *Granice zgody: autonomia zasad i dobro pacjenta*, [*The Limits of Consent: The Autonomy of Rules and the Patient's Welfare*], Warsaw 2005.

Łuków P., "Kanta odkrycie normatywności" ["Kant's Discovery of Normativity"], in: *200 lat z filozofią Kanta* [*200 years with Kant's Philosophy*], ed. M. Potępa, Z. Zwoliński, Warszawa 2006.

Łyczywek R., "O etyce zawodów prawniczych", ["On Legal Professions' Ethics"], in: *Etyka zawodowa*, ed. A. Sarapata, Warsaw 1971.

MacCannel D., *The Tourist: a New Theory of The Leisure Class*, New York 1989.

MacIntyre A., *After Virtue. A Study in Moral Theory*, Notre Dame 1984.

MacIntyre A., "Does Applied Ethics Rest on a Mistake?", in: *Applied Ethics. Critical Concepts in Philosophy*, ed. R. Chadwick, D. Schroeder, London and New York 2002, vol.1.

MacIntyre A., *Whose Justice? Which Rationality?*, Notre Dame 1988.

MacIntyre A., *Three Rival Versions of Moral Enquiry. The Gifford Lectures,* Notre Dame 1990.

Mackie J.L., "The Grounds of Responsibility", in: *Law, Morality and Society. Essays in Honour of H.L.A. Hart*, ed. P.M.S. Hacker, J. Raz, Oxford 1977.

MacNiven D., "Practical Ethics. The Idea of a Moral Expert", in: *Applied Ethics. Critical Concepts in Philosophy*, ed. R. Chadwick, D. Schroeder, London and New York 2002, vol.1.

Mannheim K., *Ideology and Utopia, an Introduction to Sociology of Knowledge*, NewYork 1954.
Marquier J., *Soft Law: Das Beispiel des OSZE-Prozesses – Ein Beitrag zur völkerrechtlichen Rechtsquellenlehre*, Bonn 2004.
Marshall G., Scott J., *Dictionary of Sociology*, 2005.
Marston A., "Guiding the profession: the 1887 code of eEthics of the Alabama State bar association", *Alabama Law Review* 1998, no. 49.
Matczak M., *Summa Iniuria. O błędzie formalizmu w stosowaniu prawa* [*On the Formalism Fallacy in Law Application*], Warsaw 2007.
Materniak-Pawłowska M., "Z polskich prac nad kodyfikacją zasad etyki adwokackiej", ["Of Polish Works on Lawyers' Ethics Rules Codification"], *Czasopismo Prawno-Historyczne* 2007, no. 2.
Mencwel A., "Trzy modernizmy", ["Three Modernisms"], in: *idem*, *Wyobraźnia antropologiczna*, Warsaw 2006.
Michalik M., "Społeczne przesłanki, swoistość i funkcje etyki zawodowej", ["Social Premises, Specificity and Functions of Professional Ethics"], in: *Etyka Zawodowa*, ed. A. Sarapata, Warsaw 1971.
Mikułowski-Pomorski J., *Komunikacja międzykulturowa. Wprowadzenie*, [*Intercultural Communication. An Introduction*], Kraków 1999.
Moore W.E., *The Professions: Roles and Rules*, New York 1970.
Morawski L., *Główne problemy współczesnej filozofii prawa. Prawo w toku przemian* [*Main Problems of Contemporary Legal Philosophy. Law under Transformation*], Warsaw 2000.
Morawski L., "Pozytywizm 'twardy', pozytywizm 'miękki' i pozytywizm martwy" ["'Hard' Positivism, 'Soft' Positivism and Dead Positivism"], *Ius et Lex* 2003, no.1.
Morawski L., "Czy sądy mogą się angażować politycznie?", ["Can Courts Engage Politically?"], in: *Państwo i Prawo* 2006, no. 3.
Nonet P., Selznick P., *Law and Society in Transition. Towards Responsive Law*, New York-Hagerstown-San Francisco-London 1978.
Najda M., Romer T., "Etyka sędziowska", ["Judicial Ethics"], *Europejski Przegląd Sądowy* 2005, no. 3.
Olechnicki K., Załęcki P., *Słownik socjologiczny*, [*Dictionary of Sociology*] Toruń 1997.
Oleszko A., *Ustrój polskiego notariatu*, [*The Structure of the Polish Notary*], Kraków 1999.
O'Neill O., "Kant: Rationality as Practical Reason", in: *The Oxford Handbook of Rationality*, ed. A.J. Mele and P. Rawling, Oxford 2004.

Opałek K., "Przedmiot prawoznawstwa a problem tzw. płaszczyzn prawa" ["The Subject of Jurisprudence and the Problem of the So-Called Planes of Law"], *Państwo i Prawo* 1969, no. 6.
Ossowska M., *Normy moralne. Próba systematyzacji,* [*Moral Norms. A Systematisation Attempt]*, Warsaw 1985.
Ossowska M., "Pojęcie wzoru i pojęcie naśladownictwa", ["The Concept of a Model and Imitation"], in: *idem*, *Ethos rycerski i jego odmiany*, Warsaw 2000.
Ossowska M., *Socjologia moralności. Zarys zagadnień*, [*Sociology of Morality. A Review of Topics*], Warsaw 2005.
Parsons T., "A Sociologist Looks at the Legal Profession", in: *idem*, *Essays in Sociological Theory*, Glencoe Illinois 1954.
Parsons T., "The Professions and Social Structure", in: *idem*, *Essays in Sociological Theory*, Glencoe Illinois 1954.
Pawlik W., "Niecnota uregulowana", ["Regulated Non-Virtue"], *Etyka* 1994, no. 27.
Pawłowski K., *Tworzenie pojęć i definiowanie w naukach humanistycznych,* [*The Creation of Concepts and Defining in Humanities*], Warsaw 1978.
Payen F., *O powołaniu adwokatury i sztuce obrończej*, [*On the Bar's Vocation and the Art of Defence*], Warsaw 1938.
Paździora M., "Uprzywilejowanie praktyki, czyli o tzw. zwrocie praktycznym w teorii i jego konsekwencjach",["Practice Privilege: on the So-Called Practical Turn in Theory and Its Consequences"], in: *Z zagadnień teorii i filozofii prawa. Ponowoczesność,* ed. M. Błachut, Wrocław 2007.
Peczenik A., "Płaszczyzny badania prawa" ["Planes of Legal Research"], *Państwo i Prawo* 1968, no. 2.
Perelman Ch., *O sprawiedliwości*, [*On Justice*], Warsaw 1959.
Perelman Ch., *Logika prawnicza. Nowa retoryka*, [*Legal Reasoning. The New Rhetoric*], Warsaw 1984.
Perelman Ch., *Imperium retoryki. Retoryka i argumentacja*, [*The Realm of Rhetoric. Rhetoric and Argumentation*],Warsaw 2004.
Pieniążek M., *Koncepcja etyki sytuacyjnej prawnika*, [*A Conception of Situational Ethics of a Lawyer*], unpublished doctoral thesis, Kraków 2005.
Pieniążek M., "Koncepcja etyki sytuacyjnej prawnika", ["The Conception of Situational Ethics of a Lawyer"], in: *Polska kultura prawna a proces integracji europejskiej*, ed. S. Wronkowska, Kraków 2005.
Pieniążek M., "Fenomenologiczne podstawy etyki zawodowej prawnika",["Phenomenological Bases of Professional Ethics of A Lawyer"], in: *Etyka prawnicza. Stanowiska i perspektywy*, ed. H. Izdebski, P. Skuczyński, Warsaw 2008.

Pieniążek M., "Kodeks czy wolny wybór? Koncepcja etyki sytuacyjnej adwokata na tle refleksji etyczno-zawodowej polskiej palestry", ["A Code or a Free Choice? The concetion of Situational Ethics of a Lawyer in the Context of the Ethical-Professional Reflection of the Polsih Bar"], in: *Etyka. Deontologia. Prawo*, ed. P. Steczkowski, Rzeszów 2008

Pieniążek M., *Etyka sytuacyjna prawnika*, [*Situational Ethics of A Lawyer*], Warsaw 2008,

Piekarski R., "Cnoty polityczne a praworządność", ["Political Virtues and the Rule of Law"], ed. J. Pawlica, Kraków 1998.

Pietrzykowski T., "'Miękki' pozytywizm i spór o regułę uznania" ["Soft Positivism and the Dispute about the Rule of Recognition"], in: *Studia z filozofii prawa*, ed. J. Stelmach, Kraków 2001.

Pietrzykowski T., *Etyczne problemy prawa. Zarys wykładu* [*Ethical Problems of Law. An Outline of a Lecture*], Katowice 2005.

Pleszczyński J., *Etyka dziennikarska*, [*Journalism Ethics*], Warsaw 2007.

Popper K.R., *Open Society and Its Enemies*, vol. 2, London 1945.

Porębski Cz., *Czy etyka się opłaca? Zagadnienia etyki biznesu* [*Does Ethics Pay Off? The Issues on Business Ethics*], Kraków 1998.

Pound R., *The Lawyer from Antiquity to Modern Times,* Minnesota 1953.

Rączka P., *Nadzór nad samorządem zawodowym*, [*Control over Self-Governing Professional Organisation*], Toruń 1999.

Rhode D.L., "Institutionalizing Ethics", *Case Western Law Review* 1995, no. 44.

Rhode D.L., "*Pro Bono* in Principle and in Practice", *Journal of Legal Education* 2003, no. 53.

Robson P., "Lawyers and the Legal System on TV: the British Experience", *International Journal of Law in Context* 2006, no. 4.

Romaniszyn K., *Rzecz o pracy i konsumpcji. Analiza antropologiczna*, [*On Work and Consumption. Anthropological Analysis*], Kraków 2007.

Romer T., Najda M., *Etyka dla sędziów. Rozważania*, [*Judicial Ethics. Reflections*], Warsaw 2007.

Rotunda R. L., Krauss M. I., *Legal Ethics in a Nutshell*, St. Paul 2003.

Russ J., *Współczesna myśl etyczna* [*Contemporary Ethical Thought*], Warszawa 2006.

Russell I.S., "The Lawyer as Public Citizen: Meeting the *Pro Bono* Challenge", *University of Memphis KC Law Review* 2003, no. 72.

Rüthers B., "Recht und Juristen unter dem Sog und Druck wechselnder politicher Systeme", in: *125 Jahre Rechtsanwaltskammer Frankfurt am Main, Oberlandesgericht Frankfurt am Main, Rechtspflege*, Frankfurt am Main 2004.

Safjan M., *Rola prawnika we współczesnym świecie*, [*The Role of a Lawyer in the Contemporary World*], Lublin 2004.

Safjan M., *Wyzwania dla państwa prawa* [*Challenges to a Law-Governed State*], Warsaw 2007.

Sagan S. ed. *Organy i korporacje ochrony prawa* [*Organs and Corporations of Law Protectioni*], Warsaw 2001.

Sarkowicz R., "O tzw. moralnym kryzysie profesji prawniczej", ["On the So-Called Moral Crisis of a Legal Profession"], in: *Studia z filozofii prawa 2*, ed. J. Stelmach, Kraków 2003.

Sarkowicz R., *Amerykańska etyka prawnicza*, [*American Legal Ethics*], Kraków 2004.

Sarkowicz R., "Uwagi o współczesnej interpretacji prawniczej" ["Remarks on the Contemporary Legal Interpretation"], in: *Polska kultura prawna a proces integracji europejskiej*, ed. S. Wronkowska, Kraków 2005.

Sarnecki P., "Pojęcie zawodu zaufania publicznego (Art. 17 ust. 1 Konstytucji) na przykładzie adwokatury", ["The Concept of a Profession of Public Trust (Art. 17 Paragraph 1 of the Constitution) on the Example of the Bar"], in: *Konstytucja – wybory – parlament. Studia ofiarowane Z. Jaroszowi*, ed. L. Garlicki, Warsaw 2000.

Sarnecki P., "Radca prawny jako zawód zaufania publicznego", ["Legal Adviser as a Profession of Public Trust"], *Radca Prawny* 2002, no. 4-5.

Scheider K., *Der deutsche Jurist als Bürokrat – Zur Beziehung zwischen der sozialen Role des deutschen Juristen und der Entwicklung der staatlichen Bürokratie*, in: *Soziologische Probleme juristischer Berufe*, ed. W. Kaupen, R. Werle, Göttingen 1974.

Schippel H., "Die allgemeinen Richtlinien für die Berufsausübung der Notare", Deutsche Notar-Zeitschrift 1963.

Schneider U.H., "O odpowiedzialności nauki prawa" ["On the Responsibility of Science of Law"], *Kwartalnik Prawa Prywatnego* 1993, no. 2.

Shaffer T.L., "Legal Ethics and the Good Client", *Catholic University Law Review* 1987, no. 36.

Shaffer T.L., Cocharn, Jr. R. F., *Lawyers, Clients and Moral Responsibility*, St. Paul 1994.

Sieckmann J-R., "On the Tension Between Moral Autonomy and the Rational Justification of Norms", *Ratio Juris* 2003, no. 1.

Sieckmann J-R., "The Concept of Autonomy", in: *Law and Legal Cultures in the 21th Century. Diversity and Unity*, ed. T. Gizbert-Studnicki, J. Stelmach, Warsaw 2007.

Siemieński F., "Jak daleko nam do państwa prawa? Pytania na marginesie postanowienia U. 1/92 Trybunału Konstytucyjnego", ["How Far Are We from the Rule of Law? Questions *A Propos* the Ruling Act 1/92 of the Constitutional Tribunal"], in: *Zagadnienia prawa konstytucyjnego. Księga pamiątkowa ku czci Profesora Tadeusza Szymczaka*, Łódź 1994.

Sierocka B., *Krytyka i dyskurs. O transcendentalno-pragmatycznym uprawomocnieniu krytyki filozoficznej* [*Criticism and Discourse. On Transcendental-Pragmatic Validation of Philosophical Criticism*], Kraków 2003.

Skarga B., "Usankcjonowanie niecnoty" ["Authorising the Non-Virtue"], *Etyka* 1994, no. 27.

Skarga B., "Wokół etyki zawodowej. Dyskusja redakcyjna", ["Around Professional Ethics. Editorial Discussion"], *Etyka* 1994, no. 27.

Skąpska G., "Zawód prawnika czy społeczna rola?", ["Lawyer's Profession or a Social Role?"], in: G. Skąpska, J. Czapska, M. Kozłowska, *Społeczne role prawników (sędziów, prokuratorów, adwokatów),* Wrocław-Warsaw-Kraków-Gdańsk-Łódź 1989.

Skowron R., "Kultura pracy *Pro Bono* w Stanach Zjednoczonych", ["The Culture of *Pro Bono* Work in the United States"], *Państwo i Prawo* 2007, no. 3.

Skuczyński P., "Metoda i przedmiot etyki prawniczej", ["Legal Ethics Method and Subject"], in: *Etyka zawodów prawniczych. Etyka prawnicza*, ed. H. Izdebski, P. Skuczyński, Warsaw 2006.

Skuczyński P., "Zaufanie (lojalność)", ["Trust (Loyalty)"], in: *Etyka zawodów prawniczych. Etyka prawnicza*, ed. H. Izdebski, P. Skuczyński, Warsaw 2006.

Skuczyński P., "Integralność", ["Integrity"], in: *Etyka zawodów prawniczych. Etyka prawnicza*, ed. H. Izdebski, P. Skuczyński, Warsaw 2006.

Skuczyński P., "Wieloznaczność w teorii etyki prawniczej", ["Ambiguity in Legal Ethics' Theory"], in: *Etyka prawnicza. Stanowiska i perspektywy*, ed. H. Izdebski, P. Skuczyński, Warsaw 2008.

Skuczyński P., "Granice odpowiedzialności dyscyplinarnej", ["Limits of Disciplinary Responsibility"], in: *Odpowiedzialność dyscyplinarna. Podstawy, procedura i orzecznictwo w sprawach studentów Uniwersytetu Warszawskiego 2000-2005*, ed. P. Skuczyński, P. Zawadzki, Warsaw 2008.

Skuczyński P., "Czy sprawiedliwość jest cnotą prawników?", ["Is Justice a Virtue of Lawyers?"], in: *Rozdroża sprawiedliwości we współczesnej myśli filozoficznoprawnej*, ed. B. Wojciechowski, M.J. Golecki, Toruń 2008.

Skuczyński P., "Soft law w perspektywie teorii prawa", ["Soft Law in Theory of Law Perspective"], in: *System prawny a porządek prawny*, ed. O. Bogucki, S. Czepita, Szczecin 2008.

Skuczyński P., "Powściągliwość sędziowska jako zasada etyki sędziowskiej", ["Judicial Cautiousness as a Principle of Judical Ethics"], in: *Dyskrecjonalność w prawie* [*Discretionality in law*], ed. T. Stawecki, W. Staśkiewicz, Warsaw 2010

Skuczyński P., *Praca pro bono a pomoc prawna i profesjonalizm prawniczy*, *Klinika. Czasopismo Fundacji Uniwersyteckich Poradni Prawnych* 2011, no. 11.

Smolak M., *Prawo, fakt, instytucja. Koncepcje teoretycznoprawne Prawniczego Pozytywizmu Instytucjonalnego* [*Law, Fact, Institution. Legal-theoretical Conceptions of Legal Posivism*], Poznań 1998.

Sobański R., "Uwagi o etyce zawodów prawniczych", ["Remarks on Ethics of Legal Professions"], *Palestra* 2003, no. 7-8.

Spaudling N. W., "The Myth of Civic Republicanism: Interrogating the Ideology of Antebellum Legal Ethics", *Fordham Law Review* 2003, no.71.

Stawecki T., "Filozofia prawa a teoria prawa: spór nierozstrzygalny czy pozorny?" [Philosophy of Law *versus* Theory of Law: an Unsolvable or a Superficial Dispute?], *Studia Iuridica* 2006.

Stawecki T., "Etyka prawnicza a filozofia prawa", ["Legal Ethics and Philosophy of Law"], in: *Etyka zawodów prawniczych. Etyka prawnicza,* ed. H. Izdebski, P. Skuczyński, Warszawa 2006.

Stawecki T., "Od perfekcjonizmu moralnego do ścisłych reguł odpowiedzialności zawodowej: droga ku globalnej etyce prawniczej?" ["From Moral Perfectionism to Precise Rules of Professional Responsibility: The Way to Global Legal Ethics?"], in: *Etyka prawnicza. Stanowiska i perspektywy*, ed. H. Izdebski, P. Skuczyński, Warsaw 2008.

Steindorff E., *Freie Berufe – Stiefkinder der Rechtsordnung?*, Köln 1980.

Steinhagen M., "Tajemnica zawodowa prawników: wyzwania i zagrożenia" ["Legal Professional Privilege: Challenges and Hazards"], *Palestra* 2004, no. 5-6.

Stelmach J., *Kodeks argumentacyjny dla prawników*, [*An Argumentative Code for Lawyers*], Kraków 2003.

Stelmach J., "Etyka dyskursu prawniczego", ["Ethics of Argumentative Discourse"], in: *Prawo a wartości. Księga jubileuszowa Profesora Józefa Nowackiego*, ed. I. Bogucka, Z. Tobor, Kraków 2003.

Stelmach J., "Ponowoczesna filozofia prawa" ["Postmodern Philosophy of Law"], in: *Studia z filozofii prawa 2*, ed. J. Stelmach, Kraków 2003.

Stelmach J., Sarkowicz R., *Teoria prawa* [*Theory of Law*], Kraków 2001.

Stelmach J., Brożek B., *Metody prawnicze. Logika, analiza, argumentacja, hermeneutyka*, [*Legal Methods. Logic, Analysis, Argumentation, Hermeneutics*], Kraków 2004.

Stier S., "Legal Ethics: The Integrity Thesis", *Ohio State Law Review* 1991, no. 52.

Strassberg M., "Taking Ethics Seriously: Beyond Positivist Jurisprudence in Legal Ethics", *Iowa Law Review* 1995, no. 80.

Struck G., *Topische Jurisprudenz*, Frankfurt am Main 1971.

Sulikowski A., *Współczesny paradygmat sądownictwa konstytucyjnego wobec kryzysu nowoczesności* [*The Contemporary Paradigm of Constitutional Judiciary in Face of Modernity Crisis*], Wrocław 2008.

Sullivan W.A., *Work and Integrity. The Crisis and Promise of Professionalism in America*, New York 1995.

Szawiel T., "Etos" ["Ethos"], in: *Encyklopedia socjologii*, Warsaw 1998, vol.1.

Sztompka P., *Thrust. Sociological Theory*, Cambridge 1999.

Szymanek K., "Perswazja, argumentacja, słaby argument, mocny argument", ["Persuasion, Argumentation, Weak Argument, Strong Argument"], in: *Studia z filozofii prawa 2,* ed. J. Stelmach, Kraków 2003.

Szymański W., *Globalizacja. Wyzwania i zagrożenia*, [*Globalisation. Challenges and Risks*], Warszawa 2001.

Szyszkowska M., "Etyka sędziego w procesie stosowania prawa" ["The Ethics of a Judge in the Process of Applying Law"], *Gazeta Sądowa* 2000, no. 9.

Ślipko T., *Zarys etyki ogólnej*, [*An Outline of General Ethics*], Kraków 2004.

Śpiewak P., *Ideologie i obywatele*, [*Ideologies and Citizens*], Warsaw 1991.

Środa M., "Słowo wstępne. Biznes i cnoty", ["Preface. Business and Virtues"], in: J. Jackson, *Biznes i moralność*, Warsaw 1999.

Świerzawski W., *Etos prawnika,* [*The Ethos of a Lawyer*], Sandomierz 1996.

Taylor Ch., *The Ethics of Authenticity*, Cambridge Massachusetts and London 2003.

Terry L.S., "U.S. Legal Ethics: The Comming of Age of Global and Comparative Perspectives", *Washington University Global Studies Law Review* 2005, no. 4.

Tobor Z., Pietrzykowski T., "Bezstronność jako pojęcie prawne", ["Impartiality as a Legal Concept"], in: *Prawo a wartości. Księga jubileuszowa Profesora Józefa Nowackiego*, ed. I. Bogucka, Z. Tobor, Kraków 2003.

Tokarczyk R., "Charakterystyka ogólna amerykańskich profesji prawniczych", ["General Characterisation of American Legal Professions"], *Palestra* 1995, no. 5-6.

Tokarczyk R., "Przedmiot etyki prawniczej", ["The Subject of Legal Ethics"], in: *Państwo, prawo, myśl prawnicza*, Lublin 2003.

Tokarczyk R., "Kształtowanie przedmiotu etyki sędziego" ["Formation of the Subject of Judicial Ethics"], *Państwo i Prawo* 2004, no. 7.

Tokarczyk R., *Etyka prawnicza,* [*Legal Ethics*], Warsaw 2005.

St. Thomas Aquinas, *Summa Theologiæ*, [*Summa Theologica*], II-II, qq. 57-122 (*On Justice*).

Torosiewicz D., *Myśli o powołaniu obrońców sądowych*, [*Reflections on the Court Advocates' Vocation*], Warsaw 1822, reprint 1917.

Toulmin J., "A Worldwide Common Code of Professional Ethics?", *Fordham International Law Journal* 1991-1992, no.15.

Tugendhat E., Wolf U., *Logisch-semantische Propädeutik*, Stuttgart 2004.

Viehweg Th., *Topik und Jurisprudenz*, 1953.

Wasilewski A., "Aktualizacja porządku prawnego – potrzeby i rygory", ["Updating Legal Framework – Needs and Rigours"], *Państwo i Prawo* 1992, no. 5.

Wasserstorm R.A., "Lawyers as Professionals. Some Moral Issues", in: *Applied Ethics. Critical Concepts in Philosophy*, ed. R. Chadwick, D. Schroeder, London and New York 2002, vol. 6.

Weizsäcker C.F. von, "O tradycji w filozofii", ["On Tradition in Philosophy"], in: *Jedność przyrody*, Warsaw 1978.

Wendel B., "Legal ethics and the separation of law and morals", *Cornell Law Review* 2005, no. 91.

Wierzbowski K., "Jedna czy dwie adwokatury? Głos w sprawie przyszłości naszego zawodu", ["One or Two Bars? A Voice in Relation to the Future of Our Profession"], *Palestra* 2002, no. 3-4.

Williams B. *Morality an Introduction to Ethics,* Cambridge 1972.

Wojtczak S., Czy prawnikom potrzebna jest mitologia?", ["Do Lawyers Need Mythology?"], in: *Etyka, deontologia, prawo*, ed. P. Steczkowski, Rzeszów 2008.

"Wokół tajemnicy adwokackiej – orzeczenia, uchwały i glosy", ["Around Legal Professional Privilege – Rulings, Resolutions and Voices"], *Palestra* 1994, no. 7-8.

Woleński J., "O pozytywizmie prawniczym" ["On Legal Positivism"], in: *Etyka a praworządność i prawo*, ed. J. Pawlica, Kraków 1998.

Woleński J., "Przeciw etyce zawodowej", ["Against Professional Ethics"], *Etyka* 1994, no. 27.

Wolfram Ch.W., "Toward a History of the Legalization of American Legal Ethics – I. Origins", *University of Chicago Law School Roundtable* 2001, no. 8.

Wolfram Ch.W., "Toward a History of the Legalization of American Legal Ethics – II. The Modern Era", *Georgetown Journal of Legal Ethics* 2002, no.15.

Wróblewski J., "Prawo i płaszczyzny jego badania", [Law and Planes of Its Study] *Państwo i Prawo* 1969, no. 6.

Wyrembak J., "Kodeks etyki lekarskiej a system prawa", ["Medical Code of Ethics and the System of Law"] *Państwo i Prawo* 2003, no.10.

"Wystąpienia przed SN w sprawie tajemnicy zawodowej", ["Pleadings in the Supreme Court Concerning Legal Professional Privilege"], *Palestra* 1994, no. 9-10.

Zajadło J., ed., *Leksykon współczesnej teorii i filozofii prawa. 100 podstawowych pojęć*, [*Lexicon of Modern Theory and Philosophy of Law. 100 Fundamental Concepts*], Warsaw 2007.

Zajadło J., "Prawo kontra etyka prawnicza" ["Law *versus* Legal Ethics"], in: *Fascynujące ścieżki filozofii prawa,* ed. J. Zajadło, Warsaw 2008.

Zajadło J., *Po co prawnikom filozofia prawa?*, [*Why Do Lawyers Need Philosophy of Law?*], Warsaw 2008.

Zima P.V., *Ideologie und Theorie. Eine Diskurskritik*, Tübingen 1989.

Zirk-Sadowski M., "Postulat etyki bezkodeksowej a stosunek prawa do moralności", ["Postulate of Ethics Without a Code *vs.* the Relationship Between Law and Morality"], *Zeszyty Naukowe Uniwersytetu Łódzkiego* 1979, no. 25.

Zirk-Sadowski M., *Rozumienie ocen w języku prawnym*, [*The Understanding of Evaluations in the Legal Language*], Łódź 1984.

Zirk-Sadowski M., "Dyskurs jako mowa regulowana wymogami moralnymi", ["Discourse as Speech Regulated by Moral Requirements"], in: *Prawo w zmieniającym się społeczeństwie,* ed. G. Skąpska et al., Kraków 1992.

Zirk-Sadowski M., *Prawo a uczestniczenie w kulturze*, [*Law and Participation in Culture*], Łódź 1998.

Zirk-Sadowski M., *Wprowadzenie do filozofii prawa*, [*An Introduction to the Philosophy of Law*], Kraków 2000.

Zirk-Sadowski M., "Pozytywizm prawniczy a filozoficzna opozycja podmiotu i przedmiotu poznania",["Legal Positivism and Philosophical Opposition of the Subject and the Object of Cognition"], in: *Studia z filozofii prawa*, ed. J. Stelmach, Kraków 2001.

Zirk-Sadowski M., "Uczestniczenie prawników w kulturze",["The Participation of Lawyers in Culture"], *Państwo i Prawo* 2002, no. 9.

Zirk-Sadowski M., "Epistemologia prawa a teorie wykładni", ["Epistemology of Law and Theories of Interpretation"], in: *Prawo-władza-społeczeństwo-polityka. Księga jubileuszowa profesora Krzysztofa Pałeckiego*, Toruń 2006.

Zirk-Sadowski M., "Postmodernistyczna jurysprudencja?", ["Postmodern Jurisprudence"], in: *Z zagadnień teorii i filozofii prawa. Ponowoczesność,* ed. M. Błachut, Wrocław 2007.

Zoll F., *Jaka szkoła prawa?*, [*What School of Law?*], Warsaw 2004.

Żywiecki W., *Etyka adwokacka*, [*Lawyers' Ethics*], Warsaw 1970.

Warsaw Studies in Philosophy and Social Sciences

Edited by Tadeusz Szawiel and Jakub Kloc-Konkołowicz

Vol. 1 Paweł Skuczyński: The Status of Legal Ethics. 2013.

www.peterlang.de

www.ingramcontent.com/pod-product-compliance
Ingram Content Group UK Ltd.
Pitfield, Milton Keynes, MK11 3LW, UK
UKHW041826100926
8556IPUK00002B/46

9 783631 641330